16/32 – Bit Microprocessors: 68000/68010/68020

Software, Hardware, and Design Applications

WUNNAVA V. SUBBARAO
Florida International University

Merrill, an imprint of
Macmillan Publishing Company
New York

Collier Macmillan Canada, Inc.
Toronto

Maxwell Macmillan International Publishing Group
New York   Oxford   Singapore   Sydney

Administrative Editor: David Garza
Production Editor: Mary M. Irvin
Art Coordinator: Lorraine Woost
Cover Designer: Russ Maselli

This book was set in Times Roman.

Macmillan Publishing Company
866 Third Avenue, New York, New York 10022

Collier Macmillan Canada, Inc.

Printing: 1 2 3 4 5 6 7 8 9   Year: 0 1 2 3
Library of Congress Catalog Card Number: 90-60538
International Standard Book Number: 0-675-21119-0

To the respectful memory of my professors

Dr. Earnest Anderson, Ph.D., P.E., North Dakota State University, Fargo, and

Dr. S. Jnanananda, Ph.D., D.Sc., Andhra University, Waltair, Andhra Pradesh, India, for their perseverance, compassion, and interest in my education,

and

To the Department of Electrical and Computer Engineering, Florida International University, Miami, for providing me with an outstanding professional atmosphere in which I could venture and complete this project

MERRILL'S INTERNATIONAL SERIES
IN ELECTRICAL AND ELECTRONICS TECHNOLOGY

PREFACE

In recent years, the single most important development in the field of digital electronics has been the microprocessor. Thanks to VLSI (very-large-scale integration), it has grown from the simple 4-bit processing element of a quarter-century ago to the complex 32/64-bit processing unit of the present time.

The Intel and Motorola corporations have been leaders in the development of microprocessors and associated electronic circuits. Currently, the two frontrunning families of microprocessors are the Intel 8086/186/286/386 family and the Motorola 68000/10/20/30 family. The Intel processors are very popular in such personal computers as the IBM PC and compatibles. The Motorola processors are equally popular in such personal computers as Apple's Macintosh, Commodore's Amiga, and Atari's ST. Most industrial controllers and systems, such as image-processing systems, robotic systems, and communication systems, are based on the Motorola 68000 family.

This book focuses on the Motorola family of microprocessors. It is written as a college-level text for electrical engineering and technology students, computer engineering and technology students, and computer science students. It can also serve as a self-teaching text for practicing engineering and technical personnel.

The book examines general software and hardware concepts of microprocessors, as well as microprocessor-based system design and implementation schemes, with specific reference to the 68000 family of processors. Descriptions of the software and hardware are sufficiently detailed to enable the reader to make use of the concepts in practical applications. Most of the software and hardware discussions are based on actual working models.

The 68000 family consists of the 16-bit 68000 processor, the 8-bit 68008 processor, the 16-bit virtual memory 68010 processor, the enhanced virtual memory 68012 processor, the 32-bit cache memory 68020 processor, and the 32-bit enhanced cache memory 68030 processor. All of the later versions are based on the original 68000. Coverage of the text includes the architecture, software, hardware, and application details of the 68000 processor, with concepts extended to the other family members. Assembly programming techniques, parallel and serial I/O (input/output) interface techniques and associated applications, interrupt and DMA (direct memory access) applications, and system implementation schemes have been given particular emphasis.

Chapter 1 presents the basic concepts of the 68000 family of microprocessors and introduces the architecture of the 68000. The special features of the 68000 family are also described. In **Chapter 2** the memory organization schemes, data structures, and addressing modes associated with the 68000 are covered, along with the instruction format and structure typical of the 68000 family. The instruction set of the 68000 is presented in **Chapter 3,** with particular emphasis on the general flow of the instruction structure, the instruction timing, and the instruction groups.

Chapter 4 deals with software and programming techniques and applications of the 68000 processor. Assembly programming methods and special software features such as macros are examined in detail. The important aspect of exception processing is covered in **Chapter 5.** In this chapter, exception processing resulting from interrupts and error conditions is described.

Chapter 6 deals with the hardware structure of the 68000 processor and the interfacing techniques with the memory and I/O. Important hardware concepts, such as address decoding, read and write bus cycle timing, and the VME and VERSA busing schemes, are introduced. This provides a foundation for the discussion on the parallel I/O interface to the 68000 and associated applications in **Chapter 7.** Important parallel interface devices, such as the 6821 PIA and 68230 PI/T, are introduced in this chapter. Data entry and display applications and position control using stepper motors are presented, along with hardware and software details. This leads to a description of the serial I/O interface to the 68000 and associated applications in **Chapter 8.** Industry standard serial interface devices, such as the 6850 ACIA and 68901 MFP, are introduced. RS-232 serial data communication and coded data transmission applications are presented, including hardware and software details.

Chapter 9 deals with the most important aspects of the interrupts and the DMA (direct memory access) schemes associated with the 68000. Such practical applications as the daisy chain of interrupts, interrupt-driven gain controllers, and interrupt-driven data-acquisition systems with A/D and D/A are presented, again with hardware and software details. General concepts of the DMA are presented through a practical application using DMA-based high-speed data transfers.

Chapter 10 introduces the 68010 virtual memory processor. The general concepts of virtual memory, virtual machines, and the operating system are discussed in detail. The additional resources of the 68010 and 68012 processors are also covered, along with memory-access fault correction schemes using virtual memory concepts.

In **chapter 11** the 32-bit 68020 and 68030 cache memory processors are introduced. The concepts of cache memory organization are discussed. Additional resources of the 68020 and 68030 processors and related performance improvements are presented. An objective comparison between the 68000 and the 68020/30 is also included to provide insight into the applications of these very powerful processors.

Finally, the book includes four appendices: Appendix A on number systems, Appendix B on the 68000 instruction set and condition uses, Appendix C on analog and digital converter devices for interfacing, and Appendix D on instruction timing for the 68000/10 processors.

The material is designed to be used in a two-semester course. For engineering and technical students, Chapters 1, 2, 3, 4, 5, and 6 can be covered in the first semester. In the second semester, Chapters 7, 8, 9, 10, and 11 can be covered. For computer science and software-oriented students, Chapters 1, 2, 3, 4, 5, and 10 can be covered in one semester. If instructors choose to introduce hardware before dealing with exceptions, they can switch the order of presentation of Chapters 5 and 6.

Each chapter is organized into four or five main sections, each dealing with an important topic. In most cases, each section has at least one example problem. The end-of-chapter problems are especially designed to supplement the material covered in the book. Most of these problems have been classroom tested. A comprehensive glossary is included at the end of the book.

The book is an outgrowth of several courses on microprocessors and digital systems taught by the author at Florida International University to engineering, technology, and computer science students. The author's association with the Motorola Corporation as a consulting professor, teaching their industrial seminars on the 68000 family of processors and applications, also significantly contributed to the book's development.

Nothing replaces a hands-on learning experience. Therefore, readers are encouraged to apply the software and hardware concepts introduced in this book to practical problems using the microcomputer system of their choice.

Acknowledgments

Many people assisted me in the preparation of this book. Students in the Electrical Engineering and Computer Science departments at Florida International University were extremely helpful. In particular, I would like to thank Jorge Salinger, Laura Ruiz, Mauracio Salinas, Fernando Gonzalez, and Mike Urucinitz of the Electrical Engineering Department for their work in conducting hardware and software experiments to support the discussions in this book.

Motorola Corporation has been very generous in donating 68000- and 68020-based systems to the university. This allowed for the concepts presented in the text to be tested on real systems. Special thanks to Ben Ledonne and Fritz Wilson of the university support service at the Motorola Corporation in Phoenix for their support and encouragement.

I would like to acknowledge the encouragement and guidance offered by our chairperson, James Story, and the professional courtesy extended to me by our dean, Gordon Hopkins, and associate dean, Manuel Cereijo, during the preparation of the book. Many thanks also to Lie Lonie Boney and Lordis Barough for their assistance in preparing the materials for presentation. I am especially grateful to my wife, Sunanda, and to my children, Madhavi and Manoj, for their immense patience and understanding during the course of the project.

Perhaps no words can express my gratitude to my teachers. They have given me a path objective, a career, and, above all, knowledge and self-esteem. Professor Earnest Anderson and Professor Edwin Anderson of North Dakota State University in Fargo and Professor D.L. Sastry, the late Professor S. Jnanananda, and Professor D.S. Sastry of Andhra University in Waltair and Masulipatam in India have been instrumental in shaping my present academic career. I remain ever grateful to them. I would also like to thank the reviewers of this edition for their important ideas and suggestions: Antony Alumkal, Austin Community College; Mike Bachelder, South Dakota School of Mines and Technology; Gary Boyington, Chemeketa Community College; George Frueh, Lincoln Technical Institute; Frank Gergelyi, Metropolitan Technical Institute; Jerry Noe, Tri Cities State Technical School; and John Skroder, Texas A&M University.

CONTENTS

CHAPTER 6
68000 Hardware Considerations and Design Applications   148

The Microprocessor Evolution

It is no exaggeration to say that the microprocessor device has revolutionized digital electronics and the computer field. Most of the currently available digital, computer, and electronic systems use some form of microprocessor. With processing capability exceeding several million instructions per second (MIPS), the microprocessor is continuously finding new applications.

The earliest form of the microprocessor was a 4-bit device (4004). It was basically used as a 4-bit ALU (arithmetic logic unit) almost a quarter-century ago. The real microprocessor era started in the early 1970s, when Intel Corporation introduced the 8080 microprocessor. This was an 8-bit microprocessor, and contained an ALU and bus interface logic on board. It also had several 8-bit registers for storing operands and addresses. Although the unit required several power supplies and a power-sequencing scheme, it found extensive applications. The success of the 8080 microprocessor led other companies to get involved in the development of different forms of microprocessors.

Immediately after launching the 8080 processor, Intel began to improve its design, which resulted in the 8085. The 8085 processor is code compatible with the earlier 8080, but can operate on a single 5-volt power supply. Almost simultaneously, Motorola Corporation introduced the 8-bit 6800 microprocessor with nonmultiplexed data and address buses. The 6800 processor also incorporates the concept of double accumulators and has an index addressing scheme. The 6800 became an instant success. Several peripheral devices to interface with the 8085 and the 6800 processors were introduced into the market by a number of vendors.

During the mid-1970s, Commodore and Rockwell International introduced the 8-bit 6502 microprocessor, which also became an instant success. This machine is similar to the 6800 processor, but includes additional addressing capabilities such as memory indirect. The design of the Apple computer was based on the 6502 processor. At about the same time, Zilog Corporation introduced the 8-bit Z80 microprocessor. The Z80 is code compatible with the 8085 processor. It has additional resources with which to store data internally, and it also has the index addressing mode of the 6800 and 6502 processors. The Z80 processor found extensive applications in the 8-bit field, even though it entered the 8-bit market late.

Most of the processors we have mentioned were developed with NMOS technology. However ultralow power requirements dictated a processor using CMOS technology. RCA Corporation introduced the first CMOS 8-bit 1802 microprocessor for low-power applications. Pacemakers and several other battery-powered devices use the 1802 type of processor. Most 8-bit processors have a 64-kilobyte address range.

Emerging applications soon demanded more processing power than 8-bit processors could provide. Intel corporation was again the leader in introducing the first 16-bit 8086 microprocessor in 1978. The internal architecture of the 8086 supports 16-bit operations. The external address bus can access 1 megabyte of memory, which was considered a great advantage. The 8086 has a 16-bit data bus. The 8088 processor is a scaled-down version of the 8086, with an 8-bit data bus. The IBM PC contributed to the great success of the 8086/88 processors.

To follow the 8086 processor, Motorola Corporation introduced the much more powerful and versatile 68000 microprocessor. It has a 16-bit data bus and an effective 24-bit address bus that can access 16 megabytes. The internal architecture of the 68000 is designed to support 8-bit, 16-bit, and 32-bit operations. There are several 32-bit data registers, each of which can be used as an accumulator. The architecture, linear address range, and versatile data-handling capability of the 68000 suited the needs of industry. Systems such as Apple's Macintosh further contributed to the popularity of the 68000 processor. During the same time frame, Zilog corporation introduced its 16-bit Z8000 processor, which is similar to the 68000 in terms of architecture.

Continuous demand by industry resulted in the development of even more powerful processors, such as the 68020 and 68030 in the 68000 family, and the 80386 in the 8086 family. The present trend of development will continue in the 1990s. In order to obtain more dedicated throughput, RISC (reduced instruction set computer chip) devices are becoming popular. But the demand for general-purpose processors will continue to rise.

Also observed in the microprocessor application market is the popularity of single-chip microcomputers and controllers, such as Intel's 8051 and Motorola's 68HC11. These 8-bit devices are suitable for 8-bit I/O interface applications. Sixteen-bit microcontroller devices are also becoming available.

All of the 8-, 16-, and 32-bit processors we have described are available in various packages using different processing techniques.

The 68000 Family of Microprocessors and Architecture

Objectives

In this chapter we will study:

The 68000 family of microprocessors

Microcomputer configuration of the 68000 family

Architectural features of the 68000

Supervisor and user modes of operation

Special features, such as the queue and pipeline

1.0   INTRODUCTION

The 68000 microprocessor, introduced by Motorola Corporation in the late 1970s, is one of the most powerful and widely used 16/32-bit processors. It is the first member of the 68000 family of processors—a family that includes the 68008, 68010, 68012, 68020, and 68030 processor devices.

Microcomputer configurations based on these processors are similar. In addition, they all have the same basic architecture as that of the 68000. The architecture consists of internal registers and pointers and arithmetic logic and control units.

The 68000 operates in two distinct modes: the **supervisor mode** and the **user mode.** These two modes of operation maintain a relative separation between the operating system programs and the user programs.[1]

All processors obtain data from the memory block, perform the appropriate operations, and store the resulting data back in the memory. Processors in the 68000 family are structured to handle the **byte** (8-bit), **word** (16-bit), and **long-word** (32-bit) data elements.[2]

An understanding of the architecture, modes of operation, and data-handling schemes is essential to the study of the 68000 microprocessor and associated designs. It will also promote understanding of the other members of the 68000 family.

The material in this chapter will provide the necessary background to understand the software and system features of the 68000 processor. The hardware concepts and designs of the 68000 will be presented in later chapters.

1.1   THE 68000 FAMILY OF MICROPROCESSORS

As mentioned previously, all processors in the 68000 family support byte, word, and long-word operations. We will now briefly introduce the important members of the 68000 family. Figure 1.1 illustrates the genealogy of these processors; they are developed using the VLSI (very-large-scale integration) MOS technology.[3]

The 68000 Microprocessor

The 68000 is the principal device of the 68000 family of microprocessors. The operating frequency of the 68000L4 is 4 MHz; for the 68000L12, the operating frequency is 12 MHz. Several other frequency versions are also available. The 68000 has a 16-bit data bus and an effective 24-bit address bus that supports 16 megabytes of address range. This microprocessor is normally contained in a 64-pin DIP (dual-in-line package), but it is also available in the 68-pin chip-carrier package.

The 68008 Microprocessor

The 68008 is the reduced-bus version of the 68000 processor. It has an 8-bit data bus and an effective 20-bit address bus that supports 1 megabyte of address range. The 68008 is contained in a 48-pin DIP. It is very cost effective in applications involving the standard 8-bit I/O (input/output) interface.

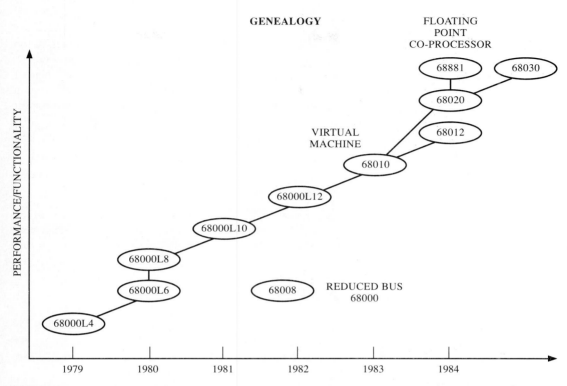

FIGURE 1.1   Genealogy of the 68000 family of microprocessors. (Courtesy of Motorola, Inc.)

The 68010 Microprocessor

The 68010 is the virtual memory microprocessor. It has all the resources of the 68000 microprocessor. In addition, it has extended internal resources to support the virtual memory management schemes. **Virtual memory** refers to a memory that is not physically present as a part of the system main memory, but is present as a part of the backup memory. This feature allows for error detection and possible error correction in memory access faults.

The 68010 is pin compatible with the 68000 microprocessor. The 68000 processor can be replaced with the 68010 in a system without any hardware changes. Additional software can then be written to support the virtual memory schemes.

The 68012 Microprocessor

The 68012 is the enhanced virtual memory microprocessor. It is architecturally identical to the 68010. It has an extended address bus that supports 2 gigabytes of address range, as well as additional control lines to support the multiprocessing activity. It is contained in an 84-pin grid-array package.

The 68020 Microprocessor

The 68020 is the cache memory microprocessor. In addition to all the resources of the 68010 microprocessor, it has internal resources to support cache memory operation. **Cache memory** is a fast-access memory that holds prefetched information; thus, it speeds up the system operation. The 68020 is truly a 32-bit microprocessor. It has a 32-bit data bus and a 32-bit address bus that support 4 gigabytes of address range. It also has additional control and interface lines to support the coprocessor interface. It is contained in a 114-pin grid-array package. The 68020 is considered to be one of the best 32-bit microprocessors, and it is one of the most widely used.

The 68030 Microprocessor

The 68030 is the enhanced version of the 68020 microprocessor. In addition to all the resources of the 68020, it has internal data cache memory and a memory management unit. These additional resources effectively enhance the throughput of the 68030 processor as compared to the 68020.[4]

The 68881 Coprocessor

The architecture of the 68881 coprocessor is different from that of other members of the 68000 family. The 68881 is capable of performing floating-point arithmetic operations to 80-bit precision. It can be interfaced to any member of the 68000 family of processors to increase the arithmetic processing power of the system.

The 68008 is the lowest member and the 68030 is the highest member of the 68000 family of processors. The gradation sequence is 68008 → 68000 → 68010 → 68012 → 68020 → 68030. These processors are upward code compatible. The software written for a lower level processor will work with a higher level processor. For example, the code written on a 68008-based system will work on a 68000-based system with a similar memory and I/O map. However, the reverse may not be true. Software written for a higher level processor, using the additional resources of that processor, will not work on a lower level processor. For example, the code written on a 68020-based system using the special resources of the 68020 will not work on a 68000-based system, which lacks those resources.[5]

The following example problem will review the concepts we have just discussed with regard to the 68000 family.

Example 1.1   The 68000 family of processors.
The 68008 and the 68000 processors support 32-bit internal operations. Their external data buses are 8 and 16 bits wide. Conceptually compute the relative speed of these two processors while transferring

1. byte-size data from memory into one of the internal registers of the processor;

2. word-size data from memory into one of the internal registers of the processor.

Solution

1. **Byte (8-bit) transfers:** The 68008 has an 8-bit data bus and transfers the byte-size data in one unit of time. The 68000 has a 16-bit data bus, out of which only 8 bits are used for byte transfers. Byte transfers, then, still take one unit of time.

2. **Word (16-bit) transfers:** The 68008 transfers a 16-bit word as two bytes. As such, it takes two units of time. By contrast, the 68000 transfers the complete word in one unit of time. Thus, for word transfers, the 68000 processor is twice as fast as the 68008 processor.

The memory and **I/O (input/output)** interface schemes are similar throughout the 68000 family of processors. This results in a well-structured microcomputer configuration, which we will now introduce.

1.2 TYPICAL MICROCOMPUTER CONFIGURATION OF THE 68000 FAMILY

Figure 1.2 illustrates the microcomputer configuration typical of the 68000 family. These microprocessors are of the **memory-mapped I/O** type, in which the microprocessor communicates with an I/O device as if it were one of the memory locations. However, there are some special instructions in the 68000 family to efficiently deal with I/O data.

General Interface Scheme

Each member of the family has appropriate control and interface buses to support the synchronous and the asynchronous devices and systems, as shown in Figure 1.2. A **bus** is a group of signal lines. In the **synchronous** type of interface, data transfers take place upon certain clocking or timing events. The peripheral devices belonging to such earlier 8-bit processors as the 8085, 6800, and Z80 operate in this manner. In the **asynchronous** type of interface, data transfers take place via **handshaking.** In this protocol, the responding device provides an acknowledgment signal to the processor during data transfers. Most of the peripherals belonging to the 68000 family and the static memory follow this protocol.[6]

There are also special interfaces. The **interrupt mechanism** is the traditional means by which to gain the attention of the processor by a slow I/O device. The **DMA (direct memory access)** is the traditional means by which to effect high-speed data transfers between the memory and I/O without the intervention of the microprocessor. Each member of the 68000 family supports both of these features explicitly. The system control interface consists of the reset, halt, and bus error detection functions. The other interfaces of the processor consist of the clock distribution network, system power distribution network, and the address decoding network. Details of all these functions will be discussed in later chapters.

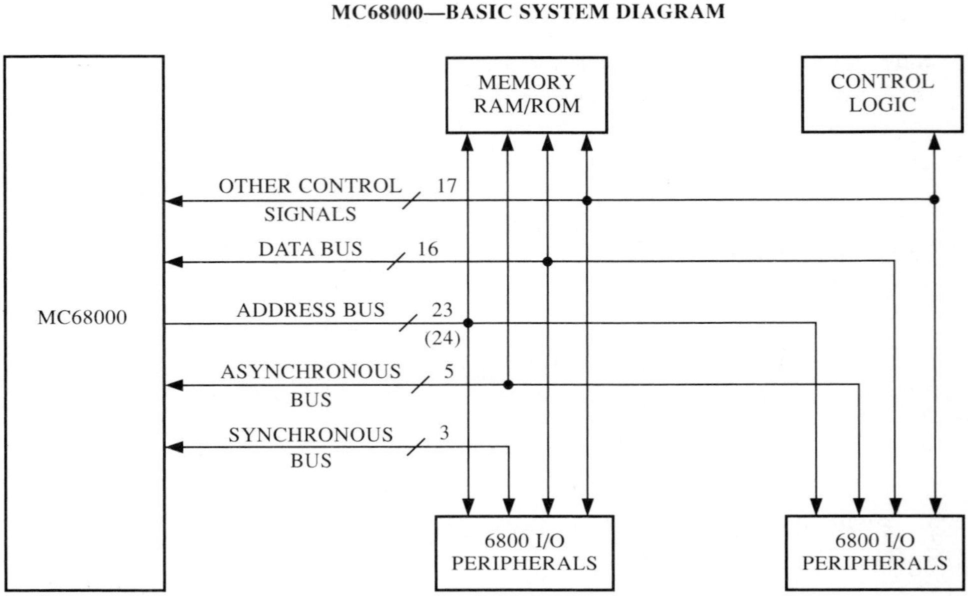

MC68000—BASIC SYSTEM DIAGRAM

FIGURE 1.2   Typical microcomputer configuration of the 68000 family of microprocessors. (Courtesy of Motorola, Inc.)

Typical 68000-Based Systems

The Macintosh from Apple Computers, Inc., the Amiga from Commodore, Inc., the ST from Atari, and the 9716 from Hewlett-Packard are some of the most popular microcomputer systems based on the 68000 microprocessor. The MEX68KECB microcomputer module from Motorola is an excellent 68000-based educational computer for learning the software and hardware features of the 68000 microprocessor and associated system designs.

An existing microcomputer system with a lower level processor can be upgraded to a higher performance processor with appropriate modifications. This is feasible because of the upward code compatibility.

The following example problem will review our discussion of the 68000-based system configuration.

Example 1.2   68000-based systems.

The 68000-based microcomputer is used in a control-system application. The processor is required to interface with the 8-bit I/O peripherals belonging to the earlier 6800 and Z80 type of processors. These devices respond to appropriate clocking events.

1. What is the preferred type of interface in the 68000? Why?

2. Suppose the 68000 system needs to be upgraded to the 68010. What additional hardware and software resources are required to accomplish this task?

Solution

1. **Interfacing the 6800 and Z80 peripherals:** Synchronous interface is preferred, since these devices are of the synchronous type.

2. **Upgrading to the 68010:** No additional hardware is required. However, to make full use of the capabilities of the 68010, memory management units may be added.

Existing software will function on the upgraded system. However, to make full use of the capabilities of the 68010, virtual memory software should be utilized.

The processing activity of a microprocessor depends on its architecture and how its internal resources are organized. The 68000 processor is rich in internal resources and has a 32-bit internal register architecture. We will now introduce these important concepts.

1.3 GENERAL ARCHITECTURE OF THE 68000 MICROPROCESSOR

The architecture of the 68000 microprocessor serves as the prototype on which all the other processors in the family are based. Figure 1.3 illustrates this internal architecture. It includes the following features:

eight 32-bit data registers, D0−D7	(Dn)
seven 32-bit address registers, A0−A6	(An)
two 32-bit stack pointers:	
user stack pointer, A7	(USP)
supervisory stack pointer, A7′	(SSP)
one 32-bit program counter	(PC)
one 16-bit status register	(SR)

In addition, the 68000 contains a 32-bit arithmetic logic unit (ALU), an instruction decoding unit, a control unit, a bus interface unit, and an execution unit. For the sake of simplicity, these resources are not indicated in the figure. For the 32-bit registers and the data structures, the byte corresponds to the lower 8 bits, the word corresponds to the lower 16 bits, and the long word corresponds to all of the 32 bits. We will now provide a functional description of the basic features.

Data Registers D0−D7 (Dn)

These eight data registers are for general-purpose data storage and processing. They handle bytes (8 bits), words (16 bits), and long words (32 bits) of data. Each of these registers can function as an accumulator. An **accumulator** is a special register that provides data operands to the ALU and stores the result from the ALU. In addition, any of

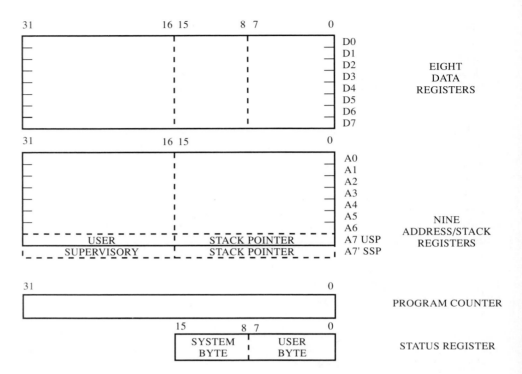

FIGURE 1.3 The internal architecture of the 68000. (Courtesy of Motorola, Inc.)

the data registers can be used for **memory indexing,** a process in which a number in the data register is added to the base address to obtain the effective address of the data operand. Operations on the data register operands affect the flag bits in the status register.

Address Registers A0–A6 (An)

These seven address registers function as address **pointers.** They store and operate on word- and long-word address operands. By means of these address operands, memory can be accessed. The address registers also can be used for general-purpose storage of operands of word and long-word size, as well as for memory indexing. The address registers do not support the byte operands. Operations on the address register operands will not affect the flag bits in the status register (except in compare-type operations).

Stack Pointers A7 (USP) and A7′ (SSP)

As previously mentioned, the 68000 microprocessor operates in two distinct modes called the user mode and the supervisor mode. The former deals with user programs; the latter, with system-level programs. In order to maintain a distinction between these modes, the 68000 has two 32-bit stack pointers: the **user stack pointer (USP or A7)** and the **supervisor stack pointer (SSP or A7′).** The 68000 can operate in only one of the modes at any given time. Either the USP or the SSP controls the system stack, depending on the mode of operation. The stack pointers can be initialized to locate the stack anywhere within the available memory space of 16 megabytes for the 68000 microprocessor. They should be initialized at the even word boundaries.

Program Counter (PC)

This 32-bit register keeps track of program space and sequentially obtains the instructions and associated operands from program space. **Program space** is that section of memory containing the program code.

Only the lower 24 bits of the program counter are brought out as the effective address bus for the 68000. This provides an address range of 16 megabytes ($2^{24} = 16$ megabytes) or 8 megawords (1 word = 2 bytes). The PC operates on an even word boundary. It advances to the next sequential program location after fetching the current instruction.[7]

Status Register (SR) and Flag Structure

Decision making in the 68000 is dependent upon the flag bits. These flag bits are contained in the status register. Figure 1.4 illustrates the details of the 16-bit status register. It is divided into two bytes—a lower byte, called the **user byte** or the **condition code register (CCR),** and an upper byte, called the **system byte.**

User Byte   This byte contains the following five flag bits:

C (Carry flag):	Set to 1 for arithmetic or logical overflow.
V (Overflow flag):	Set to 1 for overflow in twos-complement operations.
Z (Zero flag):	Set to 1 if the result of the previous operation is zero.
N (Negative flag):	Set to 1 if the most significant bit (MSB) of the operand is 1 (signifying a negative number).
X (Extend flag):	Similar to the carry flag, but not affected in the data movement operations.

When these flags are not set to the 1 condition, they remain in the 0 or reset condition. Certain instructions may not affect these flags. The details of these variations will be discussed when the instruction set is considered in the next chapter.

System Byte   This is the upper byte of the status register containing the following status information relating to the supervisor mode of operation:[8]

I2, I1, and I0 (Interrupt mask bits):	Set to the required interrupt mask level. Interrupts above this level are recognized. Can specify up to eight levels.

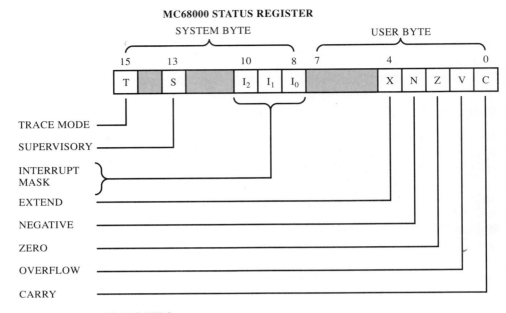

FIGURE 1.4   The 16-bit status or flag register for the 68000. (Courtesy of Motorola, Inc.)

S (Supervisor bit):	S = 0 (system in user mode).
	S = 1 (system in supervisor mode).
T (Trace bit):	T = 0 (system in run mode).
	T = 1 (system in trace mode).

The trace condition is set and used for software debugging. The system level operation is guided by the condition of the system byte. We will learn more about this byte in subsequent sections of this chapter.

It is convenient to refer to numbers in the **hex format,** especially when dealing with data and address operands. In the hex format, the decimal numbers 0–9 are represented similarly. The decimal numbers 10, 11, 12, 13, 14, and 15 are represented by the alphabetical symbols A, B, C, D, E, and F. In this book the $ sign is used to represent the hex digits. Each hex digit takes four bits; for example, $F corresponds to decimal 15 and binary 1 1 1 1. The arithmetic operations in the hex format are performed to the base 16. Appendix A provides information about the hex and other number systems.[9]

The following example problem will review our discussion of the architecture of the 68000 processor.

Example 1.3   Architecture and flags of the 68000.

The initial values of the registers D0, D1, A0, A1, USP, SSP, and the SR are as shown (in the hex format).

$$D0 = \$\,0\,0\,1\,2\,3\,4\,5\,6 \quad D1 = \$\,A\,A\,B\,B\,C\,C\,D\,D$$
$$A0 = \$\,0\,0\,6\,5\,4\,3\,2\,1 \quad A1 = \$\,0\,0\,0\,A\,5\,C\,0\,7$$
$$SR = \qquad \$\,0\,4\,0\,0$$

1. The word operand from D0 is added to the corresponding word operand from D1, with the result in D1 (ADD.W D0,D1 instruction). Show the contents of D0, D1, and SR after the addition. Take into account that the ADD instruction affects the flags.

2. The long words in A0 and A1 are added to each other, with the result in A0 (ADDA.L A1,A0 instruction). Show the contents of A0, A1, and SR after the addition. Use the same initial values.

Solution

1. **Addition of the word operands in D0 and D1:** The word operands consist of the lower four hex digits of the register contents. The hex addition is as follows:

$$
\begin{aligned}
\text{Hex word in D0} &= \$ \quad 3\ 4\ 5\ 6 \\
\text{Hex word in D1} &= \$ \quad \underline{C\ C\ D\ D} \\
\text{Hex addition} \quad &= \ 1 \quad 0\ 1\ 3\ 3
\end{aligned}
$$

There is an overflow from the fourth hex digit, which will set the carry flag and the extend flag. The word result $\$\,0\,1\,3\,3$ will be transferred to the lower word position of the D1 register. The upper word of D1 and the register D0 are not affected.
Expanding the result:

$$
\begin{array}{ccc}
 & b15 & b0 \\
\$\,0\,1\,3\,3 = & 0\,0\,0\,0\quad 0\,0\,0\,1\quad 0\,0\,1\,1\quad 0\,0\,1\,1 \\
 & \text{MSB} & \text{LSB}
\end{array}
$$

it can be seen that

the MSB = 0;	as such, the N flag = 0
the result is nonzero;	as such, the Z flag = 0
no twos-complement overflow;	as such, the V flag = 0
arithmetic overflow;	as such, the C flag = 1
	the X flag = 1

Thus, the user byte of the SR contains

$$- - - X N Z V C$$
$$0 \ 0 \ 0 \ 1 \ 0 \ 0 \ 0 \ 1 = \$ \ 1 \ 1$$

and the system byte is not affected:

$$T - S - - I2 \ I1 \ I0$$
$$0 \ 0 \ 0 \ 0 \ 0 \ 1 \ 0 \ 0 = \$ \ 0 \ 4$$

The final results are

$$D0 = \$ \ 0 \ 0 \ 1 \ 2 \ 3 \ 4 \ 5 \ 6$$
$$D1 = \$ \ A \ A \ B \ B \ 0 \ 1 \ 3 \ 3$$
$$SR = \hspace{2em} \$ \ 0 \ 4 \ 1 \ 1$$

2. Long-word addition of A0 and A1: Following the same hex addition principles,

The long-word operand in A0 = $ 0 0 6 5 4 3 2 1
The long-word operand in A1 = $ 0 0 0 A 5 C 0 7
The long-word result   = $ 0 0 6 F 9 F 2 8

This long-word result gets transferred to register A0. Register A1 is not affected. The SR also is not affected, since the operation is on the address registers, and operations on address registers do not affect flag bits.

The final results are

$$A0 = \$ \ 0 \ 0 \ 6 \ F \ 9 \ F \ 2 \ 8$$
$$A1 = \$ \ 0 \ 0 \ 0 \ A \ 5 \ C \ 0 \ 7$$
$$SR = \hspace{2em} \$ \ 0 \ 4 \ 0 \ 0$$

The processor examines the flag bits in the status register and controls the program flow accordingly. We will study more about this program flow in later chapters on software.

Other Resources

Other resources, such as the ALU, the instruction decoder, the execution unit, the bus interface unit, and the control unit are also important. The 68000 uses these resources very efficiently. They are internal to the processor and cannot be externally accessed. Their functions are as follows:

The ALU   This arithmetic logic unit performs the arithmetic and logical operations on data operands. The size of these operands may be byte, word, or long word. The flag bits in the user byte of the status register are affected as a result of ALU operations.

Instruction Decoder   This unit decodes instructions and sets up internal conditions for the execution unit.

Execution Unit   This unit performs actual operations within the processor, such as data movement.

Bus Interface Unit   This unit drives the address bus with appropriate effective address and handles data transfers on the data bus. It also generates and monitors the bus control signals necessary for the successful data transfers.

Control Unit   This unit generates appropriate control and timing signals within the processor and coordinates all processor operations.

Supervisor and User Modes of Operation

All of the processor and system resources and all the instructions are available in the supervisor mode, but some cannot be used in the user mode of programming. This condition provides a safety mechanism in that the user cannot inadvertently modify or corrupt the system-level programs and resources. The operating system software is in the supervisor mode. These modes of operation are conceptually shown in Figure 1.5.

Supervisor Mode (S=1)   This is the highest level or mode of operation. In this mode, the 68000 processor services system-level tasks, such as reset functions, interrupts, traps, tracing, and error conditions. This type of activity is known as **exception processing.** On the power-up reset condition, the S bit in the system byte of the status register is set to 1 and the 68000 enters the supervisor mode, upon which it executes the **reset routine.** This routine is always a system-initialization program. SSP is the effective stack pointer in the supervisor mode.

FIGURE 1.5 Supervisor and user modes of operation in the 68000. (Courtesy of Motorola, Inc.)

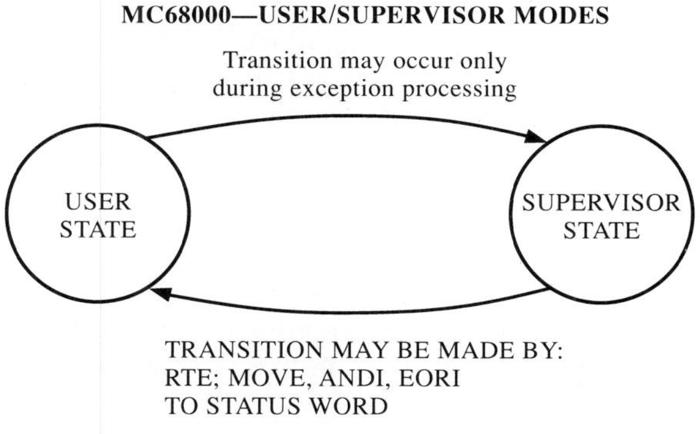

MC68000—USER/SUPERVISOR MODES

Transition may occur only during exception processing

USER STATE

SUPERVISOR STATE

TRANSITION MAY BE MADE BY:
RTE; MOVE, ANDI, EORI
TO STATUS WORD

At the end of the reset exception routine, the processor may clear the S bit in the system byte to 0. This puts the processor in the user mode.

User Mode (S=0) This is the lower level of operation. It is for this level that users write their normal programs. As we already know, some resources and instructions are not functional in this mode of operation. Any attempt to use these resources in the user mode results in an error condition whereby control is transferred to the supervisor mode. This error condition is known as a **privilege violation.** USP is the effective system stack pointer in the user mode.

Figure 1.5 illustrates the intercommunication between the two modes of operation. Exception conditions, such as reset, interrupts, errors, traps, and trace, will set the S bit in the status register to 1 and move the processor into the supervisor mode. **Traps** are special software instructions that can be used in the user mode in order to move to the supervisor mode.

The processor moves from the supervisor mode into the user mode if the S bit in the system byte is cleared to 0. This is accomplished by executing such software instructions as the RTE (return from exception), MOVE to SR (move data to status register), and others. These instructions are privileged; they can only be used in the supervisor mode.

The following example problem will review our discussion of the supervisor and user modes of operation.

Example 1.4   Supervisor and user modes in the 68000.
The initial values of the USP, SSP, and SR are as follows:

$$USP = \$ 0 0 0 0 4 8 0 C \qquad SSP = \$ 0 0 0 0 3 7 A 0$$
$$SR = \qquad \$ 2 4 0 0$$

1. Is the processor operating in the user mode or in the supervisor mode? Why?
2. Where is the system stack located?

Solution

1. **Processor operating mode:** The processor is operating in the supervisor mode, since the S bit in the system byte is 1. Expanding the system byte of the SR:

$$\$ 2 4 = \$ 0 0 1 0 0 1 \ 0 \ 0$$
$$\qquad \qquad T \quad S \qquad I2 \ I1 \ I0$$

it can be seen that the S bit is set to 1.
2. **System stack:** Because the processor is in the supervisor mode, SSP controls the system stack. As such, the system stack is located at $\$ 0 0 0 0 3 7 A 0$.

1.4 OTHER FEATURES OF THE 68000
FAMILY OF PROCESSORS

The primary objectives in using the 16/32-bit processor are to obtain more processing power and more speed. In the 68000 family, these objectives are achieved by means of the **prefetch-queue** and the **instruction-pipe** architectures.[10]

The Prefetch Queue

When the processor is internally busy with operations on data corresponding to the current instruction, the external data and address buses are relatively free. The bus unit within the microprocessor uses these buses to obtain the next instruction code from memory. This is known as **prefetching.** The internal register bank where this code is stored has memory in the form of FIFO (first in first out) and is known as the **queue.** The prefetch-queue mechanism overlaps processor activity and thus enhances speed. All members of the 68000 family have a two-word prefetch queue.

The Instruction Pipeline

The control unit within the processor sequentially arranges decoded instructions and associated operands in the form of a pipeline. The execution unit within the processor obtains information from this pipe for its operation. The pipe is structured along FIFO lines.

The internal pipeline can be formed by the control unit when the execution unit is busy with the previous operation. Thus, there is an overlap of processor activity which enhances the speed of operation. The 68020 and 68030 processors have a three-word pipe.

1.5 SUMMARY

In this chapter we introduced the 68000 family and outlined the relative features of these processors. Motorola entered the 16-bit market in the late 1970s with the 68000.

The 68000 microprocessor has an effective 24-bit address bus and a 16-bit data bus; it supports a 16-megabyte address range. The 68000 is normally contained in a 64-pin DIP package and is also available in a 68-pin grid-array package.

The 68008 is a reduced-bus version of the 68000 processor. It has an effective 20-bit address bus and an 8-bit data bus; it supports a 1-megabyte address range. It is contained in a 48-pin DIP package.

The 68010 is a virtual memory microprocessor. It contains all the resources of the 68000 and is also pin compatible with the 68000. In addition, the 68010 processor has extended internal resources to support virtual memory schemes. The 68012 processor is an enhanced version of the 68010 processor with an effective 31-bit address bus that supports 2 gigabytes of address range. The 68012 is contained in an 84-pin grid-array package.

The 68020 is a 32-bit processor with all the resources of the 68012. The address and the data buses are extended to 32 bits. It supports a 4-gigabyte address range. In addition, the 68020 processor has internal instruction cache memory and the resources to support it. The cache memory holds most recently fetched instructions and supplies them to the processor. This speeds up the system operation.

The 68030 is an enhanced version of the 68020 processor with all the resources of the 68020. In addition, it has internal data cache memory and a memory management unit, further enhancing the throughput of the 68030 as compared to the 68020 processor.

The performance gradation sequence is 68008 → 68000 → 68010 → 68012 → 68020 → 68030. The 68008 is the lowest member of the family and the 68030 is the highest. These processors are upward code compatible.

Processors in the 68000 family are provided with proper control and interface buses to support synchronous and asynchronous devices. Moreover, the interrupt and the DMA operations are fully supported.

The architecture of the 68000 microprocessor forms the basis for that of all the other members of the family. It consists of eight 32-bit data registers, seven 32-bit address registers, one 32-bit program counter, two 32-bit stack pointers, one 16-bit status register, and a 32-bit ALU. The 68000 operates in two distinct modes: the supervisor mode and the user mode. This feature serves to maintain separation between the operating system programs and the user programs.

Each member of the 68000 family has a two-word prefetch queue, which effectively speeds up processor operation. In addition, there is a three-word pipeline in the 68020 and 68030 processors, speeding up processor operation still further.

PROBLEMS

1.1   What are the physical address spaces for

(a) the 68008 and 68000 processors;
(b) the 68010 and 68012 processors;
(c) the 68020 and 68030 processors.

Specify these address spaces in bytes and words.

1.2   Does software written on a 68000-based system work with a 68020-based system having the same memory and I/O map? What happens if the memory and I/O maps are different?

1.3   Specify special conditions that would enable software written on a higher processor, such as 68010, to function on a lower processor, such as 68008.

1.4   Compute the relative speed of the processors in question in the following situations:

(a) the 68008 and 68000 transferring long words from memory into the processor internal registers;
(b) the 68008 and 68000 transferring long words from the processor internal registers into memory.

1.5   Compute the relative speed of the processors in question in the following situations:

(a) the 68000 and 68010 transferring words from memory into the processor internal registers;

(b) the 68000 and 68010 transferring words internally from one register into the other.

1.6 Is it possible for the processor to simultaneously address the devices connected to the synchronous and asynchronous buses? Why or why not?

1.7 Describe two or more advantages and disadvantages of using synchronous and asynchronous interfaces.

1.8 Suppose you are required to scale down a 68000-based system to that of a 68008. In order to make the scaled-down version functional,

(a) what hardware modifications are necessary?

(b) what software modifications are necessary?

1.9 List three differences between the data and the address registers in the 68000 family of processors.

1.10 Can the USP and the SSP be used simultaneously as stack pointers? Why or why not? Can both the stack pointers be initialized at the same location to refer to the stack? Why or why not?

1.11 The initial values of the registers in a 68000 register are

$$D0 = \$ 0 1 0 2 0 3 0 4 \qquad D1 = \$ A 0 B 0 C 0 D 0$$
$$A0 = \$ 0 0 1 3 5 7 9 8 \qquad A1 = \$ 0 0 A 9 7 5 3 2$$
$$USP = \$ 0 0 0 0 4 0 A 0 \qquad SSP = \$ 0 0 0 0 3 4 0 A$$
$$SR = \qquad \$ 0 3 0 4$$

State the contents of D0, D1, A0, A1, and the SR after each of the following operations:

(a) long word in D0 added to long word in D1, with the result in D1;

(b) byte in D0 added to byte in D1, with the result in D0;

(c) long word from A1 transferred into A0.

1.12 Using the initial conditions given in Problem 1.11, state the contents of the affected registers after each of the following operations:

(a) long word from D1 transferred into A1;

(b) long word in A0 added to long word in D1, with the result in D1;

(c) operation (b) repeated, with the result in A0.

1.13 With the initial conditions as stated in Problem 1.11,

(a) is the processor in the user mode or the supervisor mode? Why?

(b) can the processor use all the instructions, given your response to (a)? Why or why not?

1.14 How do the user and the supervisor modes differ?

1.15 The user byte of the SR is $00 initially and the interrupt mask level is set at 6. The processor is operating in the supervisor mode. The last addition operation has resulted in a word operand $FE00 in data register D7. What are the contents of the status register?

1.16 Repeat Problem 1.15 under the following conditions:

(a) byte result $00 in D6 register;

(b) long-word result $0123456B in A1 register.

1.17 Specify what happens under the following conditions:

(a) byte operand addressed in A0;

(b) stack located at an odd boundary, such as $00003401;

(c) memory reference $2345678A made by the 68000.

ENDNOTES

1. Motorola, Inc. *M68000 16/32 Bit Microprocessor Programmer's Reference Manual, Fifth Edition*. Englewood Cliffs, NJ: Prentice-Hall, 1987.

2. Motorola, Inc. *MC68000, MC68008, MC68010/12 Data Books*. Phoenix, AZ: Motorola Technical Operations, 1983.

3. Motorola, Inc. *The M68000 Family*. BR 176, Rev. 2. Phoenix, AZ: Motorola Technical Operations, 1986.

4. Reinhort, J. *Extra Functions—32-Bit Processors*. Boston: Electronic Products, 1986.

5. Motorola, Inc. *MC68020 Benchmark Report*. BR322. Phoenix, AZ: Motorola Technical Operations, 1986.

6. Motorola, Inc. *The M68000 Family*. BR176, Rev. 2. Phoenix, AZ: Motorola Technical Operations, 1986.

7. Subbarao, W. *Microprocessors: Hardware, Software, and Design Applications*. Englewood Cliffs, NJ: Prentice-Hall, 1984.

8. Stranes, T. "Design Philosophy Behind the M68000." *Byte* (Apr., May, Jun. 1983).

9. Gibson, M., and Liu, C. *Microcomputers for Scientists and Engineers*. Englewood Cliffs, NJ: Prentice-Hall, 1987.

10. Motorola, Inc. *MTT20: 68020 Course Notes*. Phoenix, AZ: Motorola Technical Operations, 1987.

2

The 68000 Memory Organization Schemes, Data Structures, and Addressing Modes

Objectives

In this chapter we will study:

Memory organization and selection schemes for the 68000
Data structures and representation for the 68000
Stack memory organization and structure for the 68000
Instruction format and structure for the 68000
Addressing modes for the 68000

2.0 INTRODUCTION

Memory access is an integral part of any computer system operation. For the 68000, memory is organized as blocks of even and odd bytes. Data are structured so that bytes can be accessed individually, words can be accessed as two bytes, and long words can be accessed as two words. This provides an efficient and reliable memory access for data operands of varying size.

The stack memory is word-aligned. The program memory, where instructions and associated operands reside, is similarly word-aligned. Thus, the complete 16-bit data bus of the 68000 is utilized, optimizing the stack and instruction fetch operations.

The 68000 processor has 14 different addressing modes with which to access memory. Depending upon the application, any of these addressing modes can be used.

An understanding of memory organization schemes and data structures is essential to the study of the addressing modes. We must first learn about these addressing modes to understand the instructions, software features, and programming techniques of the 68000, all of which will be introduced in the next chapter. Note that throughout the book, the overbar is used to represent an active low signal. For example, $\overline{LDS}$ means that the signal LDS is active when it is at the low logic level and is inactive when it is at the high logic level.

2.1 MEMORY ORGANIZATION SCHEMES AND DATA STRUCTURES

The 68000 microprocessor handles the byte, word, and long words of data. The memory is organized as 16-bit words and supports the aforementioned data elements.

Memory Organization and Selection Schemes

Figure 2.1 illustrates the memory organization and selection schemes for the 68000. The memory is structured as blocks of even and odd bytes. It can be accessed as bytes, words, or long words with the help of two strobes: $\overline{LDS}$ and $\overline{UDS}$. These are active low signals.

$\overline{LDS}$ is called the **lower data strobe.** When it is active, the lower or the odd memory byte is selected. $\overline{UDS}$ is called the **upper data strobe.** When it is active, the upper or the even memory byte is selected. When both strobes are active, both bytes are selected, providing a word access.

The odd byte is connected to the lower eight data bits, D0–D7, of the data bus. The even byte is connected to the upper eight data bits, D8–D15, of the data bus.

The 23 address lines, A1–A23, of the address bus provide an effective address range of eight megawords. The conventional A0 address line is brought out in the 68000 as the $\overline{LDS}$ and the $\overline{UDS}$ strobes. When they are active individually, these two strobes select either an odd byte or even byte. This provides an effective address range of 16 megabytes. An R/$\overline{W}$ signal from the processor is the **read/write strobe.** If this R/$\overline{W}$ strobe is at a high logic level, the processor reads the data from the memory. By the

FIGURE 2.1   (a) Memory organization and (b) selection schemes for the 68000.

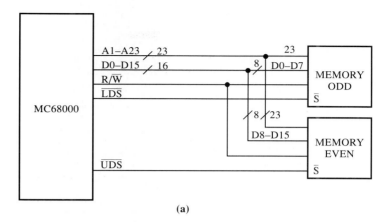

(a)

$\overline{UDS}$	$\overline{LDS}$	Memory selected
High	High	None
High	Low	Lower or odd byte selected
Low	High	Upper or even byte selected
Low	Low	Both bytes selected (word)

(b)

same token, if this signal is at a low logic level, the processor writes the data into the memory. Details of these signals will be discussed when we deal with the hardware aspects of the 68000.

Data Structures and Representation

Bytes, Words, and Long Words   Figure 2.2 illustrates how data are represented in the memory. The bytes can be accessed at the even or at the odd address boundaries. The word, consisting of two bytes, should be accessed only at the even address boundary. Similarly, the long word, consisting of two words, should be accessed only at the even address boundary. The word at the lower address corresponds to the higher word element of the long word. Word or long-word access at an odd boundary results in an error condition called the **address error.** This error condition transfers control to the supervisor mode and the operating system programs.[1,2]

BCD (Binary Coded Decimal)   The decimal numbers are represented in the BCD (binary coded decimal) format. Each BCD digit is a 4-bit element. Two BCD digits are contained in a byte. For a BCD string, the first BCD digit at the lowest address corresponds to the **MSD (most significant digit).**

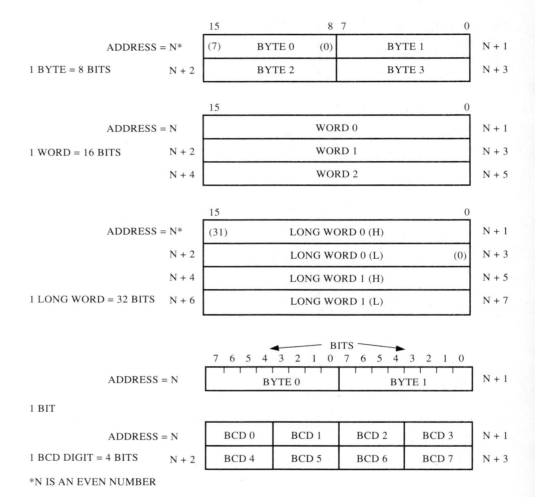

FIGURE 2.2   Data representation in memory for the 68000.

The data structures for the 68010 and 68012 processors are similar to those for the 68000. For the 68008, which has only an 8-bit data bus, the memory is byte organized. The $\overline{\text{LDS}}$ and the $\overline{\text{UDS}}$ are integrated into a single data strobe, $\overline{\text{DS}}$. A word is accessed as two sequential bytes for the 68008.[3]

The following example problem will review our discussion of data structures.

Example 2.1   Data structures for the 68000.

Suppose that we are required to store the following:

data bytes $7F and $4E at locations $0040E0 and $0040E1;
data word $CAD8 at location $0040E2;
long data word $2468A840 at the next location;
BCD data string 1234567 starting at the next location.

1. Indicate the contents of the memory for the 68000 processor.
2. What will be the contents of a long word read from location $0040E0?
3. Repeat (1) and (2) for the 68008 processor.

Solution

1. **Memory contents:** Figure 2.3(a) indicates the contents of the memory for the 68000 processor. The memory is word organized. The long word occupies two word positions, starting at $0040E4. In the long word $2468A840, the first digit, 2, is the MSD and the last digit, 0, is the LSD.

FIGURE 2.3 (a) Data structures for the 68000 microprocessor.

Even memory address	Even byte	Odd byte	Odd memory address	Data type
$0040E0	7 F	4 E	$0040E1	Byte
$0040E2	C A	D 8		Word
$0040E4	2 4	6 8		Long
	A 8	4 0		word
$0040E8	0 1	2 3	$0040E9	BCD
$0040EA	4 5	6 7	$0040EB	

(a)

For the BCD data, the leading zero is introduced by the processor, since the memory cannot be accessed at 4-bit boundaries.[4]

2. **Long word from $0040E0:** The long word from location $0040E0 will be
   MSD   LSD
   $7F4ECAD8.

3. **68008 memory organization:** Figure 2.3(b) shows the corresponding results for the 68008 processor. The memory is byte organized. A word occupies two byte locations.

FIGURE 2.3 (b) The 68008 (for Example 2.1).

Memory address			Data type
$0040E0	7	F	Byte
$0040E1	4	E	
$0040E2	C	A	Word
$0040E3	D	8	
$0040E4	2	4	Long word
$0040E5	6	8	
$0040E6	A	8	
$0040E7	4	0	
$0040E8	0	1	BCD
$0040E9	2	3	
$0040EA	4	5	
$0040EB	6	7	

(b)

The 68000 processor uses memory-mapped I/O in which the processor considers memory and I/O to be similar to one another. The memory organization for the 68000 family is linear, allowing for access of any memory location without readjusting the address mechanism. This simplifies the stack and queue operations, which will now be introduced.

Stack and Queue Organization and Structure for the 68000

A stack is a **LIFO (last-in-first-out)** data structure in the memory. Some of the internal registers of the processor are saved automatically on the stack whenever there is a change in program flow due to subroutines or exceptions. The **system stack pointer (SP)** controls the stack operation. The stack pointer is either SSP (A7′) or USP (A7), depending upon the mode of operation. The program counter is saved on the active system stack on subroutine calls and is restored from the stack on the returns. On the other hand, both the program counter and the status register are saved on the supervisor stack during the processing of exceptions, such as interrupts and traps. They are restored on return. The system stack fills from high memory to low memory.[5]

The stack is always word organized and word aligned. Byte data are put on the stack in pairs, preserving the word alignment of the stack. Saving information on the stack is known as **pushing.** Retrieving the information from the stack is known as **popping** or **pulling.** The stack pointer (SP) always points to the top of the stack, where the last element has been pushed. The SP predecrements by two for pushing a new word onto the stack. Similarly, the SP postincrements by two after pulling a word element from the stack. For long-word pushing or pulling, the SP is predecremented or postincremented by four.[6] The stack should always be accessed at even boundaries.

A queue is a **FIFO (first-in-first-out)** data structure in the memory. A queue may be implemented to fill in from high memory to low memory, or vice versa. Queues may be byte or word organized. They are very helpful in setting up memory tables and strings. There can be several queues set up in the memory. The stack and queue are very important data structures and are explicitly supported by the addressing modes of the 68000.

The following example problem on the stack and queue will promote better understanding of these structures.

Example 2.2   Stack and queue structures.
The initial values of the USP, SSP, A0, and A1 are as follows:

$$USP = \$ 0 0 0 0 4 \ 8 \ 0 \ C \qquad SSP = \$ 0 0 0 0 3 \ 7 \ A \ 0$$
$$A0 = \$ 0 0 0 0 B D 0 4 \qquad A1 = \$ 0 0 0 0 B D 1 8$$

The 68000 is executing a main user program in the user mode and the JSR (jump to subroutine) instruction has been encountered. The next instruction to be executed in the main program is at PC location $00024A08.

1. Indicate the contents of the stack.
2. The subroutine sets up a memory table in the form of a word-organized queue. A0 points to the first element and A1 points to the last element in the queue. Conceptualize the queue structure. How many words are contained in the queue?

Solution

1. **Stack:** Figure 2.4(a) shows the contents of the stack. USP is the system stack pointer, since the processor is in the user mode. The USP gets predecremented by four and the PC pointing to the next instruction in the main program gets pushed onto the stack.
2. **Queue:** Figure 2.4(b) shows the conceptual queue structure. It contains [($0000BD18 − $0000BD04) + 1] = $15 word elements.

FIGURE 2.4 (a) Contents of the stack and (b) conceptual queue structure (for Example 2.2).

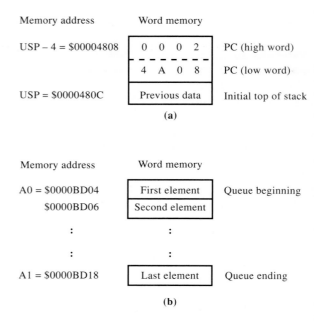

The **RTS (return-from-subroutine)** instruction restores the stored contents from the stack. RTS is the last instruction in any subroutine. On executing the RTS instruction in the subroutine of Example 2.2, the contents of the stored PC ($00024A08) are pulled from the stack and restored into the PC. This causes the main program to resume, starting at $00024A08. This is the location of the next instruction to be executed in the main program, while the subroutine is called. The SP is incremented to its original value: $0000480C.

A subroutine called by another subroutine is said to be **nested.** Suppose the first subroutine calls a second subroutine. The PC pointing to the next instruction to be executed in the first subroutine is stored on the stack, on top of the earlier stored PC (corresponding to the main routine). The processor then executes the second subroutine. At the end of the second subroutine, the RTS instruction is executed. This restores the PC corresponding to the first subroutine from the stack. At the end of the first subroutine, another RTS instruction is executed. This restores the PC corresponding to the main program from the stack. Ultimately, the SP is incremented to its original value. The available stack space determines how many of the subroutines can be nested. A similar mechanism works for nesting exceptions such as interrupts.[7]

2.2 INSTRUCTION FORMAT AND STRUCTURE

A software program consists of a sequence of instructions. These instructions are stored in program memory in the form of machine code. The **program memory** is that area in memory addressed by the program counter. The program memory is word aligned for the 68000.

Instruction Format

For the 68000, instructions are from one to five words, as shown in Figure 2.5. The first word, which is called the **operation word (op. word)** specifies the length of the instruction and the type of operation to be performed. The remaining words specify the appropriate source and destination operands. The processor obtains the source operand, performs the specified operation, and puts the result at the destination. Instructions for the 68000 have a well-defined structure enabling programmers to clearly identify the source and destination operands without ambiguity.

FIGURE 2.5 Instruction format for the 68000.

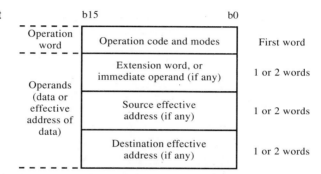

Instruction Structure

An instruction may be of the single- or the double-operand type. For the **single-operand** type, the specified operand is always the destination. For the **double-operand** type, the first operand is the source operand and the second is the destination. We will define and use three instructions for our discussion in this chapter. These instructions reference an effective address <ea> and are as follows:

CLR <ea>	Clear the contents of the specified address.
ADD <ea>,Dn	Add the contents of the effective address to the specified data register Dn (n = 1−7).
MOVE <ea>,<ea>	Move the contents of the source effective address to the destination effective address.

The CLR instruction is of the single-operand type; the other two are of the double-operand type. Figure 2.6 illustrates typical instruction structures for the 68000 processor with single and double operands. Most of the instructions are similarly structured. Also, in most cases, the data size is explicitly specified to be byte, word, or long word, as shown; thus, the same mnemonic statement may be used for different types of data.[8]

Clearly, the effective address is an integral part of the instruction. In that the 68000 has 14 distinct addressing modes to specify the effective address, it is a very powerful and versatile processor. Some of these modes deal with the register reference, some deal with the memory reference, and some deal with the control.

FIGURE 2.6 Instruction structure for the 68000.

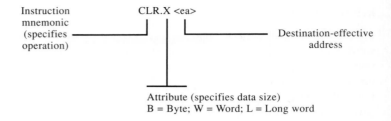

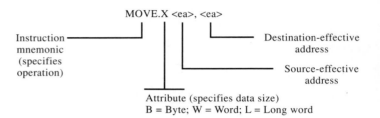

2.3 REGISTER DIRECT AND REGISTER INDIRECT ADDRESSING MODES

Motorola Corporation introduced a notation scheme to refer to the registers and operands in dealing with the addressing modes and the instructions. We will follow this notation, which is given in Figure 2.7.

Dn	Data register (n specifies the register number)
An	Address register (n specifies the register number)
Rn	Dn or An (n specifies the register number)
PC	Program counter
SR	Status register
CCR	Condition code register (user byte of the SR)
SSP	Supervisor stack pointer
USP	User stack pointer
SP	Active system stack pointer (either SSP or USP)
d8	8-bit displacement value
d16	16-bit displacement value
N	Operand size in bytes ($N = 1$, 2, or 4 for byte, word, or long-word operands)
(An)	Contents of the location addressed by An
<ea>	Effective address of the operand

FIGURE 2.7 Motorola's register and operand notation for the 68000 addressing modes and instructions.

In the register direct addressing modes, either the data or the address registers hold the data operands. On the other hand, in the register indirect addressing modes, one of the address registers holds the base address of the data operand. The register-related addressing modes are indicated in Figure 2.8.

Addressing Mode	Syntax	Effective Address <ea>
REGISTER DIRECT		
Data register direct	Dn	<ea> = Dn; n = 1–7
Address register direct	An	<ea> = An; n = 1–7
ADDRESS REGISTER INDIRECT (ARI)	(An)	<ea> = (An)
ARI with		
postincrement	(An)+	<ea> = (An) ; An+N → An
predecrement	−(An)	An−N → An ; <ea> = (An)
displacement	d(An)	<ea> = (An + d16)
index and displacement	d(An,Rn)	<ea> = (An + Rn + d8)

FIGURE 2.8 Register-related addressing modes for the 68000.

In our discussion we will use the three instructions introduced earlier:

$$CLR <ea>$$
$$ADD <ea>,Dn$$
$$MOVE <ea>,<ea>$$

We will also use the initial values of the registers and operands as given in Figure 2.9 for example problems.

It is important to note that although register A7 can be used as an address register in any of the addressing modes, extreme care should be exercised. Since A7 is the sys-

	Memory	Word
D0 = $ 1 2 3 4 0 6 7 8	Address	Data
D1 = $ A B C D E F 0 0		
A0 = $ 0 0 4 8 7 6 F 2	$0034FE74	1 A B 2
A1 = $ 0 0 3 4 F E 7 8	$0034FE76	3 C D 4
	$0034FE78	5 E F 6
	$0034FE7A	9 8 7 3
	$0034FE7C	2 4 0 8
	:	:
	$00487D6E	C D 0 2

FIGURE 2.9 Initial values for the registers and the data operands in memory.

tem stack pointer, it should remain word aligned. In the postincrement and predecrement addressing modes, A7 increments or decrements by two, even if the size of the operand is byte.

Register Direct Addressing Modes

The 68000 has two direct addressing modes: the data register direct and the address register direct.

Data Register Direct Addressing Mode (Dn; n = 1−7)   In this mode the specified data register contains the addressed operand. Examples are as follows:

CLR.L D0   Clear the long word operand in the D0 register.
             (Single-operand type; D0 is the destination.)
             D0 (before) $ I 2 3 4 0 6 7 8
             D0 (after) $ 0 0 0 0 0 0 0 0

CLR.W D1   Clear the word operand in the D1 register. The lower word in D1
             gets cleared. The upper word in D1 is not affected.
             (Single-operand type; D1 is the destination.)
             D1 (before) $ A B C D E F 0 0
             D1 (after) $ A B C D 0 0 0 0

Address Register Direct Addressing Mode (An; n = 1−7)   In this mode the specified address register contains the addressed operand. For example,

MOVEA.L A0,A1   Move the long-word operand from A0 into A1.
                  A0 is the source operand and is not affected.
                  A1 is the destination operand and is changed.
                        A0 (before) $ 0 0 4 8 7 6 F 2
                        A1 (before) $ 0 0 3 4 F E 7 8
                        A0 (after) $ 0 0 4 8 7 6 F 2 (no change)
                        A1 (after) $ 0 0 4 8 7 6 F 2 (changed)

The register direct addressing modes are very fast and efficient in conducting operations on the data operands already present in the CPU internal registers.

Register Indirect Addressing Modes

The 68000 has five indirect addressing modes: the address register indirect (ARI), the ARI with postincrement, the ARI with predecrement, the ARI with displacement, and the ARI with index and displacement. All these addressing modes provide memory reference where the data operand is located.

Address Register Indirect ARI ((An); n = 1−7)   In this mode, the specified address register contains the address of the data operand. An example follows.

MOVE.B (A1),D0   Move the byte operand in memory, the address of which is
                        contained in A1, into D0.
        Source <ea> = (A1) = $0034FE78.
        Byte operand at $0034FE78 = $5E.
        Destination <ea> = D0 register
        D0 (before) $ 1 2 3 4 0 6 7 8
        D0 (after) $ 1 2 3 4 0 6 5 E
                        Only the lower byte of D0 is changed to 5E. The other part of
                        D0 is not affected. A1 also is not affected.

ARI with Postincrement ((An)+; n = 1–7)   In this mode, too, the specified address register contains the address of the data operand. After the operand address is
used, the address register is incremented by one, two, or four, depending upon whether
the size of the operand is byte, word, or long word. This mode is very useful in setting
up and scanning the memory tables. An example follows.

MOVE.L (A1)+,D1   Move the long-word operand in memory, the address of
                        which is contained in A1, into the D1 register and postin-
                        crement A1 by four.
        Source <ea> = (A1) = $0034FE78.
        Long word at $0034FE78 = $5EF69873.
        Destination <ea> = D1 register.
        D1 (before) $ A B C D E F 0 0
        A1 (before) $ 0 0 3 4 F E 7 8
        D1 (after) $ 5 E F 6 9 8 7 3
        A1 (after) $ 0 0 3 4 F E 7 C

ARI with Predecrement (−(An); n = 1–7)   In this mode, the specified address register contains the address of the data operand. It is predecremented by one, two, or four
to generate the effective address, depending upon whether the size of the operand is
byte, word, or long word. This mode is very useful in setting up and scanning memory
tables and in multiprecision arithmetic operations. An example follows.

MOVE.W −(A1),D0   Predecrement A1 by two (since the size of the operand is
                        word), to obtain the source effective address and move the
                        word from that address into D0.
        Source <ea> = (A1−2) = $0034FE76.
        Word operand at $0034FE76 = $3CD4.
        Destination <ea> = D0 register.
        D0 (before) $ 1 2 3 4 0 6 7 8
        A1 (before) $ 0 0 3 4 F E 7 8
        D0 (after) $ 1 2 3 4 3 C D 4
        A1 (after) $ 0 0 3 4 F E 7 6

ARI with Displacement (d(An); n = 1–7)   In this mode, the specified address register contains the base address. The instruction specifies a sign-extended 16-bit displace-

ment as the extension word. The sign extension provides an effective displacement range of +32768 (+32K) for positive words and −32768 (−32K) for negative words. (Effective address computations use the sign extension for displacement and index values. Refer to Appendix A for sign-extension concepts).

The effective address is the sum of the base address and the displacement value. The contents of the address register do not change. This mode is very useful in addressing different sections of memory, with different displacement values. An example follows.

MOVE.B 0003(A1),D1   Move the byte operand from the computed source <ea> into the D1 register. Effective address computation by the processor is as shown (displacement is 16-bit d16):

$$
\begin{array}{rl}
\text{Contents of A1} & \$0034\text{FE}78 \\
+\ \text{displacement d16} & \underline{\$00000003} \\
\text{Source } <ea> = & \underline{\$0034\text{FE7B}}
\end{array}
$$

Byte operand at $0034FE7B = $73.
Destination <ea> = D1 register.
D1 (before) $ A B C D E F 0 0
A1 (before) $ 0 0 3 4 F E 7 8
D1 (after) $ A B C D E F 7 3
A1 (after) $ 0 0 3 4 F E 7 8
Only the lower byte of D1 is changed to $73. The other part of D1 is not affected. A1 also is not affected.

ARI with Index and Displacement (d(An,Rn); n = 1−7)   In this mode, the specified address register (An) contains the base address. The other address, or data, register (Rn) contains an index word (or long word), as specified. The instruction also specifies an 8-bit sign-extended displacement as a part of the extension word. The index operand can be a computed variable, which provides a dynamic addressing scheme.

The effective address is the sum of the base address, the index value, and the displacement. The contents of the address and index registers do not change. This mode is very useful in addressing different sections and blocks of memory with different index and displacement values.[9] An example follows.

MOVE.W 04(A0,D0.W),D1   Move the word operand from the source <ea> into D1. The <ea> computation by the processor is as shown (displacement is 8-bit d8).

$$
\begin{array}{rl}
\text{Contents of A0} & \$004876\text{F2} \\
+\ \text{index word from D0} & \$00000678 \\
+\ \text{displacement d8} & \underline{\$00000004} \\
\text{Source } <ea> = & \underline{\$00487\text{D6E}}
\end{array}
$$

Word operand at $00487D6E = $CD02.
D0 (before) $ 1 2 3 4 0 6 7 8
D1 (before) $ A B C D E F 0 0
A0 (before) $ 0 0 4 8 7 6 F 2

D0 (after) $ 1 2 3 4 0 6 7 8
D1 (after) $ A B C D C D 0 2
A0 (after) $ 0 0 4 8 7 6 F 2
Only the lower word of D1 is changed.

Depending upon the application, any of the preceding addressing modes can be used to specify either the source or the destination operands. In some instances, not all the addressing modes are applicable. The instruction set specifies which modes are applicable and which are not.

Any type of data structure can be set up and handled using the preceding addressing modes. For example, the predecrement and postincrement addressing modes can be used in conjunction with each other to set up a stack-type or queue-type activity. Within the same instruction, the source and destination operands can be specified by different addressing modes.

The following example problem provides a review of the register-related addressing modes.

Example 2.3   Register addressing modes for the 68000.
According to the instruction structure and the addressing modes discussed so far, specify what occurs in each of the following operations. Also, indicate the contents of the corresponding registers and the memory locations after each operation. The initial values in each case are as shown in Figure 2.9.

1. MOVE.B D1,D0
2. CLR.L −(A1)
3. MOVE.W (A1)+,0A(A0,D0.W)

Solution

1. **MOVE.B D1,D0:** D1 is the source operand. D0 is the destination operand. The source and the destination operands are specified by the data register direct addressing mode. The lower byte operand from D1 is moved to D0. Only the lower byte of D0 is changed.

   D0 (before) $ 1 2 3 4 0 6 7 8
   D0 (after) $ 1 2 3 4 0 6 0 0

2. **CLR.L −(A1):** The operand is specified by the ARI with predecrement addressing mode. A1 is predecremented by four (since the operand is long word) to obtain the effective address, and the long word at the location is cleared.

   Destination <ea> = (A1−4) = $0034FE74.
   A1 (before) $0034FE78
   A1 (after) $0034FE74

Memory address	Memory contents	
	before	after
$0034FE74	1AB2	0000
$0034FE76	3CD4	0000
$0034FE78	5EF6	5EF6
:	:	:
:	:	:

3. **MOVE.W (A1)+,0A(A0,D0.W):** The source operand is specified by the ARI with postincrement mode of addressing. The destination operand is specified by the ARI with index and displacement mode of addressing. The word from the source <ea> is moved to the destination <ea>.

Source <ea> = (A1) = $0034FE78.
Destination <ea> computation:

Contents of A0	$004876F2
+ index word from D0	$00000678
+ displacement d8	$0000000A
Destination <ea> =	$00487D74

Word at location $0034FE78 ($5EF6) is moved to location $00487D74.

A1 (before)	$ 0 0 3 4 F E 7 8
A1 (after)	$ 0 0 3 4 F E 7 C
(postincremented by four)	
Memory word at $00487D74 (before)	not known
(after)	$5EF6

The addressing modes discussed so far address the data or the address operands. We will now introduce the other modes that deal with the program control, in addition to addressing the operands.

2.4   IMMEDIATE, QUICK, ABSOLUTE, RELATIVE, AND IMPLICIT ADDRESSING MODES

Figure 2.10 illustrates the aforementioned addressing modes. In the immediate and quick addressing mode, the data is explicitly specified as part of the instruction. In the absolute addressing mode, the address of the data or of the next instruction is explicitly specified as part of the instruction. In the relative addressing mode, a displacement where the data or the next instruction is located is explicitly specified as part of the instruction. In the implicit addressing mode, instructions make implicit reference to the processor registers. We will now discuss the details of these addressing modes using the three instructions (CLR <ea>; ADD <ea>,Dn; and MOVE <ea>,<ea>) introduced earlier. The initial values of the registers and the operands given in Figure 2.11 will be used for examples.

Addressing Mode	Syntax	Effective Address <ea>
Immediate addressing	#XXX or IMM	<ea> = next one or two words of the instruction
Quick addressing	Instruction ends with Q	Data contained as part of the op.word
Absolute short addressing	XXXX or ABS.W	<ea> = next word of the instruction
Absolute long addressing	XXXXXXXX or ABS.L	<ea> = next two words of the instruction
PC relative with displacement	d(PC)	<ea> = (PC + d16)
PC relative with index and displacement	d(PC,Rn)	<ea> = (PC + Rn + d8)
Implicit	None	<ea> = PC, SR, SP. . .

FIGURE 2.10 Immediate, quick, absolute, relative, and implicit addressing modes for the 68000.

Immediate Addressing Mode (Imm)

Data are explicitly specified and contained in the extension words of the instruction. Data size can be a byte, a word, or a long word. For long-word data operands, two word extensions are required. This addressing mode is very useful in initializing the registers and the memory. Only the source operand can be specified by this addressing mode. We will use a # sign to signify the immediate operand. Examples are as follows:

	Memory Address	Word Data
D0 = $ 1 2 3 4 0 6 7 8		
D1 = $ A B C D E F 0 0		
A0 = $ 0 0 4 8 7 6 F 2	$0034FE74	1 A B 2
A1 = $ 0 0 3 4 F E 7 8	$0034FE76	3 C D 4
	$0034FE78	5 E F 6
	$0034FE7A	9 8 7 3
	$0034FE7C	2 4 0 8
	:	:
	:	:
	:	:
	$00487D6E	C D 0 2

FIGURE 2.11 Initial values for the registers and the data operands in memory.

MOVE.B #$2A,D0

Move the immediate data byte $2A into the D0 destination register.
D0 (before) $ 1 2 3 4 0 6 7 8
D0 (after) $ 1 2 3 4 0 6 2 A

MOVE.W #$BBBB,(A1)

Move the immediate data word $BBBB into memory addressed by (A1).
Destination <ea> = (A1) = $0034FE78.
Contents of $0034FE78 (before) $5EF6
                     (after) $BBBB

Quick Addressing Mode (. . . . Q)

This is a variation of the immediate addressing mode. Up to 8 bits of data can be specified as part of the operation word itself. Thus, this is a single-word instruction and operates faster than the immediate addressing mode. However, the data range is limited to 8 bits in move operations and to 8 units in arithmetic operations. In this addressing mode, all 32 bits of the destination are affected by the sign extension of the data operand. In the sign extension, the most significant bit (MSB) of the data operand is replicated to all the higher bits (see Appendix A). The instructions allowed in this mode are explicitly specified in the instruction set and end with Q (ADDQ, MOVEQ, SUBQ, and so forth). An example follows.

MOVEQ #$43,D0

Move the quick data $43 into the D0 destination register.
Data operand = $43 = 0 1 0 0 0 0 1 1
                            |
                   MSB = 0
This MSB is replicated to all the higher bits in D0 register.
D0 (before) $ 1 2 3 4 0 6 7 8
D0 (after) $ 0 0 0 0 0 0 4 3

Absolute Short and Long Addressing Modes (Abs.W, Abs.L)

In the absolute short addressing mode, a 16-bit address of the data or of the next instruction is explicitly specified as an extension word within the instruction. In the absolute long addressing mode, instead of the 16-bit address, a 32-bit address is specified as two extension words within the instruction. The short addressing mode has a range of 64 kilobytes and the long addressing mode has a range of 16 megabytes. These addressing modes are used to access the memory directly. They are also used in program control applications to specify the location of the next instruction. Examples are as follows:

CLR.L $0034FE74

Clear the long-word operand starting at memory location $0034FE74. This is the absolute long addressing mode, since a 32-bit address of the operand is specified.
Destination <ea> = $0034FE74.
Long-word operand at $0034FE74
(before) $1 A B 2 3 C D 4
(after) $0 0 0 0 0 0 0 0

MOVE.B D0,$4000   Move the byte operand from D0 into the memory location at
                         $4000. Destination of the 16-bit address is specified by the
                         absolute short addressing mode. The upper four digits of the
                         address are considered to be $0000.
                         Source operand = byte from D0 = $78
                         Destination <ea> = $00004000
                         Byte operand at $00004000 (before)   not known
                                                     (after) $78

PC Relative with Displacement Addressing Mode d(PC)

In this addressing mode, a signed displacement is specified as a part of the instruction.
This displacement is added to the contents of the PC (program counter) to obtain the
effective address of the operand.

   The displacement can be 8 or 16 bits, depending upon the instruction. For an 8-bit
displacement, the displacement range is 256 bytes; for a 16-bit displacement, it is 64
kilobytes.

   Program control instructions, such as BRANCH instructions, use this type of addressing mode. In the example that follows, we will introduce a new instruction, **BRA
(branch always).** This specifies where the next instruction to be executed is to be
found.

PC   **Instruction**
$00002000   BRA 082A(PC)   Branch to the specified effective address. The <ea>
                            calculation is as shown:
                            Contents of PC after the BRA
                            instruction* $00002002
                            + sign-extended 16-bit
                            displacement $0000082A
                                            <ea> = $0000282C
                            The program branches to $0000282C and fetches the
                            next instruction from that location.

*Recall that the PC advances to next word location after fetching the present op.word.
Thus, the PC will be at $00002002 after fetching the BRA instruction.

PC Relative with Index and Displacement Addressing Mode d(PC,Rn)

In this addressing mode, in addition to the displacement, the instruction specifies an index register. The effective address is the sum of the contents of the PC, the index register, and the displacement. The displacement is 8 bits. An example follows.

PC   **Instruction**
$00487708   MOVE.W EC(PC,D0.W),D1   Move the word operand from the source
                                    <ea> into D1. The <ea> calculation is
                                    as shown.

$$
\begin{array}{rl}
\text{Contents of PC after the MOVE instruction*} & \$0048770A \\
+ \text{ sign extended index word from D0} & \underline{\$00000678} \\
\text{Indexed address } = & \$00487D82 \\
+ \text{ sign-extended displacement}\dagger = & \underline{\$FFFFFFEC} \\
\text{<ea> } = & \$00487D6E \\
\text{Word operand from \$00487D6E } = & \$CD02 \\
\text{D1 (before)} & \$ABCDEF00 \\
\text{D1(after)} & \$ABCDCD02
\end{array}
$$

*PC advances to the next word location ($0048770A) after the MOVE instruction.
†Sign extended to 32 bits. $EC is a negative number that corresponds to $-$\$14 in twos-complement notation. (Refer to Appendix A for twos-complement concepts.)

The PC relative addressing modes are used extensively in program control applications. In addition, these addressing modes are used in applications requiring program code relocation. In such applications, the program code can be made to reside in any part of memory, and the PC can be adjusted accordingly. Any memory reference will be with respect to the adjusted PC as the base address and will be valid.

Implicit Addressing Mode

The 68000 has certain instructions that make implicit reference to the processor registers (the PC, SR, SP, and so forth). This mode works in conjunction with the other addressing modes. Sometimes it is not considered to be a separate addressing mode. An example follows.

MOVE.W #$0400,SR   Move the immediate word operand $0400 into the SR (status register).* The source operand is specified by the immediate addressing mode. Destination <ea>, which is the SR, is specified by the implicit reference.
SR (before)   not known
SR (after) $0400

*This instruction dealing with the SR is privileged and can only be used in the supervisor mode.

The following example problem provides a review of the addressing modes we have discussed.

Example 2.4   Other addressing modes for the 68000.
Use the initial values given in Figure 2.11. Specify what occurs in each of the following operations. Indicate the contents of the corresponding registers and memory locations after each operation. Consider the same initial values for each of the operations.

1. MOVE.L #$765432AC,$0034FE74
2. ADDQ.B #$04,D1
3. MOVE.W $007A(PC),SR (Contents of PC $0034FE00)

Solution

1. **MOVE.L #$765432AC,$0034FE74:** The source operand is specified by the immediate addressing mode and the destination effective address is specified by the absolute long addressing mode. The source operand is moved to the destination <ea>.

Source long word = $765432AC
Destination <ea> = $0034FE74
Long-word operand at $0034FE74 (before) = $1AB23CD4
(after) = $765432AC

2. **ADDQ.B #$04,D1:** The source operand is specified by the quick addressing mode and the destination operand is specified by the data register direct addressing mode. Add the immediate (quick) operand to the destination <ea>.

Source operand (byte) = $04.
Destination <ea> = D1 register.
Source data $04 is added to the D1 register.
D1 (before) $ A B C D E F 0 0
D1 (after) $ A B C D E F 0 4

3. **Move.W $007A(PC),SR:** With contents of PC = $0034FE00, the effective address of the source operand is $0034FE7A. The contents at that address (= $9873) are moved into SR.

SR (after) = $9873

In software applications using the 68000 microprocessor, all of the 14 addressing modes can be used in conjunction with each other. Certain addressing modes, however, may preclude some instructions. This information is available from the instruction set. Care should be taken to ensure that an invalid addressing mode is not used to specify operands. Similarly, word and long-word operands should not be accessed at the odd address boundaries. To do so would result in error conditions.

2.5 SUMMARY

In this chapter we discussed the memory organization schemes, data structures, and addressing modes for the 68000 processor.

The memory is organized as 16-bit words consisting of blocks of even and odd bytes. The bytes can be accessed individually, the words can be accessed as two bytes, and the long words can be accessed as two words. Words and long words should be accessed only at the even address boundaries. To do otherwise would result in an error condition. The 68000 processor follows memory-mapped I/O (input/output) in which the processor communicates with an I/O device as if it were one of the memory locations. The total address space for the 68000 processor can be considered as 16 megabytes or 8 megawords.

The important data structures of the 68000 are the stack and the queue. The stack is a LIFO data structure in the memory. Some of the internal registers are saved on the stack in the case of a change in program flow due to subroutines or exceptions. USP controls the stack if the processor is in the user mode; SSP controls the stack if the processor is in the supervisor mode. The stack fills from high memory to low memory on a push-type stack operation. The stack is word sized and word aligned and should only be accessed at even address boundaries.

The queue is a FIFO data structure in the memory and can be set up to fill in from high memory to low memory or vice versa. The queue is very useful in setting up tables and strings.

For the 68000, instructions are from one to five words. The first word, which is the operation word (op.word), specifies the type of operation. The rest of the words contain the appropriate extensions and operands. The structure of the instruction consists of the instruction field and the source and destination fields. Instructions may be of the single- or double-operand type. In the single-operand type, the specified operand is the destination operand on which the given operation is performed. In the double-operand type, the first operand is the source operand and the second is the destination operand. After performing the operation, the final result is put in the destination.

The 68000 has 14 different addressing modes with which to access the source and destination operands. In the register direct addressing modes, either a data register or an address register contains the specified operand. In the register indirect addressing (ARI) modes, one of the address registers contains the base address. There may be index and displacement values specified as a part of the instruction. These may be added to the base address to obtain the effective address of the operand.

In the immediate and quick addressing modes, the instruction contains the data operand. In the absolute addressing modes, the instruction contains the address of the operands. In the PC relative addressing modes, the PC contains the base address. There may be index and displacement values specified as part of the instruction. These may be added to the base address to obtain the effective address of the operand. The implicit addressing mode makes an implicit reference to some of the internal registers of the processor.

These addressing modes all can be used in conjunction with one another to specify the source and destination operands. The source operand can be specified by one addressing mode and the destination operand by another. This flexibility allows the 68000 processor to access operands conveniently and efficiently.

PROBLEMS

2.1 Draw the conceptual memory organization schemes for the following processors:

  (a) the 68008 microprocessor;

  (b) the 68010 microprocessor.

2.2 The 68000 is accessing a word operand from the memory. The memory word is $234A. Specify the following:

  (a) contents of data bus D0–D7 and D8–D15;

  (b) logic levels of the $\overline{\text{LDS}}$, $\overline{\text{UDS}}$, and R/$\overline{\text{W}}$ strobes.

2.3 What are the contents of the strobes $\overline{\text{LDS}}$, $\overline{\text{UDS}}$, and R/$\overline{\text{W}}$ and the data bus D0–D15 when the 68000 is writing the long-word operand $AABBCCDD into memory location $004000.

2.4 Suppose the $\overline{\text{LDS}}$ and the $\overline{\text{UDS}}$ connections have been interchanged in Figure 2.1. What would happen in the following situations:

  (a) the 68000 is trying to read byte operand $45 from memory location $00001000;

  (b) the 68000 is trying to write byte operand $54 into memory location $0000100B.

2.5 Long-word operands $124680AB and $78908762 are stored in sequential memory locations beginning at $00002000. BCD data string 1200340045974 is stored beginning at the next sequential location. Show how data are physically stored in the following systems:

  (a) the 68000-based system;

  (b) the 68008-based system;

  (c) the 68010-based system.

2.6 Show how the following data elements are stored in memory for a 68000-based system:

  (a) hex string $1234432156788765ABCDDCBA, starting from memory location $00004000;

  (b) the hex string given in (a), but in the form of a word-aligned queue starting from $00004040 and filling in towards high memory address.

2.7 The system stack pointer has an initial value $000034A0. Show how the following data elements are stored on the stack:

$$\text{first element} \quad \$0010$$
$$\text{second element} \quad \$0020$$
$$\vdots$$
$$\text{ninth element} \quad \$0090$$

What are the contents of the stack pointer after the ninth element has been stored?

2.8 Each subroutine call stores the program counter on the system stack. Each exception, such as interrupt, stores the program counter and the status register on the stack.

  (a) In a control system application, 128 bytes of stack space is allocated for the user mode of operation. How many subroutines can be nested if the stack is not used for any other storage?

  (b) Repeat (a) if the D0 and D1 registers are also to be stored on the stack each time a subroutine call occurs. (*Note:* separate instructions are to be written to store any registers other than the PC on the stack during subroutine calls.)

2.9 In a robotics system application using the 68000, 512 bytes of supervisor stack space is allocated. Each robotics motor requires one interrupt service routine, which nests eight subroutines.

(a) How much stack space is used up for each robotics motor application?

(b) How many of these robotics operations can be nested?

2.10 Following the instruction format of Figure 2.5, conceptualize how the following instructions are stored in the memory for a 68000-based system:

(a) CLR.L <ea>; <ea> corresponds to a 32-bit address;

(b) ADD.W <ea>,D1; <ea> corresponds to a 32-bit address;

(c) MOVE.L <ea>,<ea>; each <ea> corresponds to a 32-bit address.

2.11 Given the instruction structure of Figure 2.6, write instructions to accomplish the following tasks:

(a) clear a byte in the D7 register;

(b) move a long word from A6 into the D5 register;

(c) add the long-word contents from D6 to the long-word contents of D7, with the result in D6.

2.12 Write a sequence of instructions to accomplish the following tasks:

(a) add the word contents from D5 to the long-word contents in D6 and put the result in the D7 register;

(b) clear the long word in the D3 register and transfer the result to the A3 register.

2.13 Using the initial values as given in Figure 2.9, specify the results of the following operations:

(a) ADD.L D1,D0

(b) ADD.W A0,D1

(c) MOVE.B −(A1),−(A1)

Clearly specify the source and destination addressing modes. Show the contents of the affected registers, the SR, and the memory.

2.14 Repeat Problem 2.13 with the condition that the operations are done in sequence, affecting the values accordingly.

2.15 Transfer the long-word contents from $0034FE76 into the D1 register using the following addressing modes:

(a) ARI with displacement;

(b) ARI with index and displacement;

(c) absolute long.

Write the appropriate instruction in each case, using the same initial values given in Figure 2.9.

2.16 The PC is at location $0034FE00 after the appropriate op.word has been read, which transfers the long-word contents from $0034FE76 into the D1 register. Write the instructions needed to reach this condition using the following addressing modes:

(a) PC relative with displacement;

(b) PC relative with index and displacement;

(c) any other mode of your choice.

Use the initial values given in Figure 2.9.

2.17 Using the same initial values, specify the contents of the registers and the memory after accomplishing each of the following operations:

(a) MOVE.L −(A1),(A0)+

(b) ADD.W −(A1),−(A1)

(c) CLR.B $0034FE75

2.18 Repeat Problem 2.17, with the condition that the operations are done in sequence, affecting the values accordingly.

2.19 With the initial values of Figure 2.9, which of the following operations are valid and which generate error conditions? Why?

    (a) ADD.W $0003(A1),D0

    (b) MOVE.B $00(A1.D0.L),D1

    (c) JSR $0305

2.20 Specify the results of the following operations, using the same initial values:

    (a) ADD.L #$10101010,D0

    (b) ADDQ.L #$03,(A1)+

    (c) MOVE.L #$00100100,(A1)+

Show the contents of the affected registers, the SR, and the memory.

2.21 Repeat Problem 2.20 with the condition that the operations are done in sequence, affecting the values accordingly.

2.22 Specify whether the following are true or false:

    (a) the immediate addressing mode cannnot be used to specify the destination operand.

    (b) the quick addressing mode can be used to specify data elements of any size.

    (c) the PC relative addressing mode cannot be used to specify odd memory locations.

    (d) the implicit addressing mode cannot refer to external memory.

ENDNOTES

1. Motorola, Inc. *MC68000 Data Book*. Phoenix, AZ: Motorola Technical Operations, 1983.

2. Motorola, Inc. *M68000 16/32 Bit Microprocessor Programmer's Reference Manual, Fifth Edition*. Englewood Cliffs, NJ: Prentice-Hall, 1987.

3. Motorola, Inc. *MC68008 Data Book*. Phoenix, AZ: Motorola Technical Operations, 1983.

4. Stranes, T. "Design Philosophy Behind the M68000." *Byte* (Apr., May, Jun. 1983).

5. Gaonkar, R. *Microprocessor Architecture, Programming, and Applications with the 8085/8080A*. Columbus, OH: Merrill, 1984.

6. Stranes, T. "Design Philosophy Behind the M68000." *Byte* (Apr., May, Jun. 1983).

7. Subbarao, W. *Microprocessors: Hardware, Software,* and *Design Applications*. Englewood Cliffs, NJ: Prentice-Hall, 1984.

8. Cohen, K. "Multiprocessor Architecture." *Electronics* (May 1983).

9. Motorola, Inc. *M68000 vs. IAPX86 Benchmark Performance*. Phoenix, AZ: Motorola Technical Operations, 1986.

The 68000 Instruction Set and Programming Considerations

Objectives

In this chapter we will study:

The general instruction set of the 68000

The data movement group of instructions and applications

Binary and BCD arithmetic groups of instructions and applications

Logical and bit-manipulation groups of instructions and applications

Program and system control groups of instructions and applications

Instruction timing considerations and applications

3.0 INTRODUCTION

The 68000 has a powerful instruction set, including 56 generic instruction types. Some of these instruction types have several variations. In addition, the 14 addressing modes discussed in the previous chapter can be used in conjunction with the instructions. This provides the 68000 with tremendous software capability.[1]

The instructions are designed to follow a consistent structure. The same mnemonic statement representing an instruction can be used with appropriate attributes to refer to different operand sizes and addressing modes.

A clear understanding of how these instructions work, how they affect the status bits in the status register, and which of the addressing modes can be used is essential to the study of the software features and the programming techniques of the 68000 processor.

We will first introduce the general instruction set, categorize it into groups, and then discuss the essential features of each of the groups with appropriate illustrations. This approach will help us gain better insight into the instruction set. The material covered will provide the necessary background for writing programs using the 68000 processor.

3.1 THE GENERAL INSTRUCTION SET

Figure 3.1 indicates the general instruction set for the 68000 microprocessor in tabular form. In the first column the instruction mnemonic used in writing the assembly programs is given. The second column contains the physical description of the instruction. The third column lists the actual operation, and the last columns describe how the flags are affected in the case of each instruction. Figure 3.2 shows how the condition codes are computed. In Appendix B, details of the instruction set are presented.[2] The reader should refer to this appendix in studying the concepts covered in this chapter.

Interpretation of the Instructions

Consider the second instruction in the table in Figure 3.1. It is the ADD instruction with which we are already familiar. The description indicates that it is a binary addition. The data operands will be interpreted as binary numbers. The operation indicates that the destination operand is added to the source operand, and the final result is put in the destination. We see that all of the condition codes, known as **flags** or **status bits,** are affected by this operation. Any of them can be used for decision making in a programming sequence.

The syntax, attributes, and addressing modes for the ADD instruction are as follows (see also Appendix B):[3]

Assembler Syntax:	ADD <ea>,Dn or ADD Dn,<ea>
Attributes (size):	Byte, word, or long word.

Mnemonic	Description	Operation	Condition Codes				
			X	N	Z	V	C
ABCD	Add Decimal with Extend	$(Destination)_{10} + (Source)_{10} + X \rightarrow$ Destination	*	U	*	U	*
ADD	Add Binary	(Destination) + (Source) → Destination	*	*	*	*	*
ADDA	Add Address	(Destination) + (Source) → Destination	—	—	—	—	—
ADDI	Add Immediate	(Destination) + Immediate Data → Destination	*	*	*	*	*
ADDQ	Add Quick	(Destination) + Immediate Data → Destination	*	*	*	*	*
ADDX	Add Extended	(Destination) + (Source) + X → Destination	*	*	*	*	*
AND	AND Logical	(Destination) Λ (Source) → Destination	—	*	*	0	0
ANDI	AND Immediate	(Destination) Λ Immediate Data → Destination	—	*	*	0	0
ANDI to CCR	AND Immediate to Condition Codes	(Source) Λ CCR → CCR	*	*	*	*	*
ANDI to SR	AND Immediate to Status Register	(Source) Λ SR → SR	*	*	*	*	*
ASL, ASR	Arithmetic Shift	(Destination) Shifted by <count> → Destination	*	*	*	*	*
B$_{CC}$	Branch Conditionally	If $_{CC}$ then PC + d → PC	—	—	—	—	—
BCHG	Test a Bit and Change	~(<bit number>) OF Destination → Z ~(<bit number>) OF Destination → <bit number> OF Destination	—	—	*	—	—
BCLR	Test a Bit and Clear	~(<bit number>) OF Destination → Z 0 → <bit number> → OF Destination	—	—	*	—	—
BRA	Branch Always	PC + d → PC	—	—	—	—	—
BSET	Test a Bit and Set	~(<bit number>) OF Destination → Z 1 → <bit number> OF Destination	—	—	*	—	—
BSR	Branch to Subroutine	PC → -(SP); PC + d → PC	—	—	—	—	—
BTST	Test a Bit	~(<bit number>) OF Destination → Z	—	—	*	—	—
CHK	Check Register Against Bounds	If Dn <0 or Dn> (<ea>) then TRAP	—	*	U	U	U
CLR	Clear and Operand	0 → Destination	—	0	1	0	0
CMP	Compare	(Destination) - (Source)	—	*	*	*	*
CMPA	Compare Address	(Destination) - (Source)	—	*	*	*	*
CMPI	Compare Immediate	(Destination) - Immediate Data	—	*	*	*	*
CMPM	Compare Memory	(Destination) - (Source)	—	*	*	*	*
DB$_{CC}$	Test Condition, Decrement and Branch	If ~$_{CC}$ then Dn - 1 → Dn; if Dn ≠ -1 then PC + d → PC	—	—	—	—	—
DIVS	Signed Divide	(Destination)/(Source) → Destination	—	*	*	*	0
DIVU	Unsigned Divide	(Destination)/(Source) → Destination	—	*	*	*	0
EOR	Exclusive OR Logical	(Destination) ⊕ (Source) → Destination	—	*	*	0	0
EORI	Exclusive OR Immediate	(Destination) ⊕ Immediate Data → Destination	—	*	*	0	0
EORI to CCR	Exclusive OR Immediate to Condition Codes	(Source) ⊕ CCR → CCR	*	*	*	*	*
EORI to SR	Exclusive OR Immediate to Status Register	(Source) ⊕ SR → SR	*	*	*	*	*
EXG	Exchange Register	Rx ↔ Ry	—	—	—	—	—
EXT	Sign Extend	(Destination) Sign-Extended → Destination	—	*	*	0	0
JMP	Jump	Destination → PC	—	—	—	—	—
JSR	Jump to Subroutine	PC → -(SP); Destination → PC	—	—	—	—	—
LEA	Load Effective Address	<ea> → An	—	—	—	—	—
LINK	Link and Allocate	An → -(SP); SP → An; SP + Displacement → SP	—	—	—	—	—
LSL, LSR	Logical Shift	(Destination) Shifted by <count> → Destination	*	*	*	0	*
MOVE	Move Data from Source to Destination	(Source) → Destination	—	*	*	0	0
MOVE to CCR	Move to Condition Code	(Source) → CCR	*	*	*	*	*
MOVE to SR	Move to the Status Register	(Source) → SR	*	*	*	*	*

Λ logical AND
V logical OR
⊕ logical exclusive OR
~ logical complement

* affected
— unaffected
0 cleared
1 set
U undefined

FIGURE 3.1 The 68000 instruction set table. (Courtesy of Motorola, Inc.)

Mnemonic	Description	Operation	Condition Codes				
			X	N	Z	V	C
MOVE from SR	Move from the Status Register	SR → Destination	—	—	—	—	—
MOVE USP	Move User Stack Pointer	USP → An; An → USP	—	—	—	—	—
MOVEA	Move Address	(Source) → Destination	—	—	—	—	—
MOVEM	Move Multiple Registers	Registers → Destination (Source) → Registers	—	—	—	—	—
MOVEP	Move Peripheral Data	(Source) → Destination	—	—	—	—	—
MOVEQ	Move Quick	Immediate Data → Destination	—	*	*	0	0
MULS	Signed Multiply	(Destination)X(Source) → Destination	—	*	*	0	0
MULU	Unsigned Multiply	(Destination)X(Source) → Destination	—	*	*	0	0
NBCD	Negate Decimal with Extend	$0 - (Destination)_{10} - X$ → Destination	*	U	*	U	*
NEG	Negate	0 − (Destination) → Destination	*	*	*	*	*
NEGX	Negate with Extend	0 − (Destination) − X → Destination	*	*	*	*	*
NOP	No Operation	—	—	—	—	—	—
NOT	Logical Complement	~(Destination) → Destination	—	*	*	0	0
OR	Inclusive OR Logical	(Destination) v (Source) → Destination	—	*	*	0	0
ORI	Inclusive OR Immediate	(Destination) v Immediate Data → Destination	—	*	*	0	0
ORI to CCR	Inclusive OR Immediate to Condition Codes	(Source) v CCR → CCR	*	*	*	*	*
ORI to SR	Inclusive OR Immediate to Status Register	(Source) v SR → SR	*	*	*	*	*
PEA	Push Effective Address	<ea> → − (SP)	—	—	—	—	—
RESET	Reset External Device	—	—	—	—	—	—
ROL, ROR	Rotate (Without Extend)	(Destination) Rotated by <count> → Destination	—	*	*	0	*
ROXL, ROXR	Rotate with Extend	(Destination) Rotated by <count> → Destination	*	*	*	0	*
RTE	Return from Exception	(SP)+ → SR; (SP)+ → PC	*	*	*	*	*
RTR	Return and Restore Condition Codes	(SP)+ → CC; (SP)+ → PC	*	*	*	*	*
RTS	Return from Subroutine	(SP)+ → PC	—	—	—	—	—
SBCD	Subtract Decimal with Extend	$(Destination)_{10} - (Source)_{10} - X$ → Destination	*	U	*	U	*
S$_{CC}$	Set According to Condition	If $_{CC}$ then 1's → Destination else 0's → Destination	—	—	—	—	—
STOP	Load Status Register and Stop	Immediate Data → SR; STOP	*	*	*	*	*
SUB	Subtract Binary	(Destination) − (Source) → Destination	*	*	*	*	*
SUBA	Subtract Address	(Destination) − (Source) → Destination	—	—	—	—	—
SUBI	Subtract Immediate	(Destination) − Immediate Data → Destination	*	*	*	*	*
SUBQ	Subtract Quick	(Destination) − Immediate Data → Destination	*	*	*	*	*
SUBX	Subtract with Extend	(Destination) − (Source) − X → Destination	*	*	*	*	*
SWAP	Swap Register Halves	Register [31:16] ↔ Register [15:0]	—	*	*	0	0
TAS	Test and Set an Operand	(Destination) Tested → CC; 1 → [7] OF Destination	—	*	*	0	0
TRAP	Trap	PC → − (SSP); SR → − (SSP); (Vector) → PC	—	—	—	—	—
TRAPV	Trap on Overflow	If V then TRAP	—	—	—	—	—
TST	Test and Operand	(Destination) Tested → CC	—	*	*	0	0
UNLK	Unlink	An → SP; (SP)+ → An	—	—	—	—	—

[ ] = bit number
Λ logical AND
V logical OR
⊕ logical exclusive OR
~ logical complement

* affected
— unaffected
0 cleared
1 set
U undefined

FIGURE 3.1 *Continued.*

FIGURE 3.2 Condition code (flag) computation in the 68000 processor. (Courtesy of Motorola, Inc.)

Instruction	X	N	Z	V	C
ABCD	★	u	★	u	★
ADD	★	★	★	★	★
ADDA	—	—	—	—	—
ADDI	★	★	★	★	★
ADDQ	★	★	★	★	★
ADDX	★	★	★	★	★
AND	—	★	★	0	0
ANDI	—	★	★	0	0
ASL,ASR	★	★	★	★	★
Bcc	—	—	—	—	—
BCHG	—	—	★	—	—
BCLR	—	—	★	—	—
BRA	—	—	—	—	—
BSET	—	—	★	—	—
BSR	—	—	—	—	—
BTST	—	—	★	—	—
CHK	—	★	u	u	u
CLR	—	0	1	0	0
CMP	—	★	★	★	★
CMPA	—	★	★	★	★
CMPI	—	★	★	★	★
CMPM	—	★	★	★	★
DBcc	—	—	—	—	—
DIVS	—	★	★	★	0

Instruction	X	N	Z	V	C
DIVU	—	★	★	★	0
EOR	—	★	★	0	0
EORI	—	★	★	0	0
EXG	—	—	—	—	—
EXT	—	★	★	0	0
JMP	—	—	—	—	—
JSR	—	—	—	—	—
LEA	—	—	—	—	—
LINK	—	—	—	—	—
LSL,LSR	★	★	★	0	★
MOVE	—	★	★	0	0
MOVE from SR	—	—	—	—	—
MOVE to CC	★	★	★	★	★
MOVE to SR	★	★	★	★	★
MOVE USP	—	—	—	—	—
MOVEA	—	—	—	—	—
MOVEM	—	—	—	—	—
MOVEP	—	—	—	—	—
MOVEQ	—	★	★	0	0
MULS	—	★	★	0	0
MULU	—	★	★	0	0
NBCD	★	u	★	u	★
NEG	★	★	★	★	★
NEGX	★	★	★	★	★
NOP	—	—	—	—	—

Instruction	X	N	Z	V	C
NOT	—	★	★	0	0
OR	—	★	★	0	0
ORI	—	★	★	0	0
PEA	—	—	—	—	—
RESET	—	—	—	—	—
ROL,ROR	—	★	★	0	★
ROXL,ROXR	★	★	★	0	★
RTE	★	★	★	★	★
RTR	★	★	★	★	★
RTS	—	—	—	—	—
SBCD	★	u	★	u	★
Scc	—	—	—	—	—
STOP	★	★	★	★	★
SUB	★	★	★	★	★
SUBA	—	—	—	—	—
SUBI	★	★	★	★	★
SUBQ	★	★	★	★	★
SUBX	★	★	★	★	★
SWAP	—	★	★	0	0
TAS	—	★	★	0	0
TRAP	—	—	—	—	—
TRAPV	—	—	—	—	—
TST	—	★	★	0	0
UNLK	—	—	—	—	—

— UNAFFECTED   u UNDEFINED
0 CLEARED   1 SET   ★ SET ACCORDING TO THE RESULT

Source <ea>:   All addressing modes permissible.

Destination <ea>:   Modes An, d(PC), d(PC,Rn), and
                    immediate are not permissible. Other
                    modes can be used.

Clearly, from the preceding information, either the source or the destination operand is a data register and the other operand can be an effective address <ea>. If <ea> is the source, all addressing modes are permissible. If <ea> is the destination, some addressing modes are not allowed. The instruction can operate on byte, word, and longword operands.

Following the preceding guidelines, programmers can easily write valid instructions. For example,

ADD.L D7,D6   Add long word in D7 to the long word in
                   D6, with the result in D6.

ADD.B (A5),D3   Add the byte from memory addressed by
                   the contents of A5 to the byte in D3, with
                   the result in D3.

are valid forms of the ADD instruction. On the other hand,

ADD.W (A5),(A2)   Add the memory words addressed by (A5)
                   and (A2), with the result in memory
                   addressed by (A2).

ADD.B D6,#$12   Add the byte in D6 to the immediate data
                   $12 and put the result at the immediate
                   data location.

are invalid forms of the ADD instruction. In the former case, a data register does not appear as one of the operands. In the latter, the destination operand cannot be specified by the immediate addressing mode.

Each instruction may have several variations, depending upon the operands. Consider the first six instructions in the instruction set in Figure 3.1. They are the variations of the ADD instruction as shown in Figure 3.3. The 68000 uses the same mnemonic

---

ABCD:	**BCD** signifies that the operands are of the BCD type.
ADD:	Regular binary addition.
ADD**A:**	**A** signifies that the destination operand is an address register.
ADD**I:**	**I** signifies that the source operand is immediate data.
ADD**Q:**	**Q** signifies that the source operand is quick data.
ADD**X:**	**X** signifies that the extend flag (X) is included in the addition.

FIGURE 3.3 Variations of the ADD instruction in the 68000 instruction set.

(ADD in this case), with extensions such as **A, I, Q,** and **X,** to signify the different variations. The ABCD instruction is specifically made more symbolic to represent the BCD data, but it still belongs to the same ADD category.

The 68000 follows this consistent structure for all of its instructions. These instructions can be interpreted easily and appropriate forms written for programming and the software applications.

The Instruction Groups

The 68000 instructions may be broadly classified into the following groups:

1. data movement;
2. binary integer arithmetic;
3. BCD (binary coded decimal);
4. logic, shift, and rotate;
5. bit manipulation;
6. program control;
7. system control; and
8. special category for extended functions.

The data movement group deals with the physical movement of the source and destination operands. The integer, BCD, logic, shift, and rotate groups deal with the actual data processing operations. The program control group deals with the decision-making, conditional, and unconditional branch and jump operations. The bit-manipulation and the system control groups supplement the other operations mentioned above. We will deal with the special category in subsequent chapters.

The following example problem provides a review of the general features of the instruction set.

Example 3.1   The 68000 instruction set.
The syntax and attributes for the ADDA and ADDI are as follows, and permissible addressing modes for the effective addresses are as specified:

Syntax	*Attributes*	*Addressing Modes*
ADDA <ea>,An:	word, long word	All modes allowed for source <ea>.
ADDI #data,<ea>:	byte, word, long word	An, d(PC), d(PC,Rn), and immediate modes not allowed for destination <ea>.

1. Specify whether the following four forms are valid or not. Give the reason(s):

ADDA.L A6,A4   ADDA.B A1,A3
ADDI.W #$12AC,D7   ADDI.W #$100E,A3

2. Specify to which groups each of the instructions belongs.

Solution

1. ADDA.L A6,A4: This instruction is valid since it satisfies all of the guidelines (single-word instruction).

ADDA.B A1,A3: This instruction is not valid since the byte attribute is not allowed.

ADDI.W #$12AC,D7: This instruction is valid since it satisfies all the guidelines (two-word instruction).

ADDI.W #$100E,A3: This instruction is not valid since the destination <ea> (= A3) is not valid.

2. Group: All of the instructions are of the addition type. As such, they belong to the arithmetic group.

Any invalid instruction will generate an error condition known as an **illegal instruction exception.** We will discuss this exception in later chapters.

Figure 3.4 illustrates a standard convention introduced by Motorola to summarize the addressing modes, especially while dealing with the instruction set. We will use this convention in our discussion. The addressing modes are classified as data, memory, control, and alterable types. In the data type, the <ea> refers to a data operand. In the memory type, the memory reference is explicit as to where the data operand can be

Effective Address Modes	*Data*	*Memory*	*Control*	*Alterable*
Dn	X			X
An				X
(An)	X	X	X	X
(An)+	X	X		X
−(An)	X	X		X
d_{16}(An)	X	X	X	X
d_8(An,Rx)	X	X	X	X
xxxx (Absolute short)	X	X	X	X
xxxxxx (Absolute long)	X	X	X	X
#xxx (Immediate)	X	X		

FIGURE 3.4 Effective address classification for the 68000. (Courtesy of Motorola, Inc.)

found. In the control type, the addressing mode can be used for program control. In the alterable type, the addressed operand may change.

A single addressing mode can be classified in more than one category.[4] Consider the ARI mode (An), for example. It can be classified in all four categories. It can address data, it can address memory, it can specify a jump or a branch address for program control, and the operand addressed by this mode can be allowed to change. On the other hand, the immediate (#xxx) addressing mode belongs only to the data-type category. It cannot address memory, cannot specify a jump or branch address, and it is unalterable.

3.2   DATA MOVEMENT AND ARITHMETIC INSTRUCTION GROUPS

Data movement is an integral part of a computer system operation. The 68000 has a very powerful and efficient group of data movement instructions, as shown in Figure 3.5. The group consists of several forms of the MOVE, EXG, and SWAP instructions. The privileged instructions are indicated with an asterisk; these should be used only in the supervisor mode.

The first column specifies the instruction in mnemonic form. The second column specifies the operand size—a byte (8 bits), a word (16 bits), or a long word (32 bits). The third and fourth columns specify the operation and the syntax (or notation). The last column specifies the allowed addressing modes. We will now interpret these entries and provide some typical illustrations from each of the groups.

Data Movement Instructions

Consider the general MOVE instruction from the table in Figure 3.5. It handles byte, word, or long-word operands. Data movement is always from the source to the destination operand. The notation is MOVE <ea>,<ea>. All addressing modes are allowed for the source <ea>. Only data-alterable addressing modes, however, are allowed for the destination <ea>. Thus, any addressing mode that does not belong to both the data and the alterable types is not allowed. Referring to Figure 3.4, it can be seen that, for the MOVE instruction, the following addressing modes are not allowed for the destination effective address:

An: Not allowed, since it is not of the data type

#XXX (immediate): Not allowed, since it is not of the alterable type

MOVE instructions dealing with the status register (SR) and the USP are privileged as indicated. The EXG (exchange) instruction exchanges the long-word contents of two of the specified internal data or address registers. Similarly, the SWAP instruction exchanges (swaps) the lower and upper words in a data register.[5]

Instruction	Operand Size	Operation	Notation	Allowable Effective Address Modes
<u>MOVE</u>	8.16.32	(SOURCE) → DESTINATION	MOVE ⟨ea⟩,⟨ea⟩	SOURCE—ALL ————— DEST—DATA ALTERABLE
MOVE from SR	16	SR → DESTINATION	MOVE SR,⟨ea⟩	DATA ALTERABLE
MOVE to CC	16	(SOURCE) → CCR	MOVE ⟨ea⟩,CCR	DATA
*MOVE to SR	16	(SOURCE) → SR	MOVE ⟨ea⟩,SR	DATA
*MOVE USP	32	USP → An or An → USP	MOVE USP,An MOVE An,USP	—
MOVEA	16,32	(SOURCE) → DESTINATION	MOVEA ⟨ea⟩,An	ALL
MOVEQ	32	IMMEDIATE DATA → DESTINATION	MOVEQ # ⟨data⟩,Dn	—
EXG	32	Rx ↔ Ry	EXG Rx,Ry	—
SWAP	16	Dnlw ↔ Dnhw	SWAP Dn	—

FIGURE 3.5 The 68000 data movement group of instructions. (Courtesy of Motorola Inc.)

Figure 3.6 indicates the initial values of the registers and the memory. We will use these values for the examples in this chapter. In the general MOVE instruction, there is no overflow, and the C and V flags are reset to 0; the X flag is unaffected (see Appendix B for details). An example follows.

MOVE.L D1,D3   Move long-word data from D1 into D3.
                        D1 (before) $ 1 2 3 4 0 6 7 8
                        D3 (before) $ 0 0 0 0 0 0 0 8
                        D3 (after) $ 1 2 3 4 0 6 7 8
                        Only the N and Z flags are affected.
                        The result (new data in D3) is a positive nonzero value. As such, N = 0 and Z = 0.
                        X N Z V C (after) = 0 0 0 0 0

```
D0 = $ 1 2 3 4 0 6 7 8              Memory Address              Word Data

                                    $0034FE74                    1 A B 2
D1 = $ A B C D E F 0 0              $0034FE76                    3 C D 4
                                    $0034FE78                    5 E F 6
D2 = $ 0 0 0 0 0 0 0 4              $0034FE7A                    9 8 7 3
                                    $0034FE7C                    2 4 0 8
D3 = $ 0 0 0 0 0 0 0 8              $0034FE7E                    0 0 0 0

A0 = $ 0 0 4 8 7 6 F 2                  :                           :
                                        :                           :
A1 = $ 0 0 3 4 F E 7 8              $00487D6E                    C D 0 2
                                    $00487D70                    2 0 0 B
A2 = $ 0 0 0 0 1 0 0 0

A3 = $ 0 0 0 0 1 5 0 3

                    | System byte  |  User byte  |

SR = $ 0 4 0 0 = 0 0 0 0   0 1 0 0   0 0 0 0 0 0 0 0
                 T   S     I I I       X N Z V C
                           2 1 0
```

FIGURE 3.6 Initial values for the registers and the data operands in memory.

EXG A0,A1

Exchange the long-word contents of A0 and A1. The flags are not affected.
A0 (before) $ 0 0 4 8 7 6 F 2
A1 (before) $ 0 0 3 4 F E 7 8
A0 (after) $ 0 0 3 4 F E 7 8
A1 (after) $ 0 0 4 8 7 6 F 2
X N Z V C (after) = 0 0 0 0 0

SWAP D1

Swap the lower and the upper words in D1.
D1 (before) $ A B C D E F 0 0
D1 (after) $ E F 0 0 A B C D
The N and Z flags are affected. C and V are reset to 0, and X is unaffected. The MSB of the result is 1 ($E = 1110) and the result is a nonzero value. As such, N = 1 and Z = 0.
X N Z V C (after) = 0 1 0 0 0

We will now present an example problem to review the data movement instructions and operations.

Example 3.2   Data movement instructions.

In a control system application, the following software is run:

```
MOVE.W (A1),D1    ;move memory word addressed by (A1) into D1
SWAP   D1         ;swap the lower and the upper words in D1
EXG    D1,D3      ;exchange long words in D1 and D3
MOVE.L D3,D7      ;move long word in D3 into D7
```

Using the initial values of Figure 3.6, show the contents of the affected registers and the flags.

Solution

After the MOVE.W (A1),D1 instruction, D1 contains $ABCD5EF6. The upper word of D1 is not affected. The data operand $5EF6 is moved to the lower word position of the D1 register.

After the SWAP D1 instruction, D1 contains $5EF6ABCD.

After the EXG D1,D3 instruction, the long-word contents of the D1 and D3 registers are exchanged. D1 = $00000008; D3 = $5EF6ABCD.

After the MOVE.L D3,D7 instruction, both D3 and D7 contain $5EF6ABCD. The result is positive (MSD = $5 = 0101 and the MSB = 0) and is nonzero. As such, N = 0 and Z = 0. The X flag is unaffected. The C and V flags are reset to zero, since there is no overflow in the MOVE operation.

The final results are

$$D7 = \$5\,E\,F\,6\,A\,B\,C\,D$$

$$X\ N\ Z\ V\ C = 0\ 0\ 0\ 0\ 0$$

Binary Integer Arithmetic Instructions

These instructions deal with numbers and arithmetic operations. The 68000 processor distinguishes between signed and unsigned numbers. We will briefly discuss this concept in preparation for the discussion that follows. (Refer to Appendix A for details concerning binary and BCD numbers and arithmetic.)[6]

Consider a byte operand. In **unsigned operations** it represents a range of $00 to $FF, which corresponds to decimal values 0 to 255 as shown in Figure 3.7(a). In **signed operations,** when the MSB of the operand is 0, the operand is considered to be a positive number; when the MSB is 1, the operand is considered to be a negative number. Thus, $00 to $7F are positive numbers (decimal values 0 to 127) and $80 to $FF are negative numbers (decimal values -128 to -1 in the twos-complement form), as shown in Figure 3.7(b).

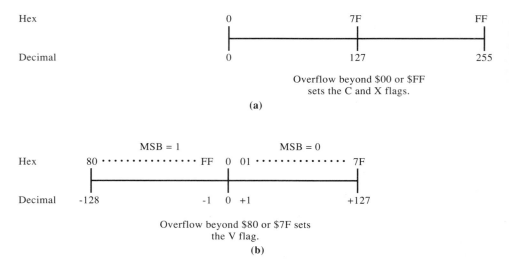

FIGURE 3.7 (a) Unsigned and (b) signed number representation.

Figures 3.8 and 3.9 illustrate the four categories of binary integer arithmetic instructions. They are ADD, SUBTRACT, COMPARE, and MULTIPLY and DIVIDE. All belong to the data processing group.

Add and Subtract Instructions There are five variations of the ADD and SUB (subtract) instructions, as shown in Figure 3.8. Except in the case of the ADDA and SUBA instructions, all five flags are affected. The C and X flags are set to 1 if there is an overflow generated from the addition operation. Similarly, the C and X flags are set to 1 if there is a borrow generated from the subtraction operation. The Z flag is set to 1 if the result of either of the operations is zero for the final operand. The N flag is set if the MSB of the result is 1. (Refer to Figure 3.2 for computation of the condition codes or flags.)

In the signed operations, the V flag is set to 1 when two positive numbers (MSB = 0 in each case) are added and a negative result (MSB = 1) is generated, or vice versa. Similarly, the V flag is set to 1 when a positive number is subtracted from a negative number and a positive result is generated, or vice versa. These conditions are known as **signed overflow.** If the signed operations are not of interest, the V flag may be ignored. An example follows using the initial values of Figure 3.6.

ADD.B #$6F,D0   Add immediate data byte $6F to byte in D0, with the result in D0. The destination <ea> is data register direct, which belongs to the data-alterable type.
Addition = $6F + $78 = $E7 = 1110 0111
D0 (before) $ 1 2 3 4 0 6 7 8
D0 (after) $ 1 2 3 4 0 6 E 7

Instruction	Operand Size	Operation	Notation	Allowable Effective Address Modes
ADD	8,16,32	(DESTINATION) + (SOURCE) → DESTINATION	ADD Dn,⟨ea⟩	ALTERABLE MEMORY
			ADD ⟨ea⟩,Dn	ALL
ADDA	16,32	(DESTINATION) + (SOURCE) → DESTINATION	ADD ⟨ea⟩,An	All
ADDI	8,16,32	(DESTINATION) + IMMEDIATE DATA → DESTINATION	ADDI # ⟨data⟩,⟨ea⟩	DATA ALTERABLE
ADDQ	8,16,32	(DESTINATION) + IMMEDIATE DATA → DESTINATION	ADDQ # ⟨data⟩,⟨ea⟩	ALTERABLE
ADDX	8,16,32	(DESTINATION) + (SOURCE) + X → DESTINATION	ADDX Dy, Dx ADDX −(Ay), −(Ax)	— —

(a)

Instruction	Operand Size	Operation	Notation	Allowable Effective Address Modes
SUB	8,16,32	(DESTINATION) − (SOURCE) → DESTINATION	SUB Dn,⟨ea⟩	ALTERABLE MEMORY
			SUB ⟨ea⟩,Dn	ALL
SUBA	16,32	(DESTINATION) − (SOURCE) → DESTINATION	SUBA ⟨ea⟩,An	ALL
SUBI	8,16,32	(DESTINATION) − IMMEDIATE DATA → DESTINATION	SUBI # ⟨data⟩,⟨ea⟩	DATA ALTERABLE
SUBQ	8,16,32	(DESTINATION) − IMMEDIATE DATA → DESTINATION	SUBQ # ⟨data⟩,⟨ea⟩	ALTERABLE
SUBX	8,16,32	(DESTINATION) − (SOURCE) − X → DESTINATION	SUBX Dy,Dx SUBX −(Ay), −(Ax)	—

(b)

FIGURE 3.8 Binary arithmetic instructions for the 68000. (a) Add-type; (b) subtract-type. (Courtesy of Motorola, Inc.)

Instruction	Operand Size	Operation	Notation	Allowable Effective Address Modes
CMP	8,16,32	(OPERAND2) − (OPERAND1)	CMP ⟨ea⟩,Dn	ALL
CMPA	16,32	(OPERAND2) − (OPERAND1)	CMPA ⟨ea⟩,An	ALL
CMPI	8,16,32	(OPERAND) − IMMEDIATE DATA	CMPI #⟨data⟩,⟨ea⟩	DATA ALTERABLE
CMPM	8,16,32	(OPERAND2) − (OPERAND1)	CMPM (Ay) +,(Ax) +	—
TST	8,16,32	(DESTINATION) − 0 (DESTINATION) TESTED → CC	TST ⟨ea⟩	DATA ALTERABLE

(a)

Instruction	Operand Size	Operation	Notation	Allowable Effective Address Modes
EXT	16,32	(DESTINATION) Sign-EXTENDED → DESTINATION	EXT Dn	—
MULS	16	(SOURCE)*(DESTINATION) → DESTINATION	MULS ⟨ea⟩,Dn	DATA
MULU	16	(SOURCE)*(DESTINATION) → DESTINATION	MULU ⟨ea⟩,Dn	DATA
NEG	8,16,32	0 − (DESTINATION) → DESTINATION	NEG ⟨ea⟩	DATA ALTERABLE
NEGX	8,16,32	0 − (DESTINATION) − X → DESTINATION	NEGX ⟨ea⟩	DATA ALTERABLE
CLR	8,16,32	0 → DESTINATION	CLR ⟨ea⟩	DATA ALTERABLE
DIVS	16	(DESTINATION) ÷ (SOURCE) → DESTINATION	DIVS ⟨ea⟩,Dn	DATA
DIVU	16	(DESTINATION) ÷ (SOURCE) → DESTINATION	DIVU ⟨ea⟩,Dn	DATA

(b)

FIGURE 3.9 (a) Compare-type instructions for the 68000; (b) multiply, divide, and sign-related instructions. (Courtesy of Motorola, Inc.)

X and C are 0, since there is no normal overflow. The MSB of the result is 1 and the result is nonzero. As such, N = 1 and Z = 0. The V flag is set since there is an overflow of the result beyond $7F. It is as if two positive numbers are added ($6F and $78) and a negative result ($E7) obtained in signed binary operations.[7]
X N Z V C (after) = 0 1 0 1 0

SUBA.W A0,A1   Subtract the word operand in A0 from the word operand in A1, with the result in A1. All 32 bits of the destination are affected. The source word is sign extended to 32 bits.

Contents of A1	$ 0 0 3 4 F E 7 8
Sign-extended word from A0	$ 0 0 0 0 7 6 F 2
Result of subtraction in A1*	$ 0 0 3 4 8 7 8 6

A1 (before) $ 0 0 3 4 F E 7 8
A1 (after) $ 0 0 3 4 8 7 8 6

Flags are not affected, since the destination <ea> is an address register.

*In subtraction operations, the source subtrahend is converted into the twos-complement form and added to the destination minuend.

Compare Instructions   There are five variations of the compare instruction, as indicated in Figure 3.9(a). The source operand is subtracted from the destination operand. The result is not stored, but is used to set or reset the flag bits in the condition code register (user byte of the SR). The processor uses this information to make decisions and control the program flow. The objective of the compare operation is to learn whether an operand has reached a particular value. The source and the destination operands (also called operand 1 and operand 2) are not affected in compare-type operations. Examples follow using the initial values of Figure 3.6.

CMP.W D1,D0   Compare the word in D1 with the word in D0 and set or reset the flags accordingly. (The word in D1 is subtracted from the word in D0. The result is not stored; D0 and D1 are not affected, but the flags change.)

Word operand in D0	$ 0 6 7 8
Word operand in D1	$ E F 0 0
Result of the subtraction =	$ 1 7 7 8

   (borrow generated)
D0 (before) $ 1 2 3 4 0 6 7 8
D1 (before) $ A B C D E F 0 0
D0 (after) $ 1 2 3 4 0 6 7 8
D1 (after) $ A B C D E F 0 0

X is not affected, but C is affected. Borrow is generated and C = 1. Nonzero positive result (MSB = 0). As such, N = 0 and Z = 0. There is no signed overflow and V = 0.
X N Z V C (after) = 0 0 0 0 1

TST.B $0007(A1)

Test the destination operand and set or reset the flags accordingly. The tested operand is not affected.

The ARI with displacement addressing mode is used for the destination <ea>.

Contents of A1 $ 0 0 3 4 F E 7 8
Sign-extended displacement $ 0 0 0 0 0 0 0 7
              Destination <ea> = $ 0 0 3 4 F E 7 F

Byte operand from $0034FE7F = $00. X is not affected, C = 0, and V = 0 (since there is no overflow in the test operation). The tested destination is positive (MSB = 0) and has a value of zero. As such, N = 0 and Z = 1.
X N Z V C (after) = 0 0 1 0 0

The TST (test) instruction is very useful in testing the operand and providing the condition code information without modifying the tested operand.

Multiply, Divide, and Sign-related Instructions   These instructions are presented in Figure 3.9(b). The EXT instruction sign extends a byte to a word (EXT.W) or a word to a long word (EXT.L). The objective of this instruction is to increase the size of the operand without changing its arithmetic value. Some instructions (ADD, SUB, for example) require that both operands be of the same size for computations. The EXT instruction is used in such instances. Notice that the operand should be contained in one of the data registers Dn.

The NEG instruction negates the operand. It subtracts the destination operand from $0 and puts the result back in the destination location. In effect, it performs a twos-complement operation on the operand. The NEGX instruction includes the X flag in the computation. Data-alterable addressing modes are allowed for NEG and NEGX instructions. Examples follow using the initial values of Figure 3.6.

EXT.L D1

Sign extend the word operand in D1 to a long word. The word operand in D1 = $ E F 0 0. The MSB = 1 (since MSD $E = 1 1 1 0) and the operand is considered negative. This MSB is replicated to all the higher bits in the D1 register.

D1 (before) $ A B C D E F 0 0
D1 (after) $ F F F F E F 0 0

D1 has the same numeric value as it did before, but the size of D1 is increased to a long word. X is not affected, C = 0, and V = 0. The resulting operand is negative (MSB = 1) and nonzero. As such, N = 1 and Z = 0.
X N Z V C (after) = 0 1 0 0 0

NEG.B D2

Negate the byte operand in D2. Subtract the byte operand in D2 from $00 and put the result back in D2.

Value to be subtracted from $ 0 0
Byte operand in D2 $ 0 4
Subtracted (negated) result = $ F C
   (borrow generated)

D2 (before) $ 0 0 0 0 0 0 0 4
D2 (after) $ 0 0 0 0 0 0 F C
All the flags are affected. Borrow is generated: C = 1 and X = 1.
The resulting operand ($FC) is negative (MSB = 1) and nonzero. As
such, N = 1 and Z = 0. Signed overflow is not generated and V =
0.
X N Z V C (after) = 1 1 0 0 1

The MULS and MULU are the signed and the unsigned multiply instructions, respectively. In the signed operations, the operands are considered to be signed binary
integers. On the other hand, in the unsigned operations, the operands are considered to
be unsigned binary integers. Similarly, the DIVS and DIVU are the signed and unsigned
division operations, respectively. In the multiply and divide operations, the destination
is always a data register Dn. In the multiply operations, the 16-bit source operand (S16)
and the lower 16 bits of the destination Dn (D16) are multiplied, and the 32-bit product
is transferred to the 32-bit destination Dn register (D32). Examples follow using the initial values of Figure 3.6.

MULU D2,D3   Multiply the word operands from D2 and D3, with the 32-bit re-
                  sult in D3. The operands are unsigned.
                  Multiplicand in D2 (before) $ 0 0 0 0 0 0 0 4
                  Multiplier in D3 (before) $ 0 0 0 0 0 0 0 8
                  D2 (after) $ 0 0 0 0 0 0 0 4
                  Product in D3 (after) $ 0 0 0 0 0 0 2 0
                  $4 × $8 = $20 = 32 decimal value. Only the N and Z flags are
                  affected. X is unaffected. C = 0 and V = 0. The result is posi-
                  tive (MSB = 0) and is nonzero. As such, N = 0 and Z = 0.
                  X N Z V C (after) = $ 0 0 0 0 0

MULS #$2,D1   Multiply the signed 16-bit operand from D1 and the source oper-
                  and ($0002), with the 32-bit signed result in D1.
                  Multiplicand word in D1 (before) $ E F 0 0
                  Multiplier source operand $ 0 0 0 2
                  Sign-extended product* = $ F F F F D E 0 0

*$EF00 × $0002 results in hex string $1DE00. Sign extending the MSB = 1 to the
higher bits results in the sign-extended product $FFFFDE00.

In the division operations, the dividend is contained in a 32-bit destination data
register Dn. The divisor is the 16-bit source operand, specified by one of the data-type
addressing modes. The dividend is divided by the divisor. The 16-bit quotient and the
16-bit remainder are placed in the destination data register, as shown:

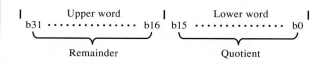

An example follows.

DIVU D2,D3   Divide the 32-bit dividend in the D3 destination register by the 16-bit divisor in the source D2 register. Place the results as shown in the preceding diagram. The operands are unsigned.

$$
\begin{aligned}
\text{32-bit dividend operand in D3 (before)} &= \$\ 0\ 0\ 0\ 0\ 0\ 0\ 0\ 8 \\
\text{16-bit divisor operand in D2 (before)} &= \$\qquad\qquad 0\ 0\ 0\ 4 \\
\text{Upon dividing, the 16-bit quotient} &= \qquad\quad \$\ 0\ 0\ 0\ 2 \\
\text{the 16-bit remainder} &= \qquad\quad \$\ 0\ 0\ 0\ 0
\end{aligned}
$$

D3 (after) $\$\ 0\ 0\ 0\ 0\ 0\ 0\ 0\ 2$

The N, Z, and V flags are affected. X is unaffected and C = 0. The quotient is positive (MSB = 0) and nonzero. As such, N = 0 and Z = 0. There is no division overflow and V = 0.

X N Z V C (after) = 0 0 0 0 0

Note: If the divisor is zero, the zero divide exception occurs.

BCD (Binary Coded Decimal) Instructions

The three BCD instructions are presented in Figure 3.10. The operand size is byte. The X flag is always involved in the computations. The ABCD (add BCD) and the $SBCD (subtract BCD) instructions use only the data register direct (Dn) or the ARI with pre-decrement (−(An)) addressing modes for both the source and the destination operands. This provides an easy and reliable access to the operands in a low-to-high value sequence, which is required for BCD arithmetic. The NBCD (negate BCD) is similar to the binary NEGX instruction. All the data-alterable addressing modes are allowed for the NBCD instruction. Only the X, Z and C flags are affected for the BCD instructions.[8] An example follows using the initial values of Figure 3.6.

Instruction	Operand Syntax	Operand Size	Operation
ABCD	Dn, Dn −(An), −(An)	8 8	$\text{Source}_{10} + \text{Destination}_{10} + X \rightarrow \text{Destination}$
NBCD	⟨ea⟩	8	$0 - \text{Destination}_{10} - X - \rightarrow \text{Destination}$
SBCD	Dn, Dn −(An), −(An)	8 8	$\text{Destination}_{10} - \text{Source}_{10} - X \rightarrow \text{Destination}$

FIGURE 3.10 BCD instructions.

ABCD D0,D3   Add the BCD byte operand in D0 to the BCD byte operand in D3, with the result in D3.

$$
\begin{aligned}
\text{Source BCD byte in D0 (before)} &\qquad 7\ 8 \\
\text{Destination BCD byte in D3 (before)} &\qquad \underline{0\ 8} \\
\text{Result of the BCD addition} &= \underline{8\ 6}
\end{aligned}
$$

D0 (before)   1 2 3 4 0 6 7 8
D3 (before)   0 0 0 0 0 0 0 8
D0 (after)   1 2 3 4 0 6 7 8
D3 (after)   0 0 0 0 0 0 8 6

There is no overflow and the result is nonzero. As such,

X N Z V C (after) = 0 0 0 0 0

In BCD operations, the operands are expected to be of the BCD type. Any other data type generates an error condition known as the illegal instruction exception.

We will now present an example problem to review the binary and BCD arithmetic operations.

Example 3.3   *Binary and BCD operations using the 68000.*

In a digital signal processing application, the following software is written as a subroutine:

```
ADD.W #$0004,D0 ;add immediate data $4 to the word in D0
MULS D2,D0      ;multiply words in D2 and D0 with result in D0
SUBQ.L #$08,D0  ;subtract quick data 8 from long word in D0
DIVU  D1,D0     ;divide long word in D0 with word in D1
RTS             ;return from subroutine
```

Consider the initial values

D0 = $12340678;   D1 = $00000006;   D2 = $00000004
SR = $ 0405 = 0 0 0 0   0 1 0 0   0 0 0 0   0 1 0 1
                                   X   N Z V C

1. What are the values of the affected registers and the SR at the end of the subroutine?
2. If [SUBQ.L #$08,D0] is changed to [SUBQ.L #$80,D0], will the software be functional? Why or why not?

Solution

1. **Results of the software:** After the addition, the destination register D0 = $1234067C. Signed multiplication of words in D2 (= $0004) and D0 (= $067C) results in a 32-bit product in D0 (= $000019F0), as shown:

$$
\begin{array}{rl}
\text{Overflow generated} & \\
\text{(see note)} & 1\ 1\ 3 \\
\$ \text{ Multiplicand} = & 0\ 6\ 7\ C \\
\$ \text{ Multiplier} \quad = & 0\ 0\ 0\ 4 \\
\hline
\text{Sign-extended 32-bit product} = & \$\ 0\ 0\ 0\ 0\ 1\ 9\ F\ 0
\end{array}
$$

Note: $C = 12 decimal; 4 × $C = 4 × 12 = 48, which is equal to $30. Digit $3 is the hex overflow to the next hex position. The hex multiplication proceeds in this fashion.

After the subtraction, the destination register D0 = $000019E8. Unsigned division of the dividend in D0 (= $000019E8) by the divisor in D1 (= $0006) is as shown, using the hex-to-decimal and decimal-to-hex conversions. ($E = 14.)

$$\text{Dividend } \$000019E8 = (1 \times 16^3) + (9 \times 16^2) + (14 \times 16) + 8 = 6632$$

Divisor $0006 = 6. The decimal division results in

$$\frac{6632}{6} = 1105 \text{ quotient, with 2 as a remainder}$$

Converting the decimal quotient 1105 into hex, we obtain

$$\text{Quotient } 1105 = (4 \times 16^2) + (5 \times 16) + 1 = \$451$$

Remainder 2 = $2.

The remainder and the quotient are put into the destination D0 as the higher and lower words, and D0 = $00020451. The quotient ($0451) is positive and non-zero and there is no division overflow. As such, the flag bits N = 0, Z = 0, and V = 0. The X flag is unaffected and the C flag is reset to zero.

The RTS instruction causes the processor to return to the calling program. The flag register is unaffected by the RTS and contains the information relating to the instruction before the RTS.

The final results are

$$\text{D0} = \$\ 0\ 0\ 0\ 2\ 0\ 4\ 5\ 1$$
$$\text{SR} = \$\qquad\quad 0\ 4\ 0\ 0$$

2. **SUBQ.L #$80,D0:** The software will not be functional. The source operand #$80 is beyond the allowed value (= $08) for the SUBQ instruction. An error condition will be generated.

Large numeric strings of data are also easily handled by the 68000 processor. The numeric string of data resides in the memory. The processor obtains the appropriately sized data from the numeric string in the memory, performs the required operations, and stores the result in the memory. We will deal with these operations when we discuss software designs; they are known as the **multiprecision arithmetic operations.**

3.3 LOGICAL AND BIT-MANIPULATION INSTRUCTION GROUPS

The logical instructions perform the logic, shift, and rotate operations. The bit-manipulation instructions deal with the individual bits of the operands. These two groups provide the 68000 with additional data processing and control capability.

Logic, Shift, and Rotate Instructions

The basic logic instructions are presented in Figure 3.11. They are the AND, OR, EOR (exclusive OR), and the NOT instructions. They operate on the byte, word, and long-word operands. Consider the two forms of the AND instruction:

AND Dn, <ea>

AND <ea>,Dn

Either the source or the destination operand has to be in one of the data registers. If the source operand is in a data register, the destination <ea> is of the memory-alterable type. If the destination operand is in a data register, the source <ea> is of the data type. In the other variation of the AND instruction:

ANDI # <data>,<ea>

the source operand is the immediate data and the destination <ea> is of the data-alterable type. In all of these cases, the processor performs the AND operation between the corresponding bits of the source and the destination operands, with the result in the destination. If the destination <ea> is the SR, then it is a privileged instruction. The logic instructions affect only the N and Z flags. The N flag is set to 1 if the MSB of the result is 1 (negative number). The Z flag is set to 1 if the result is 0. There is no over-flow in the logical operations; as such, the C and the V flags are always reset to 0. The X flag is not affected. However, if the operand is either the SR (status register) or the CCR (condition code register), all five flag bits are affected. The OR and the EOR in-structions follow the same structure as the AND, but they perform the OR and the ex-clusive OR operations between the corresponding bits of the source and the destination operands, with the result in the destination. The NOT instruction performs logical inver-sion (ones-complement form) of the operand. The operand is specified by the data-alterable type addressing modes.

The shift and rotate instructions are presented in Figure 3.12. They are the ASL and ASR (arithmetic shift left and right), LSL and LSR (logical shift left and right), ROL and ROR (rotate left and right), and ROXL and ROXR (rotate left and right through the X flag). Consider the three forms of the ASL instruction:

ASL Dx,Dy   ASL #<data>,Dy   ASL <ea>

The first two forms operate on byte, word, or long-word data operands. The destination operand is in one of the data registers. The destination operand is shifted left the number of times specified by the source operand. The shifted-out MSB goes into the C and X flag bits and 0 is shifted into the LSB for each shift operation. When the source operand is a data register, it can specify a shift number up to 64 (modulo 64). However, a shift count of 32 is sufficient to completely shift zeros into the register. When the source op-erand is a data element, the shift count is limited to 8. When an operand is shifted left

Instruction	Operand Size	Operation	Notation	Allowable Effective Address Modes
AND	8,16,32	(SOURCE) $\wedge$ (DESTINATION) $\rightarrow$ DESTINATION	AND Dn,⟨ea⟩	ALTERABLE MEMORY
			AND ⟨ea⟩,Dn	DATA
ANDI	8,16,32	IMMEDIATE DATA $\wedge$ (DESTINATION) $\rightarrow$ DESTINATION	ANDI # ⟨data⟩,⟨ea⟩	DATA ALTERABLE OR CCR OR *STATUS REGISTER
EOR	8,16,32	(SOURCE) $\oplus$ (DESTINATION) $\rightarrow$ DESTINATION	EOR Dn,⟨ea⟩	DATA ALTERABLE
EORI	8,16,32	IMMEDIATE DATA $\oplus$ (DESTINATION) $\rightarrow$ DESTINATION	EORI # ⟨data⟩,⟨ea⟩	DATA ALTERABLE OR CCR OR *STATUS REGISTER
NOT	8,16,32	$\overline{\text{(DESTINATION)}}$ $\rightarrow$ DESTINATION	NOT ⟨ea⟩	DATA ALTERABLE
OR	8,16,32	(SOURCE) $\vee$ (DESTINATION) $\rightarrow$ DESTINATION	OR Dn,⟨ea⟩	ALTERABLE MEMORY
			OR ⟨ea⟩,Dn	DATA
ORI	8,16,32	IMMEDIATE DATA $\vee$ (DESTINATION) $\rightarrow$ DESTINATION	ORI # ⟨data⟩,⟨ea⟩	DATA ALTERABLE OR CCR OR *STATUS REGISTER

FIGURE 3.11 The 68000 logic group of instructions. (Courtesy of Motorola, Inc.)

INSTRUCTION	OPERAND SIZE	OPERATION	NOTATION	ALLOWABLE EFFECTIVE ADDRESS MODES
ASL ASR	8, 16, 32 / 16	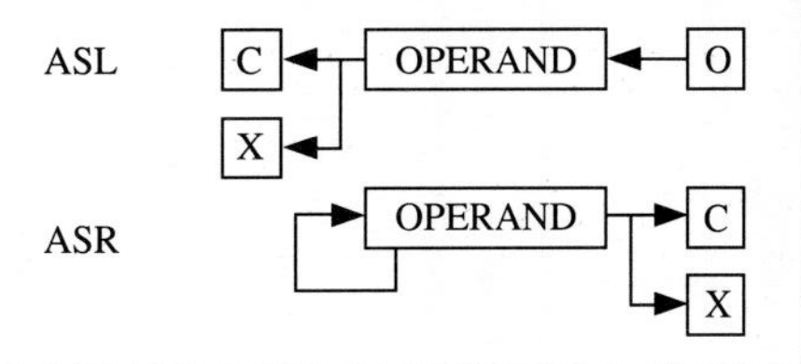 ASL / ASR	ASd Dx, Dy / ASd, #<data>, Dy / ASd <ea>	— / — / MEMORY ALTERABLE
LSL LSR	8, 16, 32 / 16	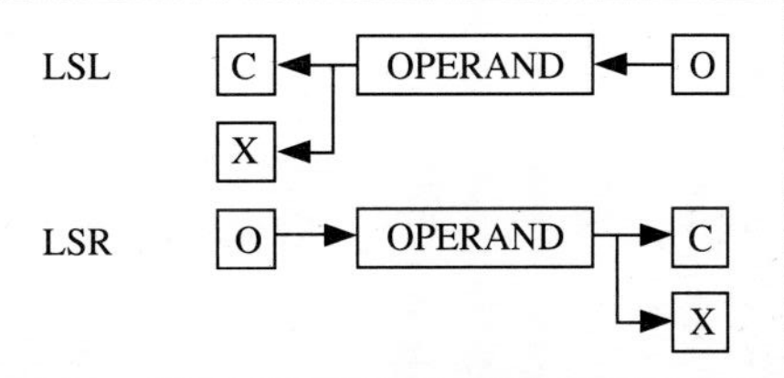 LSL / LSR	LSd Dx, Dy / LSd, #<data>, Dy / LSd <ea>	— / — / MEMORY ALTERABLE
ROL ROR	8, 16, 32 / 16	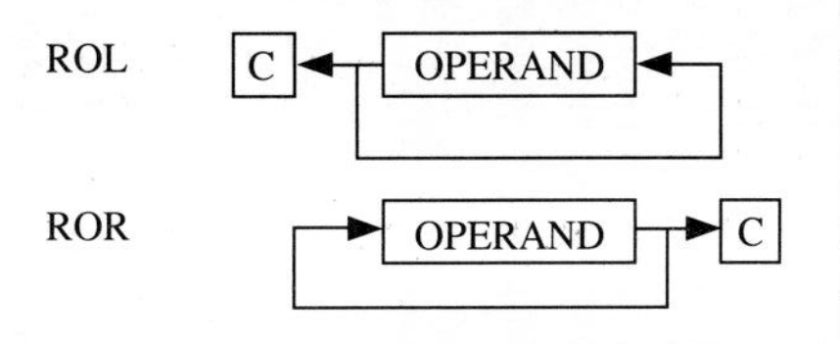 ROL / ROR	ROd Dx, Dy / ROd #<data>, Dy / ROd <ea>	— / — / MEMORY ALTERABLE
ROXL ROXR	8, 16, 32 / 16	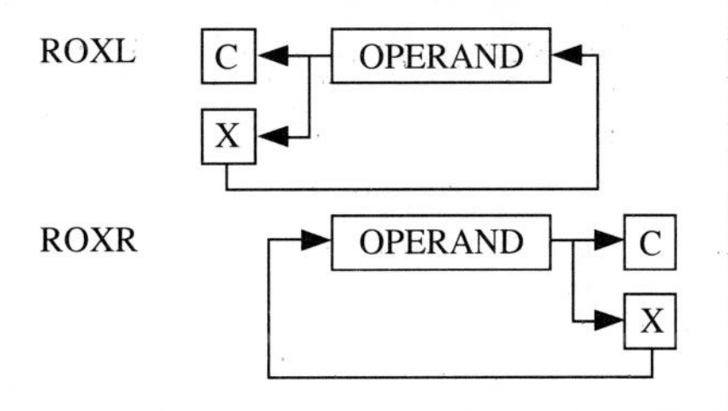 ROXL / ROXR	ROXd Dx, Dy, / ROXd #<data>, Dy / ROXd <ea>	— / — / MEMORY ALTERABLE

FIGURE 3.12 The 68000 shift and rotate instructions. (Courtesy of Motorola, Inc.)

once, it amounts to multiplying the operand by 2. Thus, shifting left by 8 positions amounts to multiplying by 256: $2^8 = 256$.

For the third form of the ASL instruction, the operand is in memory and is specified by the memory-alterable addressing modes. The operand size is a word and is shifted once to the left.

The ASR instruction is similar to the ASL, but shifts the operand in the right direction. The MSB is shifted back into itself to preserve the sign bit of the operand. The shifted-out LSB goes into the C and X bits.

In the arithmetic shift operations, the value and the sign bit of the operand can change. Furthermore, overflow can occur. As such, all five flags are affected.

The LSL and the LSR instructions are similar to the ASL and the ASR instructions. However, in case of the LSR instruction, 0 is shifted into the MSB of the operand and the LSB is shifted out for each shift. This amounts to dividing the operand by 2.

In case of the ROL instruction, the destination operand is rotated left the number of times specified by the source operand. The MSB goes into the C flag and into the LSB position, as shown in Figure 3.12. The ROR instruction is similar to the ROL, but rotates the operand in the right direction. The ROXL and the ROXR instructions are similar to the ROL and ROR instructions, but the former pair rotate the operands through the X flag.

In the logical shift operations (LSL and LSR), and in the rotate operations through the X flag (ROXL and ROXR), the signed overflow concept is not required. As such, the V flag is reset to 0 and the other four flags are affected. In the normal rotate operations (ROL and ROR), the X flag is not affected and the V flag is reset to 0. Only the other three flags are affected.

The following example problem provides a review of the logical operations.

Example 3.4   Logical operations.
The initial values of the registers and the operands are as follows:

$$D0 = \$ 1\ 2\ 3\ 4\ 0\ 6\ 7\ 8 \qquad D2 = \$ 0\ 0\ 0\ 0\ 0\ 0\ 0\ 4$$
$$A1 = \$ 0\ 0\ 3\ 4\ F\ E\ 7\ 8 \qquad X\ N\ Z\ V\ C = 0\ 0\ 0\ 0\ 0$$

Use the same initial conditions each time. Show the results of the following operations:

1. ANDI.B #$F0,D0   2. ORI.B #$F0,D0   3. EORI.B #$F0,D0
4. NOT.B D0   5. ASL.B #$2,D0   6. ASR.B #$2,D0
7. ROL.B #$2,D0   8. ROXR.B #$2,D0   9. ORI.B #$1F,CCR

Solution

$$\text{Destination byte operand in D0} = \$78 = 0\ 1\ 1\ 1\ 1\ 0\ 0\ 0$$
$$\text{Source operand} = \$F0 = 1\ 1\ 1\ 1\ 0\ 0\ 0\ 0$$

1. ANDI.B #$F0,D0: If both the source and destination bits are 1, the result bit is 1:

$$\text{Result} = 0\ 1\ 1\ 1\ 0\ 0\ 0\ 0$$
Nonzero result and MSB = 0   X N Z V C =   0 0 0 0 0

2. ORI.B #$F0,D0: If any of the source or destination bits is 1, the result bit is 1:

$$\text{Result} = 1\ 1\ 1\ 1\ 1\ 0\ 0\ 0$$
Nonzero result and MSB = 1   X N Z V C =   0 1 0 0 0

3. EORI.B #$F0,D0: If either the source or the destination bit is 1, but not both, the result bit is 1:

$$\text{Result} = 1\ 0\ 0\ 0\ 1\ 0\ 0\ 0$$
Nonzero result and MSB = 1   X N Z V C =   0 1 0 0 0

4. NOT.B D0: The operand bits are inverted:

$$\text{Result} = 1\ 0\ 0\ 0\ 0\ 1\ 1\ 1$$
Nonzero result and MSB = 1   X N Z V C =   0 1 0 0 0

5. ASL.B #$2,D0: The operand is shifted left twice:

$$\text{Result} = 1\ 1\ 1\ 0\ 0\ 0\ 0\ 0$$
Nonzero result and MSB = 1   X N Z V C =   1 1 0 1 1
Last MSB shifted out = 1: (C and X = 1)
Sign (MSB) changed at least once: (V = 1)

6. ASR.B #$2,D0: The operand is shifted right twice:

$$\text{Result} = 0\ 0\ 0\ 1\ 1\ 1\ 1\ 0$$
Nonzero result and MSB = 0   X N Z V C =   0 0 0 0 0
Last LSB shifted out = 0: (C and X = 0)
Sign (MSB) did not change: (V = 0)

7. ROL.B #$2,D0: The operand is rotated left twice:

$$\text{Result} = 1\ 1\ 1\ 0\ 0\ 0\ 0\ 1$$
Nonzero result and MSB = 1   X N Z V C =   0 1 0 0 1
Last MSB rotated = 1: (C = 1)

8. ROXR.B #$2,D0: The operand is rotated right twice through X:

$$\text{Result} = 0\ 0\ 0\ 1\ 1\ 1\ 1\ 0$$

Nonzero result and MSB = 0   X N Z V C =   0 0 0 0 0
Last LSB rotated = 0: (C and X = 0)

Note: In each of the preceding cases, the result is put back in the byte position in the D0 destination register.

9. ORI.B #$1F,CCR: The OR immediate operand $1F = 00011111 with the CCR:

$$\text{Result} = 0\ 0\ 0\ 1\ 1\ 1\ 1\ 1$$

All five flags are set   X N Z V C =   1 1 1 1 1

The AND operation forces a 0 value to the selected bits in an operand. This is called **masking.** The OR operation forces a 1 value to the selected bits in an operand. The EXOR operation selectively inverts and checks the bits in an operand.

Shift and rotate operations are suitable in data processing and logical data manipulation applications. In all cases, the operand is a complete data element. In several instances, bit-level data manipulation is required.[9]

The MC68000 has bit-manipulation instructions with which to handle bit-level operations more efficiently. We will now discuss these instructions.

Bit-Manipulation Instructions

The bit-manipulation group of instructions are presented in Figure 3.13. They are the BCHG (bit change), BCLR (bit clear), BSET (bit set), and BTST (bit test) instructions. In each case, the source operand specifies the bit number in a destination operand.[10]

With all four instructions, the specified bit is first tested and the Z flag is set or reset accordingly (Z = 1 if the tested bit is 0, and vice versa). This helps the programmer to identify the bit condition before any further bit manipulation. Only the Z flag bit is affected in this group.

The BCHG instruction changes the logic value of the tested bit from 0 to 1, or vice versa. The BCLR instruction clears the specified bit. The BSET instruction sets the specified bit. The BTST instruction tests only the specified bit.

If the destination is a data register, then any of the 32 bits can be manipulated (modulo 32), as specified by the source operand. On the other hand, if the destination is a memory location, then the bit operations are restricted to 8 bits (or a byte). The destination <ea> can be specified by the data-alterable addressing modes. The source operand can either be a data register or an immediate data element. The word-sized operands are not supported in this group of instructions. In control and I/O type of applications, bit-manipulation operations are very common.

The following example will help to clarify the bit-manipulation instructions.

Instruction	Operand Size*	Operation	Notation	Allowable Effective Address Modes
BCHG	8,32	~(bit number OF Destination) → Z ~(bit number OF Destination) → bit number OF Destination	BCHG Dn ⟨ea⟩ - - - - - - - - - - - - - BCHG # ⟨data⟩,⟨ea⟩	DATA ALTERABLE
BCLR	8,32	~(bit number OF Destination) → Z 0 → bit number OF Destination	BCLR Dn,⟨ea⟩ - - - - - - - - - - - - - BCLR # ⟨data⟩,⟨ea⟩	DATA ALTERABLE
BSET	8,32	~(bit number OF Destination) → Z: 1 → bit number OF Destination	BSET Dn,⟨ea⟩ - - - - - - - - - - - - - BSET # ⟨data⟩,⟨ea⟩	DATA ALTERABLE
BTST	8,32	~(bit number OF Destination) → Z	BTST ⟨Dn⟩,⟨ea⟩ - - - - - - - - - - - - - BTST # ⟨data⟩,⟨ea⟩	DATA (EXCLUDING IMMEDIATE)

*1. For memory operation, the data size is byte.
 2. For data register operation, the data size is long word.

FIGURE 3.13 The 68000 bit-manipulation instructions. (Courtesy of Motorola, Inc.)

___

Example 3.5   Bit manipulations.
The initial conditions of the registers and the operands are as follows:

$$D0 = \$\ 1\ 2\ 3\ 4\ 0\ 6\ 7\ 8 \qquad D1 = \$\ A\ B\ C\ D\ E\ F\ 0\ 0$$
$$X\ N\ Z\ V\ C = 0\ 0\ 0\ 0\ 0$$

It is required to test bit 0, set bit 4, clear bit 6, and change bit 31 of the operand contained in the D0 register, in the sequence stated.

1. Write a series of bit-manipulation instructions to perform this task.
2. What are the contents of the D0 register and the flags after the task has been completed?
3. If bit-manipulation instructions are not available, what alternate software approach may be used to accomplish the task?

Solution

1. **Bit-manipulation instructions:** Figure 3.14(a) shows the binary (bit) representation in the D0 register. Figure 3.14(b) shows a series of four bit-manipulation instructions to accomplish the task. In all of these operations only the Z flag is affected as indicated. The BTST instruction tests bit 0 of the D0 register, which is a zero. As such, the Z flag is set to 1. The BSET instruction tests bit 2, which is a zero, sets the Z flag to 1, and finally sets the tested bit to 1. The BCLR instruction tests bit 6, which is a one, resets the Z flag to 0 (since the tested bit is 1), and finally clears the tested bit to 0.

   The BCHG instruction tests bit 31, which is a zero; sets the Z flag to 1; and inverts the tested bit to 1. Thus, at the end of the instruction sequence, the D0 register contains:

$$b31-b28 = 1\ 0\ 0\ 1 \qquad = \$9$$
$$b27-b8 \text{ (no change)} \qquad = \$23406$$
$$b7-b0 = 0\ 0\ 1\ 1\ 0\ 1\ 0\ 0 = \$34$$

2. **Contents of D0 and the flags:** The final results are

$$\textbf{D0} = \$\ \textbf{9}\ \textbf{2}\ \textbf{3}\ \textbf{4}\ \textbf{0}\ \textbf{6}\ \textbf{3}\ \textbf{4}$$
$$\textbf{X N Z V C} = \textbf{0 0 1 0 0}$$

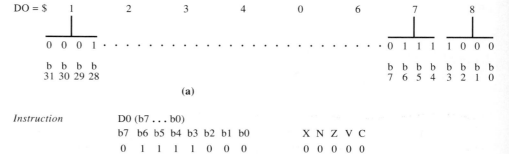

FIGURE 3.14 (a) Binary representation for the data in D0 and (b) sequence of instructions (for Example 3.5).

3. Alternate software: Logic and compare instructions must be used, involving an additional sequence of instructions.

In addition to data movement, arithmetic, logical, and bit-manipulation instructions, program and system control instructions are required for implementing software programs using the 68000. We will now discuss these instructions.

3.4 PROGRAM AND SYSTEM CONTROL INSTRUCTION GROUPS

In programming applications, it is often necessary to change the program flow conditionally or unconditionally. It is also occasionally required to stop the processor until an external event such as an interrupt occurs. In addition, it may be necessary to reset the system I/O resources under software control. The 68000 processor has appropriate program and system control instructions to support these actions.[11]

Program Control Instructions

The general program and system control instructions are presented in Figure 3.15. These instructions, all of which support program flow, are classified into three types as follows:

1. branch type: Bcc: Branch on condition
                      BRA: Unconditional branch
                      BSR: Branch to subroutine

2. jump type: JMP: Unconditional jump
                      JSR: Jump to subroutine

3. return type: RTE: Return from exception
                      RTR: Return and restore
                      RTS: Return from subroutine

Branch-Type Instructions   These instructions refer to an effective address <ea>, where the next instruction is available. The <ea> is specified by the program counter relative addressing mode (d(PC)). The displacement is specified as a part of the instruction. If the displacement is 8 bits (d8), it is a short branch operation with a 256-byte range (-128 to $+127$). If the displacement is 16 bits (d16), it is a long branch operation with a 64-kilobyte range (-32 to $+32$ kilobytes). The displacement is added to the contents of the program counter (PC) to obtain the effective address. (Recall that the PC is incremented by two after fetching the op.word; this value should be used in the computation of the <ea> in all branch operations.)

      Conditional branch instructions (Bcc) may or may not perform a desired function, depending on the current value of the processor's condition codes (or flags). Branching occurs if the specified condition is met, causing a change in the program

Instruction	Operand Size	Operation	Notation	Allowable Effective Address Modes
<u>Bcc</u>	8,16	If cc then PC + d → PC; else proceed	Bcc⟨label⟩	PC REL
<u>BRA</u>	8,16	PC + d → PC	BRA ⟨label⟩	PC REL
<u>BSR</u>	8,16	PC → −(SP); PC + d → PC	BSR ⟨label⟩	PC REL
JMP	—	DESTINATION → PC	JMP ⟨ea⟩	CONTROL
JSR	—	PC → −(SP); DESTINATION → PC	JSR ⟨ea⟩	CONTROL
<u>NOP</u>	—	PC + 2 → PC	NOP	—
*RESET	—	RESET EXTERNAL DEVICES	RESET	—
*RTE	—	(SP) + → SR;(SP) + → PC	RTE	—
RTR	—	(SP) + → CC;(SP) + → PC	RTR	—
RTS	—	(SP) + → PC	RTS	—
*STOP	16	IMMEDIATE DATA → SR; STOP PROGRAM EXECUTION	STOP #⟨data⟩	—

*Privileged

Instruction	Operand Size	Operation	Notation
TRAP	—	PC→−(SSP); SR→−(SSP); (VECTOR)→PC	TRAP #($0–$F)
TRAPV	—	If V then TRAP; else proceed	TRAPV

FIGURE 3.15 Program control instructions for the 68000. (Courtesy of Motorola, Inc.)

flow. Otherwise, the program flow remains unchanged, and the program continues with the next sequential instruction. The different forms of the Bcc instruction are indicated in Figure 3.16.

The BRA instruction causes an unconditional branch to the specified effective address. The BSR instruction stores the PC on the stack and branches to the specified sub-

FIGURE 3.16 Conditional branch instructions for the 68000. (Courtesy of Motorola, Inc.)

CC	carry clear	0100	$\overline{C}$
CS	carry set	0101	C
EQ	equal	0111	Z
GE	greater or equal	1100	$N \cdot V + \overline{N} \cdot \overline{V}$
GT	greater than	1110	$N \cdot V \cdot \overline{Z} + \overline{N} \cdot \overline{V} \cdot \overline{Z}$
HI	high	0010	$\overline{C} \cdot \overline{Z}$
LE	less or equal	1111	$Z + N \cdot \overline{V} + \overline{N} \cdot V$

LS	low or same	0011	$C + Z$
LT	less than	1101	$N \cdot \overline{V} + \overline{N} \cdot V$
MI	minus	1011	N
NE	not equal	0110	$\overline{Z}$
PL	plus	1010	$\overline{N}$
VC	overflow clear	1000	$\overline{V}$
VS	overflow set	1001	V

routine. The branch instructions generate relocatable code, since they belong to the PC relative addressing mode. Three examples of branch-type instructions follow.

PC   **Instruction**

$001000   BRA $0200(PC)   Unconditional branch to the <ea>. The <ea> computation is as follows:

PC value*   = $ 0 0 1 0 0 2
16-bit signed displacement = $ 0 2 0 0
                    <ea> = $ 0 0 1 2 0 2

*PC advances by two after fetching the op.word for the BRA instruction, thus pointing to $001002.
The <ea> is loaded into the PC.
PC (before) $ 0 0 1 0 0 2
PC (after) $ 0 0 1 2 0 2
The processor branches to $001202 and executes the program starting at that location. This is a long branch, since the displacement is 16 bits.

PC   **Instruction**

$001316   BSR $F0(PC)   Branch to the subroutine at the <ea>. The <ea> computation is as follows:

Incremented PC value   = $ 0 0 1 3 1 8
8-bit signed displacement   = $ F F F F F 0
    (twos-complement form)*
                    <ea> = $ 0 0 1 3 0 8

The original PC value (= $001318) is stored on the stack and the <ea> (= $001308) is loaded into the PC. The processor branches to the subroutine at $001308. This is a short branch, since the displacement is 8 bits.
*$F0 in twos-complement form is a negative number (= −$10). The displacement is a negative value.

PC	Instruction	
$001362	BNE $06(PC)	Branch, if not equal to zero, to the <ea>. This is a conditional branch instruction. If the operand from the previous operation is not equal to 0, the program branches to <ea>; otherwise it proceeds to the next sequential instruction.

<ea> = PC value + displacement
= $001364 + $06 = $00136A

Some assemblers support explicit extensions to distinguish between short and long branches and jumps. We will discuss these features in the next chapter when we deal with assemblers and assembly programming techniques.

Jump-Type Instructions The JMP (jump) and the JSR (jump to subroutine) instructions are similar to the BRA and BSR instructions. However, in the case of the JMP and JSR, the <ea> can be specified by any one of the control addressing modes as well as by the PC relative modes.

Return-Type Instructions The RTE (return from exception) is the last instruction to be used in an exception service routine. It restores the registers (PC, SR) that were stored on the stack when the exception occurred, and returns to the program that was being executed at the time of the exception. RTE is a privileged instruction. RTR (return and restore) is similar to RTE, but RTR restores only the user byte (or the CCR) from the stack rather than the complete SR.

The RTS (return from subroutine) is the last instruction to be used in any subroutine service routines. It restores the PC that was stored on the stack when the subroutine call was made and returns to the calling program.

System Control Instructions

These instructions control and coordinate system operation. The RESET instruction generates a reset pulse on the reset pin of the processor. In system control applications, this pulse is used to reset the I/O and the peripheral devices. The STOP instruction initializes the status register with the specified data element and stops the processor operation. The processor resumes its operation when a hardware interrupt or reset occurs. The RESET and the STOP instructions are privileged.

The NOP (no operation) instruction does not perform any task; rather, it advances the PC to the next instruction location. Software engineers and programmers use NOP instructions to fill sections of the program memory for short delays and for later replacement by active instructions.

The ILLEGAL instruction corresponds to an op.word $4AFC. It causes an illegal instruction error exception. This exception simulates the illegal error condition in the development of the operating system software.

The following example problem provides a review of the program and system control group of instructions.

Example 3.6 Program and system control instructions.

Figure 3.17 illustrates 68000-based software in an industrial application. The system is in the supervisor mode and the SR contains $2400 initially (all the flags are zero).

1. What does the main program accomplish?
2. What does the subroutine accomplish?

Solution

1. **Main program:** It initializes D0 with a data word $0008 and calls a subroutine at $00001030. After the program returns from the subroutine, it generates a reset pulse and stops the processor. When an external event such as an interrupt occurs, the program advances to the JMP instruction, which makes the program jump back to $00001000 (start).

2. **Subroutine:** This is a delay loop. It decrements the word in D0 by 1. If D0 is not decremented to 0, the BNE instruction causes the program to branch back to $00001030, which is the beginning of the delay loop. The loop is terminated when the D0 register is decremented to 0, and the program advances to the RTS instruction. The RTS causes the processor to return to the main program. For the values indicated, the delay loop runs seven times and exits the eighth time.

```
Main program
PC                  Instruction            Comment
$00001000   MOVE.W #$0008,D0      ;Move data word #$0008 into D0
$00001004   JSR     $00001030      ;Jump to subroutine at $00001030
$0000100A   RESET                  ;Generate reset pulse
$0000100C   STOP   #$2500          ;load $2500 into SR and Stop
$00001010   JMP     $00001000      ;Jump to $00001000 (start)

Subroutine
$00001030   NOP                    ;No operation
$00001032   SUBQ.W #$01,D0         ;Subtract 1 from D0 (decrement D0)
$00001034   BNE     $FA(PC)        ;If not zero, branch to ⟨ea⟩***
$00001036   RTS                    ;return from subroutine

            ⟨ea⟩ = Signed displacement + advanced PC
                 =      $FFFFFFFA + $00001036 = $00001030
```

FIGURE 3.17 Main program and subroutine (for Example 3.6).

In the software of Figure 3.17, we used absolute numbers and hex values to specify displacements and the jump and branch operations. This enabled us to show the details of the program flow at the machine level. This approach can become tedious and inefficient, however, especially if the software contains many loops and conditions. Assembly language programming, in which numbers are represented by symbols, is a better alternative in developing the software. We will learn more about these programming techniques in the following chapter.

In addition to the instruction groups discussed, the 68000 has a special group of instructions to support multiple register transfers, linking and unlinking of the stack, multiple decision schemes and software interrupts (traps). These complex instructions will be discussed in later chapters, after assembly programming concepts are introduced.

The instruction execution time is another important parameter. It specifies the actual time of execution of an instruction including calculation of the <ea> and obtaining the operands. We will now present these concepts.

3.5 INSTRUCTION TIMING CONSIDERATIONS

The 68000 is activated by a clock signal (4- to 12-MHz range). **Instruction time** refers to the time required to execute an instruction without any wait states. The fundamental unit of time is the **processor clock cycle time (T).** When the 68000 reads the op.word from the program memory, or reads the operands from memory or I/O, it is referred to as the **read bus cycle.** Similarly, when the processor writes the operands into the memory or I/O, it is referred to as the **write bus cycle.** The bus cycle in general may be a read or a write bus cycle.

Read/Write Timing

A typical bus cycle takes four clock cycles (or four **T-states**). The op.word fetch is always a read operation and takes one read bus cycle. Depending upon the instruction, the processor may perform further read operations (to obtain operands) and write operations (to write operands). In case of the 68000 and 68010/12 processors, each bus cycle involves a 16-bit data transfer. In case of the 68008, each bus cycle involves an 8-bit data transfer (due to an 8-bit data bus). The instruction timing is specified in terms of the total number of T-states and the associated read/write bus cycles.

Instruction Timing Computation

Consider the T(R/W) values shown in Figure 3.18 for the 68000. In case of the MOVE.W D1,D2 instruction, only the op.word needs to be fetched from the external memory, which involves one read operation. The source and the destination operands are within the processor; hence, the instruction does not need any further read or write bus cycles. Thus, the T(R/W) values are 4(1/0). In case of the MOVE.L (A1),(A2) in-

Instruction	T(R/W)	Comment
MOVE.W D1,D2	4(1/0)	;Move word in D1 into D2
MOVE.L (A1),(A2)	20(3/2)	;Move long word from memory addressed by (A1) into memory addressed by (A2)
MOVE.B -(A3),D6	10(2/0)	;Move byte from memory addressed by predecremented (A3) into D6

FIGURE 3.18 T(R/W) values and instruction timing for the 68000.

struction, the processor has to perform the op.word fetch and two more read operations of the memory to obtain the long-word source operand at the location addressed by the contents of A1. In addition, the processor has to perform two write operations to write the long word at the destination location addressed by the contents of A2. Thus, there are three read and two write bus cycles, corresponding to 20 T-states. The T(R/W) values are 20(3/2).

In case of the MOVE.B -(A3),D6 instruction, the processor has to perform the op.word fetch and one more read operation of the memory to obtain the byte operand from the source <ea>. The source <ea> is the predecremented A3 and involves address computation. The 68000 usually takes two additional T-states to perform the <ea> computation. There is no memory write cycle involved, since the destination operand D6 is within the processor. Thus, the T(R/W) values, including the computation time for the <ea>, are 10(2/0). If the computation time overlaps some other processor activity in the instruction, the additional T-states are not required. (See Appendices B and D for the T(R/W) values for 68000 instructions.)

We will now present an example problem to review instruction timing.

Example 3.7 Instruction timing.

The software of Figure 3.17 is repeated with the T(R/W) values indicated in Figure 3.19.

1. Explain the T(R/W) values for the JSR, RESET, BNE, and RTS instructions. (Obtain information from Appendices B and D.)

2. If the 68000 is operating at an 8-MHz clock, compute the execution time for the delay subroutine.

Solution

1. **JSR $00001030:** The processor fetches the op.word and performs two more read operations to obtain the address operand $00001030. It stores the PC in the main routine on the stack, which takes two write operations, before going to the subroutine. Thus, the T(R/W) values involve three read and two write bus cycles and 20 T-states. The T(R/W) values = 20(3/2).

Main program

PC	Instruction	Comment	T(R/W)
$00001000	MOVE.W #$0008,D0	;Move data word #$0008 into D0	8(2/0)
$00001004	JSR $00001030	;Jump to subroutine at $00001030	20(3/2)
$0000100A	RESET	;Generate reset pulse	132(1/0)
$0000100C	STOP #$2500	;load $2500 into SR and Stop	8(2/0)
$00001010	JMP $00001000	;Jump to $00001000 (start)	12(3/0)

Subroutine

PC	Instruction	Comment	T(R/W)
$00001030	NOP	;No operation	4(1/0)
$00001032	SUBQ.W #$01,D0	;Subtract 1 from D0(decrement D0)	4(1/0)
$00001034	BNE $FA(PC)	;If not zero, branch to (ea)*	10(2/0)
$00001036	RTS	;return from subroutine	16(4/0)
		*T(R/W) branch taken = 10(2/0)	
		not taken = 8(1/0)	

FIGURE 3.19 Instruction-time and execution-time computation for the 68000 (Example 3.7).

RESET: The processor needs to fetch only the op.word, involving only one read bus cycle. However, the reset pulse is held active for 128 T-states, resulting in T(R/W) values = 132(1/0).

BNE FA(PC): The processor fetches the op.word, computes the <ea>, and fetches the new op.word at the branched location, if the branch is taken. This involves two read bus cycles and address computation, resulting in T(R/W) values = 10(2/0). If the branch is not taken, the computed <ea> has to be recomputed to the original value. Thus, only one op.word fetch and two computations are involved, resulting in T(R/W) values = 8(1/0).

RTS: The processor fetches the op.word, performs two more read operations to obtain the stored PC from the stack, and fetches the new op.word from the new PC location. This involves four read bus cycles, resulting in T(R/W) values = 16(4/0).

2. **Execution time:** The delay timing loop between the NOP and the BNE instruction runs seven times (refer to Example 3.6) until D0 is decremented to 0. The loop exists the eighth time. The computation of the execution time is as follows:

$$
\begin{array}{lll}
\text{\# T-states per loop (between NOP and BNE)} & = & 18 \\
\text{\# T-states per seven loops} & = 7 \times 18 = & 126 \\
\text{\# T-states for the eighth and the last loop} & = & 32 \\
\quad \text{(BNE has only eight T-states and RTS has} & & \\
\qquad \text{to be included)} & & \\
\quad \text{Total \# T-states in the delay subroutine} & = & \underline{176} \\
\end{array}
$$

At an 8 MHz clock, each T-state = 1/8 MHz = 0.125 microsecond.

Delay routine execution time = # T-states × time/state

= 176 × 0.125

= 22 microseconds

The 68008 timing computation is similar, except that the read and write bus cycles transfer a byte of data instead of a word as in the 68000. This makes the 68008 instruction fetch and execution times (for word and long-word operands) twice as long as in the case of the 68000.

3.6 SUMMARY

In this chapter we examined the instruction set of the 68000. It has 56 generic instructions, some of which have several variations. These instructions follow a consistent structure. The same mnemonic representing an instruction can be used with appropriate attributes and extensions to refer to different operand sizes and addressing modes.

Some of the instructions for the 68000 are of the single-operand type. In such cases, the specified operand is the destination operand on which the given operation is performed. Other instructions are of the double-operand type in which the first operand is the source operand and the second is the destination operand. The final result is put in the destination.

The 68000 instruction set is subdivided into several groups: data movement, binary and BCD arithmetic, logical and bit-manipulation, program and system control, and special category.

Data movement instructions deal with the physical movement of the data operands. The binary arithmetic instructions deal with the binary arithmetic and data processing. The BCD instructions deal with decimal numbers. The binary operations are faster than the BCD operations. In the multiprecision arithmetic type of operations, the extend (X) flag bit is used to carry the result from the previous operation to the current operation.

The logical instructions deal with logical data manipulation and assist data processing operations. The bit-manipulation instructions deal with bit-level data manipulations, which are very useful in I/O applications in which a single bit must be tested or changed.

The program control instructions deal with conditional and unconditional control of the program flow. These instructions are particularly useful in controlling loops, calling subroutines, branching to specified locations on condition, and branching or jumping to specified locations unconditionally. For conditional transfers, the instruction checks the corresponding flag bits and makes the decision for a transfer.

The system control instructions deal with system functions, such as stopping the processor, resetting the peripherals, and so forth. These instructions are used at the operating system level to control and synchronize system operation. In order to enhance efficiency of the operating system activity, certain instructions dealing with the status register and the stack pointers are classified as privileged instructions. These should only be used in the supervisor mode. To do otherwise results in an error condition causing the processor to go into the supervisor mode.

Instruction timing is a very important parameter. The read or the write bus cycle takes four clock cycles (T-states) without any wait states. The op.word fetch is always a read bus cycle. An instruction may consist of several read and write bus cycles. The execution time of a program is the compounded execution time of the instructions and the program loops.

Assembly language programming, which will be covered in the next chapter, is a better way to develop software than using absolute numbers and hex values.

PROBLEMS

Note: All the problems in this section can be reworked using the 68008 processor to compare its performance with that of the 68000.

3.1 Which of the following instructions are valid and which are not valid? Give the reason.

    (a) MOVEA.L A1,A3

    (b) MOVE.W (A1),D0

    (c) MOVE.B −(D2),D3

3.2 How many words are each of the following instructions? Give the reason.

    (a) MOVE.L #$1234098A,D6

    (b) EXG A2,D4

    (c) SWAP D3

3.3 Write mnemonic instructions for the following:

    (a) move byte in D0 into memory addressed by A2;

    (b) move byte in memory addressed by A2 into D3;

    (c) move long word in memory addressed by A3 into D3;

    (d) move long word in D3 into memory addressed by A2.

3.4 Consolidate (a) and (b) of Problem 3.3 into one instruction, if possible. Is this more efficient? Why or why not?

3.5 Consolidate (c) and (d) of Problem 3.3 into one instruction, if possible. Is this more efficient? Why or why not?

3.6 Which of the following forms are allowed and which are not allowed for the ADD and SUB instructions? Give the reason.

    (a) ADDQ.L #$0F,D4

    (b) SUBI.L #$0034567C,A7

    (c) ADDX.B −(A3),−(A1)

    (d) SUB.B 0A(PC),D2

3.7 How many words are each of the following instructions? Give the reason.

    (a) ADDX.L −(A2),−(A3)

    (b) ADD.L $123C(A1,D1.W),D0

3.8 Using the information from Figure 3.4, classify each of the following addressing modes:

    (a) immediate addressing mode;

    (b) quick addressing mode;

    (c) d(PC,Rn);

    (d) An.

3.9 Which of the following instructions is likely to generate an error? Why?

    (a) SUB.W $1235,D0

    (b) MOVE.W #$2400,SR

3.10 Indicate the results of the affected registers and memory after each of the following operations using the initial values of Figure 3.6:

    (a) MOVE.L (A1),(A0)+

    (b) ADDQ.W #$07,D0

    (c) ADD.W −(A1),−(A1)

    (d) SUB.W (A1)+,(A1)+

3.11 Repeat Problem 3.10 on condition that the instructions are used in sequence.

3.12 The following program is run in sequence:

```
ADDX.W  D0,D1
SWAP    D1
EXT.L   D0
ADDX.L  D1,D0
```

Using the initial values of Figure 3.6, indicate the contents of the affected registers at each step of the sequence.

3.13 What are the contents of the affected registers and memory after each of the following operations? Use the initial values of Figure 3.6.

(a) CMP.L D0,D1

(b) CMPA.W A0,A1

(c) TST.L −(A1)

3.14 In the following program, use the initial values of Figure 3.6:

```
NEG.W  D2
MOVEA.W D2,A2
CMPA.W  A2,A1
```

What are the values of the affected registers, including the status register?

3.15 What are the results of the following operations? Use the initial conditions of Figure 3.6. Show the contents of the affected registers and the memory locations.

(a) MULU D2,D1

(b) MULS D1,D2

(c) DIVU D2,D1

(d) DIVS D1,D2

3.16 Write a sequence of instructions to add long words addressed by (A1) and (A2), with the result in a location addressed by (A3). Use any addressing modes.

3.17 Write a sequence of instructions to compute the average of word operands contained in the D0–D5 registers. (*Hint:* you may want to sign extend to long words before the actual addition!)

3.18 In a control system application as shown in the following diagram, 16-bit X and Y words are entering the 68000-based system. Registers A0 and A1 point to X and Y words. X is larger than Y and is a positive number. It is required to compute a control word Z, given by

$$Z = 0.25([X − Y]^2)$$

and output to a location addressed by A2. Write the sequence of instructions as a subroutine.

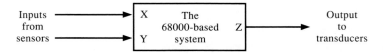

3.19 Using the initial values of Figure 3.6, compute the results of the following operations and indicate the contents of the affected registers:

    (a) AND.B D2,D1
    (b) AND.L D1,D0
    (c) EOR.W #$AA55,D1
    (d) NOT.L (A1)

3.20 Repeat Problem 3.19 on condition that the instructions are executed in sequence.

3.21 Compute the results of the following operations using the initial values of Figure 3.6 and assuming the operations are executed one at a time.

    (a) ROL.W D2,D0
    (b) ROR.L #$4,D0
    (c) ASL.W #$2,D2
    (d) LSL.L D2,D1

3.22 Repeat Problem 3.21 on condition that the instructions are executed in sequence.

3.23 Compute the results of the following operations using the initial values of Figure 3.6 and assuming the operations are executed in sequence:

    (a) BCHG.L #$1E,D0
    (b) BTST.B #$3,(A1)
    (c) BCLR.L D2,D1
    (d) BSET.B #$4,−(A1)

3.24 Write a series of instructions to invert the long-word contents of memory contained between $0034FE74 and $0034FE7C. (*Hint:* you may want to use conditional branches.)

3.25 Compute the effective address in each of the branch operations listed below. The PC value at the branch instruction is $00001040. In each case, specify the condition to be satisfied for the branch to occur.

    (a) $00001040   BEQ $4A(PC)
    (b) $00001040   BNE $FA(PC)
    (c) $00001040   BLE $FF00(PC)
    (d) $00001040   BGT $08(PC)

3.26 Write a program to clear the memory words between the locations $00002000 and $00002080.

3.27 There are 128 word X and Y binary strings in memory. A0 and A1 point to the end of the strings (the least significant words in each case), as shown:

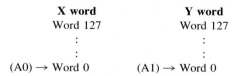

X word	Y word
Word 127	Word 127
⋮	⋮
⋮	⋮
(A0) → Word 0	(A1) → Word 0

Write a subroutine to add these strings and store the result in memory addressed by A2.

3.28 Repeat Problem 3.27, performing subtraction instead of addition.

3.29 Repeat Problem 3.27 with BCD data.

3.30 Repeat Problem 3.28 with BCD data.

3.31 Show the T(R/W) values for each of the instructions in the following software subroutine:

PC	Instruction	
$00002000	CLR.L	D0
02	CLR.L	(A1)
04	ADD.L	D0,(A1)
06	ADDQ.L	#$02,D0
08	CMPI.L	#$00000400,D0
0E	BNE	$F4(PC)
10	NOP	
12	RTS	

3.32 Analyze the software of Problem 3.31. What is being accomplished? How many times is the loop executed before the return instruction?

Indicate the contents of D0 and memory addressed by A1 when the program returns to the calling program.

3.33 The 68000 processor operates on an 8-MHz clock. Compute the time of execution of the software in Problem 3.31.

3.34 The 68000 processor operates on an 8-MHz clock. Write a subroutine that will provide a 0.1-second delay time.

ENDNOTES

1. Triebel, W., and Singh, A. *16-Bit Microprocessors: Architecture, Software and Interfacing Techniques.* Englewood Cliffs, NJ: Prentice-Hall, 1985.

2. Motorola, Inc. *M68000 16/32-Bit Microprocessor Programmer's Reference Manual, Fifth Edition.* Englewood Cliffs, NJ: Prentice-Hall, 1987.

3. Harman, T., and Lawson, B. *The Motorola MC68000 Microprocessor.* Englewood Cliffs, NJ: Prentice-Hall, 1985.

4. Motorola, Inc. *MTT8: 68000 Course Notes.* Phoenix, AZ: Motorola Technical Operations, 1987.

5. Triebel, W., and Singh, A. *16-Bit Microprocessors: Architecture, Software and Interfacing Techniques.* Englewood Cliffs, NJ: Prentice-Hall, 1985.

6. Tocci, R., and Laskowski, L. *Microprocessors and Microcomputers.* Englewood Cliffs, NJ: Prentice-Hall, 1979.

7. Harman, T., and Lawson, B. *The Motorola MC68000 Microprocessor.* Englewood Cliffs, NJ: Prentice-Hall, 1985.

8. Motorola, Inc. *MC68000, MC68008, MC68010/12 Data Books.* Phoenix, AZ: Motorola Technical Operations, 1983.

9. Stranes, T. "Design Philosophy Behind the M68000." *Byte* (Apr., May, Jun. 1983).

10. Stranes, T. "Design Philosophy Behind the M68000." *Byte* (Apr., May, Jun. 1983).

11. Motorola, Inc. *MTT8: 68000 Course Notes.* Phoenix, AZ: Motorola Technical Operations, 1987.

68000 Software Considerations and Assembly Programming Applications

Objectives

In this chapter we will study:

Assembly-level programming techniques for the 68000
Concepts of software design and implementation
Practical program development and applications
Concepts of macros and programs with macros
Special instruction groups and applications

4.0   INTRODUCTION

The required software for the 68000 microprocessor can be easily developed using assemblers and cross assemblers. **Assembly language programs** use the instruction mnemonics of the processor. **Assemblers** and **cross assemblers** are software utilities that convert assembly language programs into the appropriate form of machine code, consisting of binary 1s and 0s. Programs written in assembly language are usually more efficient with respect to code content and execution time than programs written in such higher level languages as BASIC, FORTRAN, PASCAL, and C; however, the higher level languages do provide programming ease. Industrial and I/O application programs are often written in assembly language. Assembly language programming requires a complete understanding of processor architecture, addressing modes, and the instruction set.[1]

Software usually refers to programming techniques that take into consideration system hardware resources and optimization of code content and execution time. **Programming** refers to code development to accomplish a given task. The terms *software* and *programming* are used interchangeably in most industrial circles; however, for purposes of this text, we will maintain the distinction between these terms.

Study of assembly language techniques and software considerations will provide the knowledge and background necessary to develop assembly language programs and software on 68000-based systems.

Most of the programs in this chapter are suitable for any 68000-based hardware; thus, our discussions are independent of specific hardware.

4.1   ASSEMBLY LANGUAGE SOFTWARE AND PROGRAMMING TECHNIQUES

It is impractical and tedious to use actual addresses and instruction codes in developing assembly programs. Symbols and labels can be used in place of the actual addresses if assembler utilities are available.[2]

Assembler, Cross Assembler, Linker, and Loader Utilities

Figure 4.1 illustrates a software system configuration using a host computer, an emulator, and a 68000-based target system. The software development is done on the **host system** and the code is downloaded to the **target system** for the actual operation.

In Figure 4.2 the various steps involved in the software development process are indicated. The assembly-level program is developed with the help of an editor or word-processor utility, and is known as the **source program.** The **source program file** usually has an extension (.src); for example, TEST.SRC is the source file in Figure 4.2. After correcting any typing errors, the source program is run through the assembler or the cross-assembler utility.

FIGURE 4.1 Typical system configuration for software development.

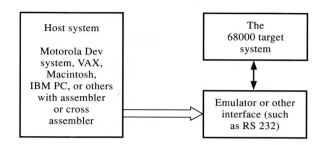

Assemblers and Cross Assemblers   These are the software utilities that convert a program in assembly language into the corresponding machine code. The machine-code program is also known as the **object code.** The corresponding file is TEST.OBJ. If the host computer has the same processor as the target system, the assembler utility is used. On the other hand, if the computer has a processor different from that of the target system, the cross-assembler utility is used. The assembler and the cross-assembler utilities are similar to each other in function. They also generate a **list file** (TEST.LST) contain-

FIGURE 4.2 Typical software development process.

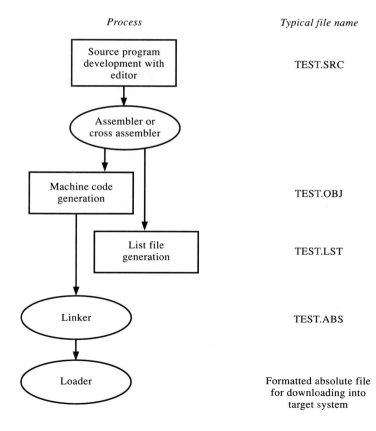

ing the machine code, the instruction mnemonics, symbols, labels, and the translated addresses and numbers. This file is very useful in debugging the programs.[3]

Linkers and Loaders The linker utility provides absolute addresses for the machine-code programs in the real operating memory environment of the target system. It also links several machine-code programs, if necessary, and provides an **absolute file** (TEST.ABS).

The loader utility provides the required format for the absolute file to be downloaded into the target system. For the 68000 family of processors, this is usually the Motorola-S format. Another common format is the INTEL-Hex format.

Writing Assembly Programs and Software Development

Most currently available assembler and cross-assembler utilities are of the two-pass type. In the first pass, symbols and labels in the assembly source program are converted into the corresponding numbers and displacement values. In the second pass, these numbers or values are substituted for the existing symbols and labels, and the machine-code file is generated. Present-day assembler and cross-assembler utilities are able to identify syntax, instruction, and operand errors at the time of assembly and display them. These errors then can be corrected and the assembly process repeated.

In developing the source program, **assembler directives** can be used. These directives are a set of commands associated with the assemblers and cross assemblers. We will introduce those directives typical of most assemblers or cross assemblers. For information on additional directives, appropriate manuals may be consulted.[4]

Figure 4.3 illustrates the assembly source program (TEST.SRC). In Figure 4.4 the assembled program listing (TEST.LST) is presented. In the discussion numbers in square brackets [ ] refer to the bracketed numbers in the figures, which correspond to important assembler directives or events.

[1] Comment directive: Usually a delimiter such as a semicolon (;) is used as an assembler comment directive to introduce the comments. The comments are provided to explain the program flow. The assembler will not generate any machine code for a comment, but will include the comment statements in the list file.

> **example:** `;test.src 8\8\87`   (at line 1)

> The preceding comment statement is listed in the assembled program listing, but it is not assembled to machine code.

[2] LLEN and OPT directives: These are the line length and the option directives, which specify the printer line length and any specific options. In our example, the line length is set at 108 columns. Option A generates an absolute file after the linker operation.

[3] ORG directive: This is the origin directive. It specifies the starting address of the assembled program.

```
                    ;this is a source program to show
                    ;the format of a typical assembly
                    ;language program.
                    ;
;test.src 8\8\87                                              ;[1]
;declaration of length, option
;and origin
            LLEN     108                                      ;[2]
            OPT      A
            ORG      $1000                                    ;[3]
;declaration of symbols and values
VALUE1      EQU      $0008                                    ;[4]
VALUE2      EQU      $0001
PORT        EQU      $A000
;move value1 into D0 and jump to
;delay subroutine
START       MOVE.W   #VALUE1,D0                               ;[5]
            BSR      DELAY                                    ;[6]
;output message to port until $
;character and back to start
            MOVEA.L  #MSGE,A0
DSPLY       MOVE.B   (A0)+,D1
            CMPI.B   #'$',D1
            BEQ      START
            MOVE.B   D1,PORT
            JMP      DSPLY
;delay subroutine. Loops until D0
;is decremented to 0.
DELAY       NOP
            SUBQ.W   #VALUE2,D0
            BNE      DELAY
            RTS
;message to be output
;
MSGE        DC       'ABCDE --$'                              ;[7]
DBUF        DS       128                                      ;[8]
            END                                              ;[9]
```

FIGURE 4.3 Assembly language source program (TEST.SRC) for 68000-based systems.

   example: ORG $1000   (at line 6)

The first instruction of the assembled program will start at PC location $1000, as can be seen from the assembled listing.

[4] EQU directive and symbols: This is the equate directive. It provides constant or computed values to the symbols.

   example: VALUE1   EQU $0008   (at line 8)

```
                         ;this is a source program to show
                         ;the format of a typical assembly
                         ;language program.
                         ;

LINE ADDR

 1                                       ;test.src 8\8\87                    ;[1]
 2                                       ;declaration of length, option
 3                                       ;and origin
 4                                       LLEN     108
 5                                       OPT      A                          ;[2]
 6                                       ORG      $1000                      ;[3]
 7                                       ;declaration of symbols and values
 8  00000008                    VALUE1   EQU      $0008                      ;[4]
 9  00000001                    VALUE2   EQU      $0001
10  0000A000                    PORT     EQU      $A000
11                                       ;move value1 into D0 and jump to
12                                       ;delay subroutine
13  00001000 303C 0008          START    MOVE.W   #VALUE1,D0                 ;[5]
14  00001004 611A 4E71          BSR              DELAY                       ;[6]
15                                       ;output message to port until $
16                                       ;character and back to start
17  00001008 207C 0000 1028     MOVEA.L  #MSGE,A0
18  0000100E 1218               DSPLY    MOVE.B   (A0)+,D1
19  00001010 0C01 0024          CMPI.B   #'$',D1
20  00001014 67EA               BEQ      START
21  00001016 13C1 0000 A000     MOVE.B   D1,PORT
22  0000101C 4EF8 100E          JMP      DSPLY
23                                       ;delay subroutine. Loops until D0
24                                       ;is decremented to 0.
25  00001020 4E71               DELAY    NOP
26  00001022 5340               SUBQ.W   #VALUE2,D0
27  00001024 66FA               BNE      DELAY
28  00001026 4E75               RTS
29                                       ;message to be output
30                                       ;
31  00001028 4142 4344          MSGE     DC       'ABCDE --$'               ;[7]
31  0000102C 4520 2D2D
31  00001030 2400
32  00001032               DBUF     DS       128                       ;[8]
33  00001132               END                                        ;[9]


    ASSEMBLER ERRORS =       0



                              SYMBOL TABLE

DBUF         00001032  DELAY    00001020  DSPLY    0000100E
MSGE         00001028  NARG     00000000  PORT     0000A000
START        00001000  VALUE1   00000008  VALUE2   00000001
```

FIGURE 4.4 Assembled program listing (TEST.LST) corresponding to the source program in Figure 4.3.

VALUE1 is a symbol for which the numerical value is $0008. The assembler replaces the symbol VALUE1 with $0008 in the assembly process by means of the EQU directive. The other symbols are VALUE2 and PORT, the numerical values of which are $0001 and $A000, respectively.

[5] Label: This is a symbolic representation of the address of a program statement. Other program statements can refer to this label as the source program is being written. The assembler configures the appropriate numerical value for the label.

    example: `START    MOVE.W  #VALUE1,D0`   (at line 13)

    START is a label, referring to the program location of $00001000, as shown in the assembled listing.

Assembly listing (Figure 4.4): The actual program starts at line 13 and reads:

```
13  00001000   303C 0008     START   MOVE.W #VALUE1,D0
```

The interpretation of the preceding line is as follows:

             13 => Line number generated by the assembler for listing convenience.

    00001000 => Hex address of the first instruction, according to the earlier ORG statement.

    303C 0008 => Op.code (303C) and the operand (0008) for the MOVE.W #VALUE1,D0 instruction. The assembler has substituted 0008 for the symbol VALUE1.

[6] Branch operations: In branch operations, the assembler configures the required displacement to branch to the location specified by the label.

    example: `BSR  DELAY`   (at line 14)

    The op.code is 611A for the preceding instruction, which contains the displacement (1A) to branch to the location $00001020. This location corresponds to the label DELAY.

[7] DC directive: This is the define constant directive. It is used to define the byte (DC.B), the word (DC.W), the long-word (DC.L), or the ASCII character constants. The ASCII characters are enclosed in single quotation marks ('').

    example: `MSGE      DC      'ABCDE --$'`   (at line 31)

    Sequential locations starting at $00001028 are filled with the ASCII values: $41 for A, $42 for B, and so on. MSGE is a label corresponding to the address $00001028.

[8] DS directive: This is the define storage directive. It is used to define storage space in memory. It can be specified as bytes (DS.B or DB), words (DS.W or DS), or long words (DS.L).

    example: `DBUF        DS        128`   (at line 32)

Storage space of 128 words (256 bytes) is defined as DBUF, starting at location $00001032.

[9] END directive: This directive signifies the end of the assembly process. Statements beyond the END directive are not recognized by the assembler.

Other Delimiters and Directives   To distinguish among operand types, certain **delimiters** are used. These delimiters depend on the assembler or the cross assembler. Some of the standard ones are as follows:

$$\$ => \text{hex data or operand}$$
$$\# => \text{immediate data or operand}$$
$$; => \text{comment beginning}$$

Symbol Table   Assemblers and cross assemblers also generate a symbol table as shown below the program listing in Figure 4.4. It provides a quick reference for the symbols and labels used in the program.

The following example problem provides a review of the assembly process of 68000 programs.

Example 4.1   Assembler usage for the 68000.
Refer to the source, assembled, and listed programs of Figures 4.3 and 4.4.

1. Are the statements

`PORT     DSPLY`

symbols or labels? Why? What are their hex values?

2. Where does the program branch after executing the instruction

`BEQ    START`   (at line 20)

What is the offset value calculated by the assembler? How is the effective address value computed?

3. What are the contents of the A0 register after executing the instruction

`MOVEA.L   #MSGE,A0`   (at line 17)

What are the details of the op.code and the operands?

Solution

1. **Symbols and labels:** PORT is a symbol, since it is declared by the EQU directive. It has a hex value $A000.

DSPLY is a label, since it is introduced in the program to identify the corresponding program location. It has a hex value of 0000100E.

$$\textbf{PORT } = \textbf{\$A000}$$
$$\textbf{DSPLY} = \textbf{\$0000100E}$$

2. **BEQ START:** If the branch condition is satisfied, the program branches to location $00001000, which corresponds to the label START. The offset or the displacement calculated by the assembler is EA, which is a part of the op.code 67EA.

$$\textbf{Offset} = \textbf{\$EA}$$

Effective address calculation:

PC value after reading the op.code $=>$ $00001016

$+$

Sign-extended displacement EA $=>$ $FFFFFFEA
(in twos-complement form)
Effective address for branch $=>$ $00001000
(corresponding to label START)

3. **Contents of A0 after the MOVEA.L #MSGE,A0 instruction:** MSGE is a label and #MSGE corresponds to the address location $00001028. As such, A0 is loaded with the value $00001028.

$$\textbf{A0} = \textbf{\$00001028}$$

Op.code and operand details: Line 17 shows

```
00001008 207C 0000 1028   MOVEA.L #MSGE,A0
```

where

00001008 $=>$ Program location of the instruction
207C $=>$ Op.code of the instruction
0000 1028 $=>$ Operand value moved into A0

Since the preceding example was used primarily to review the assembly process, we did not focus on analyzing the program. This analysis would prove useful to the reader to enhance understanding of software development.

Programming and Software Engineering Considerations

From a programmer's point of view, the program in Figure 4.4 is a 33-line program, including comments and declarations. Programmers may not be concerned about memory appropriations and code content. On the other hand, software engineers would make sure that appropriate memory was allocated for the buffer. For example, they would examine lines 32 and 33 of the listed program to ensure that the 128 words of memory space was allocated. This may be done in the following way:

Ending address of the DBUF (line 33)   => $00001132

Beginning address of the DBUF (at line 32) => $00001032
Size of the buffer in bytes   => $00000100

$0100 bytes = 256 bytes = 128 words

which is the requested memory space for the buffer.

Similarly, software engineers also would be concerned about whether the entire program was on the even boundaries and whether the entire code content was correct. Although there are some traditional distinctions between programmers and software engineers, these distinctions are rapidly vanishing as technologies continue to advance.

4.2   DATA MOVEMENT, DATA-COMPARISON SOFTWARE, AND APPLICATIONS

The majority of operations in any computer system deal with data movement between two or more locations. For example, in a file-management system, data from one section of memory may be moved into another section. Data rearrangement involves extensive data-comparison procedures, which we will now examine.

Block Transfer Applications and Software Considerations

The basis for any data movement operation is the **block transfer.** It usually involves two **pointers:** the first refers to the starting address of the source block and the second to the starting address of the destination block. In addition, there is a **loop counter,** which keeps track of the number of data elements being transferred.

Figure 4.5 shows a typical block movement sequence written as a subroutine. D0 is chosen as the loop counter and is initialized to $100 at line 10. A1 is the source pointer and A2 is the destination pointer. They are initialized to $00004000 and $00006000 at lines 11 and 12. The program loop between lines 16 and 18 transfers successive long words from the source block to destination block, until D0 is decremented to zero. In this case, the number of long words transferred are $100 or 256. At the end of the successful block transfer, the software returns to the calling program by means of the RTS instruction at line 19.

```
LINE ADDR

  1                                    ;block data move 8/8/87
  2                                    ;
  3                                       OPT A
  4                                       ORG $1000
  5                                    ;initialize A1, A2 with source
  6                                    ;and destination addresses and
  7                                    ;D0 with number of words to be
  8                                    ;transferred
  9                                    ;
 10 00001000 303C 0100        INIT MOVE.W  #$0100,D0
 11 00001004 227C 0000 4000        MOVEA.L #$00004000,A1
 12 0000100A 247C 0000 6000        MOVEA.L #$00006000,A2
 13                                    ;move data from (A1) to (A2)
 14                                    ;until D0 is decremented to 0
 15                                    ;
 16 00001010 24D9             LOOP MOVE.L  (A1)+,(A2)+
 17 00001012 5340                  SUBQ.W  #$01,D0
 18 00001014 66FA                  BNE     LOOP
 19 00001016 4E75                  RTS
 20                                    ;returns to the calling program.
 21 00001018                        END


ASSEMBLER ERRORS =    0


                         SYMBOL TABLE

INIT   00001000  LOOP    00001010  NARG    00000000
```

FIGURE 4.5 Typical 68000-based block movement sequence.

In the example problem that follows, we will consider software and timing in the block movement sequence.

Example 4.2   Block movement sequence.
Consider the sequence of Figure 4.5.

1. Specify the final values of the A1, A2, and D0 registers after the loop has been completed and the RTS instruction is being executed.

2. The system operates on an 8-MHz clock. Compute the loop execution time T(loop) to transfer $100 long words.

3. Modify any of the required instructions to transfer $0400 long words. What is the new execution time of the loop?

Solution

1. **Final values:** The data movement loop between lines 16 and 18 is run $100 times (until D0 is decremented to $0000). Each time the loop is executed, A1 and A2 are postincremented by four (because of the long-word data transfers). At the end of the loop, A1 and A2 are incremented by $0400 from their initial values.

   The final values are

$$D0 = \$00000000$$
$$A1 = \$00004400$$
$$A2 = \$00006400$$

2. **Loop execution time:** Using the T(R/W) values (refer to Chapter 3) for lines 16 through 18, we obtain

```
Line Addr                                        T(R/W)

 16          LOOP MOVE.L    (A1)+,(A2)+          20(3/2)
 17               SUBQ.W     #$01,D0              4(1/0)
 18               BNE        LOOP                10(2/0)
                                                (branch)
```

The total number of T-states is 34, as indicated. This loop is run 256 ($100) times. The clock period at an 8-MHz clock is 0.125 microsecond. Thus, the total loop execution time is as follows:

$$\text{T(loop)} = 34 \times 256 \times 0.125 = 1088 \text{ microseconds}$$

3. **Modified software:** The loop counter D0 needs to be changed to $0400 to transfer $0400 or 1024 long words. Therefore, we modify the instruction at line 10 to

```
MOVE.W    #$0400,D0
```

to accomplish the task.

   Four times as many long words are transferred; hence, the loop time increases proportionately:

$$\text{T(loop)} = 4 \times 1088 = 4352 \text{ microseconds}$$

By appropriately initializing the pointer and the counter registers, it is possible to move any amount of data. However, care should be taken not to address unavailable memory locations or odd memory locations for word and long-word transfers.

Data-Sequencing Applications and Software Considerations

In industrial and commercial applications, it is often required to arrange data either in ascending or descending order. This is accomplished by comparing the data elements and appropriately positioning them. The 68000 predecrement and postincrement addressing modes are particularly useful in such applications. Figure 4.6 illustrates data-sequencing software as a subroutine. We will now analyze and interpret the results.

```
LINE ADDR

  1                                      ;SEQ.SRC 9/24/88
  2                                      ;
  3                                      ;sequences string of words
  4                                      ;such that largest word is
  5                                      ;in the lowest location.
  6                                      ;A0 and A1 point to the
  7                                      ;beginning and end of the
  8                                      ;string
  9                                         OPT      A
 10                                         ORG      $1000
 11                                      ;save original value of A0 in A2
 12 00001000 2448                           MOVEA.L  A0,A2
 13                                      ;compare successive words. If the
 14                                      ;second word is larger, branch to
 15                                      ;EXCHG routine to swap them
 16 00001002 204A          BGAGN            MOVEA.L  A2,A0
 17 00001004 B148          NXTPR            CMPM.W   (A0)+,(A0)+
 18 00001006 620C                           BHI.S    EXCHG
 19 00001008 91FC 0000 0002                 SUBA.L   #$02,A0
 20 0000100E B3C8                           CMPA.L   A0,A1
 21 00001010 66F2                           BNE.S    NXTPR
 22 00001012 4E75                           RTS
 23                                      ;exchange the two words by swapping
 24 00001014 2020          EXCHG            MOVE.L   -(A0),D0
 25 00001016 4840                           SWAP.W   D0
 26 00001018 2080                           MOVE.L   D0,(A0)
 27 0000101A 60E6                           BRA.S    BGAGN
 28 0000101C                               END


ASSEMBLER ERRORS =     0

                        SYMBOL TABLE

BGAGN   00001002   EXCHG   00001014   NARG     00000000
NXTPR   00001004
```

FIGURE 4.6 Data-sequencing and sorting software for a typical 68000-based system. (Courtesy of Motorola, Inc.)

A0 contains the starting address of the string where the highest valued data element should be put. The next highest memory locations contain the sequentially decreasing values of the string. A1 contains the ending address of the string. At line 12, the original value of the A0 register is stored in A2 for later reference. At line 16, the stored value of A0 is restored. At line 17, two successive words of the string are compared to each other. At line 18, the subroutine branches to the EXCHG routine if the second word is larger than the first. If the words are in proper order, the program proceeds.

At line 19, A0 is decremented by two. This adjusts A0 for comparison of the next two sequential locations. At line 20, A0 is compared with A1 to check whether it is the end of the string. If it is not the end of the string, the program branches back to line 17 (label NXTPR) to start the next comparison. If it is the end of the string, the program returns to the calling program by means of the RTS instruction at line 22.

The EXCHG software module is contained between lines 24 and 27. It obtains two sequential words as a long word into D0, swaps them, and puts them back in memory. This has the effect of exchanging the words. When this happens, the program branches back to the very beginning (line 16, labeled BGAGN). This will restart the data comparison process. When the routine returns to the calling program, the data string is completely adjusted so that the highest valued element is in the lowest memory location.

The following example problem considers software and timing in the data-sequencing subroutine.

Example 4.3   Data-sequencing software.
For the software of Figure 4.6, the initial values of the A0 and A1 registers and the memory contents are as indicated in Figure 4.7.

FIGURE 4.7   Initial conditions (for Example 4.3).

(Beginning of the string) A0	$00004000
(End of the string) A1	$00004006

Memory contents at $00004000=>1234

4002	5678
4004	ABCD
4006	0E71
4008	4321

1. Following the software of Figure 4.6, specify the data comparisons and rearrangement of data.

2. What are the final values of the A0 and A1 registers?

3. How many data comparisons must be made to obtain the final string? Is this number data dependent?

Solution

1. **Data comparisons and memory contents:** Figure 4.8 shows how the data comparisons are made and the final arrangement of the data string in memory. During the [1]st comparison, data elements 1234 and 5678 are compared and swapped. During

Memory Address	Memory Contents	Memory Contents	Memory Contents	Memory Contents
$00004000	1 2 3 4 —[1]	[2]— 5 6 7 8	[4]— 5 6 7 8	[5]— A B C D
4002	5 6 7 8 —	— 1 2 3 4 —[3]	— A B C D	— 5 6 7 8 —[6]
4004	A B C D	A B C D —	1 2 3 4	[7]— 1 2 3 4 —
4006	0 E 7 1	0 E 7 1	0 E 7 1	— 0 E 7 1
4008	4 3 2 1	4 3 2 1	4 3 2 1	4 3 2 1
	(a) Initial contents	**(b)** First rearrangement	**(c)** Second rearrangement	**(d)** Final rearrangement

FIGURE 4.8   Data comparisons and rearrangement of the data string (for Example 4.3).

the [2]nd comparison, the rearranged data elements (5678 and 1234) check in proper sequence and the program proceeds to the [3]rd comparison. During the [3]rd comparison, data elements 1234 and ABCD are compared and swapped. The program then restarts from the beginning. During the [4]th comparison, data elements 5678 and ABCD are compared and swapped. The program then restarts from the beginning. During the [5]th comparison, the rearranged data elements (ABCD and 5678) check in proper sequence and the program proceeds to the [6]th comparison. The final rearranged string results after the [7]th comparison, as shown in Figure 4.8(d).

2. **Final values of A0 and A1:** The process terminates when the contents of A0 are compared and found to be equal to those of A1 (= $00004006).

$$A0 = \$00004006$$
$$A1 = \$00004006$$

3. **Number of data comparisons:** As shown in Figure 4.8, seven data comparisons are made. These comparisons are data dependent.

$$\#\text{data comparisons} = 7$$

There are some important software considerations in the preceding example. The number of comparisons, the number of times the loop gets executed, and the loop execution times are totally data dependent and do not have fixed values. When a fixed time of execution is required, this type of software should be avoided.

4.3 DATA PROCESSING APPLICATIONS AND SOFTWARE CONSIDERATIONS

Data processing involves extensive arithmetic operations on the data elements. The 68000 microprocessor has very powerful instructions to handle binary and BCD types of data.[5]

Multiprecision Addition and Subtraction Operations

Instructions employing the extended carry X (such as ADDX, SUBX) can be used to conduct multiprecision operations on binary data strings. For BCD operations, the X carry bit is always involved. In multiprecision operations, the least significant data elements are operated upon first (generating X carry). The next higher data elements are then operated upon, taking into consideration the previously generated X carry bit. The process continues until all data elements in the data string are operated upon.

Figure 4.9 illustrates a multiprecision binary addition program used in a data processing application. The source and the destination data strings are addressed by the A1 and A2 registers, respectively. The D1 and D2 registers are used as working registers.

From line 12 to line 14, the X carry bit and the D1 and D2 registers are cleared and initialized to zero. From line 17 to line 19, the two data strings addressed by A1 and A2 are sequentially added, along with the X bit, using the predecrement addressing mode. A3 contains the ending address of the destination string.

```
LINE ADDR

  1                                    ;add.src 9/25/88
  2                                    ;
  3                                    ;performs multiprecision addition
  4                                    ;on two binary strings in memory.
  5                                    ;A1-2 refers to the LSD of string1.
  6                                    ;A2-2 refers to the LSD of string2.
  7                                    ;A3 refers to the end of string2.
  8                                    ;D1 and D2 are the working registers.
  9                                      OPT     A
 10                                      ORG     $1400
 11                                    ;clear X bit, D1 and D2 registers
 12 00001400 023C 00EF                  ANDI.B  #$EF,CCR
 13 00001404 4281                       CLR.L   D1
 14 00001406 4282                       CLR.L   D2
 15                                    ;start multiprecision addition
 16                                    ;of string1 and string2.
 17 00001408 D549               AGAIN ADDX.W  -(A1),-(A2)
 18 0000140A B5CB                       CMPA.L  A3,A2
 19 0000140C 62FA                       BHI.S   AGAIN
 20                                    ;get X bit into D2 and
 21                                    ;put it along with string 2,
 22                                    ;and return to the calling program.
 23  0000140E D541                      ADDX.W  D1,D2
 24  00001410 3502                      MOVE.W  D2,-(A2)
 25  00001412 4E71                      NOP
 26  00001414 4E75                      RTS
 27  00001416                           END

ASSEMBLER ERRORS =    0

                        SYMBOL TABLE

AGAIN   00001408  NARG  00000000
```

FIGURE 4.9   Multiprecision binary addition program for a 68000-based system.

When A2 is decremented below A3, the loop is terminated. At lines 23 and 24, the X bit is effectively moved into D2 and is put with the destination string. At line 26, the routine returns to the calling program. It should be observed that addition proceeds from a high memory address (where the least significant data elements are present) toward a low memory address (where the most significant data elements are present).

The following example problem addresses software concerns in multiprecision addition.

Example 4.4   Multiprecision addition.

The initial values of registers A1, A2, and A3 and the memory contents are indicated in Figure 4.10. Using the multiprecision addition software of Figure 4.9,

A1 = $00004006		A2 = $00005006	A3 = $00005000	
Source Memory			Destination Memory	
Address	Contents(hex)		Address	Contents(hex)
$00004000	1234		$00005000	F878
4002	5678		5002	C800
4004	ABCD<=LSW		5004	A101 <=LSW
	(source)			(destination)
4006	OE71		5006	0200

FIGURE 4.10   Initial conditions for the program in Figure 4.9.

1. compute the result of the addition and indicate the contents of the destination string;
2. state the final values of the A1 and A2 registers when RTS is being executed;
3. state what would happen if the ADDX.W −(A1),−(A2) at line 17 was replaced by ADDX.L −(A1),−(A2).

Solution

1. **Results of the addition:** A1 and A2 are decremented by two to $00004004 and $00005004. They refer to the least significant words (LSWs) of the two strings. The addition proceeds from the LSWs toward the most significant words (MSWs), as follows:

		MSW	Next LSW	LSW	
Contents of −(A1)		1 2 3 4	5 6 7 8	ABCD	added to
Contents of −(A2)		F 8 7 8	C 8 0 0	A 1 0 1	added to
X carry bit	1	1	1	0	
		OAAD	1E79	4CCE	

The final addition result is 0001 OAAD 1E79 4CCE, which is put into memory sequentially as shown. The final X bit is put at memory location $00004FFE.

The final contents are

Location	Contents
$00004FFE	**0 0 0 1**
$00005000	**0 A A D**
$00005002	**1 E 7 9**
$00005004	**4 C C E**

2. **Final values of A1 and A2:** A1 and A2 are decremented up to $00004000 and $00005000 due to the ADDX.W $-(A1), -(A2)$ instruction (line 17). A2 is further decremented to $00004FFE due to the MOVE.W D2, $-(A2)$ instruction (line 24). Thus, the final values are

$$A1 = \$00004000$$

$$A2 = \$00004FFE$$

3. **Replacement by the ADDX.L $-(A1), -(A2)$ instruction:** Long-word additions would be performed. Instead of three word additions, four word additions would be performed. A1 and A2 would be decremented to final values of $00003FFE and $00004FFC; however, this task might not be intended.

There are some important software considerations in the preceding example. Even if long-word operations are more efficient than word operations, they cannot be done correctly if the operation involves an odd number of words. Similarly, if an odd number of bytes needs to be added, the corresponding instructions should be byte oriented rather than word or long-word oriented.

If the ADDX.W $-(A1), -(A2)$ instruction at line 17 is replaced by the SUBX.W $-(A1), -(A2)$ instruction, the same software will perform multiprecision subtraction operations.

The X bit should always be cleared initially when dealing with operations of the multiprecision type.

Multiplication and Division Operations

The 68000 microprocessor has signed and unsigned multiply and divide (MULS, MULU, DIVS, DIVU) instructions. The destination is always a data register Dn. Multiplication of two 16-bit unsigned operands results in a 32-bit unsigned result in the destination data register. The unsigned operands can be up to 65535 ($2^{16} - 1$) and the result can be up to 4,294,836,225 which is slightly less than 2^{32}. In signed multiplication, the multiplier and the multiplicand operands can be positive or negative and can range between -2^{15} and $+2^{15} - 1$ (or between -32768 and $+32767$). The largest positive or negative result can be up to plus or minus 2^{30}. The negative result is expressed in twos-complement notation. Since there is no possibility of obtaining any result beyond the

32-bit size, the carry and the overflow flags are always cleared to zero in multiplication operations. The N and Z flags are affected, based upon the result.

Division of a 32-bit destination operand (dividend) by a 16-bit source operand (divisor) results in a 16-bit remainder and a 16-bit quotient. The remainder and quotient occupy the upper and the lower 16-bit word positions of the 32-bit destination data register, respectively. The distinction between signed and unsigned division operations is similar to the distinction between signed and unsigned multiplication previously discussed. With division operations, it is possible to generate a quotient larger than the allowed 16 bits. In this circumstance, the overflow flag V will be set to indicate the overflow condition. Similarly, if division by 0 is performed, a zero-divide TRAP error will result.

In Figure 4.11, multiplication and division software is presented as a subroutine in a digital signal processing application. P, Q, and R are unsigned words contained in

```
LINE ADDR

   1                                    ;multiply.src   9/25/88
   2                                    ;
   3                                    ;P,Q,R unsigned words contained in
   4                                    ;ascending memory addressed by A0.
   5                                    ;W=P*Q in D0 register. Divide W by
   6                                    ;R, if R is nonzero value.
   7                                    ;U=W/R in D1 register.
   8                                    ;D2 is a working register.
   9                                        OPT     A
  10                                        ORG     $1400
  11                                    ;clear data registers
  12  00001400  4280                      CLR.L   D0
  13  00001402  4281                      CLR.L   D1
  14  00001404  4282                      CLR.L   D2
  15                                    ;move P into D0 and multiply by Q
  16                                    ;to get W = P*Q in D0 register
  17  00001406  3018            START MOVE.W    (A0)+,D0
  18  00001408  C0D8                  MULU      (A0)+,D0
  19  0000140A  2200                  MOVE.L    D0,D1
  20                                    ;check for nonzero value of R and
  21                                    ;perform division to get U=W/R in D1
  22  0000140C  3410                  MOVE.W    (A0),D2
  23  0000140E  0C42  0000            CMPI.W    #$00,D2
  24  00001412  6702                  BEQ.S     FINISH
  25  00001414  82C2                  DIVU      D2,D1
  26  00001416  4E75          FINISH RTS
  27  00001418                        END


       ASSEMBLER ERRORS =    0


                          SYMBOL TABLE

  FINISH   00001416   NARG    00000000   START    00001406
```

FIGURE 4.11   Multiplication and division software for a typical 68000-based system (Example 4.5).

memory in an ascending order, as specified by the A0 register. The product $W = P \times Q$ and the division result $U = W/R$ are to be generated. These results are to be put in the D0 and D1 registers.

In order to accomplish the intended task, all the working data registers are cleared to an all-zero condition from line 12 to line 14. At lines 17 and 18, the P and Q words are sequentially read from the memory using the postincrement mode and are multiplied together to generate a 32-bit result in the D0 register. At line 19, the result is also moved into the D1 register.

From line 22 to line 25, word R is moved from memory into the D2 register and is checked for a nonzero value. In the case of a zero value, the division operation is skipped; otherwise, it is performed, with the division result in the D1 register. In any event, the software returns to the calling program by means of the RTS instruction at line 26.

The following example problem addresses software concerns in multiplication and division operations.

Example 4.5   Multiplication and division.
Given P = $FFFF, Q = $0002, and R = $0004 in sequential memory locations, using the software of Figure 4.11,

1. compute the values of W and U and indicate the contents of the D0, D1, and D2 registers and the state of the XNZVC flags when RTS is being executed;
2. repeat (1) if the MULU and DIVU unsigned instructions are replaced by the MULS and DIVS signed instructions;
3. explain how the calling program obtains the results.

Solution

1. **Values of W, U, D0, and D1:** Unsigned multiplication is performed as follows:

P value from memory into D0 register	$FFFF
Q value from memory	$0002
Multiplication $W = P \times Q$	$0001FFFE => into D0

   Unsigned division is performed as follows:

W value from D0 into the D1 register	$0001FFFE
R value from memory into the D2 register	$0004
Division $U = W/R$: quotient	$7FFF => D1 low word
remainder	$0010 => D1 high word

   Result of unsigned multiplication:

   $$\textbf{W in D0} = \textbf{\$0001FFFE}$$

   Result of unsigned division:

   $$\textbf{U in D1} = \textbf{\$00107FFF}$$

Nonzero positive quotient result in D0 with no overflow. As such,

$$\textbf{XNZVC} = - \ \textbf{0 0 0 0}$$

2. **Signed multiplication and division results:** Signed multiplication and division are performed as follows:

> *Multiplication*
> | | |
> |---|---|
> | P value from memory into the D0 register | $FFFF (equal to -1) |
> | Q value from memory | $0002 (equal to $+2$) |
> | Signed multiplication W = P $\times$ Q | $FFFFFFFE (equal to -2) |
> | (sign extended to 32 bits and | into D0 |
> | in twos-complement form) | |
>
> *Division*
> | | |
> |---|---|
> | W value from the D0 register into D1 | $FFFFFFFE (equal to -2) |
> | R value from memory into the D2 register | $0004 (equal to $+4$) |
> | Division U = W/R: quotient | $0000 (equal to 0) |
> | | D1 low word |
> | remainder | $FFFE (equal to -2) |
> | | D1 high word |

Result of signed multiplication:

$$\textbf{W in D0} = \textbf{\$FFFFFFFE}$$

Result of signed division:

$$\textbf{U in D1} = \textbf{\$FFFE0000}$$

Zero quotient result with no overflow. As such,

$$\textbf{XNZVC} = - \ \textbf{0 1 0 0}$$

3. **Results to the calling program:** The multiplication and division results are communicated to the calling program through the contents of the D0, D1, and D2 registers. A zero value in the D2 register implies that the division has not been performed.

One of the operands (P in our case) is moved into the data register D0. This is necessary since multiplication and division instructions require that the destination operand be a data register. Also, the value of the R variable is checked before performing the division to avoid a division-by-zero error.

4.4 SPECIAL INSTRUCTION GROUPS AND APPLICATIONS

The instruction set of the 68000 family of processors also includes multiple-decision instructions (DBcc). There are several instructions related to stack and address operands, such as LINK, UNLK, PEA, and LEA. There are also instructions to move multiple registers (MOVEM) and move peripheral data (MOVEP). In all of these cases, a single instruction performs multiple operations. This provides programming convenience and improves memory utilization.[6,7]

Multiple-Decision Instructions

Figure 4.12 illustrates the sequence of multiple-decision instructions (DBcc). These instructions are used to control loops. Upon entering the DBcc instruction loop, the specified condition is checked. If the condition is true, the program exits the loop and proceeds to the next instruction in the sequence. If the condition is false, then the specified data register is decremented and is checked to see whether it is less than zero ($= -1$). If it is less than zero, the program exits the loop and proceeds to the next instruction in the sequence. Otherwise, the program branches to the specified location. Operands decremented in Dn are of word size.

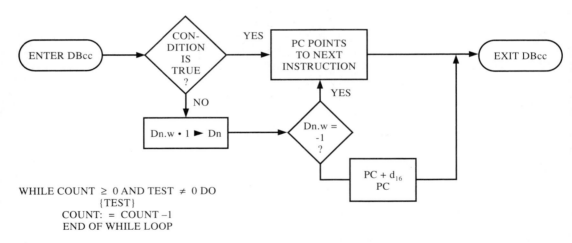

WHILE COUNT $\geq$ 0 AND TEST $\neq$ 0 DO
    {TEST}
    COUNT: = COUNT −1
END OF WHILE LOOP

FIGURE 4.12 DBcc instruction sequence. (Courtesy of Motorola, Inc.)

Figure 4.13 consists of a string-compare program using the DBcc instruction scheme. At line 13, the Z flag is set to a 1 condition. This corresponds to a false condition for the DBNE instruction (decrement and branch if not equal to zero). At line 14, two string operands addressed by (A0)+ and (A1)+ are compared. At line 15, the DBNE instruction checks whether or not the BNE condition is true (BNE true leaves Z flag = 0). BNE true implies that the two operands are different. If BNE is true, the program exits the DBNE loop and proceeds to the next instruction (NOP at line 16).

```
LINE ADDR

   1                                    ;string.src 10/21/88
   2                                    ;
   3                                    ;two strings addressed
   4                                    ;by A0 and A1 are compared
   5                                    ;for sameness, using DBcc.
   6                                    ;D1 contains number of long
   7                                    ;words to be compared.
   8                                    ;
   9                                              OPT       A
  10                                              ORG       $1000
  11                                    ;Set Z flag to 1 and
  12                                    ;start comparing strings
  13  00001000  003C  0004   START      ORI       #$04,CCR
  14  00001004  B388           AGAIN    CMPM.L    (A0)+,(A1)+
  15  00001006  56C9  FFFC              DBNE      D1,AGAIN
  16  0000100A  4E71                    NOP
  17  0000100C  4E75                    RTS
  18  0000100E                          END


ASSEMBLER ERRORS =    0


                        SYMBOL TABLE

AGAIN    00001004   NARG    00000000   START   00001000
```

FIGURE 4.13   String-compare software for a 68000-based system using the DBcc instruction.

If BNE is false (Z = 1), the DBNE instruction decrements data register D1 and checks whether it has become negative (D1 < 0). If it is negative, the program proceeds to the next instruction (NOP at line 16). Otherwise, the program branches back to the 'AGAIN' loop (line 14).

The following example problem provides a review of the concepts we have just discussed concerning DBcc usage.

Example 4.6   DBcc usage.

The initial contents of the A0, A1, and D1 registers are as follows:

$$A0 = \$00004000 \qquad A1 = \$00005000 \qquad D1 = \$000000FF$$

Memory between $4000 and $6000 is loaded with words $AAAA. The program in Figure 4.13 is run.

1. Specify when the DBNE loop is terminated. What are the contents of the D1, A0, and A1 registers when the loop is terminated?

2. Memory between $4000 and $4FFE is loaded with words $0000; between $5000 and $6000 it is loaded with words $AAAA. Repeat (1) using the same initial values for D1, A0, and A1.

Solution

1. **DBNE loop termination:** Memory between $4000 and $6000 contains word patterns $AAAA. As such, the comparison of memory addressed by A0 and A1 renders the BNE condition false (since the data strings are the same). The program loops between lines 14 and 15 until the D1 word is decremented below zero (to −1). At that point the DBNE loop is terminated.

   D1 is decremented by $FF + $01 = $100 = 256 times to get to −1. Thus, the loop is run $100 times. Due to the long-word access and the postincrement addressing modes, the A0 and A1 registers are incremented by 4 × $100 = $400, to $4400 and $5400, respectively. The final contents of the registers are

   D1 = $0000FFFF (in twos-complement form for −1)
   A0 = $00004400
   A1 = $00005400

2. **DBNE termination with modified pattern:** The first comparison itself renders the BNE condition true (since the compared data patterns are different). The DBNE loop is terminated at the first comparison. However, the A0 and A1 registers are postincremented to $4004 and $5004, respectively. The final contents of the registers are

   D1 = $000000FF
   A0 = $00004004
   A1 = $00005004

Any other data register, or any other branching condition (DBEQ, DBGE, and so forth) can be used in the DBcc instruction. However, it is important to note that the appropriate flag bits must always be preconditioned to render the DBcc condition false at the start of the loop.

Address, Stack, and Multiple-Movement Instructions

The LEA (load effective address) instruction moves a 32-bit address operand into an address register An. The PEA (push effective address) instruction stacks a specified 32-bit address operand. Both of these useful instructions do not affect the flags.

The LINK (link) instruction creates a work area on the stack and defines one of the address registers as a **frame pointer (FP)**. This pointer is used to address the work area on the stack. The UNLK (unlink) instruction effectively removes the work space from the stack. The LINK and UNLK instructions are very useful in linking and unlinking the stack area in a multitasking environment in which several tasks are run by the processor, as scheduled by the operating system.

The MOVEM (move multiple registers) instruction moves data between the specified data (Dn) and address (An) registers and the memory, or vice versa. For register-to-memory transfers, control-alterable and predecrement addressing modes are allowed. For memory-to-register transfers, control-alterable and postincrement addressing modes are allowed. The data transfers take place in the sequence indicated below. For example, in the predecrement addressing mode, the first data transfer involves the A7 register and the last data transfer involves the D0 register.

Last   First

| A7 | A6 | .... | A0 | D7 | D6 | .... | D0 | Control and postincrement addressing modes |

| D0 | D1 | .... | D7 | A0 | A1 | .... | A7 | Predecrement addressing mode |

The MOVEP instruction moves data between a specified data register and alternate even or odd bytes of memory, or vice versa. This instruction is very useful when dealing with 8-bit peripherals attached to the 68000 microprocessor. The memory can be addressed by the ARI with displacement addressing mode in the MOVEP instructions.[8]

Figure 4.14 illustrates a typical multitasking type of software. At line 6, the actual address corresponding to TABLE is loaded into the A1 register. At line 7, the PC relative addressing mode is used, and the offset corresponding to TABLE is loaded into the A2 register. At line 8, the contents of A2 are pushed to the stack.

The MOVEM instruction at line 9 moves the sequential word contents of memory addressed by A1 into the D1, D2, D3, and D4 data registers. The MOVEM instruction always follows a scanning order (D0–D7, A0–A7), regardless of the order in which they are specified. The first register to be moved (in or out) is D0, then D1, and so on until A7. Thus, the specified registers are first matched with the set sequence, and then the data movement operation is conducted.

The LINK A1, #−$0C instruction at line 13 performs several sequential operations as follows:

1. Stack A1: Stack contents of A1. SP decrements by four.

2. SP --> A1: Move contents of stack pointer (SP) into A1. This effectively links the stack to A1. A1 is now referred to as the frame pointer.

3. (SP−$0C) --> SP: Displace the SP by the specified amount of displacement (−$0C). This amounts to creating $0C (12 bytes) of work space on the stack.

The MOVEM.W D1–D4, −$8(A1) instruction at line 14 puts word operands from the D1, D2, D3, and D4 registers in the newly created work area on the stack. This amounts to passing parameters D1, D2, D3, and D4 to the other routines via the stack work area.

```
LINE ADDR

   1                                    ;special.src       11/8/88
   2                                    ;deals with special instructions
   3                                         OPT     A
   4                                         ORG     $1000
   5                                    ;task1 which initializes pointers
   6  00001000 43F8 1024 4E71TASK1 LEA      TABLE,A1
   7  00001006 45FA 001C           LEA      TABLE(PC),A2
   8  0000100A 4852                PEA      (A2)
   9  0000100C 4C91 001E           MOVEM.W (A1),D1-D4
  10                                    ;link with A1 as frame pointer
  11                                    ;and pass parameters to linked
  12                                    ;stack area
  13  00001010 4E51 FFF4           LINK     A1,#-$0C
  14  00001014 48A9 001E FFF8      MOVEM.W D1-D4,-$8(A1)
  15  0000101A 4EB8 102C 4E71      JSR      TASK2
  16  00001020 4E59                UNLK     A1
  17  00001022 4E75                RTS
  18  00001024 1234 AACB     TABLE DC.W    $1234,$AACB
  19  00001028 0026 001E           DC.W     $0026,$001E
  20                                    ;task2 here takes the passed on
  21                                    ;parameters and performs.
  22  0000102C 0B49 FFF8     TASK2 MOVEP.L -$8(A1),D5
  23  00001030 4E75                RTS
  24  00001032                     END


      ASSEMBLER ERRORS =    0

                            SYMBOL TABLE

  NARG 00000000   TABLE 00001024   TASK1 00001000   TASK2 0000102C
```

FIGURE 4.14   Linking and unlinking the stack for multitasking applications.

At line 15 the program jumps to subroutine TASK2, starting at line 22. The MOVEP.L −$8(A1),D5 instruction at line 22 moves four alternate even bytes from the work area of the stack into the D5 register. The RTS instruction at line 23 returns the program to the calling TASK1 program, which resumes at line 16.

The UNLK A1 instruction at line 16 performs the following sequential operations:

1. A1 --> SP: Restore stack pointer SP from frame pointer A1.

2. Unstack A1: Restore original value of A1. SP increments by four.

The preceding operations effectively unlink the stack and restore the original values of the frame and stack pointers. The RTS instruction at line 17 effectively returns this routine to the main calling program.

We will now review the special instructions by means of an example problem.

Example 4.7   Address, stack, and multiple-movement operations.
CPU registers Dn and An are initialized to $00000000. The stack pointer SP is initialized to $000022FE. Using the software of Figure 4.14,

1. specify the contents of the A1, A2, and D1–D4 registers after the LEA and MOVEM instructions are executed through line 9;

2. show the contents of the stack during the execution of the preceding instructions;

3. indicate the contents of the D5 register when TASK2 (line 22) is executed.

Solution

1. **Register contents:** The LEA TABLE,A1 instruction loads A1 with $00001024, which is the absolute address of TABLE. The LEA TABLE(PC),A2 instruction loads A2 with $0000001C, which is the offset of TABLE from the current PC value. The current PC value corresponds to $00001008 (op.word location + 2).

   The MOVEM.W (A1),D1–D4 instruction loads the sequential words from TABLE into the data registers D1, D2, D3, and D4. The contents of the registers are

   $$A1 = \$ 0 0 0 0 1 0 2 4$$
   $$A2 = \$ 0 0 0 0 0 0 1 C$$
   $$D1 = \$ 0 0 0 0 1 2 3 4$$
   $$D2 = \$ 0 0 0 0 A A C B$$
   $$D3 = \$ 0 0 0 0 0 0 2 6$$
   $$D4 = \$ 0 0 0 0 0 0 1 E$$

2. **Stack contents:** Figure 4.15 indicates the contents of the stack. The stack pointer decrements by two or four for word or long-word entries. The long-word contents of A2 are stored at $000022FA. The original value of A1, which is to be used as a frame pointer, is stored next at $000022F6. The current contents of the SP ($000022F6) are transferred to A1. Thus, A1 is initialized to act as a frame pointer. Furthermore, the SP is initialized to a new value equal to $000022EA ($000022F6 − displacement $0C). This effectively provides a 12-byte work area on the stack.

   Word contents from D1, D2, D3, and D4 are stored between locations $000022EE and $000022F4 in the work area by virtue of the MOVEM.W D1–D4, −$8(A1) instruction. Notice that the frame pointer A1 is used to access the stack work area. The return address $00001020 from the JSR instruction is stored in the new stack area at location $000022E6.

   When the UNLK instruction is performed, the SP and A1 registers are restored to their starting values of $000022FA and $00001024, respectively. The work area is effectively unlinked (removed) from the stack.

3. **Contents of D5:** The MOVEP.L −$8(A1),D5 instruction moves four alternate bytes (long-word equivalent) from the effective address (EA) into the D5 register. The EA

FIGURE 4.15 Stack
configuration for linking and
unlinking operations (Example
4.7).

	Operation		$\Rightarrow$ Word memory $\Leftarrow$			
			Even byte		Odd byte	Contents of stack
New stack area	$000022E6	0	0	0	0	Return address after JSR (line 16) stored
	22E8	1	0	2	0	
SP new value $\Rightarrow$	$000022EA	x	x	x	x	Existing data
	22EC	x	x	x	x	
($0C or 12 bytes of work space created on stack)	22EE	1	2	3	4	D1 word stored
	22F0	A	A	C	B	D2 word stored
	22F2	0	0	2	6	D3 word stored
	22F4	0	0	1	E	D4 word stored
A1 frame pointer initialized $\Rightarrow$	$000022F6	0	0	0	0	A1 original value stored via LINK
	22F8	1	0	2	4	
Starting SP for link $\Rightarrow$	22FA	0	0	0	0	Contents of A2 stored via PE (A2) at line 8
	22FC	0	0	1	C	
Original SP $\Rightarrow$	$000022FE	y	y	y	y	Top of stack for previous data
	$00002300	y	y	y	y	

is $000022EE. The four alternate bytes are on the even byte boundary and correspond to $12, $AA, $00, and $00. These are loaded into the D5 register with $12 in the most significant byte position. The contents of D5 are

$$\text{D5} = \$12AA0000$$

There are some important software considerations in the preceding example problem. It should be ensured that the work area created (12 bytes) is sufficient for passing on the parameters between tasks. Also, the linking process should maintain the even boundaries for both the frame and stack pointers. While unlinking the stack, the frame pointer should be at the initialized value. Address register indirect (ARI) with displacement is a very convenient mode for accessing the stack work area without modifying the contents of the frame pointer. It is possible to use any address register as the frame pointer.

FIGURE 4.16 Defining and using MACRO functions. (Courtesy of J. Salinger, FIU.)

```
;macro.src 11/11/88
;
        OPT    A
        ORG    $1400
;defining macro EXMP
EXMP    MACRO  X,Y,Z
        ADDQ.\0 #$X,Z
        NOP
        Y
        ENDM
;ENDM above defines end of macro
;using the macro EXMP
        MOVE.B #$FF,D0
        EXMP.B 8,<MOVE.B #$01,D1>,D2
        NOP
        END
```

4.5 MACROS IN SOFTWARE DEVELOPMENT

MACRO is an assembler utility. MACRO-function generation is essentially a preprocessor step in the assembly process which may result in a sequence of processor instructions. Proper parameters are passed in a MACRO-function call.

Figure 4.16 specifies the source code of a software routine containing a user-defined MACRO function EXMP with parameters X, Y, and Z. Source code following the MACRO declaration uses the processor instructions and the X, Y, and Z parameters. The ENDM assembler directive concludes the MACRO function.

The actual routine, written at the end of the program block, uses the MACRO function. The correspondence is as follows:

$$\underset{\text{parameter} =>\backslash 0}{\text{EXMP.B}} \quad \underset{X}{8,} \underset{Y}{<\text{MOVE.B } \#\$01,D1>}, \underset{Z}{D2}$$

When the source code is assembled, the assembler substitutes the actual instruction code for the MACRO function. The parameters are integrated into the code, as well. The assembled program is presented in Figure 4.17. It can be seen that the actual code has been substituted for the MACRO function.

Each time a MACRO function is used, the corresponding code is substituted. Although it takes up more program space, the MACRO program executes faster than the subroutines, since no stack activity is involved when the MACRO is used. Also, programmers can define several MACRO functions and develop software around them.

In the example problem that follows, we will review what we have learned about the MACRO.

```
LINE ADDR

     1                                    ;macro.src 11/11/88
     2                                    ;
     3                                            OPT     A
     4                                            ORG     $1400
     5                                    ;defining macro EXMP
     6                              EXMP  MACRO   X,Y,Z
     7                                            ADDQ.\0 #$X,Z
     8                                            NOP
     9                                            Y
    10                                            ENDM
    11                                    ;ENDM above defines end of macro
    12                                    ;using the macro EXMP
    13  00001400  103C  00FF                      MOVE.B  #$FF,D0
    14  00001404                                  EXMP.B  8,<MOVE.B
                                                          #$01,D1>,D2

    14  00001404  5002                  +         ADDQ.B  #$8,D2
    14  00001406  4E71                  +         NOP
    14  00001408  123C  0001            +         MOVE.B  #$01,D1
    15  0000140C  4E71                            NOP
    16  0000140E                                  END

ASSEMBLER ERRORS =    0
```

FIGURE 4.17 Assembled version of MACRO-based software from Figure 4.16.

Example 4.8   MACRO usage.
Refer to Figures 4.16 and 4.17.

1. Specify where MACROS should be declared and written.
2. Specify how the MACRO function EXMP is assembled and coded.
3. Can a MACRO function be used several times in a software routine? Explain.

Solution

1. **MACRO declaration:** Most assemblers require that MACROS should be declared and written at the very beginning of the program. This ensures that the assembler is aware of them.
2. **MACRO coding:** The qualifier \0 corresponds to either byte, word, or long word. In our particular case, it corresponds to byte. The X parameter corresponds to 8. The Z parameter corresponds to the D2 register. The Y parameter corresponds to the MOVE.B #$01,D1 instruction. When the code is assembled, the MACRO function EXMP is replaced by the actual sequence of instructions given in Figure 4.17.

3. MACRO usage: A MACRO function can be used several times in the program in which it is defined. The parameters may or may not be the same. Each time the MACRO function is used, the entire code is substituted.

Several MACROS can be defined and used in the same program. A program written with MACROS is easy to read and follow. Most software engineers now use MACRO functions extensively. It is necessary to be aware, however, of the amount of program space available when using MACRO functions. MACRO directives are dependent upon the assembler. Even though most of them are similar, an assembler manual should be consulted for details on MACRO directives.

4.6 SUMMARY

In this chapter, we introduced the assembly programming techniques with which to write 68000 assembly programs. Assemblers for the 68000 family of processors are available from several vendors. Most of the assemblers have similar directives. If the host computer has a different processor from the one for which the code is written, a cross assembler is used. Programs written in assembly language usually execute faster than programs written in such higher level languages as BASIC, FORTRAN, PASCAL, and C.

Assembler directives help in program development. In assembly language programming, symbols and labels are used in place of numbers and addresses. This greatly increases the readability of the programs. Symbols are usually specified at the beginning of the program to declare constants, address values, and variables. Labels are used within the body of the program.

Assembly-level programmers should be aware of different forms of instructions and addressing modes. They should be also familiar with the register resources and flag structure of the processor.

Most programming applications deal with some type of data movement, associated data processing, and decision making. The decision-making capability of the processor is used in program control applications. The software and the programming applications we considered in this chapter focused on program control.

Software engineers are programmers who are not only concerned with programming per se, but also with hardware resources, code integrity, execution timing, and optimization of the operating system.

Instructions such as DBcc, LINK, UNLK, MOVEM, and MOVEP are complex, each performing several operations. Use of these instructions makes for shorter, more efficient programs.

A MACRO is an assembler utility. A MACRO-function generation is a preprocessor step in the assembly process that may result in a sequence of processor instructions. When a MACRO function is used, the corresponding program code is substituted. The execution of a MACRO function does not involve any stacking operations; hence, it is faster than the execution of a subroutine. A MACRO function, however, uses more code memory.

PROBLEMS

4.1 State the difference (if any) between

(a) assemblers and cross assemblers;
(b) linkers and loaders.

4.2 Briefly outline the assembly process. What will happen if the program is written with instructions not known to the assembler?

4.3 Analyze the software in Figures 4.3 and 4.4. Does the assembled program contain the proper machine code for the listed instructions? Explain.

4.4 Write a program that will display the following message on the terminal:

MICROCOMPUTERS ARE GOOD TOOLS ; ;

Assume there is a DISPLAY subroutine available. ASCII code for the character should be put into the D0 register and the DISPLAY subroutine called in order to display the character.

4.5 Write an assembly program using 68000 mnemonics and the assembler directives discussed to accomplish the following objectives:

(a) start the program at location $1200;
(b) clear the memory words between $2000 and $2400.

4.6 Rewrite the software of Figure 4.5 to move $200 long words of data from the location starting at $6000 to the destination starting at $4000. Start the program at $00001000.

4.7 Write a routine to move $2000 words from the location starting at $6000 to the destination starting at $5000. The memory contents are as follows:

Location	Contents
$00006000	$0000
6002	$0001
6004	$0002
:	:

After the program is run, what is contained between $5000 and $5010?

4.8 Rewrite the software in Figure 4.5 using byte transfers instead of long-word transfers.

(a) Do byte transfers have a specific advantage over word or long-word transfers? Explain.
(b) What are the disadvantages of byte transfers compared to word or long-word transfers?

4.9 Rewrite the software in Figure 4.6 so that the smallest data element is at the lowest address. The data elements are given in Figure 4.7.

4.10 A 68000-based system operates on an 8-MHz clock. It is required to generate software delays in a digital control system application.

(a) Write a delay routine to generate a 1-millisecond delay.
(b) Using the software of (a), generate a 10-millisecond delay.
(c) Using the software of (b), generate a 1-second delay.

4.11 If the system was upgraded to a 68000 processor at a 16-MHz clock,

(a) Explain how the delay routines of Problem 4.10 are affected;

(b) modify the software to obtain 1-millisecond, 10-millisecond, and 1-second delays.

4.12 Write 68000-based software as a subroutine to transfer the memory block between $3000 and $3200 to another block between $3200 and $3000 as shown, without modifying the data.

Address	Block1	Block2
$3000	$1234	$029A to be put here
⋮	⋮	⋮
⋮	⋮	⋮
$3200	$029A	$1234 to be put here

4.13 Repeat Example 4.4 in the chapter given the following memory contents:

Source Address	Contents	Destination Address	Contents
$00004000	$5786	$00005000	$F88A
4002	$AAAA	5002	$CCCC
4004	$0202	5004	$1569
4006	$0987	5006	$347E

4.14 Using the memory contents indicated in Problem 4.13, write 68000-based software to add the 4-word source string to the destination string, with the final results stored at the destination.

4.15 Using the memory contents indicated in Problem 4.13, write 68000-based software to subtract the source string from the destination string, with the final result in the destination.

4.16 Write 68000-based software as a subroutine to multiply two words stored at locations $4000 and $4002, with the result stored at location $00004004. The initial contents of memory at $4000 and $4002 are $0003 and $8888, respectively. Use unsigned multiplication. What is the final result of the multiplication?

4.17 Repeat Problem 4.16 using signed multiplication.

4.18 Write software to perform unsigned division of X variable by Y variable. X and Y are stored at $5000 and $5004, respectively. The division result should be contained in the D2 register.

   If X = AABBCC00 and Y = 0008, indicate the contents of D2 after the division.

4.19 Repeat Problem 4.18 using signed division.

4.20 Rewrite the software in Figure 4.13 using DBEQ in place of DBNE to perform the same task.

4.21 What will happen if the flags are not conditioned before DBcc conditions are used?

   Can two or more DBcc conditions be nested? Explain. What precautions should be taken in nesting DBcc, if it is possible.

4.22 Rewrite the software in Figure 4.14 replacing the LINK and UNLK instructions with equivalent instructions to accomplish the same task.

Which software—with LINK and UNLK or without—is more memory efficient? Why?

4.23 The LINK A1, #−$0C instruction at line 13 of Figure 4.14 is replaced by LINK A1, #−$10.

(a) Describe the corresponding modification for the UNLK A1 instruction.

(b) Indicate the contents of the stack while the software is being executed.

(c) State the values of the A1, A2, and A7 registers after the LINK instruction is executed.

(d) State the contents of the A1, A2, and A7 registers after the modified UNLK instruction is executed.

4.24 Why are MACRO functions useful? Is there any limit to how many MACRO functions can be used? Explain.

4.25 Write a single MACRO function called CLEARD to clear all 32 bits of all the data registers.

4.26 Write a single MACRO function called CLEARA to clear all 32 bits of the A0−A6 address registers. (*Note:* Address registers cannot be directly cleared!)

4.27 A MACRO function called INIT uses ten 68000 instructions and occupies 32 words of program memory space. In a control system software application, the INIT function is used eight times with different parameters passed. When the software is assembled, how much program space is occupied by all the MACRO functions? Explain.

ENDNOTES

1. Motorola, Inc. *MC68000 Data Book*. Phoenix, AZ: Motorola Technical Operations, 1983.

2. Harman, T., and Lawson, B. *The Motorola MC68000 Microprocessor*. Englewood Cliffs, NJ: Prentice-Hall, 1985.

3. Scanlon, L.J. *The 68000: Principles and Programming*. Indianapolis: Howard W. Sams, 1981.

4. Kane, G.; Hawkins, D.; and Leventhal, L. *68000 Assembly Language Programming*. New York: McGraw-Hill, 1981.

5. Motorola, Inc. *MC68000 16/32-Bit Microprocessor Programmer's Reference Manual, Fifth Edition*. Englewood Cliffs, NJ: Prentice-Hall, 1987.

6. Motorola, Inc. *MTT8: 68000 Course Notes*. Phoenix, AZ: Motorola Technical Operations, 1987.

7. Andrews, M. *Self-Guided Tour through the 68000*. Englewood Cliffs, NJ: Prentice-Hall, 1984.

8. Stranes, T. "Design Philosophy Behind the M68000." *Byte* (Apr., May, Jun. 1983).

68000 Exception Processing Considerations

Objectives

In this chapter we will study:

General concepts of exception processing

The exception table and vectors

Reset exception processing

Interrupt exceptions and applications

Trap exceptions and applications

Error exceptions and applications

5.0 INTRODUCTION

An **exception** is a deviation from the normal processing sequence. The 68000 processor operates in the supervisor mode to handle exceptions. The supervisor mode is entered into automatically whenever the 68000 senses and services an exception routine request. An exception may be caused by an external hardware condition, an internal instruction, or an error condition.

Reset and interrupts are two exceptions caused by the system hardware. Internally generated exceptions include instructions, such as TRAPs and CHK, as well as error conditions, such as address error, bus error, privilege violation error, illegal instruction error, and zero-divide error. Other conditions, such as the TRACE mode of operation, also cause exceptions. The processor follows a specific sequence of operations in handling these exceptions.

Study of the exception processing concepts presented in this chapter will provide the necessary background to handle exception conditions in the 68000 family of processors. It will also help explain the user and supervisor modes of operation. The concepts apply to all 68000- and 68008-based systems; hence, no specific mention is made of the 68008. Exception processing for the 68010 and 68020 processors is similar to that for the 68000 processor. Due to additional resources and virtual memory schemes, however, exception processing for the 68010 and 68020 includes extra features. These features will be discussed in later chapters.

5.1 GENERAL CONCEPTS OF EXCEPTION PROCESSING

Exception processing is a privileged mode of operation in which the 68000 microprocessor operates in the supervisor mode. In this mode, the S bit in the status register is set to 1 and the SSP (supervisor stack pointer) controls the stack. Figure 5.1 indicates the 68000 exceptions with their established priority scheme and the relative timing for recognizing and starting the exception processing. Group 0 exceptions have the highest priority; Group 1 exceptions, the next highest; and Group 2 exceptions, the lowest priority. Within Group 0, the reset exception has the highest priority.

The Exception Vector Table and Exception Vectors

Exception vectors refer to memory locations from which the processor fetches the address of a routine to handle the exception. All exception vectors correspond to a long word. There are up to 256 such vectors, occupying 1 kilobyte of memory between $000000 and $0003FF. This dedicated memory is called the **vector table.**[1]

The vector table for the 68000 is presented in Figure 5.2. The two reset vectors, 0 and 1, are in the supervisor program space; all other vectors are in the supervisor data space.

Priority Group	Exception	Particulars of Occurrence
0 (Highest priority)	Reset	Hardware-activated input for system master control
	Address error	Error in addressing operands
	Bus error	Hardware memory access error
1	Trace	Single-step operation mode
	Interrupt	Hardware inputs to processor to obtain processor attention
	Illegal instruction	Nonexistent instructions or op.codes used
	Privilege violation	Privileged instructions used in user mode
2	TRAP	Software initiated
	TRAPV	Software initiated on overflow
	CHK	Data register beyond specified limits
	Zero divide	Division by zero encountered

Group 0: Current activity suspended at the end of the clock cycle. Exception processing starts within two clock cycles.

Group 1: Current activity suspended at the end of the bus cycle or the instruction cycle (for trace and interrupts). Exception processing starts before the next instruction.

Group 2: Current activity suspended within the instruction cycle. Exception processing starts as an instruction.

FIGURE 5.1 Exception grouping and priority scheme for the 68000 and the relative timing for exception processing.

Reset Exception Processing

Figure 5.3 illustrates the reset exception processing sequence. Reset is a hardware-activated input to the processor. The reset exception initializes the system; hence, the processor does not copy or store any information before starting reset exception processing, as it does for other exceptions. On power-up reset, the processor goes into the supervisor mode, turns the trace condition off, and sets the interrupt mask level at 7 (highest). This is a **cold start** of the system. Reset input can also be activated by a pushbutton while the processor is running. In this case, the processor suspends current activity at the end of the clock cycle and reinitializes the system. This is referred to as a **warm start.** A cold start requires system stabilization and requires more time than a warm start.

In either case, the processor fetches the contents of vector 0 at location $000000 from the vector table and loads them into the supervisor stack pointer (SSP). It fetches the contents of vector 1 at location $000004 from the vector table and loads them into the program counter (PC). The processor then executes the reset exception routine beginning at the location addressed by the PC. These two reset vectors are contained in the system ROM to retain their values when the power is shut off.[2]

If a bus error condition occurs while fetching vectors 0 or 1, the processor encounters a double bus fault condition and goes into a halt state. The hardware has to be de-

FIGURE 5.2 Exception vector table for the 68000. (Courtesy of Motorola, Inc.)

Vector Number(s)	Address		Space	Assignment
	Dec	Hex		
0	0	000	SP	Reset: Initial SSP
1	4	004	SP	Reset: Initial PC
2	8	008	SD	Bus Error
3	12	00C	SD	Address Error
4	16	010	SD	Illegal Instruction
5	20	014	SD	Zero Divide
6	24	018	SD	CHK Instruction
7	28	01C	SD	TRAPV Instruction
8	32	020	SD	Privilege Violation
9	36	024	SD	Trace
10	40	028	SD	Line 1010 Emulator
11	44	02C	SD	Line 1111 Emulator
12	48	030	SD	(Unassigned, Reserved)
13	52	034	SD	(Unassigned, Reserved)
14	56	038	SD	Format Error
15	60	03C	SD	Uninitialized Interrupt Vector
16-23	64	040	SD	(Unassigned, Reserved)
	92	05C		—
24	96	060	SD	Spurious Interrupt
25	100	064	SD	Level 1 Interrupt Autovector
26	104	068	SD	Level 2 Interrupt Autovector
27	108	06C	SD	Level 3 Interrupt Autovector
28	112	070	SD	Level 4 Interrupt Autovector
29	116	074	SD	Level 5 Interrupt Autovector
30	120	078	SD	Level 6 Interrupt Autovector
31	124	07C	SD	Level 7 Interrupt Autovector
32-47	128	080	SD	TRAP Instruction Vectors
	188	0BC		—
48-63	192	0C0	SD	(Unassigned, Reserved)
	255	0FF		—
64-255	256	100	SD	User Interrupt Vectors
	1020	3FC		—

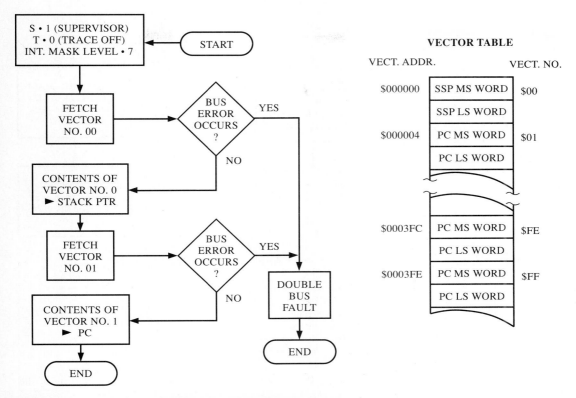

FIGURE 5.3 The 68000 reset exception sequence. (Courtesy of Motorola, Inc.)

bugged before the processor can be restarted. Hardware details relating to the reset, halt, and error conditions will be discussed in subsequent chapters.

General Scheme of Exception Processing

As previously mentioned, exception processing is carried out in the supervisor mode. When an exception (other than the reset) occurs and is recognized, the processor suspends current execution as indicated in Figure 5.1. It makes a copy of the current status register (SR) to retain the original contents. If the processor is already in the supervisor mode due to an earlier exception, it continues in that mode to service the current exception. However, if the processor is in the user mode, it moves into the supervisor mode to service the current exception. For exception processing, the stack used is the supervisor stack.[3]

The general exception sequence is presented in Figure 5.4. After setting the S bit to 1 for the supervisor mode, the trace condition is turned off (T = 0). For interrupts, the interrupt mask level is set to the new value. The processor stacks the current PC and the copied SR. For address and bus error exceptions, additional processor information is stacked. The processor then fetches the appropriate exception-vectored address from the

FIGURE 5.4 The 68000 general exception sequence. (Courtesy of Motorola, Inc.)

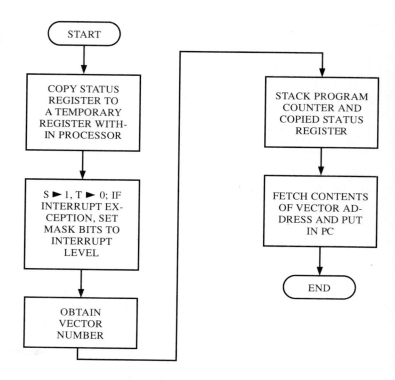

vector table and loads it into the PC. It then begins exception processing starting at the new address.[4]

The last instruction of an exception routine (other than a reset routine) is RTE (return from exception). When the RTE instruction is encountered, the processor restores the stored PC, SR, and any other information relating to the suspended process from the stack. It then resumes the execution of the suspended process.

We will now review the reset and general exception sequences with the help of an example problem.

Example 5.1   Reset and general exception sequences.

For a particular 68000-based system, the contents of the vector table are as shown:

Vector Number	Hex Address	Hex Word Contents	Assignment Type
0	000000	0000 0A00	SSP on reset
1	000004	0000 8400	PC on reset
2	000008	0000 8800	PC on bus error
⋮	⋮	⋮	⋮

1. Where are the SSP and the top of the stack initialized on power-up?
2. Where does the reset routine start? Why?
3. Are the contents of the stack memory of any particular value at the power-up reset condition? Why?
4. What are the primary differences between the reset and the general exception sequences?

Solution

1. **Initialization of the SSP and top of the stack:** Long-word contents corresponding to vector 0 at location $000000 are $00000A00. These are fetched by the processor and loaded into the SSP, which refers to the top of the stack. Thus, the top of the stack is initialized at

$$SSP = \$00000A00$$

2. **Reset routine:** Long-word contents corresponding to vector 1 at location $000004 are $00008400. These are fetched by the processor and loaded into the PC. Thus, the reset routine starts at

$$PC = \$00008400$$

3. **Initial contents of the stack:** For the reset operation, the initial contents of the stack on power-up are of no consequence. This is because the reset routine initializes the system; it does not depend on any stacked contents.

4. **Differences between reset and general exception sequences:** The following are the primary differences:

Reset Exception	General Exception
Processor registers are not stacked.	PC and copied SR are at least stacked.
Two reset vectors to initialize SSP and PC.	Only one vector, the contents of which are loaded into PC.
No RTE at the end of the reset routine, and no return address.	RTE at the end of the routine returns the processor to the suspended program.

At the end of a successful reset routine, the system is properly initialized and is ready to perform other operations and handle exception conditions. We will now study the details of the other general exceptions.

5.2   INTERRUPT EXCEPTIONS AND APPLICATIONS

Interrupts are hardware signals from the I/O devices and systems to obtain the attention of the processor. These signals are encoded and applied as $\overline{\text{IPL2}}$, $\overline{\text{IPL1}}$, and $\overline{\text{IPL0}}$ inputs to the processor. Figure 5.5 illustrates the 68000 interrupt structure. A level 7 interrupt ($\overline{\text{IPL2}}$ $\overline{\text{IPL1}}$ $\overline{\text{IPL0}}$ = 0 0 0) has the highest priority and a level 1 interrupt ($\overline{\text{IPL2}}$ $\overline{\text{IPL1}}$ $\overline{\text{IPL0}}$ = 1 1 0) has the lowest. A level 0 interrupt signifies that no interrupt is pending.[5]

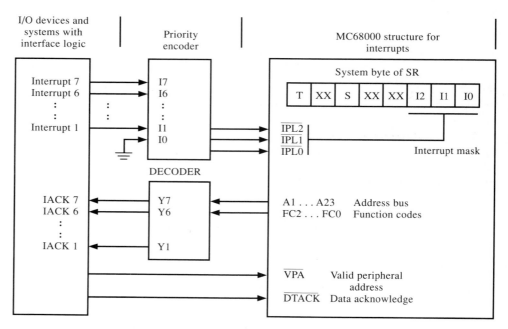

FIGURE 5.5   The 68000 interrupt structure and interface.

Interrupt Mask Levels

The I2, I1, and I0 bits of the system byte in the status register specify the **interrupt mask level.** A higher level interrupt than the mask level can interrupt the processor and be recognized. Any interrupt lower than or equal to the mask level will not be recognized; it is effectively masked out. The interrupt mask level is automatically adjusted to the interrupt level that is being recognized and serviced.

Interrupts 1 through 6 are maskable. Interrupt 7 is a **nonmaskable interrupt (NMI).** Even if the mask level is at 7, if an interrupt 7 occurs and satisfies the timing requirements, the processor must recognize and service it. When an interrupt is recognized, the processor generates an interrupt acknowledge cycle by activating the appropriate address lines (A1–A23) and the function code outputs FC2, FC1 and FC0.

An external decoder decodes this cycle and provides the corresponding interrupt acknowledge signals (IACK1–IACK7) to the interrupting devices. Hardware and timing details of these signals will be discussed in subsequent chapters.

Interrupt processing is similar to general exception processing. On recognizing the interrupt, the processor suspends current activity at the end of the instruction and makes a copy of the status register. The processor sets the S bit to 1 and moves into the supervisor mode. It then sets the interrupt mask level to a new value corresponding to the interrupt being recognized. The processor stores the current PC and the copied SR on the supervisor stack. The stored PC points to the next instruction to be executed in the suspended routine. The processor then fetches the appropriate interrupt-vectored address from the vector table and begins the interrupt exception processing starting at that vectored address.

Autovector and User Vector Methods

There are two methods, known as the autovector method and the user vector method, to obtain the interrupt vectors and service the interrupting device. In response to the IACK signal from the processor, the interrupting I/O device generates the $\overline{\text{VPA}}$ signal for the autovector method, or the $\overline{\text{DTACK}}$ signal for the user vector method.

In the **autovector method,** the processor obtains the address for the interrupt service routine directly from the vector table. Vector 25 corresponds to a level 1 interrupt and vector 31 corresponds to a level 7 interrupt. The processor reads the contents of the appropriate vector location and loads them into the PC. It begins the interrupt exception routine starting at that address.

In the **user vector method,** an interrupting device provides an 8-bit user vector number Vn (vector numbers 64 through 255) on the data bus D0–D7. The processor reads this vector number and configures the vector location by multiplying the vector number by 4. The processor reads the contents of this location and loads them into the PC. It then begins the interrupt exception routine starting at that address.

A higher level interrupt can always interrupt a lower level interrupt. The processor suspends the lower level interrupt, services the higher level interrupt, and then resumes the suspended interrupt processing. Interrupts are nested and serviced in this manner.[6]

The following example problem provides a review of interrupt exception processing.

Example 5.2   Interrupt exception processing.

Figure 5.6 illustrates an interrupt-driven 68000-based system and the exception vector table contents. The processor is executing a user program as follows:

```
PC              Mnemonic

$001200         MOVE.W  D0,D3
$001202         CLR.W   D0
$001204         NOP
$001206         JMP     (A4)
```

The internal register values are

SSP = $00000A00   USP = $0000C400   SR = $0200

FIGURE 5.6 (a) Interrupt-driven 68000-based system and (b) contents of the vector table (Example 5.2).

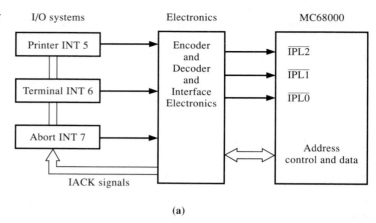

(a)

Vector #	Type	Hex address	Word Contents
0	Reset SSP	000000	0000 0A00
1	Reset PC	000004	0000 8400
:	:	:	:
29	Interrupt 5 (auto)	000074	0000 8A00
30	Interrupt 6 (auto)	000078	0000 8B00
:	:	:	:
64	User vector	000100	0000 9A44
:	:	:	:

(b)

1. Interrupt 5 from the printer occurs as the processor is executing the CLR.W D0 instruction. Will it be recognized? What are the levels of the $\overline{IPL2}$, $\overline{IPL1}$, and $\overline{IPL0}$ signals for interrupt 5?

2. Indicate the contents of the SR and the stack after interrupt 5 is recognized and is ready to be serviced. Where does the interrupt 5 exception routine start if it is autovectored?

3. When interrupt 5 is being serviced and the PC is pointing to the next instruction at $00008A4C, interrupt 7 occurs. Indicate the contents of the SR and the stack after

the interrupt is recognized and is ready to be serviced. Assume the user byte remains at the same value.

4. Assume interrupt 7 provides user vector Vn = 64 = $40. Where does the interrupt 7 exception routine start?

Solution

Figure 5.7 shows the contents of the status register and the supervisor stack.

FIGURE 5.7 (a) Status register contents and variations and (b) supervisor stack and contents as interrupts occur (Example 5.2).

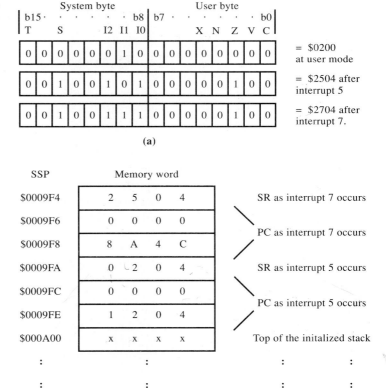

(a)

(b)

1. **Interrupt 5:** Initially, the SR contains $0200. This implies that the processor is in the user mode (S bit = 0) and the interrupt mask level is at 2 (I2 I1 I0 = 0 1 0). Interrupt 5 is higher than the mask level; thus, it is recognized.

   $\overline{IPL2}$, $\overline{IPL1}$, and $\overline{IPL0}$ inputs to the processor are active low. To signify interrupt 5, their logic levels are

$$\overline{IPL2}\ \overline{IPL1}\ \overline{IPL0} = 0\ 1\ 0$$

2. **SR and stack after interrupt 5:** The processor completes the CLR.W D0 instruction, which sets the Z flag to 1 and the other flags to zero, before attending to interrupt 5. Thus, the user byte of the SR becomes $04. The system byte remains at $02. The processor internally copies these contents of the SR (= $0204) and moves into the supervisor mode by setting the S bit to 1. It then changes the interrupt mask level to 5. Thus, the SR becomes $2504 after interrupt 5, as indicated in Figure 5.7(a).

   The PC points to the next instruction (NOP) at location $00001204. The processor stores this PC value and the copied SR on the supervisor stack, as indicated in Figure 5.7(b).

   The autovector number for interrupt 5 is 29, corresponding to vector location $000074, as indicated in Figure 5.6(b). The contents of this location (= $00008A00) are loaded into the PC. Thus, the interrupt 5 exception routine starts at

$$PC \text{ location} = \$00008A00$$

3. **Interrupt 7:** Interrupt 7 is nonmaskable; thus, it is recognized. The processor suspends the interrupt 5 routine, makes a copy of the SR, and changes the system byte to $27 (S bit = 1; mask level = 7). The SR after interrupt 7 is $2704, as indicated in Figure 5.7(a).

   The processor stacks the current PC value (= $00008A4C) and the copied SR (= $2504), as indicated in Figure 5.7(b).

4. **User vector for interrupt 7:** User vector number Vn = 64 = $40 for interrupt 7 corresponds to vector location $0100 (= 4 × $40), as indicated in Figure 5.6(b). The contents of this location (= $00009A44) are loaded into the PC. Thus, the interrupt 7 exception routine starts at

$$PC \text{ location} = \$00009A44$$

As previously discussed, the last instruction at the end of an exception routine is RTE. When RTE is encountered at the end of the interrupt 7 exception routine, the processor restores the stored SR and PC (= $2504 and $00008A4C, respectively), which correspond to the suspended interrupt 5 processing, from the stack. The processor then resumes the suspended interrupt 5 processing.

Similarly, when RTE is encountered at the end of the interrupt 5 exception routine, the processor restores the earlier stored SR and PC (= $0204 and $00001204, respectively), which correspond to the suspended user program, from the stack. The processor then resumes the suspended user program.

5.3 TRAP EXCEPTION PROCESSING AND APPLICATIONS

Traps are exceptions caused by instructions. There are 16 TRAP instructions: TRAP #0 through TRAP #15, corresponding to the vector numbers 32 through 47 of the vector table.

Using System Resources in the Supervisor Mode via Traps

Most system resources are under the control of the operating system. In the 68000 family of processors, operating system resources can only be handled in the supervisor mode. TRAP instructions are similar to software interrupts; they can be used within a program to move into the supervisor mode and use the system resources.

Similarly, traps can be used to move into the supervisor mode to use privileged instructions. Essentially, traps provide a convenient means of intercommunication between the user and supervisor modes.[7]

Trap Software Routines and Applications

Trap exception processing is similar to interrupt processing. When a TRAP instruction is encountered, the processor concludes the current instruction, copies the SR internally, and moves into the supervisor mode by setting the S bit to 1. The T (trace) bit is turned off. The processor then stores the current PC and the copied SR on the supervisor stack. The stored PC points to the next instruction after the TRAP instruction in the program.

The processor then fetches the appropriate TRAP-vectored address from the vector table, loads it into the PC, and begins the TRAP exception processing starting at that address. RTE is the last instruction in any TRAP exception routine. When the RTE instruction is encountered, the processor restores the stored PC and SR and resumes the original program.

The TRAPV instruction generates an exception (vector 7) if an overflow condition is detected in the previous operation. The TRAPV instruction is similar to the TRAP instruction, except that TRAPV does not require an operand field and will generate an exception only if the overflow (V) flag is set.

The user stack pointer (USP) is considered a system resource and can only be initialized in the supervisor mode. Figure 5.8 consists of an operating system routine writ-

```
LINE ADDR

  1                              ;TRAP.src 12/31/88
  2                              ;TRAP type exception routine
  3                              ;which initializes the USP
  4                              ;with the contents of the
  5                              ;A2 register
  6                              ;
  7                                   OPT     A
  8                                   ORG     $1200
  9                              ;load contents of A2 into USP
 10                              ;and return
 11 00001200 4E62                    MOVE.L  A2,USP
 12 00001202 4E71                    NOP
 13 00001204 4E73                    RTE
 14 00001206                         END
```

FIGURE 5.8 Operating system exception routine to initialize the USP (Example 5.3).

ten as an exception routine that initializes the USP. This routine starts at $00001200. The MOVE.L A2,USP instruction at line 11 initializes the USP with the contents of the A2 register. The RTE instruction at line 13 returns control back to the calling program.

The user can call this program via a TRAP instruction. The user must load the starting address of the exception routine at the vector table location corresponding to the TRAP being used. The user must also pass the parameter value for the USP (through the A2 register) while calling the TRAP routine.

The following example problem focuses on the software details of TRAP instruction use.

Example 5.3 Using TRAP exceptions.

Figure 5.8 shows an operating system exception routine starting at $00001200. The routine initializes the USP.

1. In order to call the routine, the TRAP #1 instruction must be used. Develop an appropriate software routine that uses TRAP #1 and initializes the USP at $00002000.
2. Is there any priority scheme associated with TRAP instructions? Explain.

Solution

1. **Software using TRAP #1:** The TRAP #1 vector number is 33, which corresponds to vector address location $0084 in the vector table of Figure 5.2. The user can load the starting address of the USP initialization routine (= $00001200) into the vector location and use the TRAP #1 instruction to call the routine.

   A software routine to accomplish the task in question is presented in Figure 5.9. Between lines 14 and 16, $00001200 is loaded into vector location $0084. At lines 20 and 21, an initialization value of $00002000 is loaded into the A2 register (to be passed on as the USP parameter for the TRAP #1 routine), and the TRAP #1 routine is called. The TRAP #1 exception routine (Figure 5.8) loads the passed-on value ($00002000) into the USP and returns to the original calling program. The JMP (A3) instruction at line 23 causes an indirect jump to the user I/O routine, the address of which is contained in the A3 register.

2. **Priority for TRAP instructions:** There is no priority scheme for TRAP instructions. This is because the TRAPs are software instructions which are executed in the sequence of their occurrence in the program.

```
LINE ADDR

  1                                  ;TRAP1.src 12/31/88
  2                                  ;TRAP1 routine initializes
  3                                  ;user stack pointer
  4                                  ;A0 = $00000000 refers to
  5                                  ;the beginning of vector table.
  6                                  ;TRAP1 routine starts at $00001200.
  7                                  ;A3 contains the address of user I/O
  8                                  ;routines.
  9                                  ;
 10                                    OPT     A
 11                                    ORG     $001100
 12                                  ;load TRAP1 address into
 13                                  ;vector location $00000084.
 14 00001100 207C 0000 0000          MOVEA.L #$00000000,A0
 15 00001106 227C 0000 1200          MOVEA.L #$00001200,A1
 16 0000110C 2149 0084               MOVE.L  A1,$0084(A0)
 17                                  ;call TRAP1 routine to initialize
 18                                  ;the user stack pointer at $00002000.
 19                                  ;pass this stack parameter through A2.
 20 00001110 247C 0000 2000          MOVEA.L #$00002000,A2
 21 00001116 4E41                    TRAP    #1
 22                                  ;jump to user I/O routines through (A3)
 23 00001118 4ED3                    JMP     (A3)
 24 0000111A                         END
```

FIGURE 5.9   TRAP1 routine initialization and use by the calling programs (Example 5.3).

In general, any TRAP #n (n = 0–15) can be used in the preceding example as long as the starting address of the exception routine is loaded into the appropriate vectored address location. Each time a TRAP routine is called, the current PC and the copied SR are stored on the supervisor stack. The user should ensure that sufficient supervisor stack space is available if several TRAP #n instructions are to be nested.

5.4   ERROR-RELATED EXCEPTIONS

The 68000 processor handles error conditions as exceptions in the supervisor mode. Operating system routines are written in the supervisor mode for the 68000 family of processors. Error-handling routines to help the user can be written by the operating system designer.

Upon detecting an error condition, the processor suspends current execution, copies the SR, and moves into the supervisor mode. It turns off the trace and stacks the copied SR and the current PC (which points to the next instruction in the suspended routine). In certain error conditions (bus and address errors, for example), additional processor information is saved on the stack. The processor then goes to the corresponding vector location in the vector table, fetches the address of the exception routine, and executes it in response to the detected error condition.

Illegal Instruction, Unimplemented Instruction, and Privilege-Violation Conditions

Illegal Instruction   The first word of an instruction is always an op.word. When the fetched op.word does not correspond to any of the defined op.words, an illegal instruction error condition occurs. Three bit patterns always force an illegal instruction error condition for the 68000 family of processors: $4AFA, $4AFB, and $4AFC. The first two patterns are reserved for Motorola; the third is for general use. This exception returns control to the operating system in case of any illegal op.codes, thus preventing unpredictable operation. The vector number for the illegal instruction is 4.

Exception processing for illegal instructions is similar to that for traps. After the instruction op.code has been fetched and decoding attempted, the processor recognizes that the execution of an illegal instruction is being attempted. It then starts the exception processing.

Unimplemented Instruction   Op.word patterns with bits 15 through 12 equaling 1010 or 1111 ($A or $F) are distinguished as unimplemented instructions. When these codes are discovered by the processor, unimplemented exception processing results. Higher level processors, such as the 68020, use these op.codes for coprocessor support and emulations. The vector numbers for the two conditions mentioned are 10 and 11.

Privilege Violation   In order to provide system security, some instructions for the 68000 dealing with the status register, stack pointer, and system operation are privileged. Examples are the following:

AND immediate to SR (for status register violation);

EOR immediate to SR (for status register violation);

MOVE to SR (for status register violation);

OR immediate to SR (for status register violation);

MOVE USP (for stack pointer violation);

RTE (return-from-exception instruction);

RESET (reset instruction);

STOP (stop-the-processor instruction).

These instructions may be used only in the supervisor mode. An attempt to use any of them in the user mode results in a privilege-violation exception.[5,7]

Exception processing for a privilege violation is similar to that for an illegal instruction. Control is returned to the operating system in case of any privilege violation, thus protecting system resources and routines from being modified by the user. The vector number for the privilege-violation condition is 8.

Uninitialized and Spurious Interrupt Exceptions

Uninitialized Interrupt In the case of the user vector method for interrupt processing, if the 68000 family I/O device is not initialized, it provides default vector number 15 during the interrupt acknowledge cycle. The processor recognizes this as an uninitialized interrupt condition and initializes exception processing.

Spurious Interrupt A spurious interrupt condition results from a bus error during the interrupt acknowledge cycle. The processor recognizes this condition and initiates spurious interrupt exception processing. The vector number for a spurious interrupt is 24.

Exception processing for uninitialized and spurious interrupts is similar to trap exception processing. These two exceptions return control to the operating system in case of an interrupt vector error, thus preventing any ambiguous interrupt processing.

Zero-Divide, CHK, and Trace Exception Conditions

Zero-Divide Exception A zero-divide exception occurs when division by zero is attempted during the execution of a divide instruction. This exception prevents the processor from going into an indefinite loop. The vector number for a zero-divide exception is 5.

CHK Exception A CHK exception occurs when the data register associated with the CHK instruction is out of bounds. This exception returns control to the operating system if boundaries are crossed in case of a multitasking operation. The vector number for the CHK exception is 6.

Trace Exception A trace exception occurs when the T (trace) bit in the system byte of the status register is set. When the T bit is set at the beginning of program execution, the processor executes one instruction at a time and goes to trace exception. In trace exception routines, the results of the instruction just executed are displayed. Essentially, the processor goes into a single-step mode for software debugging. The vector number for the trace exception is 9.

The zero-divide, CHK, and trace exceptions occur during program execution. They prevent the processor from getting hung up on errors. Appropriate exception routines that provide proper feedback to the user should be written by the operating system designer so that exception conditions can be handled efficiently.

We will now present an example problem to review the error conditions and exceptions studied thus far.

Example 5.4 *Error conditions and exceptions.*

A 68000-based system is operating in the user mode. In each of the following situations, state whether an error or exception condition will be generated. Indicate the exception vectors, as appropriate.

1. The processor tries to execute an op.code corresponding to the CLR.W A4 instruction.
2. The processor tries to execute MOVE.W D6,SR.
3. The processor tries to execute the following sequence:

```
CLR.L D0
DIVU  D0,D2
```

Solution

1. **CLR.W A4 instruction:** This is an illegal instruction, since the address register direct addressing is not defined in the CLR instruction. The processor recognizes this as an illegal instruction error condition and initiates the exception processing sequence. The vector number for the illegal instruction is 4.
2. **MOVE.W D6,SR instruction in user mode:** Moving information into the status register while in the user mode results in a privilege-violation error condition. The processor recognizes this and initiates the privilege-violation exception sequence. The vector number for the privilege violation is 8.
3. **CLR.L D0 and DIVU D0,D2 instructions in sequence:** The CLR.L D0 instruction clears the D0 register. The DIVU D0,D2 instruction attempts a division-by-zero operation, since D0 has been cleared earlier to the zero condition. The processor recognizes this and initiates the zero-divide exception sequence. The vector number for a zero-divide exception is 5.

In response to the zero-divide error in the preceding example, an exception routine will display a message:

```
division by zero attempted
```

Suppose this routine starts at address $00001400. This starting address should be loaded as a long word at location $014 (corresponding to vector number 5) during system initialization. When the zero-divide error condition occurs, the exception routine will be executed.

Address and Bus Error Conditions

Address Error   An address error occurs when the 68000 processor attempts to access a word or long-word operand or an instruction at an odd address. When the processor discovers an address error, it aborts the current bus cycle, copies the SR, and goes into the supervisor mode. It stores the copied SR, the PC (pointing to the possible next instruction), and some additional information on the supervisor stack, as shown in Figure 5.10. The supervisor stack frame for a bus error is similar.[5,6,7]

```
        b15    b14    b13 · · · · · · · · · b4   b3   b2   b1 . b0
```

SSP ⇨	Special status word (see below)	R/W	I/N	FC2	FC1	FC0
	Access address High word					
	Access address Low word					
	Instruction register Op. word					
	Status register					
	Program counter High word					
	Program counter Low word					

R/W ⇨   Read/write: write = 0 and read = 1

I/N ⇨   Instruction/not: Instruction = 0 and not = 1

FC2 FC1 FC0 ⇨   Function codes

FIGURE 5.10   Supervisor stack frame for address and bus errors for the 68000.

The stored instruction register points to the instruction in which the address error was detected. The **fault access address** refers to the actual physical address where the address error occurred. The **special status word** refers to the actual internal conditions of the processor at the occurrence of the address error. This information is useful in the software debugging process.

An address error exception prevents the 68000 processor from any word misalignment in accessing instructions or operands. The vector number for the address error is 3.

Bus Error   A bus error occurs when the processor attempts to access nonexistent memory or I/O and the interface logic activates $\overline{\text{BERR}}$ (bus error) input to the processor, as shown in Figure 5.11. Time-out circuitry in the interface logic generates the $\overline{\text{BERR}}$

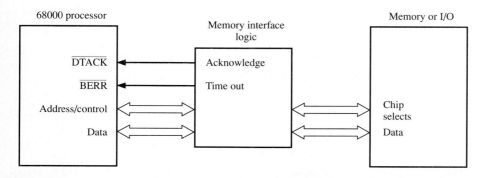

FIGURE 5.11   Memory or I/O interface, generating $\overline{\text{DTACK}}$ or $\overline{\text{BERR}}$ to the 68000.

input to the processor instead of the normal $\overline{\text{DTACK}}$ if the memory or I/O fail to respond within a given time.

Bus error exception processing is similar to address error processing. A bus error exception prevents the processor from indefinitely waiting for nonexistent memory or I/O to respond. The vector number for the bus error is 2.

The following example problem will enhance our understanding of address and bus errors.

Example 5.5   Address and bus errors.

For the 68000-based system of Figure 5.11, memory and I/O are physically contained between $000000 and $0FFFFF. The initial values of the registers are

$$\text{SSP} = \$00000A00 \qquad \text{USP} = \$00002000 \qquad \text{SR} = \$0600$$

The program of Figure 5.12 is run.

```
LINE ADDR

  1                                        ;berr.src 1/5/89
  2                                        ;demonstrates bus and
  3                                        ;address errors
  4                                        OPT       A
  5                                        ORG       $1000
  6  00001000 207C 00FF AA00 STRT          MOVEA.L   #$00FFAA00,A0
  7  00001006 227C 0000 0CC3               MOVEA.L   #$00000CC3,A1
  8  0000100C D090                         ADD.L     (A0),D0
  9  0000100E 5980                         SUBQ.L    #04,D0
 10  00001010 60EE                         BRA.S     STRT
 10  00001012                              END


     ASSEMBLER ERRORS =   0

                              SYMBOL TABLE

  NARG    00000000   STRT    00001000
```

FIGURE 5.12   Software with bus and address errors (Example 5.5).

1. The conditions given will result in an error exception sequence when the program is run. What type of error is involved? Explain.

2. Indicate the stack format for the error exception in (1).

3. The ADD.L (A0),D0 instruction at line 8 (Figure 5.12) is replaced with the ADD.L (A1),D0 instruction, and the program is rerun. Will there be an error condition now? How does the stack look for this error?

Solution

1. Error condition: There is a bus error condition. It occurs during the execution of the ADD.L (A0),D0 instruction at line 8, while trying to access the source operand. The effective address of the source operand [$00FFAA00 (contents of A0)] is beyond the available memory and I/O range, and is nonexistent. The interface logic therefore generates the $\overline{\text{BERR}}$ signal, and the processor initiates the bus error exception sequence.

2. Stack format: On detecting the bus error condition, the processor moves into the supervisor mode. The supervisor stack is used for storing the processor registers and the operands.

Figure 5.13 illustrates the supervisor stack format and the contents for the bus error exception: the PC corresponds to the next instruction (SUBQ.L #04,D0). SR is the copied status register at the time of the exception. Stored op.word $D090 corresponds to the instruction where the bus error occurred. The fault access address ($00FFAA00) is the actual physical address where the bus error fault condition occurred.

FIGURE 5.13 Supervisor stack contents for the bus error condition (Example 5.5).

SSP	Memory		word	Stored operand details
$0009F2	0 0	1	9	Special status word (see below)
$0009F4	0 0	F	F	Fault access address (high word)
$0009F6	A A	0	0	Fault access address (low word)
$0009F8	D 0	9	0	Instuction op.word
$0009FA	0 6	0	0	Copied status register
$0009FC	0 0	0	0	Program counter (high word)
$0009FE	1 0	0	E	Program counter (low word)
$000A00	x x	x	x	Top of stack (contains previous operand)

Special status word $0019 corresponds to

b15 · · · · · · · · · · b5	b4	b3	b2	b1	b0
	R/W	I/N	FC2	FC1	FC0
0 · · · · · · · · · 0	1	1	0	0	1

The stored special status word signifies that the fault occurred while reading a data operand from user data space.

3. ADD.L (A1),D0 instruction: There is an address error condition. It occurs while trying to access the source operand. The effective address of the source operand [$00000CC3 (contents of A1)] is within the physical memory, but is odd. The processor recognizes this long-word access at an odd address as an address error and initiates the address error exception sequence.

The supervisor stack format for the address error is similar to that for the bus error.

When the stack frame for the bus and address errors in the preceding example is examined, the fault conditions can be analyzed and corrected. In 68010/12 processors, additional information is stored on the stack for possible virtual memory implementation, which we will study later, in conjunction with those processors. In 68020/30 processors, word and long-word data operands can be accessed at an odd address without generating an address error condition.

Double Bus Fault Condition

This is a catastrophic failure in which the processor comes to a complete halt. The double bus fault occurs when

a bus error occurs while accessing the reset vectors;

a bus error occurs during the exception processing sequence of an earlier bus or address error; or

there are nested combinations of bus error and illegal instruction exception processing operations.

The processor also activates the **HALT output line,** which halts any peripherals connected to the halt line. This prevents a system runaway condition. Software and hardware must be debugged and the system reinitialized to recover from a double bus fault condition.[2,4,7]

5.5   SUMMARY

An exception condition is a deviation from the normal condition. The 68000 processor handles the exception in the supervisor mode.

External hardware conditions, such as reset and interrupts, cause exceptions. So do instructions, such as TRAPs and CHK, under certain conditions. Error conditions, such as privilege violations, illegal instructions, unimplemented instructions, zero-divide operations, bus errors, and address errors, also cause exceptions.

Appropriate software routines written as part of the operating system in the supervisor mode handle exceptions. On the occurrence of any type of exception, the processor moves into the supervisor mode.

One kilo byte of memory between $000000 and $0003FF of a 68000-based system corresponds to the exception vector table. This table contains the starting addresses of the exceptions. On the occurrence of an exception, the processor fetches the starting address of the corresponding exception routine from this table.

The reset exception has the highest priority; it initializes the system resources and conditions. Stacking of the registers is not done during reset exception processing. Vector 0 corresponds to the supervisor stack pointer and vector 1 corresponds to the program counter for the reset exception.

Hardware interrupts from the external I/O and peripherals are meant to obtain the attention of the processor. The interrupts follow a priority scheme involving the three interrupt mask bits of the status register. Interrupt 7 is at the highest priority level and is a nonmaskable interrupt (NMI). Interrupts 6 through 1 are at successively lower priority levels and are maskable. They can be masked by setting the interrupt mask level in the system byte of the status register to a higher level. Interrupt 0 implies that there is no pending hardware interrupt.

TRAP instructions are similar to software interrupts; they are used to move from the user mode into the supervisor mode. This allows users to employ system-level resources.

A privilege-violation error condition occurs when an attempt is made to use privileged instructions in the user mode. If an instruction code that does not correspond to any of the permissible codes is used, an illegal instruction error condition occurs. When an attempt is made to access nonexistent memory or I/O, the external logic activates $\overline{\text{BERR}}$ (bus error) input to the processor. The processor recognizes this and goes into bus error exception processing. When a word or long-word access attempt is made at an odd address, an address error condition occurs.

The processor does not stack any information for reset exception processing. For all other exceptions, the copied SR and the PC (pointing to the next instruction at the time of the exception) are stored on the supervisor stack. In the case of address and bus error conditions, additional information is also stored. This corresponds to the fault address, the instruction that caused the fault condition, the special status word, and so forth.

In the case of nested errors, a double bus fault condition causes the processor to go into a complete halt state. During the halt state, the address and data buses are tristated, and the control signals negated. The system must be debugged and reinitialized in order to recover from a double bus fault condition.

PROBLEMS

5.1 How soon does exception processing begin for the following conditions:

(a) reset from pushbutton;

(b) illegal instruction;

(c) zero-divide.

5.2 How many total exception vectors are in the vector table? How many different exceptions are serviced?

5.3 Explain why the reset exception takes two vectors, whereas all other exceptions take only one.

5.4 What is the primary difference between a cold start and a warm start? Are there any differences in terms of the exception processing with cold and warm starts?

5.5 For a 68000-based system, suppose it is necessary to initialize the supervisor stack at $00002000. The reset routine should start at $00001600. Indicate the contents of vector table locations $000 through $008.

5.6 Write a reset routine under the conditions of Problem 5.5 to reinitialize the SSP at $00003000, the USP at $00002400, and to set the interrupt mask level at 4. In addition, an interrupt 6 exception routine starting at address $00004200 is to be loaded into the appropriate autovectored location. The last instruction in the routine should be a STOP #$2200 instruction.

5.7 Consider the interrupt-driven system of Figure 5.14.

(a) The processor is executing a user program and the PC is pointing to the next instruction at $00001244. At that instant, interrupt 4 from a printer occurs. Will it be recognized? Explain.
 Indicate the contents of the stack, if the interrupt is recognized.

(b) Interrupt 4 is user vectored with a vector number 72. Interrupt 4 service routine's starting address is $00001620. What is the vector location address and what are the contents of that location?

(c) What are the contents of the status register soon after the recognition of interrupt 4?

FIGURE 5.14 An interrupt-driven 68000 system (for Problem 5.7).

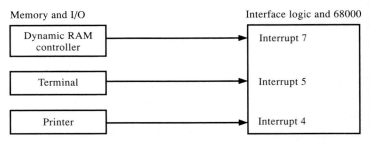

Memory and I/O

Interface logic and 68000

Initial values: SSP = $000030000; USP = $000020E0; SR = $0000

5.8 Suppose the system of Figure 5.14 is servicing interrupt 4 from the printer. The user byte of the status register is $04. Interrupt 7 from the dynamic memory controller occurs as the processor is executing the MOVE instruction in the following program segment:

```
PC value              Instruction

$000016A0             MOVE.L    #$002211CC,D2
                      ROL.W     #2,D2
```

(a) Will the interrupt be recognized? Why or why not?
(b) If the interrupt is recognized, what are the contents of the supervisor stack?
(c) Interrupt 7 is autovectored. Where does the processor go to obtain the interrupt 7 exception routine starting address?

5.9 In a particular application, the SSP and USP are initialized at $000A00 and $0009E0, respectively.

(a) How much minimum stack space is required to store the appropriate registers in the event of an interrupt?

(b) How many interrupts can be nested without running out of supervisor stack space?

5.10 Specify the advantages and disadvantages of the autovector and user vector methods. How many total user vectors are there?

5.11 In a particular 68000-based system, the starting addresses of the autovectored interrupts are as follows:

interrupt 1: $00001040
interrupt 2: $00001080
interrupt 3: $000010C0
interrupt 4: $00001100
interrupt 5: $00001140
interrupt 6: $00001180
interrupt 7: $000011C0

Indicate the contents of the exception vector table containing the preceding information. Clearly identify the vector numbers and vector locations.

5.12 What are the vector numbers and vector locations for the uninitialized and spurious interrupt exceptions?

What are the primary differences between these two interrupt conditions?

5.13 What are the vector numbers and vector locations for TRAP #3, TRAP #5, TRAP #9, and TRAP #14.

Is TRAP #15 higher, lower, or at the same priority level as TRAP #0? Explain.

5.14 Suppose it is necessary to run the operating system routine shown in Figure 5.8 as TRAP #4, which begins at a starting address of $0000140C.

What modifications should be made in this software routine so that it will be executed when the user calls TRAP #4?

5.15 Modify the software of Figures 5.8 and 5.9 so that the USP is initialized at $00004000 when TRAP #4 (starting at $0000140C) is called by the user routine.

5.16 Write a TRAP #6 routine (for a 68000 system) starting at $000016E0 to reset the system peripherals, go into a stop condition, and load SR with $2400. Indicate the contents of the appropriate vector locations.

5.17 Write a TRAP #7 routine starting at $00001700 to input a character from an I/O location at $0000F800 into the D0 register and echo the character to an output terminal at $0000F802. Indicate the contents of the appropriate vector locations.

5.18 List the errors that cause exceptions in a 68000-based system in the order of their priority, from highest to lowest. Which errors are software related and which are hardware related?

5.19 A 68000-based system is in the user mode. In the following cases specify any error or exception conditions:

(a) MOVE.B   A1,A2
(b) CLRA.W   A3
(c) DC.W $FF00
(d) ANDI.W   #$FF00,SR

5.20 With reference to Problem 5.19, specify the vector numbers and vector locations in case of error conditions.

5.21 A system is in the user mode. Identify any error or exception conditions when the software that follows is executed. Initially, D0 = $00000004; D1 = $0000FFCC.

```
LOOP MOVE.L  D1,D2
     DIVU    D0,D2
     DBEQ    D0, LOOP
     NOP
     STOP    #$0700
```

Where does the processor go in case of an error condition?

5.22 A 68000-based system memory and I/O are between $000000 and $00FFFF. The initial values of the registers are

A0 = $000FFEEA   A1 = $0000CDEF   A2 = $00000CCC   SR = $0404

Specify whether any error conditions occur in each of the following:

(a) MOVEM.L   D0–D7, (A0)
(b) MOVEP.L (A1), D2
(c) CLR.L $07(A2)

5.23 A 68000-based system memory and I/O are between $000000 and $00FFFF. The initial values of the registers are

A0 = $000FFEEA   A1 = $0000CDEF   A2 = $00000CCC   SR = $0404

USP = $00002000   SSP = $00000A00   D0 = $00000003

Specify whether there is an error condition in any of the cases that follow. If so, specify the error, the exception vector number, and the vector location. Also indicate the contents of the stack using the initial values as stated.

(a) ADD.B   (A0),D2
(b) SWAP   A1
(c) CLR.L $04(A2,D0.W)

5.24 Identify four different instances of a double bus fault condition in a 68000-based system.

5.25 Refer to the supervisor stack contents given in Figure 5.15.

(a) The processor is executing an interrupt 6 routine. When RTE is executed as the last instruction of this routine, where does the processor go? Explain.

(b) Another RTE is executed at the end of the resumed routine of (a). Where does the processor go? Explain.

(c) The routine that was suspended when interrupt 6 occurred must have been of a certain type. State the type and explain.

FIGURE 5.15 Supervisor stack contents (for Problems 5.25, 5.26, and 5.27).

SSP = $0000096C=>	2300	Current top of stack
	0000	
	1600	
	0004	
	0000	
	213C	
	xxxx	Top of stack at initialization

5.26 In Figure 5.15, the SSP pointing to the top of the stack at initialization must have been what initial value? Why?

5.27 Due to a memory read error, the entry $213C in the stack in Figure 5.15 has been read as $213B. Where will the processor go to execute the next instruction? Explain.

ENDNOTES

1. Motorola, Inc. *MC68000 Data Book*. Phoenix, AZ: Motorola Technical Operations, 1983.

2. Harman, T., and Lawson, B. *The Motorola MC68000 Microprocessor*. Englewood Cliffs, NJ: Prentice-Hall, 1985.

3. Scanlon, L.J. *The 68000: Principles and Programming*. Indianapolis: Howard W. Sams, 1981.

4. Motorola, Inc. *MC68000 16/32-Bit Microprocessor Programmer's Reference Manual, Fifth Edition*. Englewood Cliffs, NJ: Prentice-Hall, 1987.

5. Motorola, Inc. *MTT8: 68000 Course Notes*. Phoenix, AZ: Motorola Technical Operations, 1987.

6. Andrews, M. *Self-Guided Tour through the 68000*. Englewood Cliffs, NJ: Prentice-Hall, 1984.

7. Stranes, T. "Design Philosophy Behind the M68000." *Byte* (Apr., May, Jun. 1983).

68000 Hardware Considerations and Design Applications

Objectives

In this chapter we will study:

Hardware signals and buses of the 68000

Memory and I/O interface schemes and design

Control interface schemes

System-level busing schemes, such as the VERSA and the VME

6.0   INTRODUCTION

In chapters 1 through 5, our focus was on the general architectural features and software aspects of the 68000 microprocessor. In this chapter, we will explore the hardware aspects of a 68000-based system.

Generally speaking, all microprocessors have an address bus for addressing instructions and operands, a data bus for data and operand transfers, and a control bus for control and timing signals. A **bus** is a collection of signals with similar properties. The 68000 processor has additional busing features for asynchronous and synchronous data transfers, interrupt and DMA (direct memory access) transfer operations, and system control.

The material in this chapter will provide the necessary background to understand the essential hardware features of the 68000. In addition, it will provide insight into the system control and error detection schemes associated with the 68000 family. These processors follow memory-mapped I/O schemes, in which the processor communicates with an I/O device as if it were one of the memory locations. The word *memory* will be used to refer to both memory and I/O in our discussions, unless otherwise specified.

6.1   68000 HARDWARE SIGNALS AND FUNCTIONS

Figure 6.1 indicates the pin configuration of the 68000, and Figure 6.2 is a system representation. The 68000 is contained in a 64-pin DIP package or a 68-pin grid-array package. It is fabricated with either NMOS or CMOS technology. For the corresponding signal properties, appropriate data books should be referenced.[1,2]

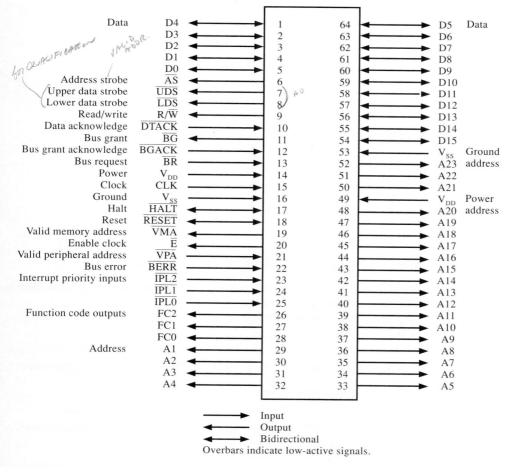

FIGURE 6.1   The 68000 pin configuration.

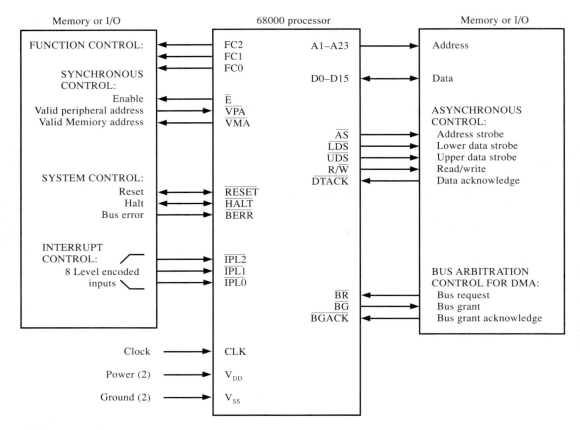

FIGURE 6.2 System representation of the 68000.

Address, Data, and Asynchronous Buses for the 68000

The **address bus** is a 23-bit (A1–A23) unidirectional tristate bus, capable of addressing 8 megawords (or 16 megabytes) of data or operands. It provides the address of the operands during the read and write bus cycles. During a read bus cycle, the processor reads the instructions or source operands from the memory. During a write bus cycle, the processor writes data into the memory. During the interrupt acknowledge cycle, address lines A1, A2, and A3 provide information about the level of interrupt being serviced. Address lines A4 through A23 are set to a high logic level.

The **data bus** is a 16-bit (D0–D15) bidirectional tristate bus, capable of transferring byte- or word-sized operands between the processor and the memory (or I/O).

The **asynchronous bus** is used to control asynchronous data transfers of varying response times between the processor and the memory or I/O units. For the 68000 processor, the asynchronous bus consists of five control signals:

1. $\overline{AS}$ (address strobe output);

2. R/$\overline{W}$ (read/write output);

3. $\overline{LDS}$ (lower data strobe output);

4. $\overline{UDS}$ (upper data strobe output); and

5. $\overline{DTACK}$ (data acknowledge input).

An $\overline{AS}$ signal signifies that the address information on the address lines is valid. An R/$\overline{W}$ signal at a high level signifies a read bus cycle; at a low level, it signifies a write bus cycle.

When $\overline{LDS}$ is low, data on lines D0 through D7 are selected. This data element is known as the **lower byte** (or the **odd byte**). When $\overline{UDS}$ is low, data on lines D8 through D15 are selected. This data element is known as the **upper byte** (or the **even byte**). When both $\overline{LDS}$ and $\overline{UDS}$ are low, data on lines D0 through D15 are selected. Figure 6.3 illustrates the data-selection scheme.[3]

$\overline{UDS}$	$\overline{LDS}$	*Data Selection*
High	High	Data not selected
High	Low	Lower byte (D0–D7) selected
Low	High	Upper byte (D8–D15) selected
Low	Low	Word (both bytes: D0–D15) selected

FIGURE 6.3 $\overline{LDS}$ and $\overline{UDS}$ signals selecting lower or upper data bytes or word of memory (or I/O).

The 68000 processor activates the $\overline{AS}$, R/$\overline{W}$, $\overline{LDS}$, and/or $\overline{UDS}$ signals along with the address information for a read or a write bus cycle. The addressed memory (or the I/O system) activates an acknowledge signal $\overline{DTACK}$ to the processor, while providing the data to the processor (read cycle), or accepting the data from the processor (write cycle). The processor does not terminate the bus cycle and insert wait states until $\overline{DTACK}$ has been generated. Thus, depending upon the speed of response of the memory or the I/O system, data transfers between the processor and these systems vary in the time they take. Consequently, we have an asynchronous data-transfer mechanism in the 68000 family of processors.[4]

Function Code Outputs

The function code outputs FC2, FC1, and FC0 provide status information about the processor, as indicated in Figure 6.4. These outputs from the processor can be used to distinguish between the user and supervisor modes of operation and between program and data space within each mode. When the processor accesses the reset vectors (vectors 0 and 1) or the program code, it is in the program space. Any other operand access is in

FC2	FC1	FC0	State	Mode
0	0	0	Reserved for Motorola	User
0	0	1	Data space	User
0	1	0	Program space	User
0	1	1	Reserved	User
1	0	0	Reserved for Motorola	Supervisor
1	0	1	Data space	Supervisor
1	1	0	Program space	Supervisor
1	1	1	Interrupt acknowledge	Supervisor

FIGURE 6.4   Function code outputs; associated states and modes.

the data space. External logic can be used to decode these function code conditions and prevent supervisor memory from being accessed when the processor is in the user mode.[5]

Other Buses and Signals

The **synchronous bus** in a microprocessor is used to control synchronous or timed data transfers between the processor and the memory or I/O. In the 68000, this bus is used to interfere with the earlier 6800 family of synchronous peripherals. In a synchronous operation, data transfers take place within a fixed time frame, as opposed to variable timing in the case of asynchronous operation. The synchronous bus for the 68000 consists of three signals used for 6800 peripheral control:

1. E (enable clock) output;
2. $\overline{\text{VMA}}$ (valid memory address) output; and
3. $\overline{\text{VPA}}$ (valid peripheral address) input.

The E clock is one-tenth the frequency of the 68000 clock input and is used to synchronize the 6800 family or similar synchronous peripherals used with the 68000. A $\overline{\text{VMA}}$ signal indicates to the 6800 family devices that there is a valid memory address on the address lines and that the device should be synchronized to the enable clock. $\overline{\text{VPA}}$ indicates to the processor that the addressed device is a synchronous device. Also, during an interrupt acknowledge cycle, $\overline{\text{VPA}}$ is used by the interrupting device to indicate an autovectoring mechanism to the processor.

The **arbitration bus** is used for direct memory access (DMA) data transfers. In such transfers, the processor releases the address, data, and control buses, and external logic controls them for direct data transfers. DMA transfers are faster than memory transfers requiring processor intervention, since no time is needed for instruction fetch cycles. The arbitration bus for the 68000 consists of three arbitration signals:

1. $\overline{\text{BR}}$ (bus request input);
2. $\overline{\text{BG}}$ (bus grant output); and
3. $\overline{\text{BGACK}}$ (bus grant acknowledge input).

The external logic requests the bus release by activating the $\overline{\text{BR}}$ line. The processor responds to this request by activating its $\overline{\text{BG}}$ output. The requesting device then acknowledges the response by activating the $\overline{\text{BGACK}}$ and subsequently takes possession of the buses. The DMA transfers take place until the external logic releases the buses and $\overline{\text{BGACK}}$.

The **interrupt control bus** is used by the external devices to request the attention of the processor. The processor recognizes these requests and services them in a level-priority scheme. The interrupt control bus for the 68000 consists of encoded $\overline{\text{IPL2}}$, $\overline{\text{IPL1}}$, and $\overline{\text{IPL0}}$ inputs (IPL stands for interrupt priority level).

The **system control bus** is used for system initialization and error control. For the 68000, it consists of the $\overline{\text{RESET}}$ and $\overline{\text{HALT}}$ bidirectional signals and the $\overline{\text{BERR}}$ (bus error) input signal.

The **clock input signal** advances the processor through the sequential states of operation. For the 68000, each read or write bus cycle (without wait states) consists of four clock cycles. Any wait states are integral multiples of clock cycles.

The 68000 operates on a 5-volt power supply. Two pins are allocated for the V_{CC} input and two for the ground connection. Some of the signals we mentioned may go into a tristate or high-Z condition under special conditions. Figure 6.5 is a summary of the 68000 signals.

We will now review the hardware aspects of the 68000 by means of an example problem.

Example 6.1   68000 signals and definitions.
The 68000 microprocessor employs a memory-mapped I/O approach, in which memory and I/O appear to be similar.

1. With 23 address lines and $\overline{\text{LDS}}$ and $\overline{\text{UDS}}$ signals, how many total memory and I/O bytes can be addressed? Explain.
2. Can the processor use the synchronous bus for I/O transfers and the asynchronous bus for memory transfers simultaneously?
3. What will be the values of the FC2, FC1, and FC0 outputs while the processor is fetching interrupt autovector 6. Why?

Solution

1. **Memory and I/O bytes:** With 23 address lines, 8 megawords ($2^{23} = 8,388,608$) of memory and I/O together can be addressed. $\overline{\text{LDS}}$ and $\overline{\text{UDS}}$ signals further select an odd or even byte within the word.

   Total memory and I/O addressing = 8 megawords = 16 megabytes

Signal Name	Mnemonic	Input/Output	Active State	Hi-Z	
				On $\overline{HALT}$	On $\overline{BGACK}$
ADDRESS BUS	A1–A23	OUTPUT	HIGH	YES	YES
DATA BUS	D0–D15	INPUT/OUTPUT	HIGH	YES	YES
ADDRESS STROBE	$\overline{AS}$	OUTPUT	LOW	NO	YES
READ/WRITE	$R/\overline{W}$	OUTPUT	READ-HIGH WRITE-LOW	NO	YES
UPPER AND LOWER DATA STROBES	$\overline{UDS}$, $\overline{LDS}$	OUTPUT	LOW	NO	YES
DATA TRANSFER ACKNOWLEDGE	$\overline{DTACK}$	INPUT	LOW	NO	NO
BUS REQUEST	$\overline{BR}$	INPUT	LOW	NO	NO
BUS GRANT	$\overline{BG}$	OUTPUT	LOW	NO	NO
BUS GRANT ACKNOWLEDGE	$\overline{BGACK}$	INPUT	LOW	NO	NO
INTERRUPT PRIORITY LEVEL	$\overline{IPL0}$, $\overline{IPL1}$, $\overline{IPL2}$	INPUT	LOW	NO	NO

BUS ERROR	$\overline{\text{BERR}}$	INPUT	LOW	NO	NO
RESET	$\overline{\text{RESET}}$	INPUT/OUTPUT	LOW	NO	NO
HALT	$\overline{\text{HALT}}$	INPUT/OUTPUT	LOW	NO	NO
ENABLE	E	OUTPUT	HIGH	NO	NO
VALID MEMORY ADDRESS	$\overline{\text{VMA}}$	OUTPUT	LOW	NO	YES
VALID PERIPHERAL ADDRESS	$\overline{\text{VPA}}$	INPUT	LOW	NO	NO
FUNCTION CODE OUTPUT	FC0, FC1, FC2	OUTPUT	HIGH	NO	YES
CLOCK	CLK	INPUT	HIGH	NO	NO
POWER INPUT (2)	V_{CC}	INPUT	—	—	—
GROUND (2)	GND	INPUT	—	—	—

FIGURE 6.5 Signal summary for the 68000. (Courtesy of Motorola, Inc.)

2. **Simultaneous usage of buses:** Synchronous and asynchronous buses cannot be used simultaneously. Address and data buses are required for each type of data transfer. The data transfers must be done one at a time.

3. **FC2, FC1, and FC0 values:** Interrupt servicing activity takes place in the supervisor mode. Interrupt vectors are in the supervisor data space (refer to Chapter 5 and Figure 6.4).

$$FC2\ FC1\ FC0 = 1\ 0\ 1$$

For the 68008 processor, there are 20 address lines (A0–A19) and 8 data lines (D0–D7). This processor can address a total of 1 megabyte of memory and I/O. There is only one data strobe $\overline{DS}$ in place of the $\overline{LDS}$ and $\overline{UDS}$ signals. $\overline{VMA}$ and $\overline{BGACK}$ signals are dropped, and the $\overline{IPL0}$ and $\overline{IPL2}$ interrupt signals are integrated for the 48-pin dip package (for the 52-pin, they are left intact). All other hardware features of the 68008 are similar to those of the 68000 processor.

6.2   MEMORY AND I/O INTERFACE SCHEMES

Memory is an integral part of any computer system. The decoded address bus provides selection signals, called **chip select (CS) signals** to the memory system. Additional selection signals, called **chip enable (CE) signals,** are used for further selection of memory systems. Data transfers take place between the processor and the selected memory on the data bus. The 68000 processor uses the asynchronous bus to control these transfers. The I/O interface is similar to the memory interface.

Memory-Device Types and Memory Concepts

Memory devices can be classified as random access or sequential access. The **random-access read/write memory (RAM)** and the **read-only memory (ROM)** systems are basically random access, in which access time to all memory locations is the same. RAM and ROM devices are used for the main operating memory of the computer system. The RAM system is suitable for information storage and retrieval; however, it is a volatile system and loses information if the power is turned off.

The industry uses either static or dynamic RAM devices. The **static RAM** device consists of an array of flip-flops contained in a matrix. Each flip-flop acts as a memory cell. Static memory devices are available in 8K-by-8 and 32K-by-8 configurations as of this writing. A 32K-by-8 RAM device has 256K (262,144) flip-flops in it.

The **dynamic RAM (DRAM)** stores information in the form of a charge on the gate of a single MOS transistor. The dynamic memory cell needs to be refreshed periodically so that charge information will not be lost due to decay. The DRAMs are denser than the static RAM devices (usually by a factor of four). One-megabit DRAM devices are common as of this writing. The DRAM interface is more complex than the static RAM interface. Moreover, the failure rate of DRAM-based systems is greater than that of static RAM-based systems. In the DRAM systems, however, error detection and correction schemes are employed to increase the reliability of the memory system. The access time of the MOS RAM (static and dynamic) is approximately 100 to 200 nanoseconds.

If simple interface and high reliability are required, static RAM systems are preferred. For high-density applications, DRAM systems with the error correction mechanism are generally preferred.

ROM devices are nonvolatile and retain information even if power to the device should be disconnected. For **mask-programmable ROMs,** the code and data contents are programmed at the factory and cannot be changed. The **erasable and programmable ROMs (EPROMs)** can be programmed with the help of EPROM programmer systems. The EPROMs are nonvolatile in the system operation. However, they can be erased using ultraviolet light or high-voltage pulses and reprogrammed with a new code and data using EPROM programmer systems. EPROM devices in denominations of 64K by 8 and 256K by 8 are common, with access times of approximately 100 to 200 nanoseconds.

NMOS and CMOS RAMs (static and dynamic) are widely used. For fast-access memories, bipolar static RAMs are preferable. The ROMs and EPROMs are basically of the MOS type. With ultralow-power CMOS RAMs and a battery backup, it is possible to obtain a nonvolatile memory system.

Sequential memory systems are nonvolatile and are suitable for backup applications. They have a larger memory capacity, but also longer access times (up to several milliseconds).

In this chapter we will concentrate on the commonly used memory system implementation with static RAM and ROM/EPROM devices.

Address Decoding, Strobing, and Memory Selection

The 68000 system memory is word organized, consisting of even and odd bytes, as illustrated in Figure 6.6. Higher order address bits are decoded and the CS signals are generated. Each CS signal selects a range of memory. Within the range, the same CS signal activates both the even and the odd memory units. $\overline{\text{UDS}}$ and $\overline{\text{LDS}}$ signals independently activate the CE inputs of the even and the odd byte sections of the memory. $\text{R}/\overline{\text{W}}$ drives the memory units for read or write selection. The low-order address lines are directly connected to the memory devices in order to select the actual location within a selected memory device.

The lower (or odd) memory byte is connected to data lines D0–D7. The upper (or even) byte is connected to data lines D8–D15. An $\overline{\text{AS}}$ (address strobe) signal enables the decoder logic and initiates the memory bus cycle. The $\overline{\text{AS}}$, $\overline{\text{LDS}}$, $\overline{\text{UDS}}$, and the control signals occur in a fixed sequence.

Read and Write Timing Considerations

Read Bus Cycle   Figure 6.7 illustrates read bus-cycle timing for word operation. Each clock cycle is divided into two **S-states.** S0 is the starting state of a bus cycle. During S0, all the strobe signals are at their inactive level. The address and data buses

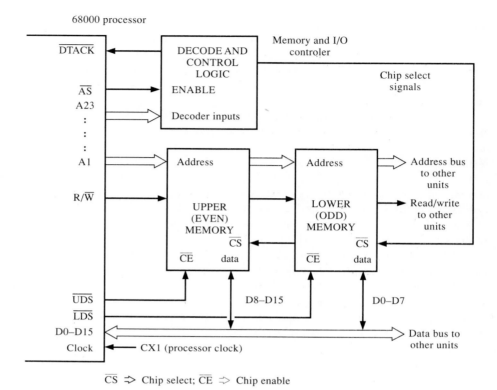

$\overline{CS} \Rightarrow$ Chip select; $\overline{CE} \Rightarrow$ Chip enable

FIGURE 6.6 Memory configuration in the 68000.

FIGURE 6.7 The 68000 read bus-cycle timing for word operation. (Courtesy of Motorola Inc.)

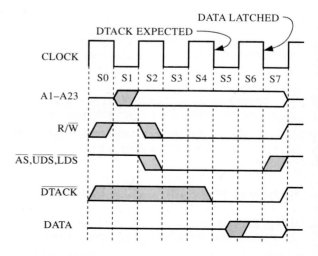

are in their tristate condition. During S1, the processor puts address information on the address bus and sets R/$\overline{\text{W}}$ to a high level to signify a read bus cycle. During S2, the strobes ($\overline{\text{AS}}$, $\overline{\text{LDS}}$, and $\overline{\text{UDS}}$) are activated.

One clock cycle (states S3 and S4) is allowed for the external logic to respond. At the end of S4, the processor expects $\overline{\text{DTACK}}$. One clock cycle after the occurrence of $\overline{\text{DTACK}}$, the processor accepts data on lines D0–D15 and internally latches it (at the end of S6, in this case). During S7, the processor deactivates all of the strobe signals and address lines. The memory system recognizes this event and deactivates $\overline{\text{DTACK}}$. This concludes the read bus cycle, whereupon the processor is ready for the next bus cycle.

The read bus cycle for byte operation is similar. The processor activates $\overline{\text{LDS}}$ for a low (or odd) byte or $\overline{\text{UDS}}$ for a high (or even) byte, but not both. Without any wait states, the read bus cycle for a word or byte operation takes four clock cycles.[6]

Write Bus Cycle   Figure 6.8 illustrates write bus-cycle timing for word operation, which is similar to read bus-cycle timing. During state S2, the processor activates the address strobe $\overline{\text{AS}}$ and sets R/$\overline{\text{W}}$ to a low level to signify a write cycle. During S3, the processor puts data on the data bus. During S4, the processor activates the $\overline{\text{LDS}}$ and $\overline{\text{UDS}}$ signals. When the memory accepts this data, it is expected to activate $\overline{\text{DTACK}}$ by the end of state S4. If $\overline{\text{DTACK}}$ occurs by the end of S4, the processor waits one more clock cycle (until the end of S6) and deactivates the strobe signals and the address and data lines. This completes the write bus cycle. For byte operations, the processor activates only $\overline{\text{LDS}}$ or $\overline{\text{UDS}}$, for odd or even bytes.

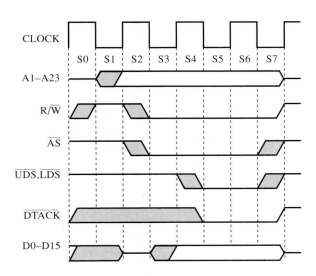

FIGURE 6.8   The 68000 write bus-cycle timing for word operation. (Courtesy of Motorola, Inc.)

Read-Modify/Write Bus Cycles   The read-modify/write operation is required by instructions such as TAS (test and set). In **TAS instruction,** the operand is read from a location into the processor. It is tested, modified, and written back at the same location.[7]

The read-modify/write bus timing is illustrated in Figure 6.9. The address content during the operand read and write cycles remains the same. Data content may change, however.

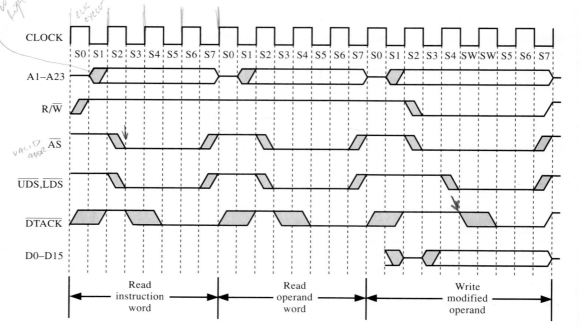

FIGURE 6.9 The 68000 read-modify/write bus-cycle timing for word operation. (Courtesy of Motorola, Inc.)

Wait States Clearly, $\overline{\text{DTACK}}$ is expected by the end of the S4 state for read and write bus cycles. If $\overline{\text{DTACK}}$ does not occur by the end of S4, the processor inserts a full clock cycle as a wait state, at the end of which $\overline{\text{DTACK}}$ is checked for.

The processor inserts wait states until either $\overline{\text{DTACK}}$ or a $\overline{\text{BERR}}$ (bus error) signal occurs. If $\overline{\text{BERR}}$ occurs, the processor aborts the bus cycle and goes into bus error exception processing, as discussed in previous chapters.

Timing Considerations of Asynchronous Inputs

$\overline{\text{DTACK}}$ is considered an asynchronous control input to the processor. The processor samples such asynchronous signals on the falling edge of the clock. On the next rising edge, the processor internally validates the sampled signal. On the next falling edge, the sampled signal is acted upon by the processor. Thus, there is an inherent clock-cycle delay to act upon a sampled asynchronous signal. From the read bus cycle of Figure 6.7, it can be observed that $\overline{\text{DTACK}}$ has been sampled at the end of S4 (a falling edge), internally validated at the end of S5 (a rising edge), and externally acted upon by the processor at the end of S6 (a falling edge). This clock-cycle delay is intended to eliminate uncertainties in bus operation. The other asynchronous inputs to the 68000 processor are $\overline{BERR}$, $\overline{BR}$, $\overline{BGACK}$, $\overline{HALT}$, $\overline{RESET}$, and $\overline{VPA}$, as indicated in Figure 6.10.

The following example problem provides a review of read and write bus cycles and timing.

FIGURE 6.10 The 68000 sampling of external asynchronous inputs. (Courtesy of Motorola, Inc.)

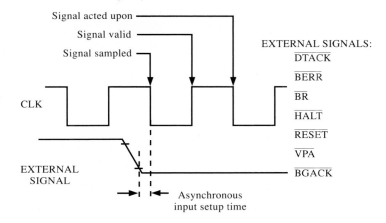

Example 6.2   68000 read and write bus-cycle timing.

The 68000 in the system of Figure 6.6 is operating at a 10-MHz clock frequency. Timings for the read and write cycles are indicated in Figures 6.7 and 6.8.

1. For the given conditions, what is the read access time?

2. Suppose the processor is reading a byte $4D from location $000FFE. What are the contents of the address bus and data bus and the logic levels of the control signals during the active read bus cycle?

3. If three wait states are inserted for writing a word at location $001000, how many clock cycles is the effective write cycle? When are the wait states inserted?

Solution

1. Read access time: The read access time is defined as the time lapse from when the address has become stable to when the data have become valid. From Figure 6.7, it can be observed that this corresponds to the time between the end of S1 and the end of S6; that is, five states, or 2.5 clock cycles. At a 10-MHz clock, each clock cycle is 100 nanoseconds. Thus,

read access time = 2.5 clock cycles = 250 nanoseconds

2. Active read-cycle operation: Location $000FFE is an even address. The even (or upper) byte is selected by the $\overline{UDS}$. Reading data $4D from $000FFE results in

Address bus (A23–A1) = $000FFE; $\overline{AS}$ is low

Data bus (D7–D0) = tristate; $\overline{LDS}$ is high(not selected)

Data bus (D15–D8) = $4D; $\overline{UDS}$ is low(selected)

R/$\overline{W}$ (read operation) = high; $\overline{DTACK}$ is low(acknowledged)

3. **Wait states during the write operation:** The wait states are inserted after state S4. Each wait state corresponds to one clock cycle. The write bus cycle without wait states takes four clock cycles. Thus,

write bus cycle with three wait states corresponds to seven clock cycles.

Wait-state insertion for the read bus cycle is similar to that for the write bus cycle for all members of the 68000 family of processors. It should be remembered that the 68008 processor is a reduced-bus version of the 68000, with a data bus only 8 bits wide.

6.3 MEMORY AND I/O SYSTEM DESIGN CONSIDERATIONS

Any microcomputer system includes RAM (read/write random access memory), ROM (read-only random access memory), and I/O (input/output) systems. RAM and I/O can be selected only during read or write operations. ROM can be selected only during read operations. CS and CE signals are generated in accordance with these constraints.

The Memory Subsystem Design

Figure 6.11 illustrates the details of a 64-kilobyte (64K-by-8) memory system. $\overline{E0}$ output of the first decoder enables the second decoder. $\overline{Y0}$ output of the second decoder drives the chip select ($\overline{CS}$) inputs of the even and odd memory units. These units consist of 32K-by-8 memory devices. $\overline{UDS}$ and $\overline{LDS}$ further drive the chip enable ($\overline{CE}$) inputs and select the even or odd unit, providing a 64K-by-8 configuration. If both units are selected, the system becomes a 32-kiloword (32K-by-16) memory system.

The 8-state shift register is the memory controller that provides the $\overline{DTACK}$ signal to the processor. Initially, all the Q outputs are at a high level (logic 1). The shift register is enabled by the corresponding chip select signal ($\overline{Y0}$ in this case), and starts shifting a logic 0 from Q0 to Q7 at each CX0 clock transition. Depending upon the response time of the memory system, proper Q output is routed as the effective $\overline{DTACK}$ input to the processor through the DTACK logic. The shift register returns to the all-1 condition when the enable signal ($\overline{Y0}$ in this case) is removed.

For the 68000 family of processors, the first kilobyte of memory corresponds to the vector table. The first eight locations correspond to the reset vectors, which should be in the ROM space. In most of the 68000-based systems, these eight locations are physical ROM locations. In some systems, additional logic is used to shift the memory

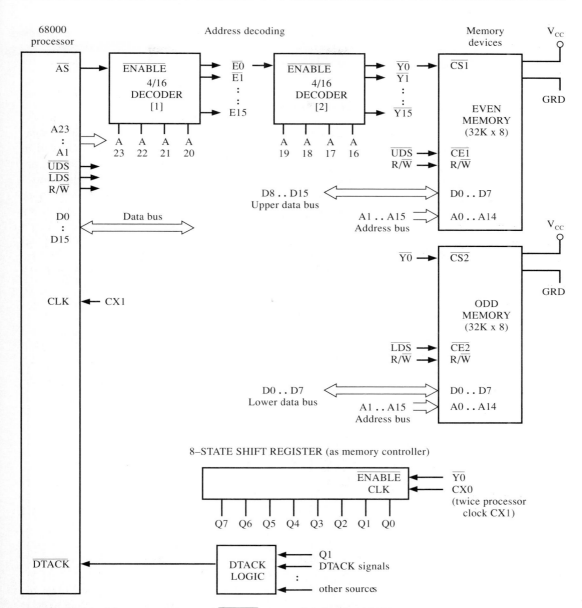

FIGURE 6.11 Memory system and $\overline{\text{DTACK}}$ generation for the 68000.

reference of these eight locations to a ROM device elsewhere in the memory map. The other part of the vector table can be contained in the RAM space. On system power-up, the reset routine initializes the vector table with proper values.

Signal Buffering Considerations

Due to electronic loading constraints, signal buffering is used to increase the drive capability of the signals. Transceivers are used to accomplish the buffering, as indicated in Figure 6.12. A **transceiver** is a logic device that can transmit a signal in either direction, depending upon the direction control. The address and the unidirectional control signals are buffered by transceiver bank [1] to go from the processor to the memory or I/O (X to Y). The data bus is buffered by transceiver bank [2], which is controlled by the R/$\overline{\text{W}}$ signal. For read operations (when the R/$\overline{\text{W}}$ signal is at a high level), data flows from the memory or I/O to the processor (Y to X), and vice versa.[8] In this conceptual framework, the memory or I/O system can be expanded to any size.

The following example problem provides a review of memory system design.

FIGURE 6.12 Signal buffering in a 68000-based system.

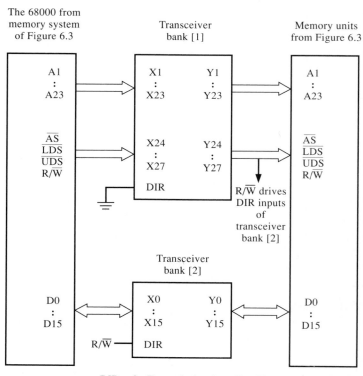

DIR = 0: Transmission from X to Y
1: Transmission from Y to X

Example 6.3   Memory system design.

Refer to the memory system of Figure 6.11.

1. Specify the memory or I/O ranges that can be selected by the $\overline{E0}$ through $\overline{E15}$ signals from the first decoder and the $\overline{Y0}$ through $\overline{Y15}$ signals from the second decoder.
2. The $\overline{Y14}$ and $\overline{Y15}$ signals are ANDed to generate an I/O chip select. What is the corresponding I/O range?
3. How much delay is there from the time the memory units are selected ($\overline{Y0}$ becoming active low) until $\overline{DTACK}$ occurs for the conditions indicated?
4. If the transceiver IC is 8 bits wide, how many such ICs are required for transceiver banks [1] and [2] in the system of Figure 6.12?

Solution

1. **Memory or I/O ranges:** The first 4/16 decoder divides the available 16-megabyte address space into 16 equal ranges of 1 megabyte each. Thus, each E output goes low for a 1-megabyte range and selects memory as follows:

$$\overline{E0} \text{ selects range } \$000000..\$0FFFFF$$
$$\overline{E1} \text{ selects range } \$100000..\$1FFFFF$$
$$\vdots \qquad\qquad \vdots$$
$$\overline{E15} \text{ selects range } \$F00000..\$FFFFFF$$

The second 4/16 decoder is activated by the $\overline{E0}$ output of the first decoder. The second decoder further divides this 1-megabyte range into 16 equal ranges of 64 kilobytes each. Thus, each Y output from the second decoder goes low for a 64-kilobyte range and selects memory as follows:

$$\overline{Y0} \text{ selects range } \$000000..\$00FFFF$$
$$\overline{Y1} \text{ selects range } \$010000..\$01FFFF$$
$$\vdots \qquad\qquad \vdots$$
$$\overline{Y15} \text{ selects range } \$0F0000..\$0FFFFF$$

2. **I/O chip select:** From the preceding solution, it can be seen that the $\overline{Y14}$ and $\overline{Y15}$ ranges are

$$\overline{Y14} = \$0E0000 \text{ through } \$0EFFFF \qquad \overline{Y15} = \$0F0000 \text{ through } \$0FFFFF$$

ANDing these two 64-kilobyte ranges would yield a 128-kilobyte I/O chip select range between $0E0000 and $0FFFFF.

3. **Delay for $\overline{DTACK}$ occurrence:** The Q1 output of the shift register goes to active zero two CX0 clock activations after the $\overline{Y0}$ signal goes active low and selects the

memory. CX0 is twice the frequency of the CX1 processor clock, and two CX0 activations correspond to one CX1 activation. Q1 is routed as the $\overline{\text{DTACK}}$ input to the processor. Thus, $\overline{\text{DTACK}}$ occurs one processor clock after the selection.

4. **8-bit transceiver ICs for buffering:** Transceiver bank [1] buffers 27 signals and requires 4 ICs. Transceiver bank [2] buffers 16 signals and requires 2 ICs.

In our discussion thus far, we have emphasized static RAMs, which are composed of flip-flop arrays. Dynamic RAMs, which involve charge storage on a capacitive element and periodic refresh of the charge, are becoming increasingly popular. Dynamic RAM devices are two to four times denser than static RAMs. However, they require complex memory controllers and use interrupts for refresh by the processor. We will discuss dynamic RAM implementation schemes along with the interrupts in subsequent chapters.

As of this writing, 64-kilobyte static memory devices and 256-kilobyte dynamic memory devices are becoming available. Some of these devices have an additional selection control input called the output enable (OE), which is similar to the CS and CE inputs. The I/O interface is essentially similar to the memory interface. Data books may be consulted for design details.[9]

6.4 CONTROL INTERFACE SCHEMES

In addition to the memory and I/O interface, processors have a control interface. The primary hardware signals that control and direct the 68000 microprocessor are $\overline{\text{RESET}}$, $\overline{\text{HALT}}$, and $\overline{\text{BERR}}$ (bus error). The DMA and interrupt signals (to be discussed later) also control the processor. In this section, we will first consider the reset and halt interface and follow with a discussion of timing signals and the bus error.

Reset and Halt Interface

Figure 6.13 illustrates the reset and halt interface with the 68000 processor. For the values shown, the MC3456 monostable produces a 100-millisecond pulse on the power-up reset. This activates both the $\overline{\text{RESET}}$ and $\overline{\text{HALT}}$ inputs to the 68000. On power-up, processors usually require more time to come to a stable state due to electronic and switching transients. The 68000 requires at least a 128-clock-cycle time equivalent to come to a stable state on the power-up condition. The 100-millisecond reset and halt pulses are more than adequate for any 68000 family member. For a reset condition to occur, both the $\overline{\text{RESET}}$ and $\overline{\text{HALT}}$ inputs should be activated to a low level.

The processor goes into the supervisor mode on reset. Reset exception processing, which is always the system initialization routine, starts as soon as the $\overline{\text{RESET}}$ and $\overline{\text{HALT}}$ are negated (go to high-level). The same sequence of operations occurs for the manual reset. The 74LS00 cross-coupled gates debounce the reset switch, providing clean $\overline{\text{RESET}}$ and $\overline{\text{HALT}}$ activation to the processor. Manual activation should last for at

MC6800 – RESET AND HALT

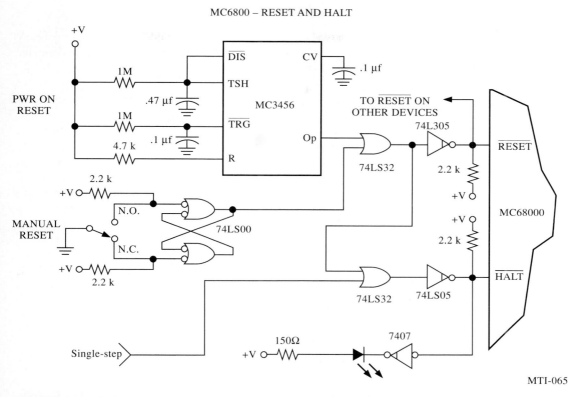

FIGURE 6.13 Reset and halt interface for the 68000. (Courtesy of Motorola, Inc.)

least ten clock cycles. (Refer to Chapter 5 for software details on reset exception processing.)

Of particular interest is the bidirectional property of the $\overline{RESET}$ line. The processor can execute a software reset instruction in the supervisor mode. The reset line then acts as an output, resetting the other peripherals connected to the 68000. When the processor drives the $\overline{RESET}$ line as an output, it goes active low for 124 clock cycles.

When the bidirectional $\overline{HALT}$ line is used as an input in conjunction with the $\overline{RESET}$ input and is activated by external circuits, the 68000 goes into a system reset condition. On the other hand, if the $\overline{HALT}$ input is activated individually, the processor is halted after the completion of the current bus cycle. In the halt state, address and data lines are put in their high-impedance state, and the control lines are negated; however, the DMA control lines are available for bus arbitration. The halt condition of the processor is used for hardware troubleshooting and single-step operation. The processor resumes the halted operation soon after the negation of the $\overline{HALT}$ input line.

When a double bus fault condition (Chapter 5) is detected, the processor uses the $\overline{HALT}$ line as an output and drives it low; this, in turn, halts any devices connected to it.

Timing Signals Associated with the 68000

The timing signals associated with the 68000 processor are indicated in Figure 6.14. A 32-MHz clock signal is derived from a crystal oscillator circuit. The 8-bit binary counter (divide-by-256) circuit provides the binary signals:

$$CX0 \text{ (divide by 2)} \qquad \text{at 16 MHz}$$
$$CX1 \text{ (divide by 4)} \qquad \text{at 8 MHz}$$
$$\vdots$$
$$CX7 \text{ (divide by 256)} \qquad \text{at 1/8 MHz}$$

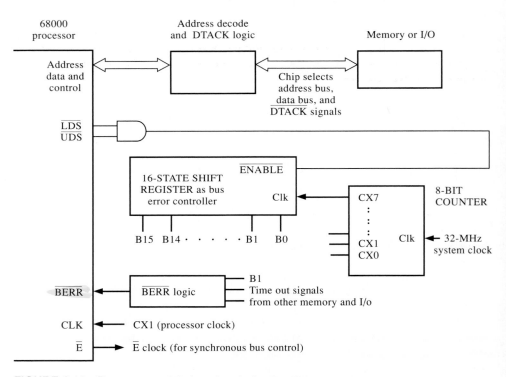

FIGURE 6.14 Bus error and timing signals for the 68000.

The CX0 signal is used for $\overline{\text{DTACK}}$ timing generation (refer to Figure 6.11). The CX1 signal runs the processor at 8 MHz. Signals CX2 through CX7 can be used by any other I/O or memory systems. In the case we are now considering, CX7 is used to drive the bus error control logic. The system clock can be changed to any value that suits the requirements.

The 68000 processor provides an E (enable) clock as an output. The E clock is one-tenth the frequency of processor clock CX1 and is used to drive the 6800 or other synchronous peripherals.

Bus Error Considerations

Of very special importance in all 68000-based systems is the bus error ($\overline{BERR}$) signal. It informs the processor that a bus error has occurred. It originates from a bus error controller, as indicated in Figure 6.14. The bus error controller is usually a **watchdog timer;** that is, a counter circuit reset to zero at the start of each bus cycle, which counts up at each clock transition. When it reaches its set maximum count, it generates a pulse signifying the time that has lapsed since the start of the last bus cycle.

The 16-state shift register acts as the bus error controller and provides the $\overline{BERR}$ signal to the processor. All the B outputs are at a high level initially. The controller is driven by the ANDed output of $\overline{UDS}$ and $\overline{LDS}$ signals from the processor. When a new bus cycle starts, either $\overline{UDS}$ or $\overline{LDS}$, or both, go to a low-active state (logic 0). Thus, the controller is enabled during each bus cycle and shifts a logic 0 from B0 to B15 at each CX7 clock transition. Depending upon the maximum allowed response time of the addressed devices, proper B output is routed as the effective $\overline{BERR}$ input to the processor through the $\overline{BERR}$ logic.

If the $\overline{DTACK}$ is given out by the addressed device within the time permitted, the bus cycle is normally terminated and the strobes ($\overline{LDS}$ and/or $\overline{UDS}$) go to the inactive logic 1 level. This restores the shift register to the all-1 condition, and the $\overline{BERR}$ activation does not occur. Otherwise, logic 0 propagates through the shift register and ultimately reaches the processor as $\overline{BERR}$ (through its selected B output). The processor then goes into the bus error condition. Software details of bus error exception processing are discussed in Chapter 5.

On occasion, a particular bus cycle may be faulty and must be rerun. External logic indicates this rerun condition to the 68000 processor by simultaneously activating the $\overline{BERR}$ and $\overline{HALT}$ inputs. On the occurrence of the rerun condition, the processor aborts the current bus cycle and goes into a halt state. After the $\overline{BERR}$ and $\overline{HALT}$ inputs are negated (return to a high level), the processor reruns the aborted bus cycle with the same address and data values. This helps the processor to correct any immediate errors due to hardware transients on the lines.

The following example problem provides a review of the control interface to the 68000.

Example 6.4   Control interface to the 68000.
The system clock is 32 MHz for the 68000-based systems illustrated in Figures 6.13 and 6.14.

1. What is the frequency of the enable output clock E?

2. What is the minimum amount of time the manual reset should last?

3. The B1 output of the bus error controller is routed as the $\overline{BERR}$ input to the processor. How much time would elapse before the $\overline{BERR}$ input goes to active low after the strobes have been activated.

Solution

1. **Frequency of the E clock:** For the conditions given, the processor clock CX1 = 8 MHz. The E clock is one-tenth the frequency of the CX1 clock. Thus,

$$\text{E clock} = \text{CX1/10} = \textbf{800 KHz}$$

2. **Manual reset timing T:** The manual reset should last for at least ten CX1 processor clock periods. Thus,

$$\text{T(reset)} = 10 \times \text{1/8 MHz} = \textbf{1.25 microseconds}$$

3. **$\overline{\text{BERR}}$ timing:** For the conditions indicated in Figure 6.14, the CX7 clock drives the bus error controller shift register. The shift register is enabled during a bus cycle, when either $\overline{\text{LDS}}$ or $\overline{\text{UDS}}$, or both, go low active. It takes two CX7 clockings after the enable to shift a logic 0 to B1 output. B1, in turn, activates the $\overline{\text{BERR}}$ input to the processor if $\overline{\text{DTACK}}$ does not occur.

   Since the CX7 clock at 1/8 MHz corresponds to 8 microseconds, two CX7 clock periods correspond to 16 microseconds. Thus, $\overline{\text{BERR}}$ occurs (in the absence of $\overline{\text{DTACK}}$) 16 microseconds after the strobe activations.

In the preceding example, a delay of up to 120 microseconds can be obtained by routing B15 as the $\overline{\text{BERR}}$ input to the processor. If more delay is required, additional counter or shift register circuits can be incorporated into the system.

6.5 68000-BASED BUSING SCHEMES

In order to support system expansion for the 68000 family of microprocessors, Motorola introduced two busing schemes: the **VERSA bus** and the **VME bus.** Both of these widely used busing schemes support 8-, 16-, and 32-bit data transfers and the associated protocols.[10,11]

The VERSA Bus

Figure 6.15 illustrates a typical VERSA busing scheme. The hardware interface consists of two edge connectors:

P1: primary connector—140-pin interface; and
P2: secondary connector—120-pin interface.

Primary Interface P1   The primary interface P1 supports 24 address lines, 16 data lines, and the associated control lines as indicated. The address, data, and control lines of the P1 interface are those of the 68000 processor.

68000-BASED VERSA MODULE

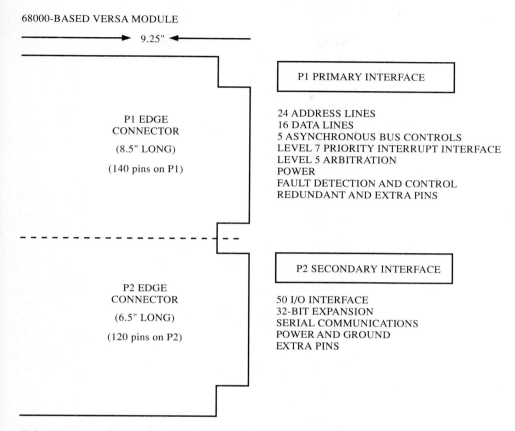

FIGURE 6.15   VERSA bus P1 and P2 particulars for 68000-based systems.

The asynchronous bus interface consists of the strobes ($\overline{AS}$, $\overline{LDS}$, $\overline{UDS}$, and R/$\overline{W}$) and the $\overline{DTACK}$. The seven-level priority interrupt interface is the standard 68000 interrupt interface. It consists of the interrupt request signals 1RQ1 through 1RQ7 and the associated interrupt acknowledge signal IACK.

Several of the VERSA modules can be bused together on a VERSA bus backplane. One or more processor modules may be used. All the signals are TTL compatible. Each module presents one unit TTL load on the corresponding input signal line. The bus drivers on each module are of the open collector type and support up to 16-unit TTL loads.

When several VERSA modules are bused together, there should be a bus arbitration scheme. The VERSA bus supports such a scheme using the five bus arbitration request signals BR0–BR4 from the requesting modules to a master controller module. The master controller responds to the requesting modules by sending a bus clear signal (BCLR), if the bus is granted.

The P1 interface supports 5, ±12, and ±15 DC voltages and an ample number of signal grounds. In addition, there are the numerous fault detection and control lines, including $\overline{\text{BERR}}$ and $\overline{\text{HALT}}$. The P1 interface is generally sufficient if extended capabilities are not required.

Secondary Interface P2 In order to expand the system to full 32-bit address and 32-bit data, a secondary interface through the edge connector P2 is used, as illustrated in Figure 6.15. This interface also supports 50 I/O lines and serial communications to other systems. Although the VERSA busing scheme is gradually being replaced by the VME busing scheme, there are still many VERSA schemes in the industry that are being expanded on an ongoing basis.

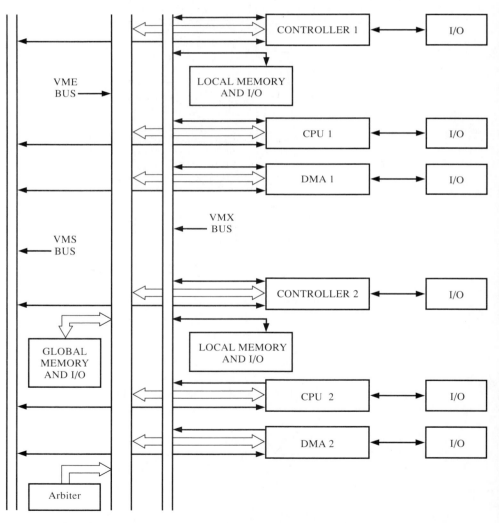

FIGURE 6.16 VME busing scheme and structure. (Courtesy of Motorola, Inc.)

The VME Bus

Redefinition of VERSA bus with emphasis on international standards has resulted in the VME bus. The VME bus interfaces with the VME modules as shown in Figure 6.16. It is an optimized busing architecture with primary P1 and secondary P2 interfaces through the respective edge connectors. Up to 16 modules can be interfaced on the backplane VME bus. These edge connectors are 96 pins each with functional groups as shown in Figure 6.17.

As illustrated in Figures 6.16 and 6.17, the VME busing architecture consists of three buses. The VME backplane bus, contained in the P1 interface connector, supports all of the global resources needed for the VME modules. The VMS serial communications bus (which is also part of the P1 interface) supports the serial communication between two or more VME modules. Similar to the VERSA busing scheme, the P1 interface in the VME scheme can handle up to 16-bit data transfers and a seven-level priority interrupt interface.

The VMX bus, which is part of the P2 interface, is a high-speed parallel bus and is local to six adjacent modules. This helps to expand the local subsystem. In most 16-bit applications, the P1 interface would be sufficient. However, if the system needs to be expanded to 32 bits, or if additional I/O or VMX capabilities are required, a P2 interface should also be used.

System expansion is very easy with the VERSA or VME busing schemes. It is sufficient to obtain card cages with the VERSA or VME backplanes and populate them with the respective VERSA or VME modules. The photos of Figure 6.18 are of typical VERSA and VME card cages and modules.

Detailed specifications are available for both busing schemes. These should be consulted for further information, such as bus arbitration methods.

We will now review the system-level busing schemes by means of an example problem.

Example 6.5   VERSA and VME busing schemes.
State which of the two busing schemes, the VERSA or the VME, is preferable in the following circumstances:

1. an A/D and D/A interface is required;
2. multiprocessing with local I/O and memory resources is required;
3. diagnostics are required.

Give reasons for each of your choices.

Solution

1. **A/D and D/A interface:** The A/D (analog-to-digital converter) is an I/O device that converts an analog input signal into a corresponding digital word and interfaces with

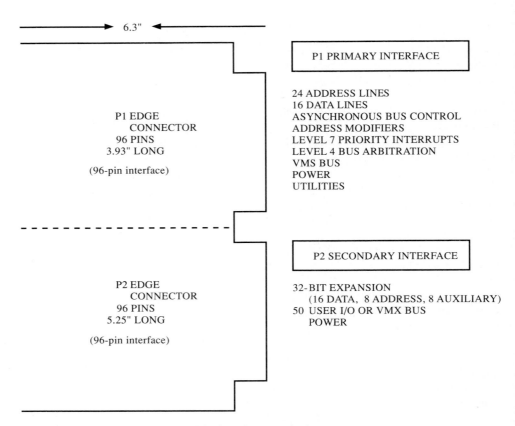

FIGURE 6.17 VME bus P1 and P2 interface particulars.

the microprocessor. The D/A (digital-to-analog converter) is another I/O device that accepts a digital word from the microprocessor and converts it into a corresponding analog voltage.

Both the VERSA and VME schemes are useful with P1 and P2 interfaces. The VME scheme, however, shares the 50 connections in P2 between I/O and VMX. If both the 50-pin I/O interface and the VMX capability are required at the same time, the VME is limited. In such situations, the VERSA bus is preferable.

2. **Multiprocessing with local resources:** Clearly, the VME busing scheme is preferable with P1 and P2 interfaces because of well-defined VMX capability for local resource expansion.

3. **Diagnostics:** The VERSA busing scheme is preferable because of its well-defined fault detection and control on the P1 interface, itself.

The VME is one of the most popular busing schemes in the industry. Even though it was developed for the 68000 family of processors, it supports other processor fami-

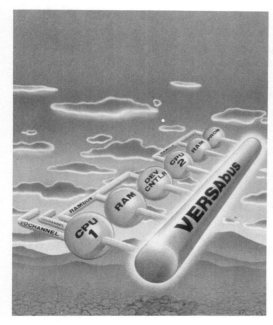

Intelligent
Peripherial controller

I/O
Transition

Hardware

FIGURE 6.18 VERSA and VME card cages and modules. (Courtesy Motorola, Inc.)

lies, such as the 8086/80286/80386. Products that are compatible with the VME bus are available from several vendors.

Other industry standard busing schemes include the Multibus-11 from Intel Corporation and the NU bus from Texas Instruments. The system-level properties of these buses are similar to those of the VME and VERSA buses. The 68000 family of processors can interface with both of these buses with equal ease.

6.6 SUMMARY

In this chapter we described the hardware signals of the 68000 processor and their properties. We also introduced the hardware interface schemes for the 68000.

Memory and I/O interface schemes are very important. The read/write random access memory (RAM) is particularly suitable for the storage and retrieval of programs and data. The static RAMs store information in flip-flop arrays. Static RAMs are the systems of choice in high-reliability applications. Dynamic RAM (DRAM) devices store information on a single MOS transistor memory cell and are denser than static RAMs. DRAM-based systems are preferable in applications requiring high density.

ROMs and EPROMs are of the read-only type and are nonvolatile. They are particularly well suited for storing permanent programs and data elements.

We also studied details of the asynchronous memory and I/O interface, as well as read and write bus-cycle timings. A bus cycle is normally terminated when the addressed memory or I/O responds to the processor with $\overline{\text{DTACK}}$. The processor introduces wait states until either $\overline{\text{DTACK}}$ or $\overline{\text{BERR}}$ occurs. The occurrence of $\overline{\text{BERR}}$ signifies a bus error. The processor responds by going into exception processing.

On considering the important system control interface schemes relating to $\overline{\text{RESET}}$, $\overline{\text{HALT}}$, and $\overline{\text{BERR}}$, we saw that simultaneous activation of both $\overline{\text{RESET}}$ and $\overline{\text{HALT}}$ results in a system reset condition. Activation of $\overline{\text{HALT}}$ alone results in a processor halt condition. Simultaneous activation of both $\overline{\text{HALT}}$ and $\overline{\text{BERR}}$ results in a bus-cycle rerun condition. Activation of $\overline{\text{BERR}}$ alone results in a bus error condition. The processor uses the reset pin as an output when executing the RESET instruction. Similarly, the processor uses the halt pin as an output when there is a double bus fault condition.

We ended the chapter with a discussion of the VERSA and VME busing schemes and interfaces. The VERSA scheme is more flexible, while the VME scheme is more efficient and universal. Other industry standard buses, such as the Multibus-11 from Intel and the NU bus from Texas Instruments, are similar to the VME and VERSA buses.

PROBLEMS

6.1 In byte-organized memory, can the $\overline{\text{LDS}}$ and $\overline{\text{UDS}}$ signals be gated together to form a single chip select? Why or why not?

6.2 Specify the conditions of the address and the data buses in the following circumstances:

(a) $\overline{\text{AS}}$ is inactive, R/$\overline{\text{W}}$ is low;

(b) $\overline{\text{AS}}$ and $\overline{\text{UDS}}$ are active, $\overline{\text{LDS}}$ is inactive, R/$\overline{\text{W}}$ is high;

(c) an external $\overline{\text{HALT}}$ signal is received by the processor.

6.3 What are the primary differences between the RAM, ROM, and backup memory, such as a disk?

(a) Can the EPROM be used where the system stack is to be located? Why or why not?

(b) Can the normal RAM be used where the reset vectors are located? Why or why not?

(c) Is it possible to use battery backup RAM in place of a disk-type backup memory? Why or why not?

6.4 In the memory system of Figure 6.6, the $\overline{\text{LDS}}$ and $\overline{\text{UDS}}$ signals have been interchanged. Specify the effect on

(a) the memory read operation of the byte, word, and long-word operands;

(b) the memory write operation.

6.5 Under the conditions given in Problem 6.4, specify how the following operands will be written into the memory:

(a) MOVE.L   D0,$1000   D0 = $3456789A

(b) MOVEP.L D0,$2000   D0 = $A9876543

6.6 Refer to the memory system with the timing waveform given in Figures 6.7 and 6.8.

(a) What are the read and write access times if the processor clock CX1 is 4 MHz?

(b) Repeat (a) with 8- and 12-MHz CX1 frequencies.

(c) Repeat (a) and (b) on the condition of four wait states.

6.7 The 68000 processor performs read-modify/write (RMW) operations while executing instructions such as TAS. Draw the RMW waveform while the processor is performing TAS at

(a) location $7000;

(b) location $700A.

6.8 For the memory system of Figure 6.11, what are the chip select (CS) ranges for

(a) the $\overline{\text{E0}}$ through $\overline{\text{E15}}$ outputs from the first decoder;

(b) the $\overline{\text{Y0}}$ through $\overline{\text{Y15}}$ outputs from the second decoder.

6.9 Design the hardware to generate chip selects to access 4K blocks of memory words as shown.

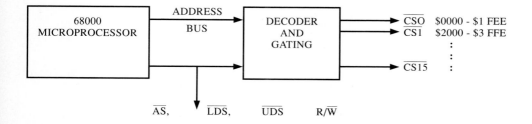

6.10 In a memory system interface to the 68000 microprocessor, the slow memory has a response time of 250 nanoseconds and the fast memory has a response time of 62.5

nanoseconds. The processor CX1 clock is 8 MHz. A 16-MHz CX0 clock signal is also available.

Design a memory controller interface to generate $\overline{\text{DTACK}}$ to the processor.

6.11 Repeat Problem 6.10 to interface memory and I/O with the following requirements:

(a) a response time of 750 nanoseconds;
(b) a response time of 15 microseconds.

6.12 Obtaining the information from data sheets, design the system shown in Figure 6.11 with real parts.

6.13 Redesign the memory system of Problem 6.12 with high-density parts, such as the 64K-by-8 and 128K-by-8 devices. The RAM should occupy the memory map starting at location $2000.

6.14 Using the 64K-by-8 RAM and EPROM/ROM devices, design a memory system for the 68000 microprocessor with the following memory map (word organized):

$000000 to $007FFE	RAM or EPROM
$008000 to $00BFFE	RAM
$00C000 to $00FFFE	EPROM/ROM
$010000 to $01FFFE	I/O space

6.15 It is necessary to protect the supervisor memory from being accessed in the user mode. Describe a scheme to accomplish this while generating chip select logic. (*Hint:* The function code signal FC2 has to be used in the logic.)

6.16 Specify the relative advantages and disadvantages of using the address, data, and control buffering of Figure 6.12.

6.17 Write software to test the memory in the $020000-to-$021FFE range.

6.18 Design a hardware or software method to test the I/O interface connected to the 68000 microprocessor, occupying a range between $010000 and $01FFFE. (*Hint:* In the 68000, I/O and memory look similar.)

6.19 Draw the waveforms of the CX0 through CX7 signals in Figure 6.14, given that the system clock is 32 MHz.

6.20 Specify all possible valid conditions of the combination of $\overline{\text{RESET}}$, $\overline{\text{HALT}}$, and $\overline{\text{BERR}}$ inputs to the processor. (*Note:* some combinations may be invalid.)

6.21 What would happen if the $\overline{\text{RESET}}$ input stayed active low all the time? Is there a possible remedy?

6.22 State two distinct conditions in which the 68000 uses its

(a) $\overline{\text{RESET}}$ output;
(b) $\overline{\text{HALT}}$ output.

6.23 For an 8-MHz 68000 system, what is the minimum time required for the power-up RESET condition? Why? Describe what happens in the following situations:

(a) the $\overline{\text{RESET}}$ input stays active for only half the time;
(b) the $\overline{\text{RESET}}$ stays active for twice the time.

6.24 With regard to the VERSA and VME busing schemes,

(a) which occupies more physical space?
(b) which is more flexible?

(c) which is more cost effective?

(d) which is more efficient?

6.25 Is it possible to interface VERSA modules onto the VME bus? If so, indicate how this can be accomplished.

6.26 Show how the interrupt levels can be increased on

(a) the VERSA busing scheme;

(b) the VME busing scheme.

6.27 Obtaining the information from appropriate data sheets, show how a system can be expanded using VERSA modules.

6.28 Repeat Problem 6.27 using VME modules.

ENDNOTES

1. Motorola, Inc. *MC68000 Data Book*. Phoenix, AZ: Motorola Technical Operations, 1983.

2. Motorola, Inc. *MC68008 Data Book*. Phoenix, AZ: Motorola Technical Operations, 1983.

3. Motorola, Inc. *MTT8: 68000 Course Notes*. Phoenix, AZ: Motorola Technical Operations, 1987.

4. Stranes, T. "Design Philosophy Behind the M68000." *Byte* (Apr., May, Jun. 1983).

5. Miller, M.A. "68000 Program Applications and Bus Cycle Timing." Chap. 4 in *The 68000 Microprocessor: Architecture, Programming, and Applications*. Columbus, OH: Merrill, 1988.

6. Harman, T., and Lawson, B. *The Motorola MC68000 Microprocessor*. Englewood Cliffs, NJ: Prentice-Hall, 1985.

7. Motorola, Inc. *MC68000 16/32-Bit Microprocessor Programmer's Reference Manual, Fifth Edition*. Englewood Cliffs, NJ: Prentice-Hall, 1987.

8. Texas Instruments, Inc. *TTL and CMOS Data Books*. Houston, TX: Texas Instruments, 1988.

9. Toshiba America, Inc. *MOS Memory Products Data Book*. Tustin, CA: Toshiba, 1988.

10. Balph, T., and Black, J. "Applications of VERSAbus Modules." *Electronic Design* (Mar. 1982).

11. Motorola, Inc. *The VME Bus Specification*. Temple, AZ: Motorola Microsystems, 1987.

CHAPTER

7

The 68000 Parallel
Interface and Applications

Objectives

In this chapter we will study:

> Architecture of the 6821 PIA and 68230 PI/T devices
>
> Interfacing the PIA and PI/T
>
> I/O applications using the 68000/6821 PIA
>
> Data entry and display applications
>
> Electromechanical applications

7.0 INTRODUCTION

Any microprocessor communicates with the external I/O (input/output) through either a parallel or a serial interface. In this chapter, we will concentrate on the parallel interface. There are several devices that support either a synchronous or asynchronous parallel interface with the 68000 family of processors. The most widely used are the **6821 PIA** for the synchronous interface and the **68230 PI/T** for the asynchronous interface.[1,2]

Study of the material in this chapter will provide the foundation for using the parallel interface in practical applications.

7.1   SYNCHRONOUS PARALLEL INTERFACE WITH THE 68000

The earlier 6800 family of peripheral devices are of the synchronous type. These devices can be interfaced easily with the 68000 family of processors by means of the synchronous bus ($\overline{E}$, $\overline{VMA}$, $\overline{VPA}$ signals).[3]

6821 PIA (Peripheral Interface Adapter) Architecture

The 6821 PIA is one of the most widely used 8-bit parallel interface devices. It is contained in a 40-pin NMOS DIP device. The structure of the PIA is indicated in Figure 7.1. It consists of two 8-bit parallel ports A and B and associated control signals CA1, CA2, CB1, and CB2. Each port consists of three internal registers:

1. ORA and ORB (output registers A and B);

2. DDRA and DDRB (data direction registers A and B); and

3. CRA and CRB (control registers A and B).

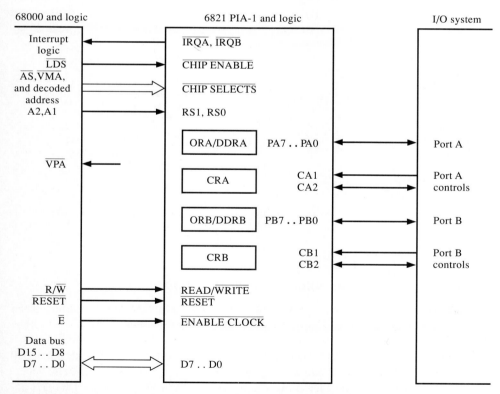

FIGURE 7.1   The 6821 PIA architecture and interface to the 68000.

The DDR and OR in each port occupy the same address. The control register determines the individual access.

Output and Data Direction Registers   The output registers (ORA and ORB) interface with the external I/O devices and systems and are capable of driving a unit TTL load. Each bit of these ports is individually programmable to be either an input or an output. The data direction registers (DDRA and DDRB) determine the direction of the output register bit. If there is a 0 in the DDR bit position, the corresponding bit is an input. If there is a 1 in the DDR bit position, the corresponding bit is an output. For example, if $07 (b7 b6 b5 b4 b3 b2 b1 b0 = 00000111) is written into DDRA, then PA7 through PA3 are configured as inputs and PA2 through PA0 are configured as outputs.

Control Registers CRA and CRB   Control register CRA determines the nature of the control lines CA1 and CA2. Figure 7.2 illustrates the typical structure of CRA. Depending upon the application, an appropriate control word can be written into CRA to configure CA1, CA2, and IRQA (interrupt request port A). The CRB format is similar to that of CRA; it configures CB1, CB2, and IRQB (interrupt request port B) lines. Bit 2 is very important in CRA and CRB. When it is 0, the data direction register is selected. When it is 1, the output register is selected.

FIGURE 7.2   PIA control register for port A (CRA).

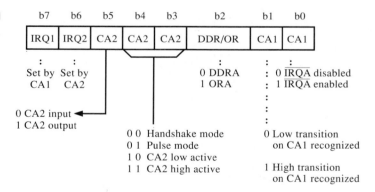

6821 PIA Synchronous Interface with the 68000

The PIA is an 8-bit device and occupies either the lower 8 bits or the upper 8 bits of the data bus. To the processor, it resembles four memory locations (ORA/DDRA, CRA, ORB/DDRB, and CRB).[4]

Figure 7.1 illustrates the synchronous interface of the 6821 PIA-1 with the 68000 microprocessor. The decoded address bus, along with the $\overline{AS}$ and $\overline{VMA}$ signals, generates the chip selects for the PIA. PIA is connected to the lower data bus D0–D7; accordingly, $\overline{LDS}$ is used to enable PIA-1. The A2 and A1 address lines drive the PIA register select inputs RS1 and RS0 and select either ORA/DDRA, CRA, ORB/DDRB, or CRB (for 00, 01, 10, 11 conditions on RS1 and RS0).

Interface logic senses the chip select signals and generates the $\overline{\text{VPA}}$ signal to the processor. $\overline{\text{VPA}}$ signifies a successful bus cycle and data transfer. The E clock initiates the data transfers and concludes the bus cycle.

Interface with any synchronous peripherals is similar to the PIA interface.

I/O Interface and Design Applications

One of the most important requirements of a digital system is the capacity for generating timing waveforms to accomplish various tasks at different intervals. With a microcomputer, such waveforms can be easily generated with great flexibility.

The following example problem deals with the initialization of the PIA in waveform generation.

Example 7.1   6821 PIA-1 I/O application: waveform generation.

In an industrial application, it is necessary to generate an 8-bit binary word, the value of which changes as $01, $02, $04, . . ., $08, and another 8-bit binary word, the value of which changes in increments of three ($00, $03, $06, . . .). Using the 68000/PIA-1 interface of Figure 7.1, develop:

1. the necessary hardware
2. the software to accomplish this task. The base address of PIA is at $020021.

Solution

1. **Hardware:** The hardware of Figure 7.1 is self-contained. To obtain two 8-bit binary words, both ports must be configured as outputs. Output drivers may be used to increase drive capability.

2. **Software:** Figure 7.3 indicates the 68000 operating assembly listings to accomplish the given task. Between lines 5 and 10, all the PIA registers are declared. Lines 11 and 12 initialize the D0 and D1 registers to $00000000 and $01. These registers will be used in the rest of the software.

   Between lines 15 and 18, all the pins of port A and port B are configured as outputs by writing $FF into the corresponding data direction registers (DDRs). At lines 21 and 22, $04 is written into CRA and CRB, which changes b2 in these control registers to 1 and provides access to the output registers instead of the DDRs.

   At lines 23 and 24, the byte contents of D0 and D1 are output to ports A and B, respectively. At line 25, the delay routine is called. At lines 26 and 27, D0 is incremented by $03 and D1 is rotated one position left. These operations provide the next binary words to be output to ports A and B. At line 28, the BRA instruction loops the program back to line 23.

   The delay routine between lines 31 and 34 produces a software delay, the value of which depends on the initial contents of D3. This delay is the amount of time during which the output port values remain the same.

```
LINE   ADDR

         1                                    ;PIA ctr 2/14/89
         2                                    ;initialize PIA
         3                                        OPT     A
         4                                        ORG     $1200
         5  00020021                DDRA EQU    $020021
         6  00020021                ORA  EQU    $020021
         7  00020023                CRA  EQU    $020023
         8  00020025                DDRB EQU    $020025
         9  00020025                ORB  EQU    $020025
        10  00020027                CRB  EQU    $020027
        11  00001200  4280          START CLR.L D0
        12  00001202  1238 0001            MOVE.B 01,D1
        13                                  ;get access to DDRA & DDRB
        14                                  ;set up Ports A & B as outputs
        15  00001206  13FC 0000 0002        MOVE.B  #$00,CRA
                      0023
        16  0000120E  13FC 0000 0002        MOVE.B  #$00,CRB
                      0027
        17  00001216  13FC 00FF 0002        MOVE.B  #$FF,DDRA
                      0021
        18  0000121E  13FC 00FF 0002        MOVE.B  #$FF,DDRB
                      0025
        19                                  ;get access to ORA & ORB
        20                                  ;and output data
        21  00001226  13FC 0004 0002        MOVE.B  #$04,CRA
                      0023
        22  0000122E  13FC 0004 0002        MOVE.B  #$04,CRB
                      0027
        23  00001236  13C0 0002 0021 LOOP MOVE.B  D0,ORA
        24  0000123C  13C1 0002 0025      MOVE.B  D1,ORB
        25  00001242  6108                BSR.S   DELAY
        26  00001244  5640                ADDQ.W  #$03,D0
        27  00001246  E319                ROL.B   #$01,D1
        28  00001248  60EC                BRA.S   LOOP
        29  0000124A  4E71                NOP
        30                                ;delay subroutine
        31  0000124C  363C 0100     DELAY MOVE.W #$0100,D3
        32  00001250  5343          AGAIN SUBQ.W #$01,D3
        33  00001252  66FC                BNE.S   AGAIN
        34  00001254  4E75                RTS
        34  00001256                      END

    ASSEMBLER ERRORS =      0
                                    SYMBOL TABLE

  AGAIN  00001250   CRA  00020023   CRB  00020027  DDRA  00020021
  DDRB   00020025   DELAY 0000124C  LOOP 00001236  ORA   00020021
  ORB    00020025   START 00001200
```

FIGURE 7.3 The 68000 listings for timing-signal generation with PIA.

It is possible to interface another PIA to the upper part of data bus. The control registers can be appropriately configured in a manner similar to that described in Example 7.1 to effectively use the control signals. We will deal with interfacing the second PIA in another example which follows.

Example 7.2   Interfacing a second PIA.

In the control system application described in Example 7.1, it is now necessary to interface a second PIA, PIA-2, onto the upper part of the data bus.

1. Describe how this can be accomplished.
2. What is the memory map of PIA-2 given the conditions described?
3. It is required that a low-to-high transition be recognized on CA1 to enable the interrupt and generate a positive pulse on CA2 for PIA-2. Explain the sequence of events that will accomplish this task.

Solution

1. **PIA-2 interface:** The PIA-2 interface is similar to the PIA-1 interface of Figure 7.1, with the following modifications:

PIA-2	**68000**
Connect D0–D7 data lines	to D8–D15 data lines
$\overline{\text{CHIP ENABLE}}$	to $\overline{\text{UDS}}$
Other control, address, and chip selects	same as PIA-1

2. **Memory map of PIA-2:** PIA-2 occupies the upper (or even) byte locations compared to PIA-1. Thus, the base address of PIA-2 is at $020020.

   The memory map of PIA-2 is as follows:

   ORA/DDRA at $020020

   CRA   at $020022

   ORB/DDRB at $020024

   CRB   at $020026

3. **Control word in CRA of PIA-2 for CA1 and CA2 control:** Using the CRA format of Figure 7.2, it can be seen that writing a control word

$$\text{b7 b6 b5 b4 b3 b2 b1 b0}$$
$$0 \quad 0 \quad 1 \quad 0 \quad 1 \quad 1 \quad 1 \quad 1 \quad = \$2F$$

into CRA of PIA-2 defines CA2 as a pulse output, recognizes the CA1 low-to-high transition from the I/O, and activates the $\overline{\text{IRQA}}$ interrupt line to the 68000.

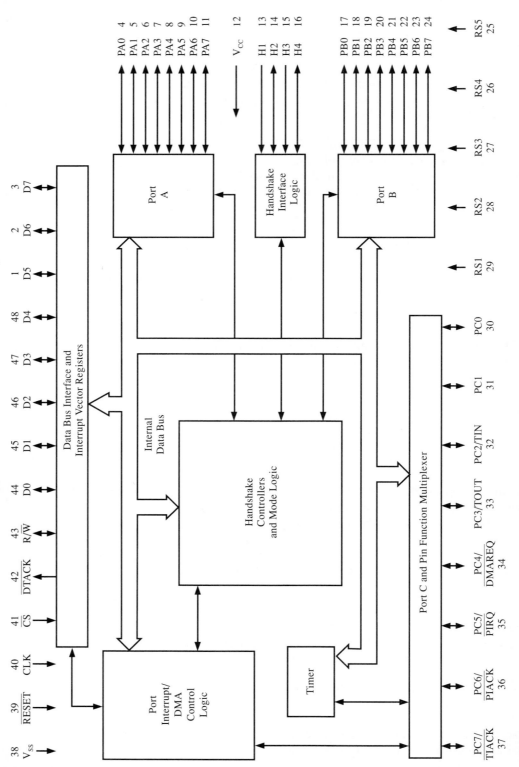

FIGURE 7.4 The 68230 PI/T pin diagram and architecture. (Courtesy of Motorola, Inc.)

Consider port A of PIA-2 to be configured as input. In response to the CA1 transition and corresponding interrupt, the 68000 will access and read port A of PIA-2. Whenever the I/O port is accessed, a CA2 positive pulse, equal to the duration of one E clock, will be generated. The I/O device recognizes this pulse on CA2 and moves to the next I/O operation.[5]

The I/O device generates a low-to-high transition on CA1 when the next I/O data are available on port A. I/O operation becomes repetitive. The pulse-mode operation is equally valid when the port is configured as an output and the processor is writing data to the I/O device.

7.2 THE 68230 PARALLEL INTERFACE AND TIMER (PI/T)

Figure 7.4 illustrates the pin configuration and general architecture of the 68230 PI/T device. It is contained in a 48-pin DIP package and is fabricated with HMOS technology. The 68230 PI/T consists of two bidirectional 8-bit ports A and B and a multipurpose 8-bit port C. The bits are individually programmable to be either inputs or outputs for all three ports. In addition, there is a 4-bit H port for handshake operations. The H1 and H2 lines are associated with port A. The H3 and H4 lines are associated with port B. Port C can be configured to handle the interrupts and the DMA functions.

Registers and I/O Ports

The 68230 PI/T consists of 23 active 8-bit registers as shown in Figure 7.5. Information written into the appropriate registers by the 68000 processor controls the 68230 operation. Some of the PI/T registers are read-only and contain the status information of the I/O operations. The 68000 processor reads this information and performs the appropriate I/O functions as defined by the software. The 68230 PI/T device is very complex; however, we will present some of the basic features. For further detail, data sheets should be consulted.

Port Control Registers (PGCR, PACR, PBCR) The modes of operation of ports A and B and port H (handshake) are controlled by the control words written into the port general control register (PGCR) and the port A/B control registers (PACR/PBCR). These control registers are illustrated in Figure 7.6.

Data Direction Registers (PADDR, PBDDR, PCDDR) The direction of each bit in the port is determined by the contents of these registers. If there is a 1 in a bit position, the corresponding port bit is an output; if there is a 0, the corresponding port bit is an input. For example,

$$1\ 1\ 1\ 1\ 0\ 0\ 0\ 0$$

written into PADDR configures the lower four bits of port A as inputs and the upper four bits as outputs.

Number*	Symbol	Name	Function
1	PGCR	Port General Control Reg.	Controls port modes
3	PSRR	Port Service Request Reg.	Controls service routines
5	PADDR	Port A Data Direction Reg.	Controls direction PA
7	PBDDR	Port B Data Direction Reg.	Controls direction PB
9	PCDDR	Port C Data Direction Reg.	Controls direction PC
B	PIVR	Port Interrupt Vector Reg.	Contains interrupt vector
D	PACR	Port A Control Reg.	Controls H1/H2
F	PBCR	Port B Control Reg.	Controls H3/H4
11	PADR	Port A Data Reg.	Contains I/O data PA
13	PBDR	Port B Data Reg.	Contains I/O data PB
15	PAAR	Port A Alternate Data Reg.	Contains instant PA
17	PBAR	Port B Alternate Data Reg.	Contains instant PB
19	PCDR	Port C Data Reg.	Contains I/O data PC
1B	PSR	Port Status Reg.	Contains status H1–H4
1D	—	—	Not used
1F	—	—	Not used
21	TCR	Timer Control Reg.	Controls timer modes
23	TIVR	Timer Interrupt Vector Reg.	Contains timer vector
25			
27	CPRH	Counter Preload Reg. High ⎤	
29	CPRM	Counter Preload Reg. Med. ⎬	Contains 24-bit preloaded number
2B	CPRL	Counter Preload Reg. Low ⎦	
2D	—		
2F	CNTRH	Counter Reg. High ⎤	
31	CNTRM	Counter Reg. Med. ⎬	Acts as a 24-bit counter
33	CNTRL	Counter Reg. Low ⎦	
35	TSR	Timer Status Reg.	Contains status of counters
37	—	—	Not used
39	—	—	Not used
3B	—	—	Not used
3D	—	—	Not used
3F	—	—	Not used

*Relative address increment with respect to the base address.

FIGURE 7.5   The 68230 PI/T register structure.

Data Registers (PADR, PBDR, PCDR)   These registers contain the latched I/O data. Input data is latched during a read operation and output data is latched during a write operation. When the alternate data registers are used, however, I/O data is not latched, and is instantaneous.

Other Registers (PSRR, PSR, PIVR, TIVR)   The PSRR controls the service requests of the interrupts, DMA, and the signal lines H1–H4. The PSR contains the status

FIGURE 7.6 (a) The PGCR control register and (b) the PACR control format.

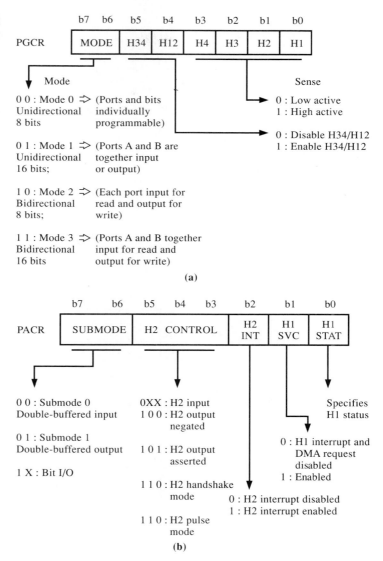

(a)

(b)

of the handshake port H. The PIVR and TIVR contain the 8-bit address for the interrupt vectors to be used by the processor. The other counter/timer-related registers are for timing applications.

Interfacing the 68230 PI/T

Figure 7.7 diagrams the required connections between the 68000 and the 68230. The 68230 PI/T is driven by the 68000 processor clock. The decoded address bus, gated

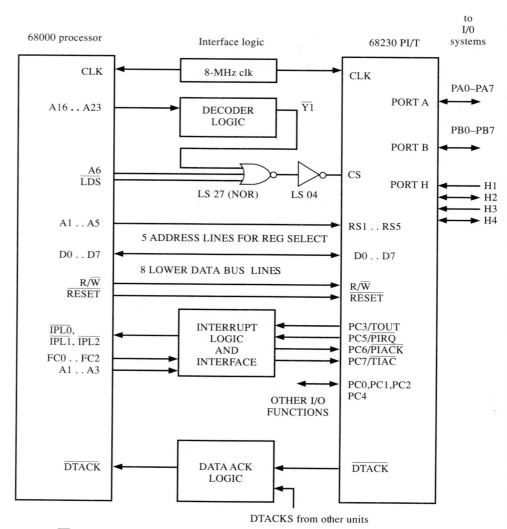

FIGURE 7.7 Interfacing the 68230 PI/T and the 68000.

with $\overline{\text{LDS}}$, generates the chip select $\overline{\text{CS}}$ signal to the 68230. The lower address lines A5–A1 drive the register select input lines RS5–RS1 to select one of the 23 active registers from the register bank.[6]

The PI/T data lines D7–D0 are connected to the lower byte of the data bus D7–D0, since the 68230 is selected via $\overline{\text{LDS}}$. The R/$\overline{\text{W}}$ and $\overline{\text{RESET}}$ signals from the processor directly drive the corresponding inputs of the PI/T. The multifunction port signals PC3, PC5, PC6, and PC7 are interfaced with the 68000 through the interrupt control logic as indicated. PC0, PC1, PC2, and PC4 are available for any other I/O interface. Ports A, B, and H are used for the I/O interface.

We will now review the concepts introduced thus far with the help of an example problem.

Example 7.3   The 68230 PI/T interface.
Consider the interface diagrammed in Figure 7.7.

1. What is the address range for the 68230?
2. Where are PGCR, PADDR, and PBDDR located?
3. Suppose it is necessary to program port A as an 8-bit output port and port B as output on lines PB7–PB2 and input on lines PB1 and PB0. Configure the appropriate registers.

Solution

1. **Address range:** The $\overline{Y1}$ output of the address decoder network is active low for the address range $010000 to $01FFFF. (Refer to Section 6.3 of Chapter 6.) It is further gated with the A6 and $\overline{LDS}$ signals. The $\overline{CS}$ signal is generated when $\overline{Y1}$, $\overline{LDS}$, and A6 are all at a low level. There is a redundant memory map for the 68230 on the odd address boundary as shown:

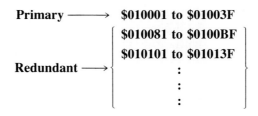

Primary ⟶ $010001 to $01003F

Redundant ⟶ { $010081 to $0100BF
$010101 to $01013F
⋮
⋮
⋮ }

2. **Locations of PGCR, PADDR, and PBDDR:** Following the given address range and Figure 7.5, all the registers are sequentially mapped at odd byte locations as shown (primary):

PGCR located at 010001

PADDR located at 010005

PBDDR located at 010007

Redundant locations are also possible.

3. **A and B ports (refer to Figure 7.6):** Both ports are used in the unidirectional 8-bit mode (mode 0). As such, PGCR, PADDR, and PBDDR should be initialized as indicated in the diagram that follows. The H port is not used, and PACR and PBCR need not be initialized.

		b7	b6	b5	b4	b3	b2	b1	b0
Mode 0	PGCR	0	0	0	0	0	0	0	0
Port A output	PADDR	1	1	1	1	1	1	1	1
Port B: PB0 and PB1 inputs; others output	PBDDR	1	1	1	1	1	1	0	0

In the preceding example, because of the selection of the 68230 due to the $\overline{\text{LDS}}$ signal, the registers are mapped at consecutive odd byte locations. By changing $\overline{\text{LDS}}$ to $\overline{\text{UDS}}$ and connecting the data bus of the 68230 to the upper byte of the 68000 data bus (D8−D15), the 68230 can be easily mapped at consecutive even bytes. To make full use of the 16-bit data bus of the 68000, one PI/T device is interfaced with the lower byte and a second PI/T is interfaced with the upper byte of the data bus.

7.3   DATA ENTRY AND DISPLAY SYSTEMS

In any computer system, data entry and data display are of utmost importance. A simple data entry mechanism may be a switch or a keyboard. A complex data entry mechanism may involve sophisticated sensors. In either case, the processor reads an input port and interprets and validates the entered data.

Similarly, a simple data display may be a light-emitting diode (LED). Complex data display may involve sophisticated graphics on a terminal. In either case, the processor sends the processed data to an output display port.

The Keyboard and Hex Display Interface

As illustrated in Figure 7.8, the keyboard/display interface to the 68000 through the 68230 PI/T combines data entry and display concepts. The keyboard encoder (74C922) activates one of the X columns and scans the Y rows to detect if any key has been pressed. When a key is pressed, the 74C922 encodes the X and Y data to corresponding binary data on its ABCD outputs. In addition, a data-valid signal is generated on its DV output whenever a valid key is pressed.

System Hardware and Software Considerations

Hardware   The encoded ABCD signals and the DV signal from the encoder are interfaced to port B. Two 7-segment display devices are interfaced to port A. These devices (7300 series) have internal decoders and drivers and display the pressed key in hex format. For this application, port A is configured as an output port and port B as an input port.

FIGURE 7.8   Keyboard/display interface with the 68000 through the 68230 PI/T. (Courtesy of Aldo Aden and Ignacio Martinez: FIU.)

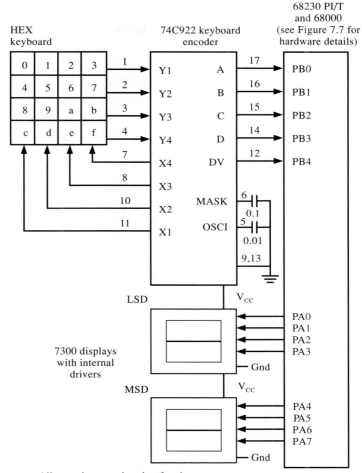

All capacitors are in microfarads.

Software   Figure 7.9 is the system flowchart. The assembled listings for the keyboard/display interface are indicated in Figure 7.10.

Between lines 15 and 21 in the listings, the initializations are accomplished. The 68230 is configured to operate in mode 0 by loading 00 into the PGCR. Port B is configured as input and port A as output by loading 00 and FF into the respective data direction registers PBDDR and PADDR.

The main routine between lines 23 and 36 calls the **keycode subroutine** to obtain valid key code. It then sends the valid key code to port A to be displayed. The main routine also calls the **check subroutine** to check whether any new key has been pressed. This is necessary to ensure that the same key is not being recognized all the time. When a second key is pressed, the main routine shifts the old key code to the MSD position,

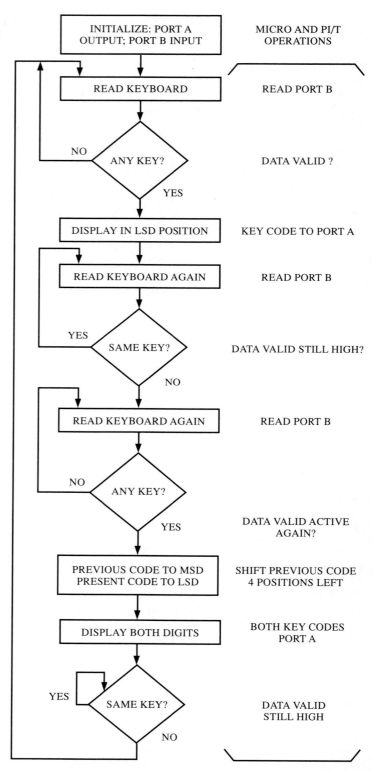

FIGURE 7.9 Flowchart for the keyboard/display I/O interface to the 68230 PIT/68000 system.

```
LINE   ADDR
1; KEYBOARD/DISPLAY INTERFACE
2; ADEN/MARTINEZ/SUBBARAO 7/86   F.I.U
3; READS AND DISPLAYS VALID KEY CODE
4;
5                          LLEN     108
6                          OPT      A
7                          ORG      $1000
8; 68230 PI/T REGISTERS DEFINED
9  00010001  PGCR      EQU      $010001 ;GENERAL CONTROL REG
10 00010005  PADDR     EQU      $010005 ;PA DATA DIR REG
11 00010007  PBDDR     EQU      $010007 ;PB DATA DIR REG
12 00010011  PADR      EQU      $010011 ;PA DATA REG
13 00010013  PBDR      EQU      $010013 ;PB DATA REG
14 00002000  STKP      EQU      $002000 ;STACK POINTER VALUE
15; INITIALIZE REGISTERS AND PI/T PORTS
16 00001000 13FC 0000 0001 INIT MOVE.B   #$00,PGCR;MODE0
                 0001
17 00001008 13FC 0000 0001      MOVE.B   #$00,PBDDR; PB INPUT
                 0007
18 00001010 13FC 00FF 0001      MOVE.B   #$FF,PADDR;PA OUTPUT
                 0005
19 00001018 267C 0001 0011      MOVEA.L  #PADR,A3;A3 REFERS PADR
20 0000101E 287C 0001 0013      MOVEA.L  #PBDR,A4;A4 REFERS PBDR
21 00001024 2E7C 0000 2000      MOVEA.L  #STKP,A7;STACK DEFINED
22;KEY PROCESSING AND DISPLAY MAIN ROUTINE:
23 0000102A 4280         MAIN   CLR.L    D0;CLEAR D0
24 0000102C 4281                CLR.L    D1       ;CLEAR D1
25 0000102E 6116         AGAIN  BSR.S    KEY CODE
26 00001030 1680                MOVE.B   D0,(A3) ; TO DISPLAY
27 00001032 4E71                NOP
28 00001034 1200                MOVE.B   D0,D1    ;SAVE OLD KEY
29 00001036 6120                BSR.S    CHECK    ;SAME KEY CHECK
30 00001038 610C                BSR.S    KEYCODE  ;GET KEY CODE
31 0000103A E909                LSL.B    #4,D1    ;OLD KEY TO MSD
32 0000103C D001                ADD.B    D1,D0    ;TWO KEY CODE
33 0000103E 1680                MOVE.B   D0,(A3)  ;DOUBLE DISPLAY
34 00001040 6116                BSR.S    CHECK    ;SAME KEY CHECK
35 00001042 60E6                BRA.S    MAIN     ;LOOP BACK
36 00001044 4E71                NOP
37;KEY CODE ROUTINE:READS PB: OBTAINS KEY CODE AS LOW NIBBLE IN D0
38 00001046 1014         KEYCODE MOVE.B  (A4),D0;READ KEY
39 00001048 0800 0004            BTST    #4,D0   ;DATA VALID ?
40 0000104C 67F8                 BEQ.S   KEY CODE
41 0000104E 0200 000F            AND.B   #$0F,D0
42 00001056 4E75                 RTS
43;CHECK ROUTINE:CHECKS IF SAME KEY AND LOOPS UNTIL NEW KEY
44 00001058 1014         CHECK MOVE.B    (A4),D0;READ KEY
45 0000105A 0800 0004            BTST    #4,D0
46 0000105E 66F8                 BNE CHECK
47 00001064 4E75                 RTS
48 00001066                      END
```

FIGURE 7.10   The 68230/68000-based keyboard/display system listings.

puts the new code in the LSD position, and displays it (lines 31 to 33). The program then goes back into the main loop.

The **keycode routine** between lines 38 and 42 reads port B and loops until the data-valid signal is high (signifying that a key has been activated). It then puts the valid key code in the lower nibble of the D0 register and returns to the main routine.

The **check routine** between lines 44 and 47 checks whether the same data-valid signal is present, signifying that the same key has been kept pressed.

The following example problem provides a review of the keyboard/display interface with the 68000/68230 system.

Example 7.4   Keyboard/display interface with 68000/68230 system.
Consider the hardware and software of Figures 7.8, 7.9, and 7.10.

1. What happens when the same key is kept pressed continuously?

2. The keys are pressed in sequence as follows:

1 2 3 4 5

Indicate how the keys are displayed.

Solution

1. **Same key:** It will be displayed in the LSD position. The program goes into an indefinite check loop and will not recognize any other key. This concept is known as **key lockout.**

2. **Key display:** After two key entries, the MSD is cleared to the 0 condition. The display is as follows:

	MSD	LSD
after 1st key	0	1
after 2nd key	1	2
after 3rd key	0	3
after 4th key	3	4
after 5th key	0	5

The preceding example sheds light on the initialization of the appropriate registers of the 68230 PI/T. In I/O applications, it is usually necessary to analyze the existing software and predict the results, as we have done in the second part of the problem.

The keyboard and segment displays may be replaced by other data entry and display mechanisms. The concepts we have discussed remain valid. Modifications, such as software switch debouncing, can be accomplished by checking the key code for sameness with a delay in between.

Other Forms of Keyboard and Interface Schemes

The hex keyboard we have examined is of limited scope. The computer and other keyboards have up to 128 key positions. A 128-position keyboard can be wired as a 16-by-8 XY matrix; however, the key positions can be conveniently located. Figure 7.11 shows a conceptual 128-position keyboard interface with the 68000 through the 68230 PI/T port B.

FIGURE 7.11 Conceptual 128-key position keyboard interface to the 68000.

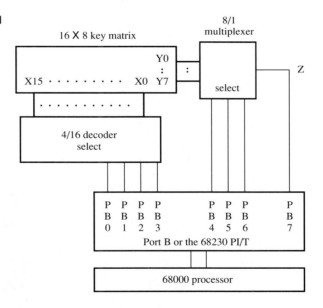

The processor activates one line of the 16-column input lines (X0–X15) through a 4/16 decoder connected to lines PB0 through PB3 of the PI/T. It then senses one line of the eight-row output lines (Y0–Y7) through an 8/1 multiplexer driven by the lines PB4 through PB6 of the PI/T. The Z output of the multiplexer is connected to the PB7 line. When a key is pressed, the Z output goes active for a unique combination of the digital word on lines PB0 through PB6. This essentially generates a 7-bit binary code for the 128-position keyboard.

In the case described, only port B of the PI/T is used. PB0 through PB6 must be configured as outputs and PB7 as input. The software generates a sequential 7-bit word on lines PB6 through PB0. When a key is pressed, the PB7 input is activated. The processor senses this condition and matches the 7-bit code on lines PB6 through PB0 to the pressed key. Additional software can process this binary information to generate other key codes, such as ASCII. The concept can be extended to any size key matrix.

In order to display one of the 128 keys, more sophisticated display units, such as the terminal or alphanumeric type, are required.

7.4   ELECTROMECHANICAL APPLICATIONS

Many industrial applications depend on position control, which can be accomplished with the help of **stepper motors.** Stepper motors can be controlled by microprocessors for flexibility and accuracy. In this section, we will describe a 68000-driven electromechanical position control system using the stepper motor.[7,8]

FIGURE 7.12   Typical stepper motors. (Courtesy of Airpax, Inc.)

Rotational and Linear Stepper Motors

In Figure 7.12, we see some typical stepper motors. They are available in the range of 0.9 to 7.5 degrees per step. Each stepper motor has four windings: W0, W1, W2, and W3. When the code on these windings changes in a given sequence, the stepper rotates one step either clockwise or counterclockwise, as indicated in Figure 7.13. **Linear steppers** have an internal gear mechanism to convert rotational motion into linear motion.

	W Code (hex)	W3	W2	W1	W0	Function
Counter-clockwise ↑	0 F	1	1	1	1	Standby
	0 3	0	0	1	1	First CW code
	0 9	1	0	0	1	Move one step
	0 C	1	1	0	0	Move one step
	0 6	0	1	1	0	First CCW code
Clockwise ↓	0 F	1	1	1	1	Standby

0: Activates the stepper coil.
1: Deactivates the stepper coil.

FIGURE 7.13 W code word for stepper-motor windings.

Stepper-Motor Interface Considerations

Hardware Figure 7.14 shows interface of a 7.5-degree resolution stepper motor with the 68000/68230 PI/T system. The four windings (W0–W3) are connected to port A of the 68230 PI/T through optoisolators and high-current drivers, as shown. **Optoisolators** prevent the inductive transients from the motor windings from feeding back into the microcomputer module. The sensor inputs on port B provide an S control word for the stepper movement. The format of the S control word is as follows:

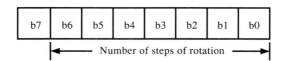

| b7 | b6 | b5 | b4 | b3 | b2 | b1 | b0 |

←———— Number of steps of rotation ————→

b7 = 0 Clockwise
    1 Counterclockwise

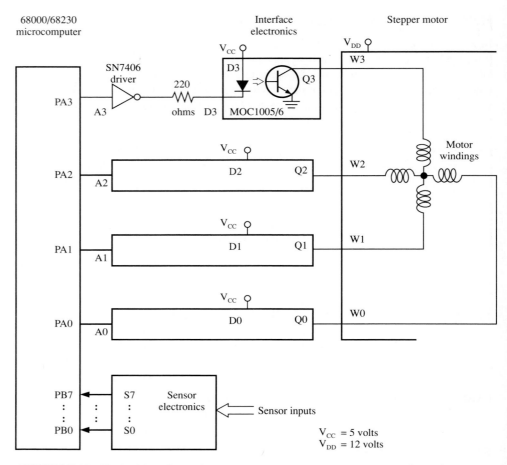

FIGURE 7.14 Typical interface of the stepper motor and the 68000/68230 PI/T system. (Courtesy of J. Wongchang, J. Launez, and F. Chorlett, FIU).

If the stepper code does not change, the stepper will not rotate and stays in the same position. When the code is changed, there is some delay before the stepper responds. A delay of 10 to 100 milliseconds is typical.

Software The operating listings for the preceding stepper-motor system are given in Figure 7.15. Between lines 5 and 21, the required PI/T registers are declared and initialized. The 68230 PI/T is set up for mode 0 operation, with handshake lines disabled. Port A is configured as an output port and port B as an input port. The D2 and D3 registers are loaded with the first stepper code words for the clockwise and counterclockwise routines, as depicted in Figure 7.13.

```
LINE   ADDR
  1;stepper 2/89
  2                                     OPT     A
  3                                     ORG     $1200
  4;declare 68230 registers
  5 00010001                    PGCR    EQU     $010001
  6 00010005                    PADDR   EQU     $010005
  7 00010007                    PBDDR   EQU     $010007
  8 00010011                    PADR    EQU     $010011
  9 00010013                    PBDR    EQU     $010013
 10 0001001D                    PACR    EQU     $01001D
 11 0001001F                    PBCR    EQU     $01001F
 12;initialize Port A output & Port B input
 13 00001200 13FC 0000 0001 INIT MOVE.B  #$00,PGCR
             0001
 14 00001208 13FC 0000 0001      MOVE.B  #$00,PACR
             001D
 15 00001210 13FC 0000 0001      MOVE.B  #$00,PBCR
             001F
 16 00001218 13FC 0000 0001      MOVE.B  #$00,PBDDR
             0007
 17 00001220 13FC 00FF 0001      MOVE.B  #$FF,PADDR
             0005
 18;initialize stepper codes
 19 00001228 143C 0033           MOVE.B  #$33,D2 ;cw code
 20 0000122C 163C 0066           MOVE.B  #$66,D3 ;ccw code
 21 00001230 183C 00FF           MOVE.B  #$FF,D4
 22;read X from PB and rotate stepper accordingly
 23 00001234 1039 0001 0013 READ MOVE.B  PBDR,D0
 24 0000123A 6708               BEQ.S   NULL    ;null routine
 25 0000123C E308               LSL.B   #1,D0
 26 0000123E 640C               BCC.S   CW    ;clockwise routine
 27 00001240 651A               BCS.S   CCW   ;counterclockwise
 28 00001242 60F0               BRA.S   READ
 29 00001244 13C4 0001 0011 NULL MOVE.B  D4,PADR
 30 0000124A 60E8               BRA.S   READ
 31 0000124C 13C2 0001 0011 CW   MOVE.B  D2,PADR
 32 00001252 6118               BSR.S   DLY  ;delay routine
 33 00001254 E21A               ROR.B   #1,D2
 34 00001256 5500               SUBQ.B  #2,D0
 35 00001258 66F2               BNE.S   CW
 36 0000125A 60D8               BRA.S   READ
 37 0000125C 13C3 0001 0011 CCW  MOVE.B  D3,PADR
 38 00001262 6108               BSR.S   DLY  ;delay routine
 39 00001264 E31B               ROL.B   #1,D3
 40 00001266 5500               SUBQ.B  #2,D0
 41 00001268 66F2               BNE.S   CCW
 42 0000126A 60C8               BRA.S   READ
 43 0000126C 2A3C 0000 61A8 DLY  MOVE.L  #25000,D5
 44 00001272 4E71          AGAIN NOP
 45 00001274 0485 0000 0001      SUBI.L  #01,D5
 46 0000127A 66F6               BNE.S   AGAIN
 47 0000127C 4E75               RTS
```

FIGURE 7.15   The 68000 assembly listings for the stepper-motor interface.

The **READ module** between lines 23 and 28 reads the S control word, checks it, and branches to the appropriate routines. The **NULL module** at lines 29 and 30 outputs the null code to the stepper and branches back to the READ module.

The **CW module** between lines 31 and 36 outputs the clockwise code to the stepper, calls the **DLY subroutine** for the stepper-response delay, and generates the next clockwise sequential code (ROR.B #1,D2 instruction). It then goes into the CW loop until the D0 register (which contains information about bits b6 through b0 of the S control word) is decremented to zero. In effect, this amounts to rotating the stepper in the clockwise direction, as specified by the S control word. Finally, the CW module branches back to the READ module.

The **CCW module** between lines 37 and 42 is similar to the CW module. It rotates the stepper in the counterclockwise direction as specified by the S control word. It also branches back to the READ module.

The **DLY module** between lines 43 and 47 generates the delay required for the stepper motor to respond.

We will now review the stepper-motor interface by means of an example problem.

Example 7.5   The stepper-motor interface.
Consider the stepper-motor interface described in Figures 7.13, 7.14, and 7.15.

1. Explain in detail how the CCW module works.

2. Assume an 8-MHz processor clock. Compute the approximate delay value for the DLY routine.

3. The S control word is $0F = 0 0 0 0 1 1 1 1. How many times will the stepper rotate and in which direction?

Solution

1. **The CCW module:** This module is contained between lines 37 and 42 of Figure 7.15. The software details are as follows:

```
CCW    MOVE.B   D3, PADR    ; output counterclockwise
                              code to stepper.
       BSR.S    DLY         ; call the delay routine.
       ROL.B    #1,D3       ; generate next CCW code in
                              the upward sequence.
       SUBQ.B   #2,D0       ; subtract 2 from D0. D0
                              contains left shifted S
                              control word.
       BNE.S    CCW         ; branch back to CCW until
                              D0 is decremented to
                              zero.
       BRA.S    READ        ; branch back to READ
                              module.
```

2. **DLY routine timing Td:** The T(R/W) values for the instructions in the DLY routine are as follows (refer to Section 3.5 of Chapter 3):

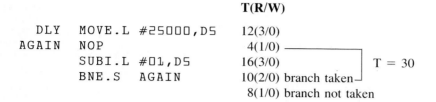

		T(R/W)
DLY	MOVE.L #25000,D5	12(3/0)
AGAIN	NOP	4(1/0)
	SUBI.L #01,D5	16(3/0)
	BNE.S AGAIN	10(2/0) branch taken
		8(1/0) branch not taken

T = 30

The AGAIN loop is run 25,000 times. Each time it takes 30 T-states, as shown. At 8 MHz, each T-state corresponds to 125 nanoseconds. Thus, the approximate delay time is as follows:

$$Td = 25,000 \times 30 \times 125 \text{ nanoseconds} = 93.75 \text{ milliseconds}$$

3. **Stepper rotation:** For the S control word:

$$\$0F = 0\ 0\ 0\ 0\ 1\ 1\ 1\ 1$$

The rotation is clockwise, since b7 = 0. The stepper rotates 15 times.

In the preceding example, we have introduced the very practical modular software approach. It involves writing independent software modules with local parameters and using them in conjunction with each other to generate system-level software activity.

Position Control Systems

Several stepper motors can be connected to a microcomputer, with each stepper controlling one axis. For example, an XY plotter system could have three steppers: X, Y, and Z. The X and Y steppers would control the X- and Y-axis motions and the Z stepper would control the Z-axis pen motion. Such a system is illustrated in Figure 7.16. Port A of PI/T-1 drives the X and Y steppers. Ports B and C of PI/T-1 accept the control words from the X and Y steppers. Port A of PI/T-2 drives the Z stepper and port B of PI/T-2 accepts the control word from the Z stepper.

The software involves reading each control word and moving the corresponding stepper accordingly. Software for each stepper is similar to that presented in Figure 7.15. Care should be taken to avoid control of one stepper affecting control of another.

A **robotic system** is a more complex position control system in which as many as ten stepper motors control individual movements. A parallel printer interface involves controlling three or more stepper motors. The system interface and the software, however, are similar to those we have described.[9]

FIGURE 7.16   X-, Y-, and Z-position control system using three stepper motors and a microcomputer interface.

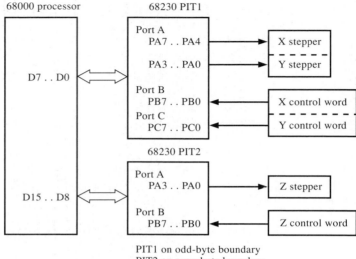

68000 processor   68230 PIT1

Port A
PA7 . . PA4 → X stepper
PA3 . . PA0 → Y stepper

D7 . . D0

Port B
PB7 . . PB0 ← X control word
Port C
PC7 . . PC0 ← Y control word

68230 PIT2

Port A
PA3 . . PA0 → Z stepper

D15 . . D8

Port B
PB7 . . PB0 ← Z control word

PIT1 on odd-byte boundary
PIT2 on even-byte boundary

7.5   SUMMARY

In this chapter we introduced the parallel I/O interface with the 68000 processor. Two of the most popular and widely used devices are the 6821 PIA and the 68230 PI/T.

The 6821 PIA (peripheral interface adapter) is a synchronous 8-bit parallel interface device, belonging to the earlier 6800 microprocessor. It has two individually programmable 8-bit I/O ports, A and B, along with the associated control signals. The PIA contains six internal registers and occupies four bytes of memory space. The processor communicates with the external I/O with the help of these registers.

The 68230 PI/T (parallel interface and timer) is an asynchronous parallel interface device belonging to the 68000 family of processors. It has three individually programmable 8-bit I/O ports, A, B, and C. In addition, it has a 4-bit handshake control, port H. The PI/T contains 23 active 8-bit internal registers and occupies 23 bytes of memory space. The PI/T communicates with the external I/O with the help of these registers.

The 68000 family of processors uses memory-mapped I/O in which the I/O interface is similar to the memory interface. The PIA/68000 interface uses the synchronous bus. In the case of the PI/T, the asynchronous bus is used.

In the waveform-generation I/O application (Example 7.1), we described the interface of the 68000 and 6821 PIA and the PIA initialization schemes. Waveform generation can be extended to generate any required timing sequence for digital words.

In our discussion of data entry and display systems, we described the interface of external I/O units, such as keyboards and segment displays, to the 68000/68230 PI/T systems. Keys can be electrically wired as an XY matrix. The processor generates a digital word and drives the interface logic for the matrix-type keyboard. The processor then senses the key closure through the interface logic and generates the appropriate key code for the closed key using software routines.

The stepper-motor interface to the 68000/68230 PI/T system emphasizes electro-mechanical position control applications. Any complex position control system can be easily implemented by means of stepper motors and microcomputer control. A three-stepper system can control XY plotters and a pen-motion mechanism. A robotic system is a more complex position control system in which up to ten stepper motors control individual movements.

PROBLEMS

7.1   Using the 68000/6821 PIA interface, develop a waveform-generator system in which

   (a) port A resembles an 8-bit up counter and port B an 8-bit down counter;
   (b) modification of the software results in a 16-bit shift register type system.

7.2   Describe the details of the 68000/6821 PIA interface with PIA-1 base address at $020021 and PIA-2 base address at $020020.

7.3   For the I/O system of Figure 7.7, specify the address locations of all of the 68230 PI/T registers

   (a) in the primary address range;
   (b) in the redundant address range.

7.4   Redesign the I/O system of Figure 7.7 so that the 68230 is contained between $010001 and $010003F, without any redundancy.

7.5   Configure and write proper words into the appropriate PI/T registers so that

   (a) PA7 through PA3 are outputs and PA2 through PA0 are inputs,
   (b) PB7 through PB0 are bidirectional, and
   (c) handshake lines are not used.

7.6   Configure and write proper words into the appropriate PI/T registers so that

   (a) ports PA and PB are 16-bit bidirectional,
   (b) port H is low active, and
   (c) the H interrupts are disabled.

7.7   Redesign the I/O system of Figure 7.7 interfacing two 68230 PI/T devices. The memory map indicates PI/T-1 base address at $010000 on an even byte boundary; PI/T-2 base address at $010001 on an odd byte boundary.

7.8   Given the conditions of Problem 7.7, describe the memory map of both 68230 devices in detail.

7.9   State whether the system of Figure 7.7 will function properly under the following conditions:

   (a) $\overline{LDS}$ and $\overline{UDS}$ are interchanged.
   (b) $\overline{LDS}$ is inactive all the time.

   Briefly explain your answers.

7.10 Design an I/O system with two 68230 PI/T devices and conceptualize how to accomplish the following tasks:

   (a) Drive 32 individual relay coils by the 68230 ports.
   (b) Drive 16 individual relay coils and read in a 16-bit I/O control word.

7.11 Repeat Problem 7.10, with the system driving all 32 relay coils, but also accepting 32-bit control information on the same ports. (*Hint:* External multiplexers may be required.)

7.12 With information from the data sheets, fully explain the operation of the keyboard and the 74C922 interface with the 68000/68230 system.

7.13 Redesign the keyboard/display interface system to allow for an extended display to 4 hex digits. Port C may be used to drive the extra display digits.

Write the software to achieve the display shift. (The old digit is to be shifted to the MSD position and the newest digit is to be displayed in the LSD position.)

7.14 Analyzing the software of Figure 7.10,

(a) specify the condition of the display at the time of power-up;
(b) at the beginning of the program;
(c) when the program is running in the loop and the system reset is activated.

7.15 The following keys have been activated in sequence:

$$1\ 3\ 2\ 4\ 5\ 7\ 6\ 8\ 0\ 9$$

Using the software of Figure 7.10, show how they are displayed in pairs.

7.16 Modify the software of Figure 7.10 so that

(a) before any key is pressed, 00 will be displayed;
(b) before any key is pressed, a flashing FF will be displayed.

7.17 With reference to the software of Figure 7.10, what will be displayed if two keys are pressed simultaneously? What is this condition called?

7.18 Design the hardware and software for the ASCII keyboard interface indicated below. You may use the system video monitor to display the typed characters.

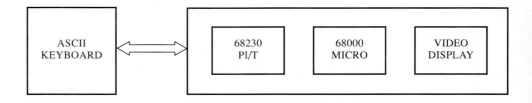

7.19 For the system of Problem 7.18, develop software that will result in key lockout.

7.20 Repeat Problem 7.19 so that key rollover will occur (that is, keys will be identified in the order of the scanning sequence of the keyboard).

7.21 With reference to Example 7.5, design a stepper-motor controller system in which the stepper completes the clockwise rotation of 360 degrees, reverses to perform the counterclockwise rotation, and so on.

(a) In intervals of 100 milliseconds per step.
(b) In intervals of one second per step.

7.22 Redesign the stepper-control system of Example 7.5 so that each time the stepper is activated it goes through

(a) a 30-degree rotation;
(b) a 60-degree rotation.

7.23 Design a solar tracking system according to Figure 7.17. Stepper 1, containing optical sensors, rotates between 0 and 180 degrees in 24 steps and identifies the maximum intensity position. Stepper 2, containing the solar plates, then rotates to the maximum intensity position. The solar stepper position should be changed once every ten minutes. Also develop the software for this system.

FIGURE 7.17   For problems 7.23 and 7.24

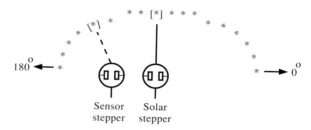

Sensor   Solar
stepper   stepper

7.24 Repeat Problem 7.23 so that the solar stepper position

    (a) is updated every minute;

    (b) is updated continuously.

    (*Hint:* The sensor stepper has to scan all 24 positions before moving the solar stepper.)

7.25 A conveyor-belt system is illustrated in Figure 7.18. The S input controls both steppers, as shown in the accompanying table. Consider 7.5-degree steppers. Slow movement corresponds to 24 steps per minute. Fast movement corresponds to 96 steps per minute. Design the system with hardware and software.

7.26 In the preceding problem, the S3 input is a safety input. Design a safety system in which power will shut down and an alarm will sound if S3 is active high for more than a minute on a continuous basis.

FIGURE 7.18   For problems 7.25 and 7.26

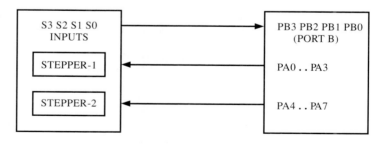

S2	S1	S0	STEPPER-1	STEPPER-2
0	0	0	STILL	STILL
0	0	1	STILL	CW SLOW
0	1	0	STILL	CW FAST
0	1	1	STILL	CCW SLOW
1	0	0	CW SLOW	STILL
1	0	1	CW FAST	STILL
1	1	0	CCW SLOW	STILL
1	1	1	STILL	STILL

S CONTROL
TABLE

ENDNOTES

1. Motorola, Inc. "Data Sheets on 6821 PIA." In *Microcomputer Components Data Book*. Phoenix, AZ: Motorola Technical Operations, 1986.

2. Motorola, Inc. *68230 PI/T Data Book*. Phoenix, AZ: Motorola Technical Operations, 1986.

3. Motorola, Inc. *MC68000 Data Book*. Phoenix, AZ: Motorola Technical Operations, 1983.

4. Miller, M.A. "Parallel Interfacing the 68000." Chap. 5 in *The 68000 Microprocessor: Architecture, Programming, and Applications*. Columbus, OH: Merrill, 1988.

5. Subbarao, W. *Microprocessors: Hardware, Software, and Design Applications*. Englewood Cliffs, NJ: Prentice-Hall, 1984.

6. Andrews, M. *Self-Guided Tour through the 68000*. Englewood Cliffs, NJ: Prentice-Hall, 1984.

7. Airpax, Inc. *Data Book on Stepper Motors*. Cheshire, CT: Airpax, 1988.

8. Fu, K.; Gonzalez, R; and Lee, C. "Introduction." Chap. 1 in *Robotics: Control, Sensing, Vision, and Intelligence*. New York: McGraw-Hill, 1987.

9. Scherer, V., and Peterson, W. *The MC68230 PI/T Provides an Effective Interface*. App. Note #854. Austin, TX: Motorola Microprocessor Group, 1982.

The 68000 Serial Interface and Applications

Objectives

In this chapter we will study:

Principles of serial data communication

Architecture of the 6850 ACIA and interface with the 68000

Implementation of the RS-232 serial interface

Architecture of the 68901 MFP and interface with the 68000

System applications using the serial interface.

8.0 INTRODUCTION

Slower I/O systems, such as keyboards, terminals, modems, and other electromechanical units, usually communicate with fast processors through a serial interface. This reduces the number of external connections to the processor interface.[1]

Of the several serial interface and communication devices, the 6850 asynchronous communications interface adapter (ACIA) and the 68901 multifunction peripheral (MFP) are widely used with 68000-based systems. The **6850 ACIA** belongs to the earlier 6800 family and has standard RS-232 interface properties. The **68901 MFP** is a 68000-family serial interface device and has additional ports and interrupt processing logic associated with it.

Study of the material in this chapter will provide background knowledge of serial data communication concepts. It will also help the reader develop practical applications using the serial interface.

8.1 SERIAL DATA COMMUNICATION CONCEPTS

The information sending station is called the **transmitter** and the information receiving station is called the **receiver.** In serial communications, data travels between the transmitter and the receiver serially on a single line, one bit at a time. The **American Standard Code for Information Interchange (ASCII),** as shown in Figure 8.1, is the most widely used 7-bit code for serial data communications.[2]

LSD \ MSD		0 000	1 001	2 010	3 011	4 100	5 101	6 110	7 111
0	0000	NUL	DLE	SP	0	@	P	'	p
1	0001	SOH	DC1	!	1	A	Q	a	q
2	0010	STX	DC2	"	2	B	R	b	r
3	0011	ETX	DC3	#	3	C	S	c	s
4	0100	EOT	DC4	$	4	D	T	d	t
5	0101	ENQ	NAK	%	5	E	U	e	u
6	0110	ACK	SYN	&	6	F	V	f	v
7	0111	BEL	ETB	'	7	G	W	g	w
8	1000	BS	CAN	(	8	H	X	h	x
9	1001	HT	EM	)	9	I	Y	i	y
A	1010	LF	SUB	*	:	J	Z	j	z
B	1011	VT	ESC	+	;	K	[	k	{
C	1100	FF	FS	,	<	L	\	l	|
D	1101	CR	GS	−	=	M	]	m	}
E	1110	SO	RS	.	>	N	↑	n	~
F	1111	SI	VS	/	?	O	←	o	DEL

FIGURE 8.1 ASCII codes used in microcomputer systems.

Figure 8.2 illustrates a typical asynchronous serial data frame. The **start bit** signifies the beginning of the serial data frame. The next seven bits (b6−b0) represent the ASCII-coded data element. The next bit is the **parity bit,** which is used for error checking. If even parity is used, the total number of 1s in the data frame should be an even number, including the parity bit. If odd parity is used, the total number of 1s in the data frame should be an odd number. If the parity does not check out at the receiving end, the data frame is in error and will be rejected. The last bits are the **stop bits,** signifying the end of the data frame. There may be one or two stop bits per serial frame.

FIGURE 8.2 Typical serial data frame using ASCII code.

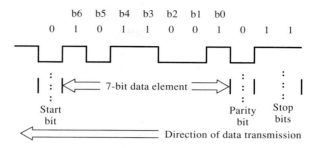

The rate of data transmission is specified in bits per second and is known as the **baud rate.** The transmitter and the receiver are adjusted to the same baud rate. The receiver recovers the data element from the received serial data frame.

The following example problem will further clarify basic serial data communication concepts.

Example 8.1   Serial data communications.
Refer to Figures 8.1 and 8.2.

1. Specify what ASCII character is being transmitted.
2. What is the type of parity, even or odd?
3. If the data transmission rate is 300 baud, how many ASCII characters can be transmitted per second on a continuous basis?

Solution

1. **ASCII character:** The data element contained in b6–b0 is

$$1\ 0\ 1\ 1\ 0\ 0\ 1 = \$59$$

which corresponds to ASCII character Y.
2. **Parity:** Including the start and parity bits, the total number of 1s in the data frame is equal to 4, which is an even number. Thus, the data frame has even parity.
3. **Characters per second:** Each serial frame, composed of the start, data, parity, and stop bits, is 11 bits long and represents one character. At 300 baud, the number of frames per second = 300/11 = 27.2. Thus, 27 characters per second can be transmitted.

A baud rate of 300 is relatively slow, but is standard for such electromechanical equipment as keyboards and terminals. With electronic high-speed serial devices, such as modems, higher rates of up to 9600 baud are quite common. Other codes, such as the

8-bit **Extended Binary Coded Decimal Interchange Code (EBCDIC),** are also very popular. In any event, the basic concepts of the serial data communication remain the same.[3]

8.2   6850 ACIA GENERAL ARCHITECTURE

The ACIA is a 24-pin DIP device fabricated with NMOS technology. It is one of the industry standard serial communication devices. In Figure 8.3, the pin configuration and internal architecture of the 6850 ACIA are diagrammed.[4,5]

Registers and I/O Ports

As shown in Figure 8.3(b), the ACIA consists of four registers:

> the control register (CR);
>
> the status register (SR);
>
> the transmit data register (TDR); and
>
> the receive data register (RDR).

The **control register (CR)** is a write-only register and is written by the processor to configure the ACIA mode of operation.

The **status register (SR)** is a read-only register and is at the same address space as the CR. It contains the status of the events associated with the ACIA. The processor reads and interprets the status information and performs the appropriate operations.

The **transmit data register (TDR)** is a write-only register. The processor writes the 8-bit word to be transmitted into this TDR. The parity and control units in the ACIA insert proper parity, start, and stop bits to the data element and generate a complete serial frame. The transmit control logic in the ACIA shifts this frame serially on the **transmit data (TXD) line.**

The **receive data register (RDR)** is a read-only register and is at the same address space as the TDR. It receives the serial data on the **receive data (RXD) input line** and converts it into an 8-bit parallel word. The parity and control units within the ACIA check and separate the parity, start, and stop bits. The processor reads this 8-bit data in the RDR when it is ready. Any parity error information is sent to the status register.

The **ready-to-send (RTS)** and **clear-to-send ($\overline{\text{CTS}}$) lines** are handshake signals between the ACIA and the I/O units. The **data carrier detect ($\overline{\text{DCD}}$) signal** is an input to the ACIA and signifies that the transmission carrier is in progress. The **register select (RS) line** is used to select between the CR/SR and the TDR/RDR pairs.

The **receive clock (RXCLK)** and the **transmit clock (TXCLK)** are the shift clock inputs. They are conditioned by the internal clock generator logic for appropriate receive and transmit baud rates.

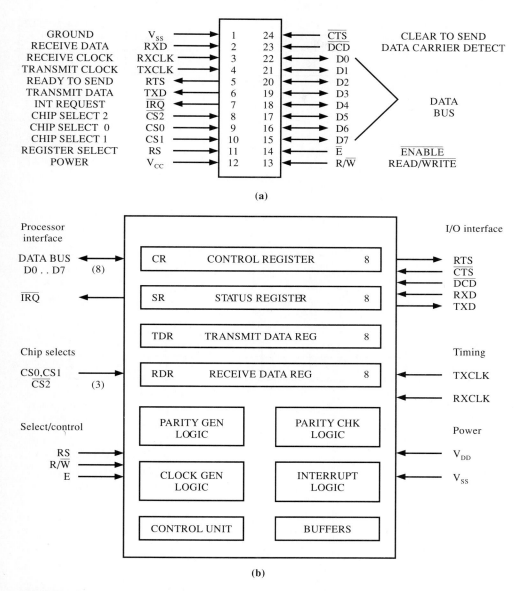

FIGURE 8.3   (a) The 6850 ACIA pin diagram and (b) architecture.

Modes of Operation and Status Conditions of the ACIA

The contents of the control register, as shown in Figure 8.4(a), control the modes of operation of the 6850. The ACIA can activate the interrupt line $\overline{\text{IRQ}}$, on occurrence of such events as filling of the RDR, emptying of the TDR, and activation of the $\overline{\text{CTS}}$. The interrupts can be enabled or disabled by bit 7. RTS output can be configured to be active

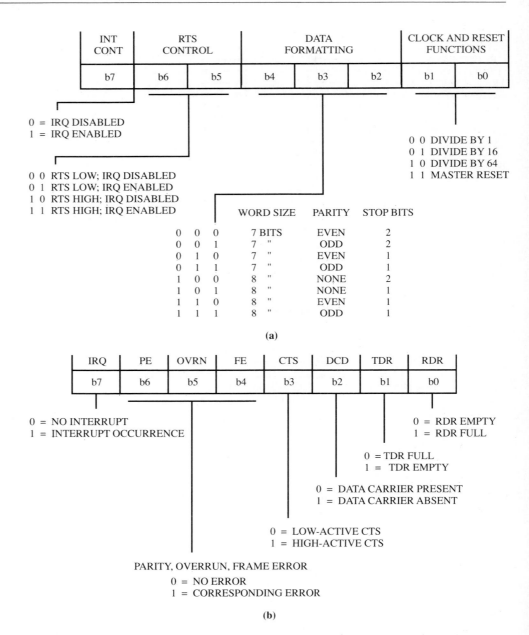

FIGURE 8.4   (a) The 6850 ACIA control register (CR) format and (b) status register format.

high or low, and the associated interrupt activation can be enabled or disabled by bits 6 and 5. Data formatting can be accomplished by bits 4, 3, and 2. The reset and the clock functions are controlled by bits 1 and 0.

The status register illustrated in Figure 8.4(b) contains status information on the 6850 signals and events. If the interrupt has occurred, b7 is set. Bits 6, 5, and 4 are set for parity, overrun, and frame errors, respectively. A **parity error** occurs when an even parity is detected instead of an expected odd parity, or vice versa. An **overrun error** occurs when new data is shifted into the RDR, destroying the old data before it is read by the processor. A **frame error** occurs when the stop bits are not detected as expected at the end of the frame.

Bit 3 specifies the activity on the $\overline{\text{CTS}}$ line. Bit 2 is set if the data carrier is absent. Bit 1 is set if the TDR is empty. Bit 0 is set if the RDR is full. The processor reads these status conditions and responds accordingly. Reading or writing into the corresponding registers clears the flag conditions in the SR.

The following example problem will clarify the internal architecture of the ACIA.

Example 8.2   6850 ACIA architecture.
In a data transmission application, 6850 is at address space \$010041 for CR/SR and at \$010043 for TDR/RDR.

1. Specify the conditions under which each of the registers are addressed.
2. Control word \$45 is written into the control register CR. Specify the data format being transmitted or received.

Solution

1. **Register map (refer to Figure 8.3):** Register select input RS is used to select the CR/SR pair (when RS = 0) or the TDR/RDR pair (when RS = 1). The R/$\overline{\text{W}}$ signal further selects the individual registers as indicated:

Addressed Location	RS	R/$\overline{\text{W}}$	Register Selected
010041	0	0	CR (Write only)
		1	SR (Read only)
010043	1	0	TDR (Write only)
		1	RDR (Read only)

2. **Control word \$45 [refer to Figure 8.4]:**

b7	b6	b5	b4	b3	b2	b1	b0
0	1	0	0	0	1	0	1
IRQ disabled	RTS high active		7-bit odd-parity word; 2 stop bits			Divide by 16	

The data transmission and receiving is configured for a 7-bit odd-parity word with two stop bits. RXCLK and TXCLK are divided by 16 for the proper baud rate. RTS is active high and the interrupt is disabled.

The contents of the control register and the associated modes of operation can be changed under program control. Thus, it is possible to transmit and receive data in a variety of formats and at different baud rates.

8.3 THE 6850 ACIA INTERFACE WITH THE 68000 AND APPLICATIONS

The 6850 ACIA belongs to the earlier 6800 family and requires a synchronous bus interface to the processor. The 68000/6850 ACIA interface is similar to the 68000/6821 PIA interface described in Chapter 7.

68000/6850 Interface Considerations

In serial data communications, the intelligent unit is known as the **DTE (data terminal equipment.)** The I/O unit that is communicating with the DTE is known as the **DCE (data communication equipment).** Figure 8.5 illustrates the DTE/DCE interface. The 68000/6850 system is the DTE. The I/O system (a terminal or printer, for example) is the DCE. The DTE and the DCE communicate on a standard RS-232 serial link.[6]

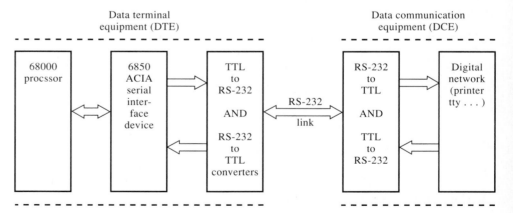

FIGURE 8.5 The DTE/DCE interface in serial data communications.

In Figure 8.6, the system of Figure 8.5 is detailed. The ACIA requires a synchronous clocking signal for data transfers. This signal is provided by the E clock of the 68000 processor. The address decoder provides an active low $\overline{Y1}$ select signal for the address range $010000 to $01FFFF (refer to Section 6.3 of Chapter 6). It is further gated by the $\overline{VMA}$ (valid memory address) signal from the processor and generates the

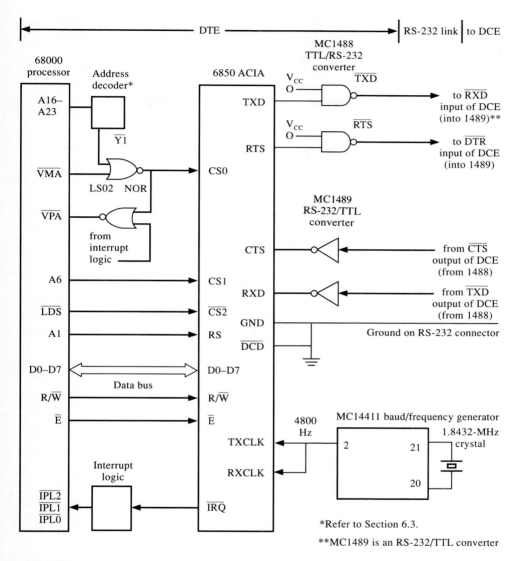

FIGURE 8.6 The 68000/6850 DTE, RS-232, and DCE functional interface.

CS0 chip select for the ACIA. The A6 address line activates the CS1 chip select. The $\overline{\text{LDS}}$ signal activates the $\overline{\text{CS2}}$ chip select. The A1 address line drives the register select (RS) input. The other control connections are as shown. The ACIA can be put on the upper byte of the data bus by using the $\overline{\text{UDS}}$ signal in place of the $\overline{\text{LDS}}$.[7]

For the connections shown in Figure 8.6, the 6850 occupies the following memory map, at the odd byte boundary: $010041 for CR/SR (control register/status register); $010043 for TDR/RDR (transmit register/receive register).

The MC14411 baud/frequency generator IC accepts a 1.8432-MHz crystal input and generates several clock rates. For our illustration, we have chosen a 4800-Hz signal for the activation of the TXCLK and RXCLK inputs.

For better noise immunity, RS-232 lines are driven by enhanced logic voltage swings. Noise immunity is achieved by the MC1488-type TTL–to–RS-232 converter and driver device. This device is powered by higher voltages ($V_{DD} = +12$ volts; $V_{EE} = -12$ volts). It converts TTL levels to RS-232 levels. RS-232 levels follow negative logic convention. Negative voltage in excess of -3 volts is regarded as logic 1; positive voltage in excess of $+3$ volts is regarded as logic 0. Thus, there is a minimum 6-volt swing on the RS-232 lines. This provides sufficient noise immunity for the RS-232 interface.

On the receiving end, signals coming from the RS-232 lines are converted to TTL levels by the MC1489-type RS-232–to–TTL converter. The double logic inversion caused by the MC1488 and 1489 converters does not cause any system logic mismatch and is totally transparent to the user.

RS-232 Interface Application

For most of the standard RS-232 interface applications, approximately four connections are used, as shown in Figure 8.6. The TXD and RXD lines are the serial transmit and receive data lines. The RTS output of the ACIA is gated as the $\overline{DTR}$ (data-terminal-ready) signal to the RS-232 interface. The $\overline{CTS}$ (clear-to-send) signal from the RS-232 is gated as the $\overline{CTS}$ input to the ACIA. The $\overline{DCD}$ (data-carrier-detect) input to the 6850 is connected to ground and is always activated.

When the DTE (68000/6850) is in the receive mode, it expects the DCE to activate the $\overline{CTS}$ line, signifying that the serial data are coming on the RXD line. The processor polls the SR of the ACIA for any error conditions and for $\overline{CTS}$ activity. If there are no errors, and if the $\overline{CTS}$ is active, the processor polls to see if the RDR is full. A full RDR implies that the incoming serial data have already been converted into the parallel byte form and are available in the RDR. The processor reads the RDR and accepts the incoming data.

During the transmit mode, the processor polls to see whether the TDR is empty. If it is empty, the processor writes the data byte (to be transmitted serially) into the TDR. During this write operation, the RTS line is activated and is communicated to the DCE as the $\overline{DTR}$. The DCE checks for the $\overline{DTR}$ active condition and goes into its routine to accept the transmitted data.

We will now present an example problem dealing with the hardware and software aspects of the RS-232 interface and serial data communications.

Example 8.3   RS-232 data communications.
Design (1) operating hardware and (2) software based on Figure 8.6. The system will receive ASCII characters on RXD from the DCE at 300 baud with a start bit, seven data bits, odd parity, and two stop bits.

Echo the same character to the DCE on the TXD line. The DTE and DCE follow the standard RS-232 interface format discussed earlier.

```
LINE   ADDR

  1                                      ;RS232.SRC 11/22/88
  2                                      ;F.I.U
  3                                       OPT     A
  4                                       ORG     $1000
  5                                      ;DECLARE 6850 ACIA REGISTERS
  6 00010041            ACCR             EQU $010041 ;CONTROL REG
  7 00010041            ACSR             EQU $010041 ;STATUS  REG
  8 00010041            ACTDR            EQU $010041 ;TRANSMIT REG
  9 00010043            ACRDR            EQU $010043 ;RECEIVE  REG
 10;master reset and initialize the 6850 ACIA
 11 00001000 13FC 0003 0001              MOVE.B #$03,ACCR ;MASTER RESET
             0041
 12 00001008 13FC 0045 0001              MOVE.B #$45,ACCR ;INITIALIZE
             0041
 13;checks parity, overrun, frame, DCD errors and CTS activity
 14 00001010 1039 0001 0041 INPT MOVE.B ACSR,D0
 15 00001016 0200 007C              ANDI.B #$7C,D0 ; ANY ERRORS ?
 16 0000101A 66F4                   BNE.S INPT    ; IF SO LOOP
 17;no errors: proceed to check if the RDR is full
 18 0000101C 1039 0001 0041 RECV MOVE.B ACSR,D0
 19 00001022 0200 0001              ANDI.B #$01,D0
 20 00001026 67F4                   BEQ.S RECV
 21 00001028 1239 0001 0043         MOVE.B ACRDR,D1;RDR INTO D1
 22;transmit the received character, if the TDR is empty
 23 0000102E 1039 0001 0041 TNSM MOVE.B ACSR,D0
 24 00001034 0200 0002              ANDI.B #$02,D0 ;IS TDR EMPTY?
 25 00001038 67F4                   BEQ.S  TNSM
 26 0000103A 13C1 0001 0041         MOVE.B D1,ACTDR
 27 00001040 4E71                   NOP
 28 00001042 60CC                   BRA.S INPT
 29                                  ;
 30;
 31                                  ;
 32 00001044                         END


    ASSEMBLER ERRORS =     0
```

FIGURE 8.7 The 68000 software listings for the DTE/DCE interface.

Solution

1. **Hardware:** The hardware of Figure 8.6 is self-contained. The internal control register of the 6850 should be configured to obtain a baud rate of 300 from the 4800-Hz external RXCLK and TXCLK inputs. This can be achieved by selecting the divide-by-16 option.

2. **Software:** The actual 68000 software listings to accomplish the task are given in Figure 8.7. It is necessary to reset the 6850 at the outset to eliminate any residual conditions from previous operations.

   Between lines 10 and 12, the control register is configured for master reset. It is reinitialized with $45 for the communication format as shown:

b7	b6	b5	b4	b3	b2	b1	b0
0	1	0	0	0	1	0	0
IRQ disabled	RTS high active		7-bit odd-parity word; 2 stop bits			Divide by 16	

Between lines 13 and 17, the software polls the status register of the 6850 until the CTS input goes active and the error-free condition is detected. It then proceeds to the RECV module.

In the RECV module between lines 18 and 22, the software reads the received data byte when the RDR becomes full. The 6850 strips the start, parity, and stop bits from the incoming serial data on the RXD line, converts the serial data into a parallel data element, and places it in the RDR.

The character echo is accomplished by transmitting the received character back to the DCE by means of the TNSM module. Between lines 23 and 27, the software polls the status register until the TDR is empty. When the TDR is empty, the software writes the received data byte into it to be transmitted back (echoed) to the DCE unit. The 6850 adds the start, parity, and stop bits to the data in the TDR, generates a data frame, and serializes it on the TXD line. The BRA.S INPT instruction at line 28 loops the program back to line 14 for the next character.

The software we have just described can be very easily converted to terminal input and output software. The NOP instruction at line 27 can be changed to an RTS instruction and the current software can be called as a subroutine by a main program.

For example, the JSR INPT instruction in a main program enters the software at line 14, reads an input character from the terminal, and echoes it to the terminal. It then returns to the main program with the value of the input character in the D1 register.

The DCE system should have RS-232–compatible software in it. In the system of Figure 8.6, the RTS output of the 6850 ACIA goes high when the TDR is loaded with new data. This manifests as low on the $\overline{DTR}$ line. The DCE system should poll this condition and accept the data accordingly.

8.4 68901 MFP (MULTIFUNCTION PERIPHERAL) GENERAL ARCHITECTURE

In addition to serial communication, need often arises for attendant control, timing, I/O, and interrupt functions. The 68901 MFP of the 68000 family is a multifunction device that is becoming an industry standard for integrated serial, parallel, timing, and interrupt applications. In this section, we will examine the architecture of the MFP. The MFP data book should be used as an additional reference.[8]

Internal Architecture of the MFP

Figure 8.8 illustrates the pin configuration and internal architecture of the 68901 MFP. The device is contained in a 48-pin DIP and is fabricated with HMOS technology. It includes the following features:

four timers for timing applications;

one USART for serial data communications;

one GPIP for 8-bit parallel I/O and external interrupt inputs; and

control logic for the coordination of the various functions.

The A, B, C, and D timers accept external clock inputs from the XTL1 and XTL2 lines and provide timed pulses on the TAO, TBO, TCO, and TDO lines. In addition, the A and B timers can accept external timing inputs on the TAI and TBI lines and measure their time duration.

The **USART (universal synchronous/asynchronous receiver and transmitter)** provides serial output on the SO line. It accepts serial input on the SI line. The receive and transmit clocks are accepted on the RC and TC inputs and are used for the respective data-shifting operations within the USART.

The **GPIP (general purpose I/O and interrupt port)** has 8-bit parallel I/O capability on the 10–17 lines. These lines can also be configured as eight external interrupts, allowing the MFP to function as an interrupt controller. The associated interrupt control logic interfaces with the processor on the $\overline{\text{IRQ}}$ and the $\overline{\text{IACK}}$ lines. The $\overline{\text{IEO}}$ and $\overline{\text{IEI}}$ (interrupt enable output and input) signals are used for daisy chaining the priority interrupts.

The 68901 MFP communicates with the processor on an 8-bit data bus D0–D7. There are twenty-four 8-bit registers in the 68901, which are selected by the five register select inputs, RS1–RS5. The select and control logic consists of the $\overline{\text{CS}}$ (chip select), $\overline{\text{DS}}$ (data strobe), and R/$\overline{\text{W}}$ (read/write) inputs and the $\overline{\text{DTACK}}$ (data acknowledge) output.

The RESET input provides the 68901 reset operation. The CLK input advances the internal states of the MFP.

In this section we will discuss some details of the registers dealing with the GPIP, USART, and timers, emphasizing the utility of the MFP in serial communication applications. We will deal with the interrupt-related registers in Chapter 9.

Register Structure and Modes of Operation

Figure 8.9 is a tabular representation of the MFP's internal register structure. Contents written into the appropriate registers determine the mode of operation of the MFP. Similarly, some of the status registers contain status information about events occurring in the MFP. The processor reads this status information, interprets it, and performs appropriate operations as determined by the software.[9]

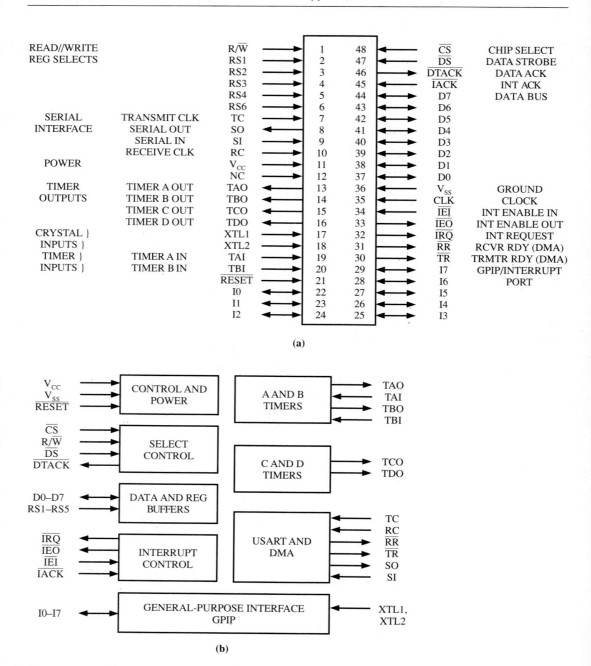

FIGURE 8.8 (a) Pin diagram of the 68901 multifunction peripheral (MFP) and (b) architecture.

Number*	Symbol	Name	Function
0 1	GPIP	General-purpose I/O register	I/O and interrupt interface
0 3	AER	Active edge register	Specifies edges
0 5	DDR	Data direction register	Specifies GPIP direction
0 7	IERA	Interrupt enable register A	Interrupt enable/disable
0 9	IERB	Interrupt enable register B	Interrupt enable/disable
0 B	IPRA	Interrupt pending register A	Pending interrupts
0 D	IPRB	Interrupt pending register B	Pending interrupts
0 F	ISRA	Interrupt in-service register A	Interrupt service specify
1 1	ISRB	Interrupt in-service register B	Interrupt service specify
1 3	IMRA	Interrupt mask register A	Masks interrupts
1 5	IMRB	Interrupt mask register B	Masks interrupts
1 7	VR	Vector register	Interrupt vector number
1 9	TACR	Timer A control register	Specifies timer A
1 B	TBCR	Timer B control register	Specifies timer B
1 D	TCDCR	Timers C and D control register	Specifies timers C and D
1 F	TADR	Timer A data register	Timer A count number
2 1	TBDR	Timer B data register	Timer B count number
2 3	TCDR	Timer C data register	Timer C count number
2 5	TDDR	Timer D data register	Timer D count number
2 7	SCR	Synchronous character register	Specifies synchronous character
2 9	UCR	USART control register	Specifies USART
2 B	RSR	Receiver status register	Receiver status
2 D	TSR	Transmitter status register	Transmitter status
2 F	UDR†	USART data register	Receiver/transmitter data

*Relative increment with respect to the base address.
†Receive register in read mode; transmit register in write mode.

FIGURE 8.9 The 68901 MFP internal register structure.

GPIP (General-Purpose I/O and Interrupt) Port The following three registers determine the mode of operation of the GPIP port:

> GPIP (general-purpose I/O register): at displacement $01;
>
> AER (active edge register): at displacement $03; and
>
> DDR (data direction register): at displacement $05.

Zero in a bit position of the DDR makes the corresponding GPIP line an input, and vice versa. Zero in a bit position of the AER causes an interrupt to be generated on the falling edge of the corresponding GPIP input line, and vice versa. These interrupts can be masked out by the interrupt mask registers, whereupon the GPIP inputs become normal inputs.

Timers A, B, C, and D The timer data registers TADR, TBDR, TCDR, and TDDR at displacement addresses $1F, $21, $23, and $25 can be loaded with 8-bit numbers. These registers act as down counters and produce pulses on the TAO, TBO, TCO, and TDO outputs when they are decremented to zero from the preloaded condition. The timer control registers TACR, TBCR, and TCDCR at displacement addresses $19, $1B, and $1D determine the mode of operation of the timer registers. Figure 8.10 illustrates the format of the TCDCR, which controls timers C and D. A delay mode implies that the timer registers are decremented after the prescaling of the input clock. The format of the TACR and TBCR registers is similar to that of the TCDCR, but the TACR and TBCR individually control the A and B timers.

FIGURE 8.10 Timer C and D control register (TCDCR) format.

CC2 DC2	CC1 DC1	CC0 DC0	Timer C operation mode Timer D operation mode
0	0	0	Timer stopped
0	0	1	Delay mode: divide-by-4 prescale
0	1	0	" " 10 "
0	1	1	" " 16 "
1	0	0	" " 50 "
1	0	1	" " 64 "
1	1	0	" " 100 "
1	1	1	" " 200 "

USART Operation and Control The USART can be configured to operate in a synchronous or an asynchronous mode, with different word formats and baud rates. The UDR (USART data register) at displacement address $2F acts as a receive data register during receive operations and as a transmit data register during transmit operations. The UCR (USART control register) at displacement address $29 controls the USART modes as shown in Figure 8.11.

The RSR (receive status register) and TSR (transmit status register) at displacement addresses $2B and $2D contain the receiver and transmitter status information as shown in Figure 8.12. In our discussion, we will focus on asynchronous serial communications, since they are more widely used. The MFP is also capable of synchronous communications. These involve synchronous protocols and are more complex than asynchronous communications.

We will now present an example problem to enhance our understanding of the MFP architecture and register formats.

FIGURE 8.11 USART control register (UCR) format.

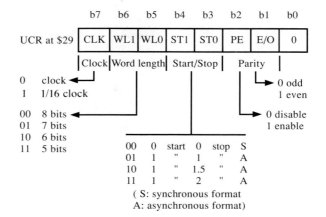

b7	BF	1⇒	receive buffer full
b6	OE	1⇒	overrun error
b5	PE	1⇒	parity error
b4	FE	1⇒	frame error
b3	B*	1⇒	break condition (all 0 data with no stop bits)
b2	CIP*	1⇒	character in progress
b1	SS*	1⇒	synchronous strip enable
b0	RE	1⇒	receiver enable (processor writes this bit)

*These bits have different meaning in synchronous communications.

(a)

b7	BE	1⇒	transmit buffer empty
b6	UE	1⇒	underrun error
b5	AT	1⇒	auto turnaround (receiver enabled after transmit)
b4	END	1⇒	end of transmission after which transmitter disabled
b3	B*	1⇒	break character to be transmitted next
b2	H*	HL = 00 ⇒ SO high Z	
b1	L*	01 ⇒ SO low [SO output control]
		10 ⇒ SO high	
		11 ⇒ loop back (transmitter and receiver are internally connected)	
b0	TE*	1⇒ transmitter enable	

*The processor writes these bits.

(b)

FIGURE 8.12 (a) USART receive status register (RSR) and (b) transmit status register (TSR) structure.

Example 8.4   68901 registers and architecture.

In a particular data communication application, the MFP is initialized with the following hex values in the registers:

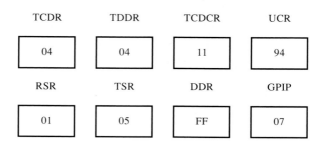

TCDR	TDDR	TCDCR	UCR
04	04	11	94

RSR	TSR	DDR	GPIP
01	05	FF	07

Using the information presented on the 68901 MFP,

1. specify how the GPIP is configured;

2. specify how the USART is configured;

3. specify how timers C and D are configured.

Solution (Refer to Figures 8.9 through 8.12.)

1. GPIP: $FF = 1\ 1\ 1\ 1\ 1\ 1\ 1\ 1$ is written into the DDR. It defines each bit of GPIP port (I7–I0) as an output. The GPIP register contents $07 = 0\ 0\ 0\ 0\ 0\ 1\ 1\ 1$ are output to the port making

$$I7-I0 \Rightarrow 0\ 0\ 0\ 0\ 0\ 1\ 1\ 1$$

2. USART: $94 = 1\ 0\ 0\ 1\ 0\ 1\ 0\ 0$ is written into the UCR. As such, the USART is configured for an 8-bit odd-parity word with one start and 1.5 stop bits. The shift clock is 1/16 of the respective RC (receive) and TC (transmit) clock inputs.

$$RSR \text{ contains } \$01 = 0\ 0\ 0\ 0\ 0\ 0\ 0\ 1$$

and

$$TSR \text{ contains } \$05 = 0\ 0\ 0\ 0\ 0\ 1\ 0\ 1$$

By writing 1 into b0 of RSR and TSR, both the receiver and the transmitter are enabled. The SO (serial output) is held at high level (b2 of TSR = 1) during inactive transmission.

3. Timers C and D:

$$\text{TCDR and TDDR contain } \$04 = 0\ 0\ 0\ 0\ 0\ 1\ 0\ 0$$

and

$$\text{TCDCR contains } \$11 = 0\ 0\ 0\ 1\ 0\ 0\ 0\ 1$$

Both timers are configured for a delayed and prescaled mode. Divide-by-4 prescaling has been selected (b4 and b0 = 1 in TCDCR). Further divide-by-4 action has been selected (b2 = 1 in TCDR and TDDR). This provides divide-by-16 action for both timer outputs TCO and TDO with reference to the crystal clock input.

The unused registers of the MFP do not effect the other operations. The reset condition of the MFP leaves most of these registers in a default state, which leaves the MFP in an inactive condition with disabled interrupts.

8.5 68901 MFP INTERFACE WITH THE 68000 AND APPLICATIONS

The 68901 MFP is a 68000-compatible I/O device. The multifunction capabilities of the 68901 make the I/O interface and applications very efficient and powerful.

68000/68901 and I/O Interface Considerations

Figure 8.13 illustrates the interface details of the 68901 with the 68000 processor and the I/O systems. The address decoders (refer to Section 6.3 of Chapter 6) generate the required chip select to the MFP. The system reset signal drives the MFP to reset the MFP and set default values in the registers. The R/$\overline{\text{W}}$ signal is interfaced directly for read/write operations.[10]

The MFP is mapped on the lower data byte D7−D0 to facilitate direct transfers of the interrupt vector numbers from the MFP to the processor. The $\overline{\text{LDS}}$ signal drives the $\overline{\text{DS}}$ (data strobe) input for the lower byte data transfers. The A5−A1 address lines drive the register select lines RS5−RS1 to address one of the internal 24 registers of the MFP. The $\overline{\text{DTACK}}$ is fed back to the processor through the interface logic. The clock input is the same as that for the processor. Another MFP can be mapped on upper byte of the data bus by using the $\overline{\text{UDS}}$ signal in place of the $\overline{\text{LDS}}$. Both MFP devices together occupy the 16-bit data bus for effective word transfers.

The SO and SI (serial out and serial in) lines are interfaced to the serial I/O unit. The 2.4576-MHz crystal activates the MFP for proper timing of the timers and the USART. The TCO and the TDO timer outputs are fed back as the RC and the TC clock inputs. The GPIP I/O port drives an LED display. For the conditions of Figure 8.13, the base address of the MFP is $040000. The GPIP is located at $040001, and so on.

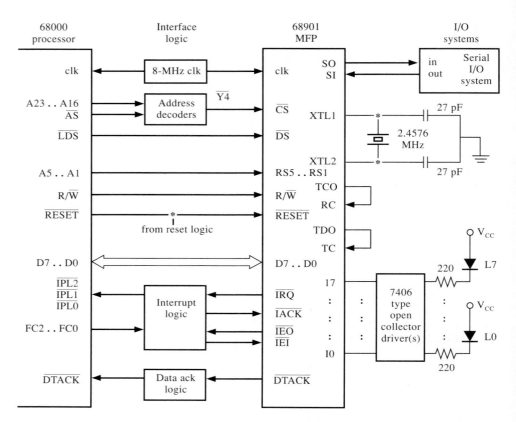

FIGURE 8.13 The 68901 MFP interface with the 68000 and with I/O systems (Example 8.5).

Coded Data Communication System

In order to maintain security, data may be coded during data communications. The 68000/68901 system of Figure 8.13 is well suited for such an application. The data are transmitted on the SO line to the I/O system in a coded form and are echoed back on the SI line of the MFP. The microprocessor reads and further codes the data, and displays the data on the GPIP port LED bank. The coding used for the data communication is the data inversion. The coding used for the display is to advance to the next ASCII value. The characters to be transmitted are in a memory buffer. A0 refers to the starting address and A1 refers to the ending address of the buffer.

Figure 8.14 indicates the 68000-based software for this coded data communication system. Between lines 6 and 16, the MFP registers that are relevant to this application are defined. Between lines 17 and 32, the MFP is initialized as follows (refer to Example 8.4 for details):

```
LINE   ADDR

  1;MFP.SRC CODED DATA COMMUNICATION
  2;fiu 2/89
  3;
  4                        OPT A
  5                        ORG $1000
  6;DEFINE 68901 MFP REGISTERS
  7 00040000   BASE       EQU $040000   ;BASE REG
  8 00040001   GPIP       EQU BASE+$01  ;GPIP PORT
  9 00040005   DDR        EQU BASE+$05  ;DATA DIR REG
 10 0004001D   TCDCR      EQU BASE+$1D  ;TIMER C/D CONTROL
 11 00040023   TCDR       EQU BASE+$23  ;TIMER C DATA REG
 12 00040025   DDR        EQU BASE+$25  ;TIMER D DATA REG
 13 00040029   UCR        EQU BASE+$29  ;USART CONTROL REG
 14 0004002B   RSR        EQU BASE+$2B  ;RCVR STATUS REG
 15 0004002D   TSR        EQU BASE+$2D  ;TNSMT STATUS REG
 16 0004002F   UDR        EQU BASE+$2F  ;USART DATA REG
 17;INITIALIZE GPIP AS OUTPUT
 18;INITIALIZE TIMERS C&D IN DIVIDE BY 16 MODE
 19;
 20 00001000 13FC 00FF 0004 INIT1 MOVE.B  #$FF,DDR ;GPIP OUT
            0005
 21 00001008 13FC 0000 0004       MOVE.B  #$00,GPIP
            0001
 22 00001010 13FC 0002 0004       MOVE.B  #$02,TCDR
            0023
 23 00001018 13FC 0002 0004       MOVE.B  #$02,TDDR
            0025
 24 00001020 13FC 0011 0004       MOVE.B  #$11,TCDCR
            001D
 25;USART FURTHER CONFIGURED FOR FURTHER DIVIDE BY 16
 26;1 START, 8 DATA, ODD PARITY & 1 1/2 STOP BITS
 27;
 28 00001028 13FC 0094 0004 INIT2 MOVE.B #$94,UCR ;FORMAT
            0029
 29 00001030 13FC 0001 0004       MOVE.B  #$01,RSR ;ENABLE
            002B                                    RCVR
```

FIGURE 8.14   Coded data communication software for the 68901/68000-based system (Example 8.5).

GPIP is configured as an 8-bit parallel output port;

USART is configured for 9600 baud, 8 data bits with 1 start and $1\frac{1}{2}$ stop bits, and odd parity;

Timers TC and TD are in a divide-by-16 mode.

Between lines 33 and 40, the transmit character routine is performed. The character from the memory buffer referenced by the A0 register is read into D0. It is coded by logical inversion and transmitted on the SO output. This is accomplished by checking bit 7 of the TSR for logical 1 (signifying that the USART transmit buffer register UDR is empty) and then writing the data byte in D0 into the UDR, if it is empty.

```
30 00001038 13FC 0005 0004        MOVE.B  #$05,TSR ;ENABLE
            002D                                   TSMTR
31 00001040 4E71                  NOP
32 00001042 4E71                  NOP
33;READ IT FROM CHARACTER BUFFER SEQUENTIALLY, CODE IT
34;AND TRANSMIT. A0 BEGINNING AND A1 END OF BUFFER
35 00001044 1018           START MOVE.B  (A0)+,D0 ;IN D0
36 00001046 0A00 00FF            EORI.B   #$FF,D0 ;INVERT IT
37 0000104A 0839 0007 0004 TRSMT BTST.B   #$7,TSR
            002D
38 00001052 67F6                  BEQ.S    TRSMT
39 00001054 13C0 0004 002F        MOVE.B   D0,UDR  ;CHRCTR IN
40 0000105A 4E71                  NOP              ;PORT
41;RECEIVE CODED CHARACTER FROM SERIAL PORT INTO D1
42 0000105C 0839 0007 0004 RCEVE BTST.B #$7,RSR
            0028
43 00001064 67F6                  BEQ.S    RCEVE
44 00001066 1239 0004 002F        MOVE.B   UDR,D1  ;CHRCTR INTO D1
45 0000106C 0A01 00FF            EORI.B   #$FF,D1 ;INVERT IT
46;CODE AGAIN AND SEND IT TO GPIP LED DISPLAY
47;
48 00001070 0601 0001      DSPLY ADDI.B   #$01,D1 ;NEXT
49 00001074 13C1 0004 0001        MOVE.B   D1,GPIP
50;SHORT DELAY AND CHECK END OF BUFFER
51 0000107A 343C 0F00            MOVE.W   #$0F00,D2
52 0000107E 5342            LOOP SUBQ.W   #$01,D2
53 00001080 66FC                  BNE.S    LOOP
54 00001082 B3C8                  CMPA.L   A0,A1      ;END OF BUFFER
55 00001084 66BE                  BNE.S    START    ;NO: TO START
56 00001086 60FE            WAIT BRA.S    WAIT;WAIT LOOP
57 00001088 4E71                  NOP
58;
59;
60 0000108A                       END

   ASSEMBLER ERRORS =      0
```

FIGURE 8.14 *Continued.*

Between lines 41 and 49, the receive character routine is performed. The echoed character from the serial I/O on the SI input is read into D1 after checking that the receive buffer is full. It is decoded by logical inversion. It is further coded to be the next ASCII character by adding 1 to it. Finally, it is output to the LED display on the GPIP output port.

Between lines 50 and 53, a delay routine is incorporated. At lines 54 and 55, the program checks for the end of the buffer. If the end of the buffer is not indicated, the program loops back to start. At line 56, the program goes into an indefinite wait loop.

The following example problem provides a review of the 68000/68901 interface and the coded data communication.

Example 8.5   68000/68901 coded data communication.
Consider the hardware and software of Figures 8.13 and 8.14.

1. What are the baud rates for data transmission and receiving?
2. Show how character A will be transmitted on the SO line.
3. Show how character A will be displayed on the LED array.
4. When does the WAIT loop at line 56 end? Why is it used?

Solution

1. **Baud rates:** The TCDR, TDDR, and the TCDCR are effectively configured for a divide-by-16 mode for the crystal input clock. Thus, TCO and TDO timer outputs (connected as RC and TC inputs) are at

$$2.4576 \text{ MHz}/16 = 153.6 \text{ KHz}$$

The UCR (USART control register) is configured for a divide-by-16 mode to obtain effective shift baud rates, given by

Receive baud rate = RC/16 = 9600 baud

Transmit baud rate = TC/16 = 9600 baud

2. **Transmission of character A:**

ASCII code for character A $= 0\ 1\ 0\ 0\ 0\ 0\ 0\ 1 \Rightarrow \$41$

Inverted code for character A $= 1\ 0\ 1\ 1\ 1\ 1\ 1\ 0 \Rightarrow \$BE$

The 68901 adds the start, odd-parity, and $1\frac{1}{2}$ stop bits to the preceding inverted data. The transmitted data on SO will be as shown:

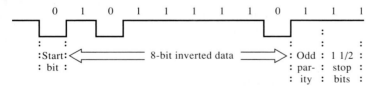

3. **Display on the LED array:** The received character in the inverted form is inverted back to the original character A. It is then coded to be the next ASCII character B. The ASCII code for B is $42; thus, the LED array displays

$$\$42 \Rightarrow 0\ 1\ 0\ 0\ 0\ 0\ 1\ 0$$

0 LED off; 1 LED on.

4. **WAIT loop:** The WAIT loop can be terminated only by an external interrupt or reset condition. In situations requiring external excitation, the software wait loops are used.

The coding in the preceding example is simple. However, it can be made as complex as required. The $1\frac{1}{2}$ stop-bit concept implies that the second stop bit is only half the period of the shift clock. However, the shift clock is 1/16 the frequency of the TC and the RC clock inputs. As such, the half stop bit can be accurately sampled by the RC and TC clocks. The half stop bit is intended to make the data frame more efficient.

8.6 SUMMARY

In this chapter we introduced some important serial data communication concepts. For interfacing slower peripherals and systems to a fast processor, serial communication is preferable to parallel communication. The standard asynchronous serial data frame consists of a stop bit, a data element, a parity bit, and one or two stop bits. The parity bit is for error checking. With serial interface, the number of external connections to the processor interface are reduced. This results in a cost efficient, less complex interface.

One of the industry standard serial communication devices for RS-232 serial communications is the 6850 ACIA (asynchronous communication interface adapter) of the earlier 6800 family. It consists of four internal registers: the control register, the status register, the transmit register, and the receive register. It accepts an 8-bit parallel word from the processor, converts it into RS-232 format, and serializes the data frame for transmission on the serial data link. Similarly, it accepts the serial data from the data link, checks the parity, removes the extra bits in the serial frame, converts it into an 8-bit parallel word, and supplies it to the processor.

We described interfacing the 68000 using the 6850 ACIA. We also described the industry standard RS-232 serial interface using the 6850 ACIA, including the details of a hardware and software application.

The 68901 MFP (multifunction peripheral) is a very useful device belonging to the 68000 family. We described its internal architecture and the particulars of the 68000/68901 MFP interface. The MFP device has integrated capabilities for serial data communications, timing, parallel I/O, interrupts, and DMA. It is particularly useful as a serial communication device.

The coded data communication example we presented was meant to provide a practical application of the MFP device and also illustrate the concept of data security in transmission and receiving. It should be noted, however, that there are more efficient data security methods than the one we considered.

PROBLEMS

8.1 Configure the control register of the ACIA to
(a) transmit an 8-bit odd-parity word with one stop bit;
(b) transmit a 7-bit even-parity word with two stop bits.

Consider an active low RTS in both cases. Use the divide-by-64 option at a 300 baud rate. Interrupts are disabled.

8.2 Repeat Problem 8.1 assuming that the data are to be received rather than transmitted.

8.3 The following message has been transmitted using the divide-by-16 option at 1200 baud with a 7-bit odd-parity format with one start bit and two stop bits:

6850   IS ACIA

(a) Specify the word frame for each of the characters using ASCII code.
(b) Specify the contents of the control register.

8.4 Repeat Problem 8.3 when an 8-bit frame with two stop bits and no parity is used.

8.5 Can the TX and RX baud rates be different? Explain.

(a) If they can be different, how can this be accomplished?
(b) What additional hardware would be required to achieve different baud rates for TX and RX?

8.6 Redesign the RS-232 interface of Figures 8.6 and 8.7 for data communications at

(a) 110 baud;
(b) 4800 baud.

8.7 For the 6850 ACIA/RS-232 interface, design the necessary hardware and software

(a) to receive 256 characters of data as a block at 600 baud and store the data in a buffer, with a 7-bit even-parity character format;
(b) to transmit the data at 300 baud after the entire block has been received.

8.8 Design a 6850-based coded data transmission system that will

(a) receive an ASCII character and also transmit the next highest ASCII character;
(b) receive an ASCII character and also transmit the next lowest ASCII character.

8.9 Repeat Problem 8.8 so that the higher and lower ASCII characters are transmitted for each received character as shown:

Received characters:	B	K	M
Transmitted characters:	A C	J L	L N

8.10 Can the 68901 MFP perform several functions simultaneously in real time? Can it operate at a frequency different from that of the processor? Explain your answers.

8.11 Using Example 8.4, with the crystal at 2.84596 MHz,

(a) what are the TCO and TDO frequencies?
(b) if the TCO and TDO are used as the RC and TC clock inputs, what are the effective shift rates of the receive and transmit shift registers of the 68901?

8.12 Reconfigure the 68901 MFP so that the GPIP has the lower nibble as the input and the upper nibble as the output. Specify the control words to be written into the appropriate registers.

(a) When outputting data on the GPIP, how do the pins configured as inputs behave?
(b) When entering the data, what is read on the pins configured as outputs?

8.13 Reconfigure timers C and D for

(a) delayed divide-by-64 prescale activity for both;

(b) delayed divide-by-200 prescale activity for both with additional divide-by-4 action in the 68901.

8.14 Can the C and D timers of the 68901 MFP count external events? Why or why not?

8.15 In the system of Figure 8.13, specify the redundant locations for the 68901 MFP registers.

8.16 Redesign the system of Figure 8.13 to allow for two MFP devices occupying the lower and upper memory bytes. Indicate all of the hardware details.

8.17 Redesign the software of Figure 8.14 so that reverse coding is done while transmitting a received character. For example

Received character code A $\Longrightarrow$ 0 1 0 0 0 0 0 1 $\Longrightarrow$ $41

Transmitted character code $\Longrightarrow$ 1 0 0 0 0 0 1 0 $\Longrightarrow$ $82

8.18 Redesign the system of Figure 8.13 so that

(a) the receive and the transmit baud rates are 1200;

(b) the receive baud rate is 1200, but the transmit baud rate is 600.

8.19 Repeat Problem 8.17 so that there is reverse coding and also code inversion. For example,

Received character code A $\Longrightarrow$ 0 1 0 0 0 0 0 1 $\Longrightarrow$ $41

Reverse code $\Longrightarrow$ 1 0 0 0 0 0 1 0 $\Longrightarrow$ $82

Inverted reverse
code for transmission $\Longrightarrow$ 0 1 1 1 1 1 0 1 $\Longrightarrow$ $7D

ENDNOTES

1. Harman, T., and Lawson, B. *The Motorola MC68000 Microprocessor*. Englewood Cliffs, NJ: Prentice-Hall, 1985.

2. Gaonkar, R. *Microprocessor Architecture, Programming, and Applications with the 8085/8080A*. Columbus, OH: Merrill, 1984.

3. Gibson, M., and Liu, C. *Microcomputers for Scientists and Engineers*. Englewood Cliffs, NJ: Prentice-Hall, 1987.

4. Motorola, Inc. *Data Sheets on M6850 ACIA*. Phoenix, AZ: Motorola Technical Operations, 1986.

5. Subbarao, W. *Microprocessors: Hardware, Software, and Design Applications*. Englewood Cliffs, NJ: Prentice-Hall, 1984.

6. Triebel, W., and Singh, A. "8086 Microprocessors." Chap. 12 in *16-Bit Microprocessors: Architecture, Software and Interfacing Techniques*. Englewood Cliffs, NJ: Prentice-Hall, 1985.

7. Melear, C. *Asynchronous Communications for MC6850*. App. Note #817. Austin, TX: Motorola Microprocessor Group, 1981.

8. Motorola, Inc. *MC68901 MFP Data Book*. Phoenix, AZ: Motorola Technical Operations, 1984.

9. Brown, G. *Serial I/O, Timer, and Interface Capabilities of the 68901*. App. Note #896. Austin, TX: Motorola Microprocessor Group, 1984.

10. Motorola, Inc. *MC68000 Data Book*. Phoenix, AZ: Motorola Technical Operations, 1983.

The 68000 Interrupt and DMA Interface and Applications

Objectives

In this chapter we will study:

Interrupt interface schemes associated with the 68000

Interrupt expansion schemes and daisy chaining

Interrupt-driven system applications

The DMA interface and controllers

DMA system interface design

9.0 INTRODUCTION

An interrupt is the traditional way in which the attention of the processor is obtained by an external device or a peripheral. By contrast, DMA (direct memory access) is the traditional way of obtaining control of the processor buses and is used by I/O systems for high-speed data transfers.

Interrupts are handled in the supervisor mode. The terms $\overline{\text{IRQ}}$ and $\overline{\text{INT}}$ are used interchangeably in this chapter to refer to the interrupt request. Study of the material to be presented will help the reader understand the interrupt and DMA structure of the 68000 family of processors so as to implement interrupt-based I/O systems and DMA-based data transfers.

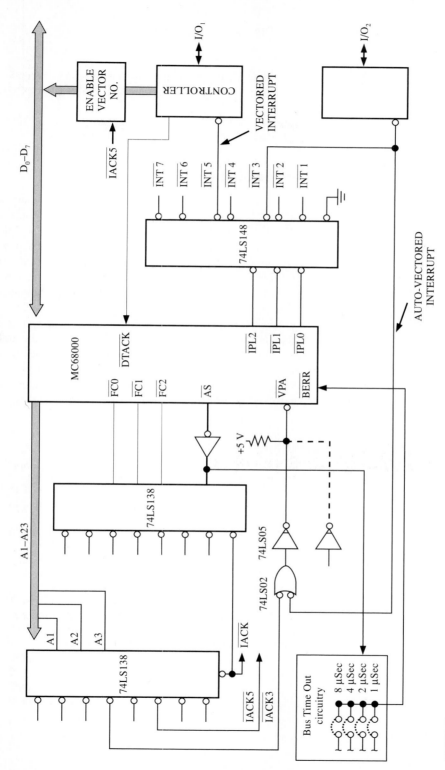

FIGURE 9.1 Autovector and user vector interrupt logic associated with the 68000. (Courtesy of Motorola, Inc.)

The reader is advised to review the concepts in Chapter 5 related to exception vectors and interrupts (Sections 5.1 and 5.2) before proceeding further.

9.1 INTERRUPT INTERFACE CONSIDERATIONS

Autovectored and User-vectored Interrupt Logic

Figure 9.1 (p. 237) illustrates the autovectored and user-vectored interrupt logic associated with the 68000 processor. The I/O-2 device generates interrupt request $\overline{INT3}$, which is encoded onto the $\overline{IPL2}$, $\overline{IPL1}$, and $\overline{IPL0}$ inputs of the processor by the 74LS148 encoder. In response to $\overline{INT3}$, the processor generates an $\overline{IACK3}$ interrupt acknowledge signal, which is gated as $\overline{VPA}$ input to the processor for **autovectoring.** During the interrupt acknowledge cycle, the FC2, FC1, and FC0 outputs of the processor remain at the 111 condition; the A3, A2, and A1 address lines contain the interrupt number that is being acknowledged. In this case, A3, A2, and A1 will be at 011.

The I/O-1 device generates interrupt request $\overline{INT5}$. The processor generates the corresponding $\overline{IACK5}$ interrupt acknowledge signal, which is routed to the interrupt controller of the I/O-1 device. In response to $\overline{IACK5}$, the controller provides the interrupt vector number on the data bus and activates the $\overline{DTACK}$ input to the processor for **user vectoring.** In either case, the processor goes to the appropriate vector location as outlined in Chapter 5, and executes the interrupt service routine in the supervisor mode.[1]

Priority		Channel	Description
highest	$0F	1 1 1 1	GPIP interrupt I7
	$0E	1 1 1 0	GPIP interrupt I6
	$0D	1 1 0 1	Timer A
	$0C	1 1 0 0	Receive buffer full
	$0B	1 0 1 1	Receive error
	$0A	1 0 1 0	Transmit buffer empty
	$09	1 0 0 1	Transmit error
	$08	1 0 0 0	Timer B
	$07	0 1 1 1	GPIP interrupt I5
	$06	0 1 1 0	GPIP interrupt I4
	$05	0 1 0 1	Timer C
	$04	0 1 0 0	Timer D
	$03	0 0 1 1	GPIP interrupt I3
	$02	0 0 1 0	GPIP interrupt I2
	$01	0 0 0 1	GPIP interrupt I1
lowest	$00	0 0 0 0	GPIP interrupt I0

FIGURE 9.2 The 68901 MFP interrupt channels and priority structure. (Courtesy of Motorola, Inc.)

Interrupt Controllers

An **interrupt controller** is a device that can prioritize interrupts, provide vector numbers to the processor, and keep track of the occurrence of the interrupts. The 68901 MFP introduced in the previous chapter is such an interrupt controller belonging to the 68000 family. The MFP handles 16 interrupt channels (8 from the internal sources and 8 from the external GPIP lines I0–I7 used as interrupt inputs). In Figure 9.2 the priority structure of these interrupt channels is indicated. (Refer to Chapter 8 for 68901 MFP details.) The MFP controls these interrupts using

the interrupt enable registers A and B (IERA and IERB);

the interrupt mask registers A and B (IMRA and IMRB);

the interrupt pending registers A and B (IPRA and IPRB);

the interrupt in-service registers A and B (ISRA and ISRB); and

the interrupt vector register (VR).[2]

Figure 9.3 illustrates the format of the IERA and IERB. These two registers enable or disable the interrupts. If the bit is set (= 1), the corresponding interrupt is enabled. If the bit is reset (= 0), the corresponding interrupt is disabled. When the interrupt is enabled, its occurrence will be recognized by the MFP, and the $\overline{IRQ}$ will be asserted to the processor. All the other interrupt-related registers have bit maps similar to that of the IERA/IERB.

Interrupts are masked for a channel by clearing the appropriate bit to 0 in the mask registers IMRA/IMRB. When an interrupt is enabled but masked, it will be recognized by the MFP, but the $\overline{IRQ}$ will not be asserted to the processor. Instead, the corresponding bit in the interrupt pending registers IPRA/IPRB will be set. The processor can poll these registers to determine if an interrupt has occurred.

	b7	b6	b5	b4	b3	b2	b1	b0
IERA at dis $07	GPIP 7	GPIP 6	TIMER A	R. BUFF empty	RCV error	T. BUFF empty	TMIT error	TIMER B

	b7	b6	b5	b4	b3	b2	b1	b0
IERB at dis $09	GPIP 5	GPIP 4	TIMER C	TIMER D	GPIP 3	GPIP 2	GPIP 1	GPIP 0

	b7	b6	b5	b4	b3	b2	b1	b0
VR at dis $17	V7	V6	V5	V4	IV3	IV2	IV1	IV0

:⟵[User-written ⟶:⟵] MFP-supplied ⟶:

dis ⟹ displacement address of the MFP registers.

FIGURE 9.3 Structure of the interrupt enable registers, IERA and IERB, and the vector register, VR.

When a bit in the ISRA/ISRB is set, it implies that the corresponding interrupt vector number has been given to the processor and that the interrupt routine is in progress.

For external GPIP interrupt inputs, the active edge register (AER) of the MFP is used to specify the edge activation. A zero in a bit position makes the corresponding interrupt active on a high-to-low transition, and vice versa.

The interrupt vector number is contained in the vector register (VR), as indicated in Figure 9.3. The upper four bits are written by the user during initialization. The lower four bits are written by the MFP according to the priority scheme of Figure 9.2.

Interrupt Expansion and the Daisy-Chain Mechanism

In 68000-based systems, the MFP interrupt controllers are assigned to one of the seven possible interrupt levels of the processor. Each MFP supports up to 16 interrupts (8 internal and 8 external). However, in systems that are I/O-based to a large extent, there may be a requirement to increase the number of interrupt inputs. This can be accomplished by **daisy chaining** the interrupt controllers, as shown in Figure 9.4. The controller closest to the processor (MFP 1, in this case) has the highest priority. It is always enabled by keeping its interrupt enable input, $\overline{\text{IEI}}$, grounded.

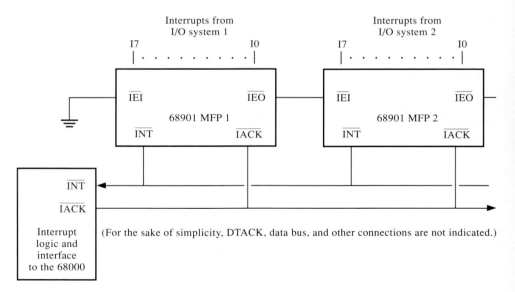

FIGURE 9.4   Interrupt expansion using the daisy-chain mechanism.

When the processor recognizes the interrupt request on the common $\overline{\text{INT}}$ line, it sends the acknowledge signal $\overline{\text{IACK}}$ to the controllers. Suppose the interrupt request has come from MFP 1. MFP 1 accepts the $\overline{\text{IACK}}$ signal, puts the corresponding vector number on the data bus, and activates the $\overline{\text{DTACK}}$ to the processor. At the same time, it negates its interrupt enable output, $\overline{\text{IEO}}$. This, in turn, disables the next controller by deactivating its interrupt enable input, $\overline{\text{IEI}}$.

On the other hand, if we assume that MFP 2 has generated the $\overline{\text{INT}}$, MFP 1 activates its $\overline{\text{IEO}}$ output and enables the MFP 2 controller during the interrupt acknowledge cycle. MFP 2, in turn, supplies the vector number to the processor in response to the $\overline{\text{IACK}}$ signal. This enable and disable process continues until the end of the chain.

In the preceding case, it can be seen that a single $\overline{\text{INT}}$ line can be expanded to handle 32 interrupts (16 from each controller). The number of entries in the vector table and the electronic loading on the lines determine the practical upper limit for the number of controllers on the daisy chain.[3]

The following example problem provides a review of the interrupt interface to the 68000 and the daisy-chain mechanism.

Example 9.1   68000 interrupt interface and daisy chain.

Assume that the $\overline{\text{IRQ}}$ outputs from the daisy-chained controllers of Figure 9.4 activate the $\overline{\text{IRQ5}}$ input to the 68000 system. ($\overline{\text{IRQ}}$ and $\overline{\text{INT}}$ refer to the same thing.)

1. Interrupt I7 from I/O system 2 and interrupt I6 from I/O system 1 occur simultaneously and activate the $\overline{\text{IRQ5}}$ line to the processor interface logic. Which interrupt will be recognized? Assume the interrupts are enabled and are not masked.

2. Suppose it is required to disable all the other interrupts except the GPIP interrupts for both controllers. In addition, GPIP interrupts I4–I0 should be masked out. What words should be written into the interrupt enable and mask registers?

3. If the upper four bits of the vector register for MFP 1 are loaded with $4, what vector number is supplied to the processor by MFP 1 for GPIP interrupt I6?

Solution

1. **Interrupt recognition:** MFP 1 is of higher priority than MFP 2 in the daisy chain. Thus, interrupt I6 from MFP 1 will be recognized.

2. **Disabling and masking of interrupts:** Refer to the bit map of the IERA/IERB (Figure 9.3).

> 0 in the bit position disables the interrupt;
> 1 in the bit position enables the interrupt.

The mask registers IMRA/IMRB have a similar bit map.

> 0 in the bit position masks the interrupt;
> 1 in the bit position does not mask the interrupt.

To enable all the GPIP interrupts, disable the others, and additionally mask the I4–I0 interrupts, the bit patterns should be written as follows:

b7	b6	b5	b4	b3	b2	b1	b0	register
1	1	0	0	0	0	0	0	into IERA
1	1	0	0	1	1	1	1	into IERB
1	1	0	0	0	0	0	0	into IMRA
1	0	0	0	0	0	0	0	into IMRB

3. **Vector number for I6:** Refer to Figure 9.2. The channel priority number for I6 is 1110 = $E. This will be loaded into the lower four bits of its vector register by MFP 1. The upper four bits are written by the user to be $4 = 0100. Thus, the vector for the I6 interrupt corresponds to

$$0\ 1\ 0\ 0\ 1\ 1\ 1\ 0 = \$4E$$

9.2 INTERRUPT-DRIVEN SYSTEM APPLICATIONS

As we already know, the interrupt is a convenient means by which to obtain the attention of the processor. We will now emphasize this concept by describing practical applications involving the interrupt-driven gain controllers, DRAM systems, and data-acquisition systems.

Interrupt-Driven Gain Controller

Figure 9.5 illustrates a digital gain-controller system. The 68901 MFP discussed earlier is used as an interrupt controller. The GPIP drives a summing amplifier-type D/A (digital-to-analog) converter. The D/A converter, in turn, drives a power amplifier and a DC motor.[4]

The internal B timer of the MFP is used to generate a timed interrupt to the processor. The $\overline{IRQ}$ output from the MFP drives level 1 of the interrupt ($\overline{IRQ1}$) of the 68000 processor through the encoder device. Each time the timer is decremented to zero from a preloaded value, an interrupt is generated by the timer. The 68901 routes that interrupt to the processor as $\overline{IRQ1}$.

When the processor recognizes this interrupt, it generates a higher gain digital word on the GPIP output, up to the maximum allowed. The processor increases the gain from a minimum to a maximum value and restarts the gain process. This has the effect of increasing the motor speed to a maximum at regular time intervals, reducing the speed to a minimum, and then starting the process again. In industry, such systems are used to control conveyer belts.

We will now discuss the design details by means of an example problem.

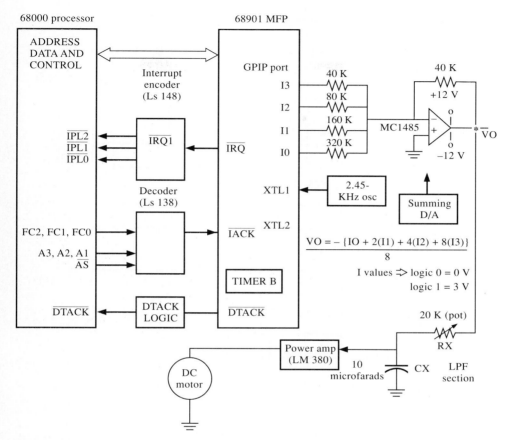

FIGURE 9.5   The 68000-based interrupt-driven gain controller system (Example 9.2).

Example 9.2   Interrupt-driven gain controller

For the system of Figure 9.5, the MFP occupies the memory map starting at base address \$040000 (GPIP at \$040001. . .). Develop (1) the operating hardware and (2) the software so that the motor speed increases to the next value up in 20-second intervals.

Solution

1. **Hardware:** The hardware of Figure 9.5 is self-contained. If increased drive capability is required, additional power amplifier stages can be incorporated. The XTL1 clock input for the MFP is driven by a 2.456-KHz oscillator. The low-pass filter (LPF) effectively removes any switching transients from the D/A converter.

2. **Software:** The software initializes the appropriate MFP interrupt and timer-related registers (refer to Sections 8.4, 8.5, and 9.1). It increases the digital gain word to the next value up on each timer interrupt occurrence. This digital word is then output to

the GPIP port. (The word is converted to an analog voltage and drives the motor at the appropriate speed.)

Figure 9.6 details the MFP initialization process. The unused registers are loaded with the inactive words on system reset. The flowchart and the 68000 program listings for the interrupt-driven gain controller are presented in Figures 9.7 and 9.8, respectively.

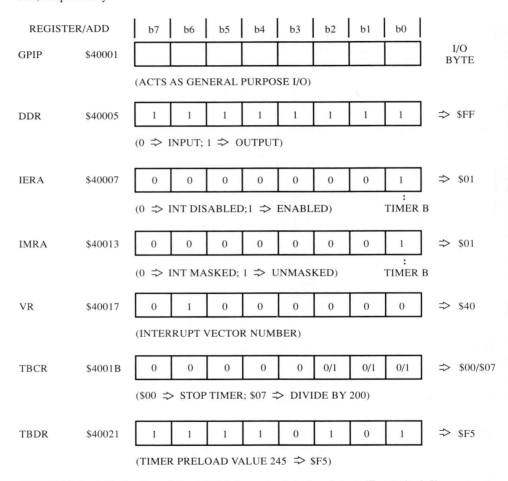

FIGURE 9.6 Initialization of the MFP interrupt-related registers (Example 9.2).

Between lines 6 to 23 in the listings, all the MFP registers used in the software are declared and initialized. Timer B has an internal priority of 8 (refer to Section 9.1), which presents an effective device interrupt vector of $40 + $08 = $48 to the processor. This refers to a vector address of

$$4 \times \$48 = \$120$$

FIGURE 9.7 Flowchart for the interrupt-driven gain controller using the 68901 MFP with the 68000.

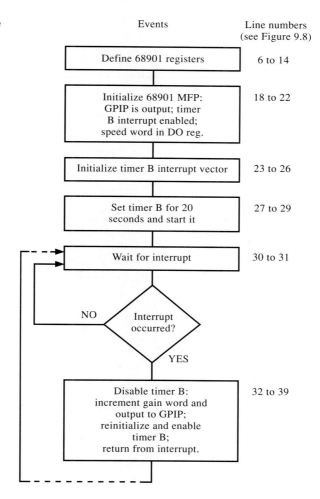

Events   Line numbers (see Figure 9.8)

Define 68901 registers — 6 to 14

Initialize 68901 MFP: GPIP is output; timer B interrupt enabled; speed word in DO reg. — 18 to 22

Initialize timer B interrupt vector — 23 to 26

Set timer B for 20 seconds and start it — 27 to 29

Wait for interrupt — 30 to 31

Interrupt occurred? — NO / YES

Disable timer B: increment gain word and output to GPIP; reinitialize and enable timer B; return from interrupt. — 32 to 39

At line 25, the interrupt service routine address of $2000 is loaded into this vector address location of $120.

At lines 28 and 29, the timer data and control registers (TBDR and TBCR) are loaded with $F5 and $07. This enables timer B with a prescale factor of 200. Timer B counts down and generates an interrupt when it is decremented to zero from the preset value of $F5 (= 245). With a 2.45-KHz XTL1 clock, this generates a 20-second delay between successive interrupts as shown:

$$\textbf{Delay} = (\textbf{prescale factor}) \times (\textbf{preset value}) \times (\textbf{XTL1 period})$$
$$= (\textbf{200}) \times (\textbf{245}) \times (\textbf{1/2.45 KHz}) = \textbf{20 seconds}$$

At lines 30 and 31, the system goes into a wait loop and waits for the above interrupt to occur.

```
LINE   ADDR
  1                                      ;int controller
  2                                      ;FIU 9/7/88
  3                                      ;
  4                                         OPT      A
  5                                         ORG      $1000
  6                                      ;68901 register  declarations
  7   00040000                          BASE     EQU       $040000
  8   00040001                          GPIP     EQU       BASE+$01
  9   00040005                          DDR      EQU       BASE+$05
 10   00040007                          IERA     EQU       BASE+$07
 11   00040013                          IMRA     EQU       BASE+$13
 12   00040017                          VR       EQU       BASE+$17
 13   0004001B                          TBCR     EQU       BASE+$1B
 14   00040021                          TBDR     EQU       BASE+$21
 15                                      ;initialize MFP: GPIP is output
 16                                      ;Timer B interrupt enabled
 17                                      ;initialize D0 with speed word
 18   00001000  13FC 00FF 0004  START MOVE.B  #$FF,DDR
                 0005
 19   00001008  103C 0000             MOVE.B  #$00,D0     ;MINIMUM SPEED
 20   0000100C  13C0 0004 0001        MOVE.B  D0,GPIP
 21   00001012  08F9 0000 0004        BSET.B  #0,IERA
                 0007
 22   0000101A  08F9 0000 0004        BSET.B  #0,IMRA
                 0013
 23   00001022  13FC 0040 0004        MOVE.B  #$40,VR
                 0017
 24                                      ;interrupt address $2000 into $120
 25   0000102A  21FC 0000 2000        MOVE.L  #$2000,$120
                 0120
 26   00001032  4071                  NOP
 27                                      ;set Timer B for 20 seconds
 28   00001034  13FC 00F5 0004        MOVE.B  #$F5,TBDR
                 0021
 29   0000103C  13FC 0007 0004        MOVE.B  #$07,TBCR ;start timer
                 001B
 30   00001044  60FE          WAIT BRA.S    WAIT        ;wait for
 31   00001046  60FC               BRA.S    WAIT        ;interrupt loop
 32                                  ORG      $2000  ;interrupt routine
 33   00002000  13FC 0000 0004        MOVE.B  #$00,TBCR ;disable timer
                 001B
 34   00002008  5200                  ADDQ.B  #$01,D0    ;next gain word
 35   0000200A  13C0 0004 0001        MOVE.B  D0,GPIP    ;output to GPIP
 36   00002010  13FC 00F5 0004        MOVE.B  #$F5,TBDR ;20 sec timer
                 0021
 37   00002018  13FC 0007 0004        MOVE.B  #$07,TBCR ;start timer
                 001B
 38   00002020  4071                  NOP
 39   00002022  4073                  RTE
```

FIGURE 9.8 Software listings for the interrupt-driven gain controller using the 68901 MFP (Example 9.2).

When the timer B interrupt is generated once every 20 seconds, the processor goes to the interrupt service routine between lines 32 and 39 (starting address $2000). The interrupt service routine stops timer B by loading $00 into the TBCR. It increments and outputs the digital gain word in the D0 register to the GPIP. It re-loads the timer B data register with $F5 and restarts it. The last RTE instruction returns the processor to the wait loop.

The timer B interrupt is communicated to the processor as a level 1 interrupt. The processor interrupt mask level in the system byte should be initialized to zero for recognizing a level 1 interrupt. With few modifications to the preceding software, it is possible to obtain a different result, as we will see in the following example.

Example 9.3   Modified interrupt-driven gain controller.

Modify the software in Figure 9.8 so that the gain will not be increased if it is already at the allowed maximum.

Solution

The maximum allowed gain word is $FF in the D0 register. The D0 register should only be incremented if its byte content is less than $FF. The interrupt routine between lines 33 to 39 should be modified as shown:

```
          MOVE.B    #$00,TBCR    ;disable timer B
          CMP.B     #$FF,D0      ;compare D0 with $FF
          BEQ.S     FINAL        ;if equal branch to final inst
          ADDQ.B    #$01,D0      ;if not increment D0 by 1
FINAL     MOVE.B    D0,GPIP      ;output new gain word to GPIP
          MOVE.B    #$F5,TBDR    ;set timer to 20 seconds
          MOVE.B    #$07,TBCR    ;start timer B
          NOP
          RTE                    ;return (to wait loop)
```

It should be noted that when the system reaches the maximum gain condition, it stays at that condition.

Dynamic Random Access Memory (DRAM) Interface

Because of their higher density, DRAMs are fast replacing the static RAMs in large memory systems. DRAMs store binary information in the form of charge on MOS transistor cells. These cells have to be **refreshed** (rewritten) periodically, so that the charge will not decay and the information will not be lost. The typical refresh time for a mem-

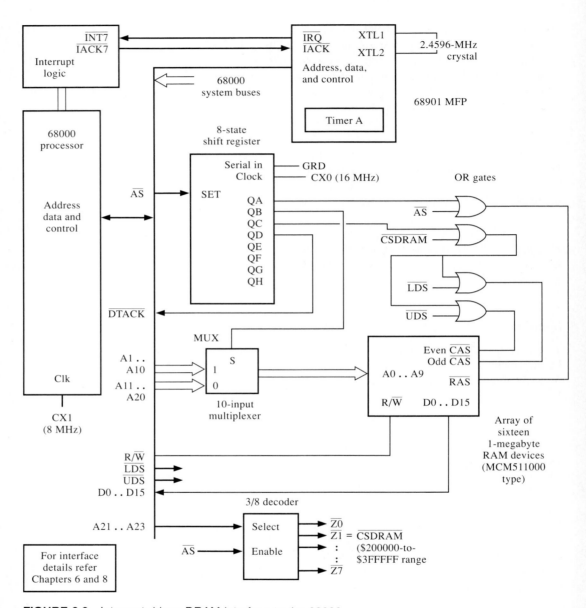

FIGURE 9.9   Interrupt-driven DRAM interface to the 68000.

ory cell is 2 milliseconds. This refresh activity can be easily controlled with the help of interrupts and software techniques.[5,6]

A 1-megabyte DRAM device (such as the Motorola MCM511000) is organized as 512 rows by 2,048 columns. During the first half of the bus cycle, the row address is presented to the DRAM and the $\overline{RAS}$ (row address strobe) is activated. All 512 cells on that row present their information internally to sense amplifiers. During the second half of the bus cycle, the column address is presented and the $\overline{CAS}$ (column address strobe) is activated. One out of the 2,048 columns is selected, and the appropriate data bit is thus addressed. For refreshing, it is sufficient that the row address be supplied and RAS activated.

Twenty address lines are required to access one out of a million locations. Externally, ten row address lines (A1–A10) and ten column address lines (A11–A20) are multiplexed to drive the ten address lines of the DRAM (pins A0–A9). Internally, these twenty effective address lines are adjusted in groups of nine and eleven (to address one out of 512 rows and one out of 2,048 columns).

Figure 9.9 illustrates a 1-megaword DRAM system interface with a 68000 processor, occupying the range between $200000 and $3FFFFF. The 68901 is used as an interrupt controller to generate a nonmaskable interrupt (level 7), once every 2 milliseconds. The processor recognizes this interrupt and executes 512 sequential NOP instructions contained in system ROM or EPROM. For the system shown, $\overline{RAS}$ is generated while the address lines A1–A9 from the 68000 change in sequence. This has the effect of refreshing the 512 rows (of all the 16 DRAM devices) in sequence. The DRAM is selected only when the $\overline{CSDRAM}$ and $\overline{CAS}$ signals are generated. This happens only when the locations in the DRAM are addressed.

If the DRAM is not refreshed within 2-millisecond intervals, the information may be lost. The highest priority interrupt is used (in this case, interrupt level 7) so that the processor will not mask it and will respond to the refresh operation.

In Figure 9.10, the DRAM refresh software listings are given. During the system initialization (reset routine), the DRAM module is called as a subroutine to initialize the interrupt controller (in this case, the 68901 MFP). (Refer to Chapter 8 for a description of the MFP/68000 interface.) Timer A, with an internal interrupt priority of $D, is used in this application to generate a 2-millisecond delay.

Between lines 6 and 11, the MFP registers required for this application are declared. At line 14 the vector register of the MFP is loaded with $40. When timer A generates an interrupt, the corresponding vector number is

$$\textbf{\$40 + priority of timer A = \$40 + \$D = \$4D}$$

The corresponding exception vector location is

$$\textbf{4} \times \textbf{vector number = 4} \times \textbf{\$4D = \$134}$$

At line 15, this vector location is loaded with the starting address of the interrupt service routine (INTR module).

```
LINE    ADDR

  1                                          ;ram.src 3/6/89
  2                                          ;DRAM software refresh
  3                                                 OPT      A
  4                                                 ORG      $1300
  5                                          ;68901 register declarations
  6   00040000                              BASE     EQU      $040000
  7   00040007                              IERA     EQU      BASE+$07
  8   00040013                              IMRA     EQU      BASE+$13
  9   00040017                              VR       EQU      BASE+$17
 10   00040019                              TACR     EQU      BASE+$19
 11   0004001F                              TADR     EQU      BASE+$1F
 12   00004E71                              NOP      EQU      $4E71
 13                                          ;initialize 68901 for refresh
 14   00001300  13FC 0040 0004    DRAM MOVE.B   #$40,VR
                0017
 15   00001308  21FC 0000 1336         MOVE.L   #INTR,$134
                0134 4E71
 16                                          ;enable timer A interrupt
 17   00001312  08F9 0005 0004         BSET.B   #5,IERA
                0007
 18   0000131A  08F9 0005 0004         BSET.B   #5,IMRA
                0013
 19                                          ;timer  A for 2 milliseconds
 20   00001322  13FC 0031 0004         MOVE.B   #$31,TADR
                001F
 21   0000132A  13FC 0006 0004         MOVE.B   #$06,TACR
                0019
 22   00001332  4E71                   NOP
 23   00001334  4E75                   RTS
 24                                          ;interrupt routine corresponds
 25                                          ;to 512 locations of NOP codes
 26   00001336  4E71 4E71    INTR DCB.W           512,NOP
 27   00001736  4E73                   RTE
 28   00001738                         END

ASSEMBLER ERRORS =      0
```

FIGURE 9.10 Listings for the DRAM refresh software.

Between lines 17 and 22, the timer A interrupt is enabled and the timer A data and control registers are conditioned to generate an interrupt every 2 milliseconds. At line 25, the subroutine returns to the calling program.

The interrupt routine INTR starts at line 26. The NOP codes are sequentially arranged by means of the DCB.W 512,NOP assembler statement. When interrupt 7 occurs, these 512 NOPs are executed and the program returns to the interrupted program by means of the RTE instruction at line 27.

The following example problem provides a review of the interrupt controller and the DRAM implementation.

Example 9.4   Interrupt-driven DRAM implementation.

Consider the DRAM system and software of Figures 9.9 and 9.10.

1. Specify the relative timing of the $\overline{\text{RAS}}$, MUX, $\overline{\text{CAS}}$, and $\overline{\text{DTACK}}$ signal generation.
2. Specify how timer A is configured to generate an interrupt once every 2 milliseconds.
3. What percentage of processor time is taken for refresh?

Solution

1. **$\overline{\text{RAS}}$, MUX, and $\overline{\text{CAS}}$:** $\overline{\text{AS}}$ is generated each time a bus cycle is initiated. $\overline{\text{RAS}}$ is generated one CX0 (16 MHz) clock period after the $\overline{\text{AS}}$ signal. $\overline{\text{RAS}}$ latches the row address on the DRAM pins.

   MUX is generated two CX0 clock periods after the $\overline{\text{AS}}$ signal. This presents the column address to the DRAM pins.

   $\overline{\text{CAS}}$ is generated three CX0 clock periods after the $\overline{\text{AS}}$ if the $\overline{\text{CSDRAM}}$ signal is activated. $\overline{\text{CAS}}$ latches the column address on the DRAM pins; the DRAM is selected only after $\overline{\text{CAS}}$.

   $\overline{\text{DTACK}}$ is generated four CX0 clock periods after the $\overline{\text{AS}}$ signal. This is a proper timing sequence for data transfers.

2. **Timer A interrupt:** Bit 5 of the interrupt enable and interrupt mask registers (IERA and IMRA) is set to 1, enabling the timer A interrupt. When the timer counts down to zero from the preloaded number, an interrupt is generated. Timer A is decremented by the XTL1 clock. The timing calculation is as follows:

   $$\text{TACR loaded with } 6 = 100 \text{ prescale factor}$$
   $$\text{TADR loaded with } \$31 = 49$$
   $$\text{XTL1 crystal clock} = 2.4596 \text{ MHz}$$

   Thus,

   $$\textbf{Timer A countdown period} = \frac{\textbf{100} \times \textbf{49}}{\textbf{2.4596} \times \textbf{10}^{\textbf{6}}} = \textbf{2 milliseconds}$$

3. **Percentage of processor time for refresh:** Refresh time corresponds to executing 512 NOP instructions. Each NOP instruction takes four CX1 processor clock periods. The timing calculation is as follows:

   $$\text{CX1 8-MHz processor clock} = 125 \text{ nanoseconds cycle time}$$
   $$\text{NOP execution time} = 4 \times 125 = 500 \text{ nanoseconds}$$
   $$= 0.5 \text{ microseconds}$$
   $$\text{512 NOP execution time} = 512 \times 0.5 = 256 \text{ microseconds}$$

These 512 NOPs have to be executed once every 2-millisecond refresh interval. Thus,

$$\text{Percentage refresh time} = \frac{256 \text{ microseconds}}{2 \text{ milliseconds}} \times 100 = 12.8 \text{ percent}$$

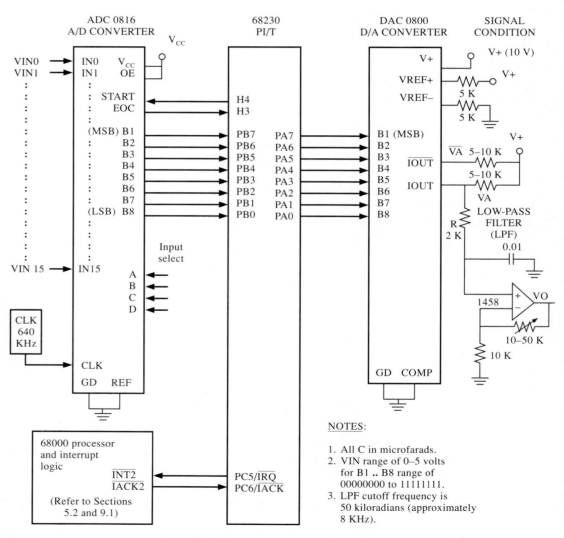

FIGURE 9.11 Interrupt-driven A/D and D/A interface to the 68000. (Courtesy of Laura Ruiz and José Zarut, FIU)

Software refresh eliminates the need for additional hardware. In the preceding case, 12.8 percent of the processor time is devoted exclusively for refreshing 1-megaword of memory. Interrupt stacking and unstacking takes a few more clock cycles. In small-to-medium systems, such an arrangement is acceptable. However, for larger systems with more memory, hardware refresh is used with the help of memory management units.

9.3 THE INTERRUPT-DRIVEN DATA-ACQUISITION SYSTEM AND APPLICATIONS

The usefulness of any microprocessor-based system is greatly enhanced when it is interfaced with the analog word. This can be accomplished easily with the help of A/D (analog-to-digital) and D/A (digital-to-analog) converters. The processor-to-A/D interface can be interrupt driven to make efficient use of the processor time.[7]

The A/D and D/A Interface

Figure 9.11 illustrates a typical A/D and D/A interface to the 68000 microprocessor through the 68230 PI/T (refer to Chapter 7 for PI/T details). ADC 0816 is an 8-bit 16-channel A/D converter device. By means of the select word DCBA, any one of the 16 input channels (VIN0–VIN15) can be selected. DCBA = 0000 selects VIN0, and DCBA = 1111 selects VIN15.

All of these analog voltages are signal conditioned and filtered before being applied to the A/D converter. Figure 9.12 illustrates a typical signal-conditioning system.

FIGURE 9.12 Analog signal conditioning for VIN inputs to the A/D converter.

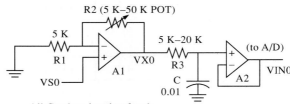

All C values in microfarads

A1: Noninverting amplifier
$$VX0 = (1 + R2/R1) \, VS0$$
R3 and C compose a low-pass filter with a radian cutoff frequency of
$wo = 1/(R3 \times C)$ radians sec.

A2: Voltage follower with unity gain. Its output is
$$VIN0 = [1/1 + jw/wo)] \, [VX0]$$
where w is the radian frequency of VS0 input and j is the imaginary operator.

For low frequencies less than wo, VIN0 = VX0.

The signal input VS0 is buffered by high-input impedance noninverting amplifier A1. The A1 amplifier has an effective voltage gain of $1 + (R2/R1)$. VS0 input should be in the range of 0 to 5 volts for this system. The R3-C network provides low-pass filter action to remove switching transients. The A2 amplifier is a voltage follower, the output (VIN0) of which is applied as input0 (IN0) to the A/D converter of Figure 9.11.

The A/D converter digitizes the applied analog input voltage VIN and produces a corresponding 8-bit digital word on its B1–B8 outputs. A 640-KHz clock drives the A/D converter. The converter is interfaced to port B of the 68230 PI/T. The H3 and H4 handshake lines control the A/D. A pulse from the microcomputer on the H4 line to the START input of the A/D converter starts the conversion of the selected VIN input.

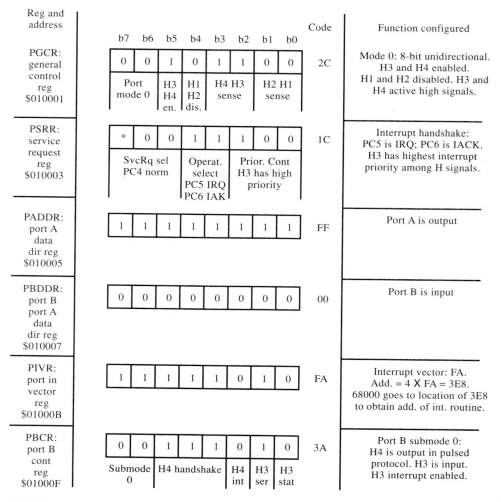

FIGURE 9.13 The 68230 PI/T register initialization for the data-acquisition system.

When the conversion is complete, the A/D converter generates a pulse on its EOC (end of conversion). It is connected to the H3 handshake input of the 68230 which in turn, generates an interrupt to the processor on its PC5/$\overline{\text{IRQ}}$ line. In this application, $\overline{\text{IRQ}}$ drives a level 2 interrupt ($\overline{\text{INT2}}$).

The DAC 0800 D/A converter is interfaced to port A of the 68230 PI/T as indicated. This 8-bit D/A converts the processed digital word on its B1–B8 inputs (sent by the processor on its port A) into a corresponding analog voltage VA. VA is filtered using the low-pass filter (LPF) amplifier to remove any step and switching transients and to provide a reconstructed analog voltage VO. The LPF has a cutoff frequency of 8 KHz, which is sufficient in most audio, control, and instrumentation systems.[8]

FIGURE 9.14 Flowchart for the 68000-based data-acquisition system (Example 9.5).

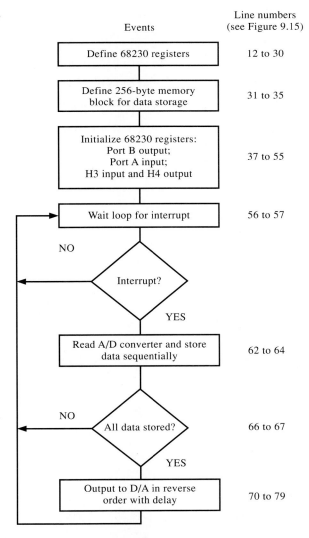

Events	Line numbers (see Figure 9.15)
Define 68230 registers	12 to 30
Define 256-byte memory block for data storage	31 to 35
Initialize 68230 registers: Port B output; Port A input; H3 input and H4 output	37 to 55
Wait loop for interrupt	56 to 57
Interrupt?	
Read A/D converter and store data sequentially	62 to 64
All data stored?	66 to 67
Output to D/A in reverse order with delay	70 to 79

```
LINE   ADDR
  1                                    LLEN 108
  2                                    OPT A
  3                            *
  4                            * ADC/DAC SYSTEM INTERFACE
  5                            *
  6                            * MOTOROLA 68000
  7                            * 2/7/87
  8                            *
  9                            * Laura Ruiz
 10                            *
 11                                    ORG $900
 12  00010001           PGCR EQU $010001 ; Port General
 13                                      ; Control Register
 14  00010003           PSRR EQU $010003 ; Port Service
 15                                      ; Request Register
 16  00010005           PADDR EQU $010005 ; Port A Data
 17                                      ; Direction Register
 18  00010007           PBDDR EQU $010007 ; Port B Data
 19                                      ; Direction Register
 20  0001000B           PIVR EQU $01000B ; Port Interrupt
 21                                      ; Vector Register
 22  0001000D           PACR EQU $01000D ; Port A Control
 23                                      ; Register
 24  0001000F           PBCR EQU $01000F ; Port B Control
 25                                      ; Register
 26  00010011           PADR EQU $010011 ; Port A Data
 27                                      ; Register
 28  00010013           PBDR EQU $010013 ; Port B Data
 29                                      ; Register
 30                            *
 31  00000900 4280             CLR.L D0
 32  00000902 247C 0000 2100   MOVEA.L #$2100,A2 ;memory block
 33                                              ;to store data
 34  00000908 163C 00FF        MOVE.B #$FF,D3   ;ctr to store 256
 35                                      ; bytes in memory
 36                            *
 37                            * Initializing registers
 38                            *
 39  0000090C 13FC 0000 0001   MOVE.B #$00,PBDDR ;port B: input
                   0007
 40  00000914 13FC 00FF 0001   MOVE.B #$FF,PADDR ;port A: output
                   0005
 41  0000091C 13FC 002C 0001   MOVE.B #$2C,PGCR   ;mode 00,H34
                   0001
```

FIGURE 9.15 Software for the 68000-based data-acquisition system (Example 9.5). (Courtesy of Laura Ruiz, FIU).

```
42                                              ;enabled high
43  00000924  13FC  00FA  0001      MOVE.B #$FA,PIVR ;vector int
              000B
44  0000092C  227C  0000  03E8      MOVEA.L #$3E8,A1;vector add(FA*4)
45  00000932  22BC  0000  2000      MOVE.L #$00002000,(A1);interrupt
46                                              ;routine address
47  00000938  13FC  001C  0001      MOVE.B #$1C,PSRR ;PIRQ,PIACK
              0003
48                                  ;enable H3 at highest priority
49  00000940  1039  0001  0013      MOVE.B PBDR,D0; H4 first pulse.
50                                  ; Wait for interrupt from ADC when
51                                  ; conversion is ready
52                                  ;
53  00000946  13FC  003A  0001  WAIT MOVE.B #$3A,PBCR ;00 submode
              000F                    ; and pulsed input handshake
54                                  ; mode.  H3 enabled.
55                                  ;
56  0000094E  60F6                    BRA WAIT
57  00000950  60F4                    BRA WAIT
58                                  ; Interrupt routine : read port B;
59                                  ; output to port A
60                                  ;
61                                      ORG $2000
62  00002000  13FC  0038  0001      MOVE.B #$38,PBCR; H3 disabled
              000F
63  00002008  1039  0001  0013      MOVE.B PBDR,D0   ; read input
64  0000200E  14C0                  MOVE.B D0,(A2)+ ;store in memory
65  00002010  5343                  SUBQ #1,D3       ;decrement ctr
66  00002012  4A03                  TST.B D3         ;check if done
67  00002014  6704  4E71            BEQ FINAL
68  00002018  4E73            BACK  RTE    ;return from interrupt
69                                *
70  0000201A  13E2  0001      FINAL MOVE.B -(A2),PADR;data to port A
71            0011                  *
72  00002020  183C  0040            MOVE.B #$40,D4   ;delay
73  00002024  0404  0001      DELAY SUBI.B #1,D4
74  00002028  66FA                  BNE DELAY
75                                *
76  0000202A  0603  0001            ADDI.B #1,D3     ;increment ctr
77  0000202E  0C03  00FF            CMPI.B #$FF,D3   ;check if done
78  00002032  66E6                  BNE FINAL        ;send more data
79  00002034  60E2                  BRA BACK         ;if 256 data sent,
79  00002036                        END              ;start back ADC

    ASSEMBLER ERRORS =     0
```

FIGURE 9.15 *Continued.*

A Typical Data-Acquisition System

With appropriate software, the A/D and D/A system of Figures 9.11 and 9.12 can be integrated into a useful data-acquisition and instrumentation system. For the 68000-based system under consideration, the 68230 PI/T resides at the address map between $010001 and $01003F. Port A is configured as an 8-bit output port to drive the D/A converter. Port B is configured as an 8-bit input port to accept the A/D data.

    The handshake signals H3 and H4 are configured for pulse handshake on port B. A pulse will be generated on H4 whenever port B is accessed. This pulse starts the A/D conversion. When the A/D conversion is complete, H3 input will be activated by the A/D converter. This interrupts the processor, which, in turn, reads the digitized data on port B. This interrupt handshake between the 68230 PI/T and the 68000 is accomplished by configuring the PC5 (port C, pin 5) as an $\overline{\text{IRQ}}$ to the processor and the PC6 (port C, pin 6) as the IACK to the 68230 (refer to Figure 9.11).

    The user vector method is employed in this application to provide the interrupt vector to the processor. The DCBA switches are set to 0000 to select VIN0 as the analog input. Figure 9.13 (p. 254) illustrates the 68230 initialization required for this application.

    The flowchart and operating listings for a 68000-based computer using the preceding data-acquisition system are given in Figures 9.14 (p. 255) and 9.15 (pp. 256–257). The software configures the 68230 PI/T ports and the CPU registers. The interrupt routine reads the A/D data (from port B), stores up to 256 data bytes, and outputs the stored data in the reverse order to the D/A (on port A). Finally, the software loops back for the next digitization.

    We will now analyze the software and the system response with the help of an example problem.

Example 9.5   Data-acquisition system.
Consider the data-acquisition system hardware and software of Figures 9.11 through 9.15.

1. Analyze the software. Where is the A/D data stored?
2. Where does the interrupt service routine start?
3. VIN0 is as shown in the following diagram. Plot reconstructed VO output to scale.

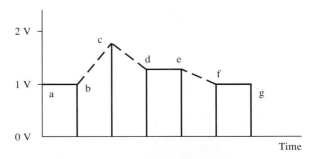

Solution

1. **Software analysis:** Between lines 12 and 28, all the PI/T registers used in this application are defined. Between lines 31 and 36, registers D0, A2, and D3 are initialized with $00000000, $2100, and $FF, respectively.

   Between lines 38 and 43, the PI/T registers are initialized according to Figure 9.13. At lines 44 and 48, $00002000 is stored at vector location 3E8 and port C is configured for interrupt activity (PC5 is an $\overline{\text{IRQ}}$ and PC6 is an $\overline{\text{IACK}}$). Accessing port B (at line 49) generates the first H4 pulse to start the A/D process. Between lines 53 and 56, the processor enables the H3 interrupt and goes into a wait loop— waiting for the interrupt to occur at the end of the conversion.

   On occurrence of the H3-activated interrupt, the processor fetches the interrupt routine address ($00002000) from the vector location $3E8 and starts the interrupt exception routine (line 62). At line 62, the H3 interrupt is disabled so that the processor will not be reinterrupted by the A/D while it is servicing the interrupt that already has been recognized.

   At lines 63 and 64, the processor reads the A/D byte from port B and stores it in the memory in an ascending order. If 256 bytes of the A/D data are stored, the program branches to the final module (lines 65 to 67). Otherwise, the program returns to the wait loop by means of the RTE instruction at line 68.

   The final module is contained between lines 70 and 79. It outputs 256 bytes of the stored A/D data in the memory to the D/A converter through port A in a descending order. The delay loop (lines 72 to 74) provides delay between successive D/A samples. After all 256 samples are output, the program branches back to line 68 and the RTE instruction at line 68 returns the program to the wait loop.

2. **Interrupt service routine:** This routine starts at location $00002000 (line 62).

3. **VO waveform:** The digitized and stored data (256 bytes) are output to the D/A converter in the reverse order, with delay between the samples (lines 70 to 79 of the software). Thus, the reconstructed VO analog signal looks backward, as diagrammed, when compared to the corresponding VIN0 input.

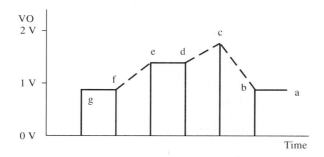

Interrupt-driven data-acquisition systems are extremely useful in industrial applications. Data processing may be more involved than a signal reversal, and data storage well over 256 bytes. The general hardware and software concepts of the data-acquisition and the A/D and D/A interface schemes remain the same, however.

We will now present another example problem in which the importance of D/A conversions and associated waveform generation are emphasized.

Example 9.6   Waveform generation using D/A.

With reference to Example 9.5, suppose it is necessary to generate a triangular waveform at the output of the D/A converter (connected to port A PADR). Assume all the initialization conditions of Example 9.5.

1. Develop the operating software.
2. How is the frequency of the waveform changed?

Solution

1. **Operating software:** The flowchart and the 68000-based program listings to accomplish the task are given in Figure 9.16. The D0 register is used as the count register. It is incremented and output to port A (with a delay) if the count is between $00 and $FF. This provides a positive-going ramp at the output of the D/A. If the D0 register equals $FF while it is being incremented, it is then decremented and is output to port A (with a delay). This provides a negative-going ramp at the output of the D/A. The positive- and negative-going ramps generated in sequence provide the required triangular waveform.

2. **Changing the frequency:** The frequency can be changed by changing the delay counter parameter in the instruction MOVE.W   #$40,D4. If the number $40 is increased, the frequency proportionally decreases.

In the preceding example, the maximum frequency will be obtained if the delay routine is deleted.

9.4   DIRECT MEMORY ACCESS (DMA) CONSIDERATIONS

DMA techniques help accomplish high-speed data transfers between memory and memory, memory and I/O, and vice versa. The DMA operations are performed with the help of DMA controller devices. These controllers obtain the address, data, and the control buses from the processor and implement the DMA transfers. During the DMA transfers, the processor is logically disconnected from the buses.

General Architecture of the DMA Controllers

Figure 9.17 illustrates a typical DMA system organization. The I/O device requests the controller for DMA operation. The DMA controller, in turn, requests the processor, ob-

FIGURE 9.16 (a) Flowchart and (b) 68000 assembly program listings for the triangular waveform generation (Example 9.6).

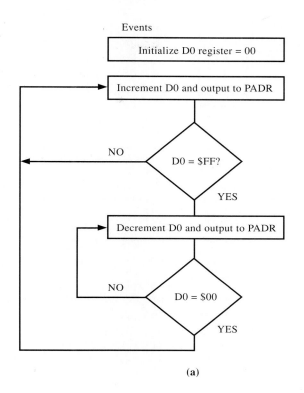

(a)

```
; all the initialization conditions of previous example
; are used in this software
; initialize D0 to $00
        MOVE.B    #$00,D0
UP      ADDQ.B    #$01,D0     ;increment D0
        BSR.S     DELAY
        MOVE.B    D0,PADR     ;output D0 to port A
        CMP.B     #$FF,D0
        BEQ.S     DOWN        ;if D0 = $FF branch to DOWN
        BRA.S     UP
DOWN    SUBQ.B    #$01,D0     ;DECREMENT D0
        BSR.S     DELAY
        MOVE.B    D0,PADR     ;output D0 to port A
        CMP.B     #$00,D0
        BEQ.B     UP          ;if D0 = $00 branch to UP
        BRA.S     DOWN
DELAY   MOVE.W    #$40,D4     ;delay counter initialize
LOOP    DBNE      D4,LOOP     ;delay loop
        RTE
```

(b)

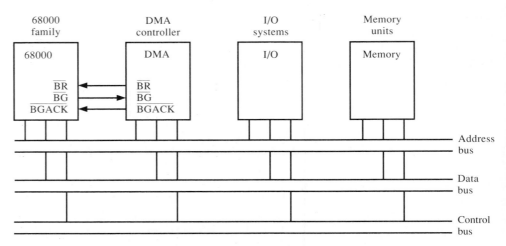

FIGURE 9.17 General concept and architecture for the DMA system.

tains the buses, and performs the DMA data transfers between memory and memory, memory and I/O, and vice versa.[9,10]

Figure 9.18 illustrates the typical DMA bus request timing for the 68000 family of processors. To request the buses, the DMA controller activates the $\overline{\text{BR}}$ (bus request) signal to the processor. The processor recognizes this request and activates the $\overline{\text{BG}}$ (bus

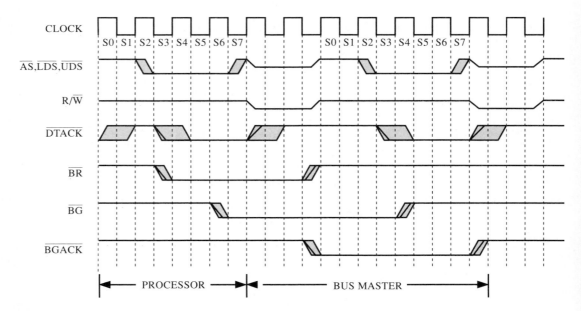

FIGURE 9.18 DMA bus request, bus grant, and acknowledge timing. (Courtesy of Motorola Inc.)

grant) signal to the controller. The controller, in turn, sends the $\overline{\text{BGACK}}$ (bus grant acknowledge) signal to the processor and takes control of the buses. The DMA controller is the bus master until the $\overline{\text{BGACK}}$ is deactivated. The controller drives the address and control buses and performs the DMA operations. The processor regains control of the buses after the $\overline{\text{BGACK}}$ is deactivated.

The 68440 and 68450 DMA Controllers

The 68440 and 68450 are industry standard DMA controller devices belonging to the 68000 family. The 68440 has two DMA channels, while the 68450 has four DMA channels. These devices are pin compatible with one another and are contained in a 64-pin DIP or a 68-pin grid-array package. They are fabricated with HMOS technology. The devices are similar with respect to internal architecture. Both have signals similar to those of the 68000 processor.

Figure 9.19 illustrates the signal organization for the 68440/450 devices. The higher order address bus (A8–A23) is multiplexed with the 16-bit data bus (D0–D15). These buses are demultiplexed by external logic and are connected to the 68000 system bus. There are two modes of operation for DMA controllers: the CPU mode and the DMA mode.

In the **CPU mode of operation,** the processor is the bus master. The DMA controller resembles an external device. The control signals R/$\overline{\text{W}}$, $\overline{\text{LDS}}$, $\overline{\text{UDS}}$, and $\overline{\text{AS}}$ behave as inputs to the DMA controller. The $\overline{\text{DTACK}}$ signal behaves as an output. The processor effectively writes or reads information from the DMA controller.

In the **DMA mode of operation,** the processor releases the control of the buses, and the DMA controller becomes the bus master. The aforementioned signals behave in a manner opposite to that described. The controller generates all the 68000-compatible signals appropriate for data transfers.

The multiplexer control signals control the demultiplex logic for the data and address buses to appropriately interface the 68000 system bus. The DMA controller communicates with the I/O systems via the device control signals $\overline{\text{REQ}}$, $\overline{\text{ACK}}$, $\overline{\text{PCL}}$, $\overline{\text{DTC}}$, and $\overline{\text{DONE}}$.

The DMA controller communicates with the processor via the bus arbitration signals $\overline{\text{BR}}$, $\overline{\text{BG}}$, and $\overline{\text{BGACK}}$, and via the interrupt signals $\overline{\text{IRQ}}$ and $\overline{\text{IACK}}$.

Figure 9.20 illustrates the internal register structure of the 68440/68450-type DMA controllers. Each channel consists of 17 registers. In addition, each device has a general control register, GCR. Some of these registers are initialized by the processor to set up the DMA operation. Others present the status information to the processor. We will discuss the details of these registers in the following section.

Modes of Operation of the DMA Controllers

When the controller is serving as the bus master, it is in the DMA mode of operation, performing the data transfers. This DMA mode allows for two distinct modes: the single-address mode and the dual-address mode.

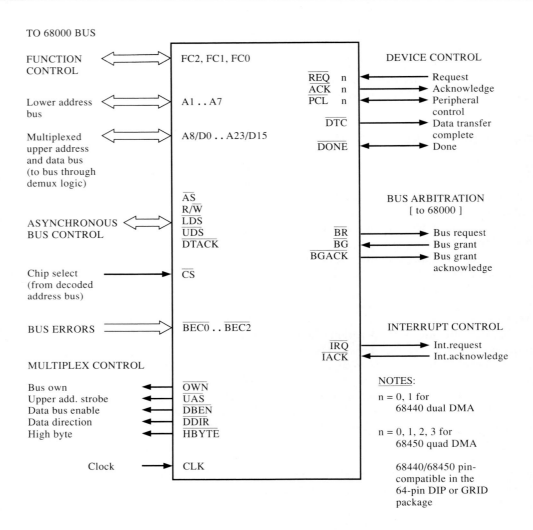

FIGURE 9.19 Signal configuration for the 68440/450 DMA controller devices.

In the **single-address mode,** the data transfers are between the I/O and memory. The controller changes the memory address for successive transfers, but the I/O address remains the same. The I/O device is activated by the $\overline{\text{ACK}}$ signal from the controller. The data transfer takes only one bus cycle.

In the **dual-address mode,** the transfers are between memory and memory. In this mode, the controller contains the source and the destination addresses in the MAR and DAR registers. Any external peripheral device has sequential address space similar to that of memory. The controller generates the source address and reads the source oper-

OFFSET	FUNCTION	#BITS	REGISTER	
$FF	Sets mode of operation	8	general control register	GCR
$04	Sets device control	8	device control register	DCR
$05	Sets operation control	8	operation control register	OCR
$06	Sets sequence control	8	sequence control register	SCR
$07	Sets channel control	8	channel control register	CHCR
$2D	Sets channel priority	8	channel priority register	CPR
$00	Contains channel status	8	channel status register	CSR
$01	Contains channel errors	8	channel error register	CER
$25	Contains interrupt vector	8	normal interrupt vector register	NIVR
$27	Contains error interrupt vector	8	error interrupt vector register	EIVR
$29	Contains memory function codes	8	memory function code register	MFCR
$31	Contains device function codes	8	device function code register	DFCR
$39	Contains base function codes	8	base function code register	BFCR
$0A	Contains memory transfer count	16	memory transfer counter	MTCR
$1A	Contains base transfer count	16	base transfer counter	BTCR
$0C	Contains memory address	32	memory address register	MAR
$14	Contains device address	32	device address register	DAR
$1C	Contains base address	32	base address register	BAR

Notes:

GCR	always at $FF	
Channel 0	between $00 and $3F	
Channel 1	between $40 and $7F	
Channel 2	between $80 and $BF	for 68450 only
Channel 3	between $C0 and $FF	for 68450 only

FIGURE 9.20   *Internal register architecture for the 68440/450.*

and into an internal temporary register, TEMP, during the first bus cycle. It generates the destination address and writes the operand (in the temporary register) into the destination location. Thus, it takes two bus cycles for word or byte transfers.

The DMA controllers are complex devices; data books should be consulted for further details.

We will now present an example problem to review DMA concepts, controllers, and architecture.

Example 9.7   DMA concepts and controller architecture.
Review the material covered in Section 9.4 to answer the questions that follow.

1. How many total registers are there for the 68440 and the 68450 devices? Explain.
2. Can all the channels operate simultaneously? Why or why not?
3. Specify the relative address locations of MAR and BAR for channel 2, in the case of the 68450 controller.
4. At what point does the DMA controller gain control of the buses? Under what conditions?

Solution

1. **Number of registers:** Each channel has 17 registers. In addition, each device has the common GCR and a temporary register, TEMP, to hold data in the dual-address mode. Thus,

   the 68440 DDMA has 2 × 17 + GCR + TEMP = 36 registers

   the 68450 QDMA has 4 × 17 + GCR + TEMP = 70 registers

2. **All channels:** Only one channel becomes operational at any given time. This is because of the bus activity. Each channel can be individually initialized, however.

3. **MAR and BAR (refer to Figure 9.20):** For channel 2, the relative base address is $80. As such,

   the MAR is at $80 + $0C = $8C

   the BAR is at $80 + $1C = $9C

   (*Note:* To obtain the effective addresses, the chip select base address should be added.)

4. **Control of the buses:** After receiving the $\overline{\text{BGACK}}$ from the DMA controller, the processor concludes the current bus cycle. The address, data, and control buses (specifically, R/$\overline{\text{W}}$, $\overline{\text{LDS}}$, $\overline{\text{UDS}}$, and $\overline{\text{AS}}$) go into a high-impedance state. At that point, the DMA controller gains control of the buses.

9.5   THE DMA INTERFACE AND APPLICATIONS

Figure 9.21 illustrates a typical 68000/DMA/I-O interface. This is in the single-address mode. The I/O system is activated by the $\overline{\text{ACK}}$ signal from the DMA controller. DMA channel 0 is used in this application.

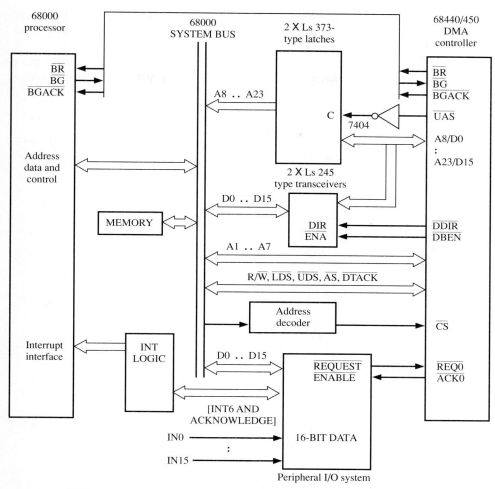

FIGURE 9.21 The 68000/DMA/I/O peripheral interface (Example 9.8).

DMA Sequence of Operations

The peripheral I/O system activates the $\overline{REQ}$ input to the DMA controller and initiates the DMA operation. The controller, in turn, activates the bus request ($\overline{BR}$) signal to the processor. The processor responds back to the controller by activating the $\overline{BG}$ output. The processor also completes the current bus cycle. The controller accepts the $\overline{BR}$ and sends the $\overline{BGACK}$ acknowledge signal to the processor. This signal is held low active by the controller until the DMA data transfers have been completed. When $\overline{BGACK}$ is low, the data, address, and control buses of the 68000 remain in a high-impedance state (refer to Chapter 6, Section 6.1). The DMA controller takes control of these buses, becomes the bus master, and begins the data transfers.

Figure 9.22 specifies the typical sequence of events during single-address mode transfers from the I/O units to the system memory. Other types of DMA transfers follow a similar sequence of events.

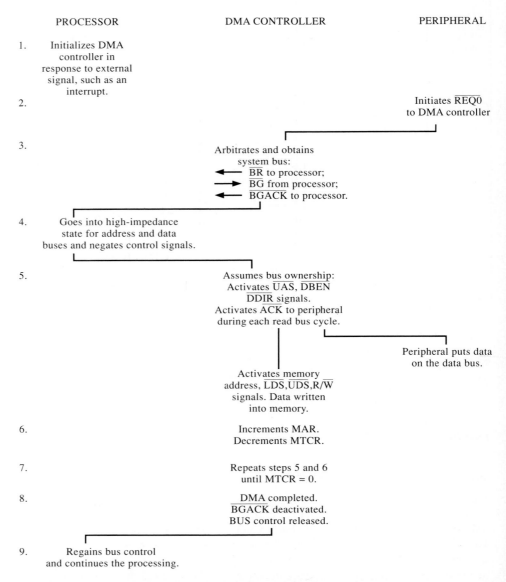

FIGURE 9.22 Sequence of DMA operations in the single-address mode.

DMA Channel Initialization

The DMA controller must be initialized in accordance with the system application before any DMA activity takes place. For single-address transfers, the processor writes the starting address of the memory, the size and number of data operands to be transferred, the direction of transfer, and other such information into the appropriate registers of the DMA controller. For dual-address-mode transfers, the source and destination operand addresses are written into two separate registers.

After the first initialization, further reinitialization of the controller can be done internally by the controller, itself, if it is operated in the reload condition.

We will now present an example problem to review the DMA sequence of operations and initialization schemes.

Example 9.8   DMA sequence and initialization.
Suppose a 1-kiloword transfer of data to memory from a peripheral I/O port is required, using the DMA system of Figure 9.21. The DMA controller occupies the memory map between $012000 and $0120FF.

DMA channel 0 in the single-address mode is used. Memory for DMA transfers starts at $00002000.

1. Using the 68440 DMA controller, illustrate the initialization of the DMA internal registers.
2. If the 68440 is replaced by a 68450 controller, will there be any change in the initialization? Why or why not?
3. Interrupt 7 (a nonmaskable interrupt) is being serviced when the DMA request comes to the processor from the controller. Will it be recognized? If so, specify the sequence of events.

Solution

1. **Initialization:** Figure 9.23 illustrates the required initialization of the 68440 channel 0 registers (refer to Section 9.4 for the register map). The device control register (DCR) is initialized for a burst mode of transfer for word-sized operands. In addition, the I/O is activated by $\overline{\text{ACK}}$. The rest of the register initialization is self-explanatory.
2. **68450 Initialization:** For channels 0 and 1, the initialization sequence remains the same for the 68440 and 68450 devices, since these devices have the same memory map.
3. **Interrupt and DMA:** As soon as the DMA request comes, the processor must respond, even if it is servicing an interrupt level 7. It issues the bus grant signal and

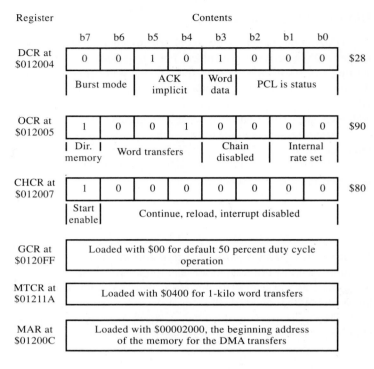

FIGURE 9.23 Initialization of the DMA registers (Channel 0).

The other registers are not explicitly used, and the default conditions on reset are acceptable.

concludes the current bus cycle. It releases the control of the buses to the DMA controller on the occurrence of the $\overline{\text{BGACK}}$ signal.

Only one DMA channel can be serviced at a given time. Two such channels can be serviced (one at a time), if a 68440 controller is used. For four such channels, the 68450 controller should be used. The initialization scheme for each channel is similar to the scheme we have described. The DMA channels are prioritized by the controller.

DMA Software Considerations

In DMA applications, the software basically initializes the DMA controller. When the peripheral is ready for DMA operation, it usually interrupts the processor. The processor recognizes this interrupt and initializes the DMA controller. Thereafter, the DMA request can occur at any time. The DMA request should not be allowed prior to, or during, the initialization of the DMA controller.

We will now introduce the software for DMA operations with the help of an example problem.

Example 9.9   Software for DMA operations.
In the DMA system of Figure 9.21, interrupt 6 is activated by the peripheral I/O to initialize DMA channel 0. One-kiloword transfers, as specified in Example 9.8, are required.

```
LINE    ADDR
  1                                      ;DMA INITIALIZATIONS
  2                                      ;9/9/88   F.I.U.
  3                                      OPT A
  4                                      ORG $1000
  5                                      ;68440/450 registers defined
  6   00012000                           BASE      EQU     $012000
  7   00012004                           DCR       EQU     $012004
  8   00012005                           OCR       EQU     $012005
  9   00012007                           CHCR      EQU     $012007
 10   0001200A                           MTCR      EQU     $01200A
 11   0001200C                           MAR       EQU     $01200C
 12   0001200F                           GCR       EQU     $01200F
 13   00001200                           INT6      EQU     $00001200
 14   00000078                           VECTOR    EQU     $0078
 15                                      ;
 16                                      ;initialize interrupt 6 vector address
 17   00001000  21FC 0000 1200 STRT MOVE.L    #INT6,VECTOR
                0078
 18   00001008  6006 4E71           BRA       TASK
 19   0000100C  4E71                NOP
 20   0000100E  60F0                BRA       STRT
 21                                  ;processor performing a task
 22   00001010  4E71           TASK NOP
 23   00001012  5482                ADDQ.L    #$02,D2
 24   00001014  60FA                BRA       TASK
 25                                  ;Int #6 routine to initialize DMA
 26                                      ORG       $00001200
 27   00001200  13FC 0000 0001      MOVE.B    #$00,GCR
                200F
 28   00001208  13FC 0090 0001      MOVE.B    #$90,OCR
                2005
 29   00001210  13FC 0080 0001      MOVE.B    #$80,CHCR
                2007
 30   00001218  33FC 0400 0001      MOVE.W    #$0400,MTCR
                200A
 31   00001220  23FC 0000 2000      MOVE.L    #$00002000,MAR
                0001 200C
 32   0000122A  4E71                NOP
 33   0000122C  4E73                RTE
 34 ;
 35 ;
 36 ;
 37   0000122E                      END

      ASSEMBLER ERRORS =       0
```

FIGURE 9.24   DMA initialization software for the 68000/68440-450 system (Example 9.9).

1. Develop 68000-based operating software to initialize the DMA controller.
2. Compute the actual time of the DMA transfers, using the software developed. Consider the system (processor and controller) to be operational at 8 MHz.

Solution

1. **DMA initialization software:** In Figure 9.24, the operating software using the 68000 is given. Between lines 6 and 14, the relevant channel 0 registers of the controller (a 68440/450 device) are defined. At line 17, the interrupt 6 vectored address of $00001200 is loaded into the exception table at location $0078. This is the interrupt 6 autovector location.

   Between lines 18 and 24, the processor goes into a TASK routine. A task can be any processing activity the processor is involved in. For simplicity, we have chosen a three-instruction loop. The processor responds to the interrupt, if the interrupt is enabled, and appropriately initializes the DMA channel.

   Between lines 25 and 33, the interrupt 6 service routine is contained. This routine initializes the DMA registers as specified in Example 9.8. After the initialization, when the DMA request occurs, the processor gives up the buses to the DMA controller to transfer the data, as outlined previously.

2. **Time for DMA transfers:** After the DMA channel has been set up, the transfer time is that of the 1-kiloword transfers. The DMA is set up for single-address transfers from the I/O peripheral to the system memory.

   Each word transfer takes one bus cycle, which corresponds to four clock cycles. Thus, the timing is as follows:

$$\text{Clock cycle time at 8 MHz} = 0.125 \text{ microseconds}$$
$$\text{Bus cycle time} = 4 \times 0.125 = 0.5 \text{ microseconds}$$
$$\text{1-kiloword DMA time} = 1{,}024 \times 0.5 = 512 \text{ microseconds.}$$

Examples 9.8 and 9.9 involve the single-address mode of DMA operation. The dual-address mode of DMA operation is similar to the single-address mode; for the dual-address mode, however, each byte or word transfer takes two bus cycles for 68000-based systems.

9.6 SUMMARY

In this chapter we considered interrupt and DMA applications related to the 68000 microprocessor.

The external interrupts are properly encoded and applied to the $\overline{\text{IPL2}}$, $\overline{\text{IPL1}}$, and $\overline{\text{IPL0}}$ inputs of the 68000 processor. A level 0 interrupt signifies that there is no pending interrupt. Interrupt levels 1 through 7 are set on priority, with level 2 higher than level 1, and so on. Level 7 is a nonmaskable interrupt (NMI).

These interrupts can be autovectored or device (user) vectored. In autovectoring, the processor goes to a fixed vector location. The autovectoring scheme is simple and is preferable when a fixed number of interrupt vectors is satisfactory for the application. The device-vectoring scheme is more involved, but it provides the scope for interrupt expansion. In device vectoring, the interrupting device supplies the corresponding vector number.

In order to increase the effective number of interrupts, a daisy-chain mechanism with a device-vectoring scheme is used. In the daisy chain, the device closest to the processor has the highest priority; the device farthest away has the lowest priority.

Interrupt processing is done in the supervisor mode. After stacking the program counter and the copied status register, the 68000 processor obtains the interrupt-vectored address from the appropriate vector location and executes the corresponding interrupt service routine.

We described the following interrupt-driven systems: the gain-controller system, the data-acquisition system, and the dynamic memory system. The discussions helped to provide insight into practical interrupt applications. The gain-controller application is widely used in industry; for example, in setting up proper motor speeds. In the data-acquisition system application, A/D and D/A interfaces to the processor are involved. The dynamic memory system application deals with interrupt-driven timing in memory system designs.

Whenever there is a requirement for high-speed data transfers, DMA (direct memory access) methods are used. In such methods, an external DMA controller obtains the control of the processor buses and implements data transfers without the intervention of the processor.

The industry standard 68440 and 68450 DMA controllers belonging to the 68000 family were introduced in this chapter. The 68440 is a dual-channel DMA controller. The 68450 is a quad-channel DMA controller. The devices are compatible with one another.

When there is a requirement for DMA-type data transfers, the DMA controller arbitrates and wins the system buses from the processor. The processor goes into a high-impedance condition for data and address buses and certain control signals. It goes into the inactive condition for other control signals. The DMA controller generates the required signals for data transfers and acts as the bus master.

DMA transfers can be between memory and I/O or between memory and memory. In the former case, they are single-address transfers. The DMA controller activates the peripheral at a single fixed address and the memory at a sequential address in the same bus cycle. Thus, the single-address mode is the fastest, and is well suited for DMA transfers between memory and I/O ports.

When data transfers are from memory to memory, they are dual-address transfers. The DMA controller reads the source operand (byte or word) into an internal temporary register during one bus cycle, and writes it into the destination location during the next bus cycle. Dual-address transfers take two bus cycles for byte or word transfers in 68000-based systems.

In all DMA applications, the DMA controller must be properly initialized by the processor before the actual operation. Otherwise, unpredictable results may occur.

PROBLEMS

9.1 Assume that interrupt 5 is being serviced.

(a) Another level 5 interrupt occurs. Will it be recognized? Why or why not?

(b) Interrupt 7 occurs under the conditions of (a). Will it be recognized? Why or why not?

(c) Interrupt 7 is being serviced. Another level 7 interrupt occurs. Will it be recognized? Why or why not?

9.2 In an 8-MHz 68000 system, $\overline{IRQ6}$ and $\overline{IRQ4}$ occur at the same time.

(a) Which will be recognized? In order to be recognized, specify the required duration of the interrupt.

(b) The $\overline{IRQ6}$ routine takes 32 microseconds; the $\overline{IRQ4}$ routine takes 64 microseconds. If they occur at the same time, specify the required duration of each in order to be recognized.

9.3 There are two methods of servicing interrupts: the autovector method and the user-vector method. Outline the advantages and disadvantages of each of these methods. Also specify applications particularly well suited to one or another of the methods.

9.4 Is the user stack involved in servicing interrupts? Explain.

(a) If subroutines are used in interrupt service routines, which stack is used? Why?

(b) Which stack is used when an interrupt occurs during a user subroutine execution?

9.5 Assume $\overline{IRQ6}$ is being serviced. $\overline{IRQ7}$ occurs while the processor is fetching the op.code for the instruction

$$\text{MOVE.L} \quad \#\$734512A6,D1$$

(a) How many T-states have to elapse before $\overline{IRQ7}$ is serviced? Explain.

(b) Considering that the SSP is at \$00003ABA at the time of the occurrence of $\overline{IRQ6}$, and the USP is at \$00004000, indicate the contents of the appropriate stack when $\overline{IRQ7}$ has been recognized.

9.6 The daisy chain is an accepted means of interrupt expansion. Outline the advantages and the disadvantages of the daisy-chain mechanism.

(a) In which applications is the daisy chain not the method of choice?

(b) In which applications is the daisy chain particularly useful?

9.7 In the daisy-chained system of Figure 9.4, suppose it is necessary for I/O system 2 to have higher priority. How should the system be redesigned?

9.8 For the system of Figure 9.4,

(a) how many external devices can be interfaced? Why?

(b) including the internal interrupt sources of the 68901 MFP, how many total interrupt requests can be handled? Why?

Note: Problems 9.9, 9.10, 9.13, 9.14, 9.16, 9.18, and 9.22 can be used as the basis for special projects involving hardware and software implementation.

9.9 Refer to Figures 9.5 and 9.8. Redesign the hardware and the software so that

(a) the motor speed gradually increases to a maximum and stays there;

(b) the motor speed varies between a maximum and a minimum on the occurrence of each timer interrupt.

9.10 In a servo belt system, it is required to increase the motor speed to a maximum, have it remain stable for 10 units of time, and then gradually reduce it to minimum. The system is repetitive. Consider one unit of time as the occurrence of the timer interrupt.
Design the hardware and the software needed to implement this system.

9.11 How many steps of gain variation are possible in the system of Figure 9.5 considering all the possible software features?

9.12 For the DRAM system of Figure 9.9, specify what could happen if a lower level interrupt, such as level 1, were used for the refresh operation.

9.13 Suppose the DRAM system of Figure 9.9 has to be expanded to accommodate an additional 1 megabyte of DRAM starting at $400000. Specify the hardware details.

9.14 Given the conditions of Problem 9.13, suppose it is necessary to modify the software of Figure 9.10 to refresh the 2 megawords of total DRAM. Redesign the software and implement it.

9.15 What is the maximum amount of DRAM that can be software refreshed using no more than 30 percent of processor time?

9.16 Redesign the data-acquisition system described in Section 9.3 so that

(a) the buffer to store the A/D data is 4 kilobytes;
(b) the stored data is output to D/A with an attenuation of two units.

9.17 Additional signal shaping and processing are possible with data-acquisition system software. Redesign the software of Problem 9.16 so that the digital attenuation is 2 on even samples and 4 on odd samples.

9.18 The data-acquisition system can be easily converted into a digital voltmeter as shown in the following diagram. Digits 3 and 4 should display a voltage between 0.0 V and 9.9 V. Digit 2 should display + or −. Digit 1 should display a flashing 1 if there is an overload condition.

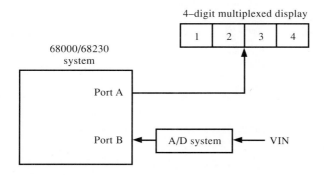

Design and implement the system.

9.19 Specify the complete address map for all four channels of the 68450 DMA controller. Why is there only one GCR for all four channels?

9.20 Draw the timing diagrams for the asynchronous bus signals when the DMA controller is in the following modes:

(a) the CPU mode, in which the controller resembles an I/O device to the processor;

(b) the DMA mode, in which the controller is the bus master and controls the data transfers.

9.21 With reference to the data books on 68440/450 controllers,

(a) discuss the bus arbitration scheme involving $\overline{BR}$, $\overline{BG}$, and $\overline{BGACK}$ for single-operand transfers and block transfers (assume 1-kiloword transfers);

(b) describe the handshake between the DMA controller and the peripheral device.

9.22 Redesign the system of Figure 9.21 using all-CMOS logic for minimum power operation.

9.23 Specify a sequence of operations similar to that of Figure 9.22 for

(a) dual-address transfers;

(b) port-to-port transfers.

9.24 Repeat Example 9.9 for the following transfers:

(a) 1 kiloword from memory to I/O;

(b) 10 kilowords from memory to I/O.

9.25 Repeat Problem 9.24 for memory-to-memory transfers with the DMA controller in the dual-address mode.

9.26 Compute the DMA timing assuming the conditions of Problem 9.24. Repeat the computation for the conditions of Problem 9.25.

ENDNOTES

1. Davis, R. *Prioritized Individually Vectored Interrupts*. App. Note #819. Austin, TX: Motorola Microprocessor Group, 1981.

2. Motorola, Inc. *MC68901 MFP Data Book*. Phoenix, AZ: Motorola Technical Operations, 1984.

3. Motorola, Inc. *MTT8: 68000 Course Notes*. Phoenix, AZ: Motorola Technical Operations, 1987.

4. Andrews, M. *Self-Guided Tour through the 68000*. Englewood Cliffs, NJ: Prentice-Hall, 1984.

5. Motorola, Inc. *MCM511000 Data Sheets*. Phoenix, AZ: Motorola Semiconductor Group, 1988.

6. Wilcox, A. *68000 Microcomputer Systems*. Englewood Cliffs, NJ: Prentice-Hall, 1987.

7. Miller, M.A. "Parallel Interfacing the 68000." Chap. 5 in *The 68000 Microprocessor: Architecture, Programming, and Applications*. Columbus, OH: Merrill, 1988.

8. Subbarao, W. *Microprocessor Hardware, Software, and Design Applications*. Englewood Cliffs, NJ: Prentice-Hall, 1984.

9. Motorola, Inc. *M68440/68450 DMA Controller Data Books*. Phoenix, AZ: Motorola Technical Operations, 1987.

10. Clements, A. *Microprocessor Systems Design: 68000 Family of Processors*. Boston: PWS-KENT, 1988.

10

68010 and 68012 Architecture, Organization, and Applications

Objectives

In this chapter we will study:

> Virtual memory and virtual machine schemes
> The additional resources of the 68010 and 68012
> Virtual memory implementation schemes
> Exception processing associated with virtual memory

10.0   INTRODUCTION

The **68010 virtual memory microprocessor** has more internal resources than the 68000 microprocessor. The additional resources are needed to implement designs based on virtual memory. Externally, the 68010 is pin compatible with the 68000 and can access 16 megabytes of logical memory.[1]

The **68012 extended virtual memory microprocessor** is similar to the 68010 internally, but has an extended address bus (A1–A29 and A31) that can address 2 gigabytes of logical memory.[2]

When there is a large logical memory space, but only limited physical memory space (due to hardware limitations), a virtual memory scheme is used. Such a scheme allows for effective implementation of a computer system in the logical address space while operating in the actual hardware physical memory space.

Study of the material in this chapter will help the reader understand the virtual memory concepts that are fundamental to the implementation of virtual memory system designs using the 68010 and 68012 microprocessors.

10.1   VIRTUAL MEMORY AND VIRTUAL MACHINE CONCEPTS

For most microcomputer systems, only a fraction of the memory and I/O resources of the processor are available. Virtual memory and virtual machine concepts allow the system to operate as if full system resources were available, even when only a fraction of them are physically represented. This enhances the scope of software and hardware development of the microcomputer systems.[3]

Virtual Memory Schemes

Virtual memory gives the computer user the impression that the entire memory space is available for use. It is memory that is not present in the real-time physically accessible memory, although it is in the logical memory space of the processor and is contained in backup memory, such as disk. When the processor tries to access this memory, a memory-access fault occurs. The processor attempts to correct this fault by moving the contents from the virtual memory into the physical memory. The processor may move some of the physical memory contents into backup memory in order to create space for the virtual memory contents to be brought in. Figure 10.1 illustrates a virtual memory scheme.

Virtual Machine Schemes

The extension of virtual memory concepts to cover other nonexistent hardware resources, such as the I/O, leads to virtual machine schemes. There may be several local operating systems under a governing operating system. Each of these local operating systems can access the I/O resources belonging to the others through the governing op-

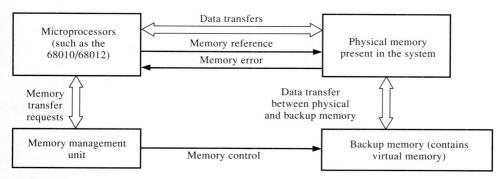

FIGURE 10.1   Virtual memory concepts in computer systems.

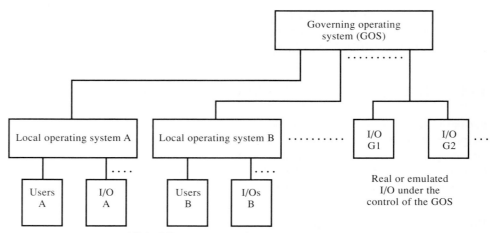

All the I/O resources may be real or emulated (virtual).

FIGURE 10.2 Virtual machine scheme concepts.

erating system, as shown in Figure 10.2. These I/O resources may be real, or they may be emulated by the governing operating system.[4]

During emulation, the governing operating system mimics the corresponding I/O properties. However, the local operating system addressing these resources considers them to be part of its own system. Hence, the concept of the virtual machine: The local operating system looks like a user to the governing system, and like a governing operating system to the user.

We will now present an example problem to review what we have learned about virtual memory and the virtual machine.

Example 10.1 Virtual memory and virtual machine concepts.

In a database management system using the 68010 processor, the memory map for physical memory and I/O is as follows:

$$\text{System ROM/EPROM/RAM} \Rightarrow \text{\$000000 to \$00FFFF (64 kilobytes)}$$
$$\text{System/User RAM} \Rightarrow \text{\$010000 to \$04FFFF (256 kilobytes)}$$
$$\text{System I/O} \Rightarrow \text{\$100000 to \$1003FF (1,024 bytes)}$$

Assume that appropriate virtual memory management software and hardware have been implemented.

1. The MOVE.W (A1),D1 instruction is executed with A1 = $0C000E. Conceptualize the sequence of events. How is the virtual memory scheme implemented, if implementation is possible?

2. Now suppose A1 = $012345AE. Can the scheme be implemented?

3. Suppose it is necessary to implement an additional I/O system between $1A2300 and $1A23FF. Conceptualize the implementation scheme for this virtual machine.

Solution

1. **Virtual memory implementation:** The 68010 processor has a 16-megabyte logical space between $000000 and $FFFFFF. Currently, the 68010 is accessing memory at $0C000E. It is outside the physical memory, but is contained in the logical memory space. Therefore, the virtual memory scheme is possible.

   In Figure 10.3, the conceptual events in the virtual memory implementation scheme are indicated. When the memory-access fault is detected, the fault correction software and the memory management hardware will move the virtual memory section (in which the current reference is made) into the real physical memory. The memory reference pointer (A1, in this case) will be readjusted to correspond to the remapped memory. Thus, the referenced memory will be made available to the processor for the data movement operations.

   After the fault has been corrected, the processor resumes its earlier activity. The fault correction software is really bus error exception processing software (details to be discussed later).

2. **Memory access at $012345AE for 68010- and 68012-based systems:** The virtual memory scheme cannot be implemented for the 68010, since the location $012345AE is beyond its logical space. However, in the case of the 68012 processor, the location is in the logical space and the virtual memory scheme can be implemented.

3. **Virtual machine (I/O between $1A2300 and $1A23FF):** When a reference is made to this nonexistent I/O, the processor will implement the virtual memory schemes as

FIGURE 10.3 Virtual memory concepts (Example 10.1).

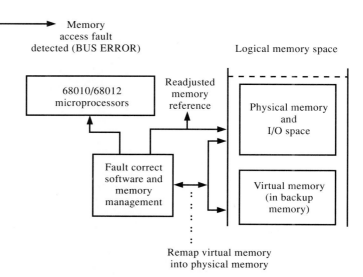

we have outlined, with additional emphasis on the emulation of the I/O device properties and associated operating systems.

In the preceding problem, mention was made of the virtual memory section from the backup memory being moved into the physical memory area. The functional details of this important virtual memory implementation concept are shown in the flowchart of Figure 10.4. A part of the physical memory is assigned as a memory buffer. This buffer is used for all the virtual memory transfers. A 64-kilobyte area between $040000 and $04FFFF is chosen as the memory buffer for our particular case.

When a virtual memory reference is made, the virtual memory implementation software checks whether the memory buffer area has been filled by an earlier virtual memory reference. If it has, the software moves the contents of the buffer into the corresponding backup memory. The software also readjusts any previously adjusted memory pointers to their original values.

When the buffer becomes available, the software moves the memory block containing the virtual memory reference from the backup memory into the buffer area. Also, the original pointer values are stored and adjusted to refer to the buffered area. After these adjustments, any related virtual memory reference will be accessed from the buffer area.

FIGURE 10.4 Virtual memory implementation flowchart.

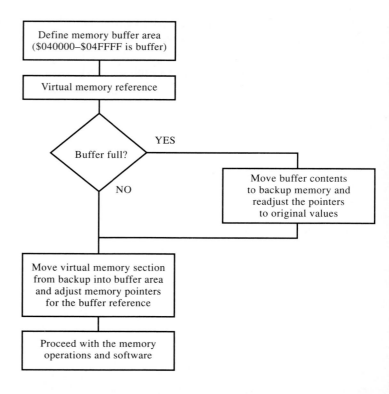

FIGURE 10.5   A/D converter virtual machine emulation flowchart.

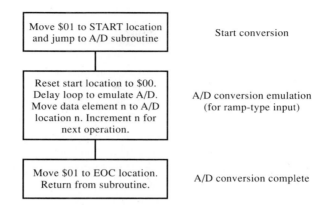

Move $01 to START location and jump to A/D subroutine	Start conversion
Reset start location to $00. Delay loop to emulate A/D. Move data element n to A/D location n. Increment n for next operation.	A/D conversion emulation (for ramp-type input)
Move $01 to EOC location. Return from subroutine.	A/D conversion complete

The flowchart for an A/D converter type of virtual machine emulation scheme is given in Figure 10.5. All the hardware signals are emulated by memory locations. A start pulse to the A/D converter starts the actual conversion process (refer to Chapter 9 on A/D conversions). This is accomplished by writing a 1 to a memory location (START) which mimics the A/D start input and the calling of an A/D subroutine.

The subroutine resets the start location and generates a delay corresponding to the actual conversion time of the A/D device. It then writes a data element, n (the initial value of n would be $00), into the memory array designated to hold the A/D data. Finally, the software writes $01 into the EOC (end-of-conversion) location which mimics the end-of-conversion pulse and returns the program to the calling routine.

It can be seen that the virtual machine emulation is software intensive and mimics hardware operations by writing into appropriate memory locations.

We will now present an example problem to review the actual implementation schemes of virtual memory and virtual machines.

Example 10.2   Virtual memory/machine implementation schemes.
The memory buffer for a virtual memory implementation scheme is between $040000 and $04FFFF (64 kilobytes), as shown in Figure 10.4. A 64-kilobyte block ($0000 to $FFFF) containing the virtual memory reference address will be moved from the backup memory into the buffer each time virtual memory implementation takes place. (Refer to Example 10.1 for the memory map of the 68010-based system.)

1. The MOVE.W (A1),D1 instruction is executed with A1 = $0C000E. Specify the actual memory block moved from the backup memory into the buffer memory.
2. What adjusted value will be in the memory pointer A1?
3. For an 8-bit A/D conversion emulation as a virtual machine, how many bytes of A/D data array are required for emulating a linear ramp signal?
4. Answer the preceding question for emulating a triangular wave.

Solution

1. **Memory block moved into the virtual memory buffer:** Memory pointer A1 refers to an address $0C000E which is not in the physical memory of the system, but which is in the logical memory space contained in the backup memory. Therefore, virtual memory implementation is possible. The memory block containing the virtual memory reference $0C000E is between $0C0000 and $0CFFFF. Thus, memory block $0C0000 to $0CFFFF is moved into the buffer between $040000 and $04FFFF.

2. **Adjusted memory pointer A1:** The original A1 pointer contents ($0C000E) are stored in memory (possibly in the supervisor stack), and the pointer is adjusted to hold $04000E. The pointer refers to the corresponding location in the memory buffer after the memory movement.

3. **Linear ramp A/D emulation:** The 8-bit linear ramp data are between $00 and $FF in increments of 1. This requires a 256-byte memory array. In addition, two byte locations are required to emulate the START and EOC signals, for a total of 258 locations. Thus, a 258-byte array is required.

4. **Triangular wave A/D emulation:** A triangular wave takes positive-going and negative-going ramps, for a total of 512 byte-sized data elements. Considering the START and EOC locations, the required memory array is 514 bytes.

The preceding concepts regarding virtual memory and virtual machine schemes apply to all processors having the proper resources. In the next few sections, we will describe these resources with reference to the 68010 and 68012 processors.

10.2 ARCHITECTURE OF THE 68010 AND 68012 MICROPROCESSORS

Figure 10.6 illustrates the general architecture and busing features of the 68010 and 68012 microprocessors. They contain all the resources of the 68000 microprocessor, with additional registers to handle the virtual memory and virtual machine schemes.

Additional Register and Busing Resources

Internally, the 68010 and 68012 processors have a 32-bit vector base register (VBR). In addition, they have two 3-bit registers: the SFC (source function code) register and the DFC (destination function code) register. These registers help to implement the virtual memory management schemes.

VBR (Vector Base Register) This register contains a 32-bit base address, which is meant to relocate the exception vector table. This allows for a multioperating system in a multiuser environment. Each local operating system may have a different value written into the VBR. This leads to different exception tables for different local operating sys-

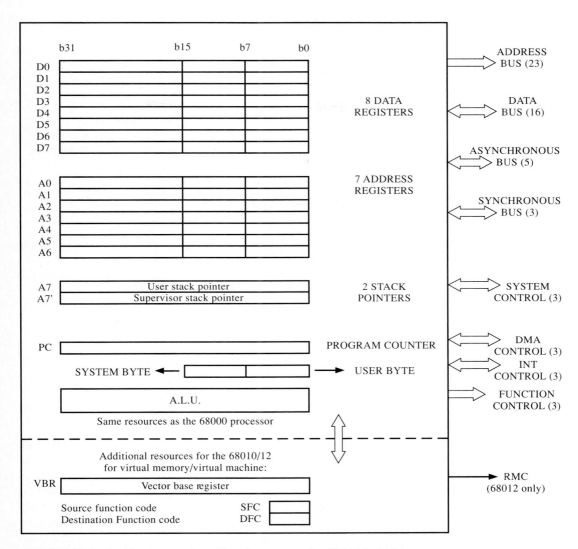

FIGURE 10.6 Architecture and additional resources for 68010/68012-type microprocessors.

tems. The default VBR value (on system reset) is $00000000, which matches that of the 68000 exception table. This table corresponds to the governing operating system. The VBR can be accessed only in the supervisor mode (using the MOVEC instruction).

SFC and DFC (Source and Destination Function Code Registers) These registers contain information about the function codes (FC2, FC1, and FC0). They can be accessed in the supervisor mode using the MOVEC instruction. This provides easy ac-

FC2	FC1	FC0	Cycle Type
0	0	0	Reserved
0	0	1	User data
0	1	0	User program
0	1	1	Reserved
1	0	0	Reserved
1	0	1	Supervisor data
1	1	0	Supervisor program
1	1	1	CPU space

FIGURE 10.7 The 68010/68012 function code table.

cess to the program or data space for virtual memory and virtual machine schemes. In Figure 10.7 the function code table for the 68010 and 68012 is given. The FC2 FC1 FC0 = 1 1 1 condition is designated as the CPU space, which is further classified as follows:

$$FC2 \; FC1 \; FC0 = 1 \; 1 \; 1 \quad \text{and} \quad A4-A23 = 1 \ldots 1$$

is the interrupt acknowledge cycle;

$$FC2 \; FC1 \; FC0 = 1 \; 1 \; 1 \quad \text{and} \quad A1-A23 = 0 \ldots 0$$

is the breakpoint cycle (details to be discussed later).

Busing The 68010 is pin compatible with the 68000 processor. Thus, the 68010 processor is contained in a 64-pin DIP or 68-pin grid-array package, as is the 68000. The 68012, however, has seven more address lines (A24–A29 and A31) to address 2 gigabytes of memory. An additional control line, $\overline{RMC}$ (read modify write control), is included for multiprocessor interfacing. To minimize noise, the 68012 has two additional ground pins. It is contained in a standard 84-pin grid-array package. It is not hardware compatible with the 68000/68010 processors; thus, hardware must be specially designed for the 68012.

The Breakpoint (BKPT) Concept for the 68010 and 68012 When the BKPT #n (n = 0–7) instruction is executed, it results in illegal instruction exception processing. The function codes and the address bus can further be decoded to generate a hardware breakpoint condition for system debugging.

Additional Instructions and Modified Instructions

The table of Figure 10.8 indicates additional instructions (new) and instructions that have been modified for the 68010 and 68012 virtual memory processors. The MOVEC, RTD, and the MOVES are new instructions and support the virtual memory implemen-

Instruction	Syntax	Operation	Type
Move control register	MOVEC Rn,Rc MOVEC Rc,Rn	Move long word between Rn (An or Dn) and Rc (SFC,DFC,VBR,USP)	Privileged and new
Return and deallocate stack	RTD #n	Return from subroutine and deallocate #n bytes from stack (n is even)	Normal and new

Move alternate address space	MOVES ⟨ea⟩,Rn
	
	MOVES Rn,⟨ea⟩
		Move between effective address and Rn (SFC and DFC are preconditioned)	Privileged and new

Move status register	MOVE SR,⟨ea⟩	Move from status register to effective address	Modified to be privileged

FIGURE 10.8   Additional and modified instructions for the 68010/68012.

tation. The MOVE SR,<ea> instruction has been modified to be a privileged instruction. This facilitates the coexistence of the multiuser and local operating systems under a governing operating system. Local operating systems of users are prevented from accessing the status register. An attempt at such access causes an exception and takes the processor to the governing operating system (S bit = 1 in system bytes). The governing operating system controls the local operating systems, which are really in the user mode.

Loop Mode   The 68010 and 68012 processors go into a loop mode of operation in executing a three-instruction loop involving the DBcc (decrement and branch on condition). The processor keeps the three instructions in the internal instruction queue and executes them until the loop condition is satisfied. This circumvents the external memory access bus cycles and greatly speeds up the loop operation. Data sheets for the 68010 and 68012 specify those instructions that are eligible for the loop mode of operation.[5,6]

The VBR is usually relocated for each local operating system. The stack is sometimes deallocated (for the governing operating system to input or retrieve information). Similarly, the SFC and DFC registers are reconditioned to address any memory space. These capabilities are unique to the 68010 and 68012. The rest of the software of these processors is similar to that of the 68000 processor.

We will now present an example problem to review the additional resources of the 68010 and 68012 processors and associated software considerations.

Example 10.3   68010/12 additional resources and software.
In Figure 10.9, an initialization routine for the 68010 and 68012 processors is given. Assume that the TRAP #14 call, passing parameter 228 in the D7 register, returns the control to the governing operating system.

```
LINE   ADDR

 1;M68010.SRC 68010/12 :FIU    11/25/88
 2                                      CHIP     68010
 3                                      OPT A
 4                                      ORG $1000
 5;MOVE VECTOR TABLE TO NEW ADDRESS
 6 00001000 4E71             START   NOP
 7 00001002 207C 0000 0000           MOVEA.L #$0,A0      ;A0=0
 8 00001008 227C 0000 2000           MOVEA.L #$2000,A1 ;A1=$2000
 9 0000100E 103C 00FF                MOVE.B  #$FF,D0     ;D0=FF
10 00001012 22D8             AGAIN   MOVE.L  (A0)+,(A1)+
11 00001014 51C8 FFFC                DBRA    D0,AGAIN
12;INITIALIZE VBR AND TRAP #1 VECTOR AT $84
13 00001018 247C 0000 2000 REINT     MOVEA.L #$2000,A2
14 0000101E 4E7B A801                MOVEC   A2,VBR    ;VBR=$2000
15 00001022 257C 0000 3000           MOVE.L  #$3000,$0084(A2)
            0084
16 0000102A 4EB8 1036 4E71           JSR     FCODE
17 00001030 1E3C 00E4                MOVE.B  #228,D7   ;TO SYSTEM
18 00001034 4E4E                     TRAP    #14
19 00001036 267C 0000 0000 FCODE     MOVEA.L #$0,A3
20 0000103C 7207                      MOVEQ   #$07,D1
21 0000103E 4E7B 1000                MOVEC   D1,SFC  ;SFC=111
22 00001042 0E53 2000                MOVES.W (A3),D2
23 00001046 4E74 0008                RTD     #$8
24 0000104A 4E71                     NOP
25;
26 0000104C                          END


ASSEMBLER ERRORS =     0

                         SYMBOL TABLE

AGAIN    00001012  FCODE   00001036  NARG    00000000
REINT    00001018  START   00001000
```

FIGURE 10.9 Initialization software for 68010/12 processors (Example 10.3).

1. What tasks are being accomplished in the software? Specify any special features of 68010/12 software.

2. Where is the TRAP #1 routine configured to start after this initialization program has been run?

3. For running the program, what mode should the processor be in? Why?

4. If the initial value of the corresponding stack pointer is $0700, diagram the stack frame and its contents.

Solution

1. **Software:** Between lines 6 and 11, 256 long words of the original vector table (starting at $000000) are copied to memory starting at $2000. Of particular importance is the AGAIN loop. The 68010 and 68012 processors keep this instruction sequence in the internal queue for fast execution.

Between lines 13 and 15, the vector base register is initialized to $2000. It relocates the vector table at $00002000. The default vector table remains at $00000000.

The vector location $2084 (corresponding to the TRAP #1 vector at the offset of $84 in the relocated vector table) is loaded with $3000. The JSR instruction at line 16 takes the program to the FCODE module.

The FCODE module is contained between lines 19 and 24. The SFC is loaded with $07, which corresponds to FC2 FC1 FC0 = 1 1 1, and refers to the CPU space (see Figure 10.7). The MOVES.W (A3),D2 instruction forces FC2 FC1 FC0 = 1 1 1 and address lines A1–A23 to the 0 . . . 0 condition during the source operand fetch. This emulates a break condition externally. The RTD instruction returns the program to the REINT module, deallocating the stack by eight words.

Finally, control is given to the governing operating system by means of the TRAP #14 call at lines 17 and 18.

2. **TRAP #1 routine:** The vector offset for TRAP #1 is $84. With the VBR at $2000, the reinitialized TRAP #1 vector location is at $2084, into which $00003000 is loaded. Thus, the TRAP #1 routine would start at $00003000.

3. **Mode of operation:** The processor must be in the supervisor mode, since MOVEC and MOVES are privileged instructions and can only be used in the supervisor mode.[7]

4. **The stack frame and contents:** The processor is in the supervisor mode. The corresponding supervisor stack frame is as follows:

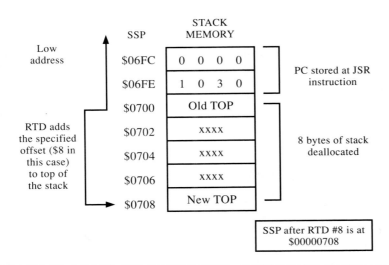

The deallocated space on the stack is usually used by the governing operating system for passing the parameters between local operating systems. The concept of emulation is also demonstrated in the software. While accessing the source operand with the MOVES.W (A3),D2 instruction, a breakpoint condition has been created (or emulated). Detailed discussions on system emulations are beyond the scope of this book; however, references at the end of the chapter may be consulted for further study.

10.3 MEMORY FAULT CORRECTION SCHEMES

Memory-access faults (or memory faults) are corrected using virtual memory schemes. There are two methods by which to implement these schemes: the **instruction restart method** and the **instruction continuation method,** both widely used in the computer industry. The 68010 and 68012 processors follow memory-mapped I/O concepts. The memory fault correction schemes are equally applicable for the I/O units of these processors.

The Instruction Restart Method

Each instruction is organized as a sequence of microcoded modules. Figure 10.10 illustrates a microinstruction scheme for a typical instruction:

$$\text{MOVE.W} \quad -(An), -(Am)$$

The instruction op.word is prefetched (during the previous microinstruction module A) and stored in the instruction queue. The microinstruction modules A, B, and C must be sequentially executed for successful execution of the instruction. The memory-access fault can occur during the A, B, or C module.

In the instruction restart method, if a memory fault occurs in any micromodule, it is corrected (if possible) using virtual memory concepts. Then the complete instruction is repeated. For this to happen, the processor should have the internal resources with which to copy all the original values of the registers. Although this puts a tremendous resource burden on the processor, the instruction restart method is considered to be superior to the instruction continuation method. The instruction is finally executed as a complete unit.

The Instruction Continuation Method

The microinstruction sequence for this method is similar to the sequence of Figure 10.10. The memory fault can occur during the A, B, or C module.

In the instruction continuation method, the memory fault is corrected (if possible) using virtual memory concepts. The instruction execution then continues from the corresponding microinstruction module where the fault was detected and corrected. In this method, it is not necessary to copy the register values, but any interdependence of the destination address and source address (as in the case of MOVE.L $\quad -(An), -(An)$) may result in inaccurate results. This method is easy to implement, however, and is sufficiently accurate for most applications.

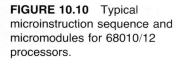

FIGURE 10.10 Typical microinstruction sequence and micromodules for 68010/12 processors.

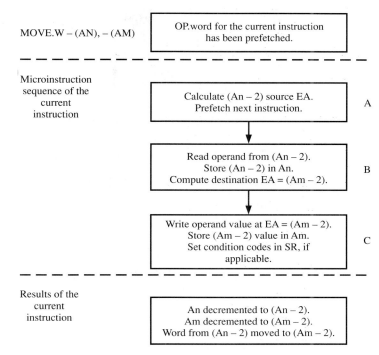

MOVE.W – (AN), – (AM)

OP.word for the current instruction has been prefetched.

Microinstruction sequence of the current instruction

Calculate (An – 2) source EA.
Prefetch next instruction.

A

Read operand from (An – 2).
Store (An – 2) in An.
Compute destination EA = (Am – 2).

B

Write operand value at EA = (Am – 2).
Store (Am – 2) value in Am.
Set condition codes in SR, if applicable.

C

Results of the current instruction

An decremented to (An – 2).
Am decremented to (Am – 2).
Word from (An – 2) moved to (Am – 2).

The 68010/68012 Memory Fault Correction Methods

The 68010 and 68012 microprocessors use the instruction continuation method. To the extent possible, Motorola Corporation designed the instruction micromodules to be functionally independent so as to minimize the fault interaction. These processors use virtual memory schemes to correct memory-access faults. A memory-access fault cannot be corrected if it is not within the logical memory space of the processors.

We will now further address the memory fault correction schemes with the help of an example problem.

Example 10.4   Memory fault correction schemes.
Suppose the 68010 or 68012 processor must execute the following instruction:

$$\text{MOVE.L} \quad -(A1), -(A3)$$

1. Conceptualize the microinstruction sequence.

2. Outline the sequence of events if a memory-access fault occurs while accessing the upper word of the source operand.

3. Outline the sequence of events if a memory-access fault occurs while addressing the lower word location of the destination operand.

Solution

1. **Microinstruction sequence:** The sequence is illustrated in Figure 10.11. It consists of five microinstruction modules: A, B, C, D, and E.

2. **Memory-access fault in source operand:** Referring to Figure 10.11, the memory-access fault occurs during micromodule B. The processor already has completed module A. If possible, the processor corrects the memory-access fault during module B. The microinstruction sequence continues from B to complete the rest of the instruction.

3. **Memory-access fault at destination:** The access fault occurs during micromodule E. The A, B, C, and D modules already have been executed. If possible, the processor corrects the fault during module E, which is the last module. The execution then continues to the next instruction.

FIGURE 10.11 Microinstruction sequence for the MOVE.L   −(A1),−(A3) instruction (Example 10.4).

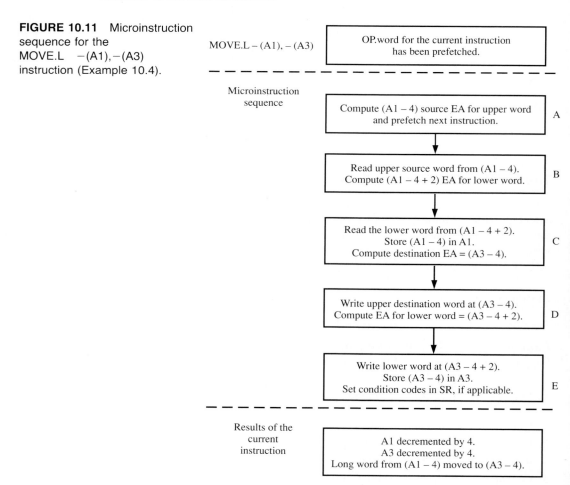

In most cases, the op.word for the next instruction is prefetched during the first module of the current instruction. If a fault occurs in prefetching the next op.word, the current instruction is completed first. The memory fault correction for the prefetched op.word begins after the completion of the current instruction.

10.4 BUS ERROR EXCEPTION PROCESSING ASSOCIATED WITH VIRTUAL MEMORY

As previously stated, the 68010 and 68012 processors can correct memory-access faults using a virtual memory scheme, if the faults occur within the logical space of the processors. The scheme is implemented as a modified bus error exception. The processor must store more information on the stack for the modified bus error exception to be able to correct memory-related faults. If the memory-access fault occurs beyond the logical memory space, the processor reverts to normal bus error exception processing. These exceptions are handled in the supervisor mode.

Modified Bus Error (BERR) Exception Processing

In Figure 10.12, the exception vector table for the 68010 and 68012 processors is given. It is similar to that of the 68000, with a few additions; for example, the format error (vector 14 at offset $038).

Figure 10.13 illustrates the 68010 and 68012 supervisor stack frame for the bus and address error conditions. The processors may stack up to 29 words for memory-related bus error or address error faults. At relative location $06 from the top of the stack, the format and the vector offset entries are of particular importance. If the 4-bit format is 1000, it refers to a long stack frame with 29 words. If the 4-bit format is 0000, it refers to a short stack of 4 words, as shown. Virtual memory schemes are not implemented if the shorter frame is used. The 12-bit vector offset is the relative offset of the exception in the vector table. This value is $008 for the bus error, $024 for the trace, and so on. The stack used is the supervisor stack.

In all types of exceptions, the program counter and the copied status register are automatically stacked. At the conclusion of the exception processing routine, the RTE (return from exception) is executed. The RTE instruction examines the format code (0000 or 1000) and accordingly unstacks either 4 or 29 words into the appropriate registers. Even though the address error stack frame appears to be similar to the bus error stack frame, virtual memory schemes are not implemented for the address error. The address error deals with misaligned access of word or long-word operands at the odd address boundary for the 68000, 68010, and 68012 processors.

Of particular importance is the **special status word** at stack relative location $08. Detailed in Figure 10.14, the special status word reflects the conditions of the bus activity at the time of the exception. This information is useful in developing appropriate error correction routines using virtual memory principles.

Appropriate software dealing with the normal bus error exception or the modified bus error exception should be written as a part of the governing operating system.

Vector Number(s)	Address		Space[6]	Assignment
	Dec	Hex		
0	0	000	SP	Reset: Initial SSP[2]
1	4	004	SP	Reset: Initial PC[2]
2	8	008	SD	Bus Error
3	12	00C	SD	Address Error
4	16	010	SD	Illegal Instruction
5	20	014	SD	Zero Divide
6	24	018	SD	CHK Instruction
7	28	01C	SD	TRAPV Instruction
8	32	020	SD	Privilege Violation
9	36	024	SD	Trace
10	40	028	SD	Line 1010 Emulator
11	44	02C	SD	Line 1111 Emulator
12[1]	48	030	SD	(Unassigned, Reserved)
13[1]	52	034	SD	(Unassigned, Reserved)
14	56	038	SD	Format Error[5]
15	60	03C	SD	Uninitialized Interrupt Vector
16-23[1]	64	040	SD	(Unassigned, Reserved)
	92	05C		—
24	96	060	SD	Spurious Interrupt[3]
25	100	064	SD	Level 1 Interrupt Autovector
26	104	068	SD	Level 2 Interrupt Autovector
27	108	06C	SD	Level 3 Interrupt Autovector
28	112	070	SD	Level 4 Interrupt Autovector
29	116	074	SD	Level 5 Interrupt Autovector
30	120	078	SD	Level 6 Interrupt Autovector
31	124	07C	SD	Level 7 Interrupt Autovector
32-47	128	080	SD	TRAP Instruction Vectors[4]
	188	0BC		—
48-63[1]	192	0C0	SD	(Unassigned, Reserved)
	255	0FF		—
64-255	256	100	SD	User Interrupt Vectors
	1020	3FC		—

NOTES:
1. Vector numbers 12, 13, 16 through 23, and 48 through 63 are reserved for future enhancements by Motorola. No user peripheral devices should be assigned these numbers.
2. Reset vector (0) requires four words, unlike the other vectors which only require two words, and is located in the supervisor program space.
3. The spurious interrupt vector is taken when there is a bus error indication during interrupt processing. Refer to Paragraph 4.4.4.
4. TRAP #n uses vector number 32 + n.
5. MC68010/MC68012 only. See Return from Exception Section.
   This vector is unassigned, reserved on the MC68000 and MC68008.
6. SP denotes supervisor program space, and SD denotes supervisor data space.

FIGURE 10.12 Exception vector table for the 68010/12 processors. (Courtesy of Motorola, Inc.)

FIGURE 10.13 Stack frame for bus and address errors in 68010/12 processors.

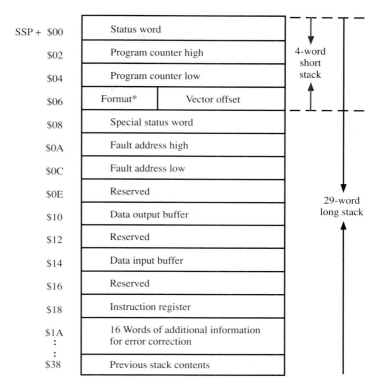

SSP + $00	Status word
$02	Program counter high
$04	Program counter low
$06	Format* / Vector offset
$08	Special status word
$0A	Fault address high
$0C	Fault address low
$0E	Reserved
$10	Data output buffer
$12	Reserved
$14	Data input buffer
$16	Reserved
$18	Instruction register
$1A : :	16 Words of additional information for error correction
$38	Previous stack contents

4-word short stack

29-word long stack

*Format 0000 for short stack and 1000 for long stack.

b15	b14	b13	b12	b11	b10	b9	b8	b7	b6	b5	b4	b3	b2	b1	b0
RR	*	IF	DF	RM	HB	BY	RW	*	*	*	*	*	FC2	FC1	FC0

RR ⇨ Rerun; 0 for processor and 1 for software rerun
IF ⇨ Instruction fetch   DF ⇨ Data fetch
RM ⇨ Read, modify, write cycle   HB ⇨ High byte
BY ⇨ Byte/word transfer for 1/0   RW ⇨ Read/write for 1/0
* ⇨ Reserved   FC2, FC1, FC0 ⇨ Function codes

FIGURE 10.14 Special status word for 68010/68012 processors.

We will now present an example problem to review what we have learned about the modified bus error and associated stack frame.

Example 10.5   68010/12 exceptions and supervisor stack frame.
Figure 10.15 indicates the contents of the stack after a certain type of exception has occurred. The top of the stack is at $0600.

FIGURE 10.15 Supervisor stack frame and contents for the 68010/12-based system (Example 10.5).

SSP	SUPERVISOR STACK				CONTENTS	
	b15 ·························· b0					
$0600	0010	0011	0000	0000	$2300	SR
$0602	0000	0000	0000	0000	$0000	PC
$0604	0001	0000	0100	0010	$1042	
$0606	1000	0000	0000	1000	$8008	[1]
$0608	0001	0001	0000	0101	$1105	[2]
$060A	0000	0000	1000	0001	$0081	[3]
$060C	0010	0000	0100	1000	$2048	
$060E	0000	0000	0000	0000	$0000	[4]
$0610	Other words of the 29-word frame					
⋮	⋮					
$0638	Previous stack contents					

[1] FORMAT/VECTOR
[2] SPECIAL STATUS WORD
[3] FAULT ADDRESS
[4] RESERVED WORD

1. What type of exception has occurred? Can a virtual memory scheme be implemented?
2. What are the conditions at the time of this exception, as indicated in the special status word?
3. What is the fault address?

Solution

1. **Type of exception:** The format/vector offset word at stack location $0606 is $8008. This is interpreted as follows:

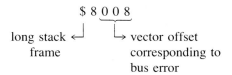

A bus error exception has occurred, with a long stack frame. Virtual memory implementation is possible.

2. **Conditions:** Examining the special status word $1105 at stack location $0608 and comparing it with the special status word format of Figure 10.14, we observe

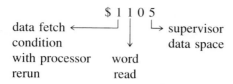

At the time of the exception (bus error), the processor is attempting to read a word from the supervisor data space.

3. **Fault address:** The stack contents at $060A and $060C contain the fault address.

Fault address = $00812048

The governing operating system software uses the stack information in attempting to correct memory-related faults. It should be remembered that the governing operating system is the original or default operating system. It is functional in the supervisor mode. All the local operating systems are functional in the user mode.

Correction of Memory-related Faults Using Virtual Memory Schemes

The most important application of the virtual memory implementation scheme is to correct memory-access faults. If the memory reference is made to memory that is physically nonexistent, but logically existent, the processor can implement the virtual memory scheme upon receiving the $\overline{BERR}$ (bus error) signal. The processor moves the required memory block from the backup memory into the main memory and readjusts the memory pointer reference. It then reruns the bus cycle where the fault occurred and continues with the rest of the instruction and the program.

Virtual memory software is written as part of the modified bus error exception processing. If the memory reference is beyond the logical address space and a bus error occurs, a normal bus error exception will be executed, as we have already mentioned.

In Figure 10.16 the operating listings of a 68010-based system are given. In this software a memory-access fault is simulated and is being corrected. This is written as part of the governing operating system in the supervisor mode. The system has the following memory map:

System ROM/EPROM/RAM $\Rightarrow$ $000000 to $00FFFF (64 kilobytes)

System/User RAM $\Rightarrow$ $010000 to $04FFFF (256 kilobytes)

RAM buffer $\Rightarrow$ $040000 to $04FFFF (64 kilobytes)

System I/O $\Rightarrow$ $100000 to $1003FF (1,024 bytes)

The governing and local operating system programs are contained in the system ROM/ EPROM/RAM. The RAM buffer is used for virtual memory implementation and data transfers.

```
         LINE   ADDR

            1                                 ;virtual memory and memory
            2                                 ;fault correction, fiu 3/88
            3                                     CHIP    68010
            4                                     OPT     A
            5                                     ORG     $1400
            6                                 ;VBR reconfigured at $2000
            7  00001400 41F8 2000                 LEA     $00002000,A0
            8  00001404 4E7B 8801                 MOVEC   A0,VBR
            9  00001408 217C 0000 1420            MOVE.L  #CORRECT,$08(A0)
                        0008
           10                                 ;fault generation
           11  00001410 47F9 0081 2048            LEA $00812048,A3
           12  00001416 3013                      MOVE.W  (A3),D0
           13  00001418 4E71                      NOP
           14                                 ;return to system
           15  0000141A 1E3C 00E4                 MOVE.B  #228,D7
           16  0000141E 4E4E                      TRAP    #14
           17;modified bus error routine if in
           18;logical space. Else normal bus error
           19  00001420 4E54 FFF0       CORRECT LINK    A4,#-$10
           20  00001424 2E2C 000E               MOVE.L  $0E(A4),D7
           21  00001428 0C87 00FF FFFC          CMPI.L  #$FFFFFC,D7
           22  0000142E 6208                    BHI.S   NORMAL
           23;trap #2 routine does memory management
           24;block transfer between backup and main
           25;memory and adjust memory reference.
           26  00001430 4E42                    TRAP    #2
           27  00001432 4E71                    NOP
           28  00001434 4E5C                    UNLK    A4
           29  00001436 4E73                    RTE
           30;to normal bus error
           31  00001438 2A78 0008       NORMAL  MOVEA.L $0008,A5
           32  0000143C 4E5C                    UNLK    A4
           33  0000143E 4ED5                    JMP     (A5)
           34  00001440                         END

         ASSEMBLER ERRORS =     0

                                 SYMBOL TABLE

         CORRECT    00001420   NARG   00000000  NORMAL     00001438
```

FIGURE 10.16 Bus error/memory-access fault correction software for the 68010 (Example 10.6).

At lines 7 and 8, the VBR is initialized to $2000. This is the base address for the new vector table. At line 9, the modified bus error exception routine address (CORRECT) is loaded into new bus error vectored location $2008.

This system does not have physical memory beyond $04FFFF (refer to Section 10.1). Hence, the instructions

LEA $00812048,A3   and   MOVE   (A3),D0

at lines 11 and 12 simulate a bus error condition. Location $812048 is beyond the physical memory, but is contained in the logical memory. While executing the instruction

MOVE.W (A3),D0

the processor receives a $\overline{BERR}$ signal when the source operand is addressed. The processor then stacks the internal register and control information on the stack (see Figure 10.15).

The processor goes to the modified bus error routine (CORRECT) between lines 19 and 29. The fault address is stored at an offset $0A with reference to the current SSP (supervisor stack pointer). The A4 register is configured as the frame pointer by the LINK instruction. At lines 20 and 21, the logical address limit is checked against the fault address. If the fault address is beyond the logical address, the program goes to the normal bus error exception routine (NORMAL) at line 31.

The modified bus error routine is executed via the TRAP #2 routine. This is the memory fault correct software. It transfers 64 kilobytes from the RAM buffer into the backup memory to create space for the new virtual memory data to be brought in. It then transfers a 64-kilobyte block (±32K) around the fault address from the backup memory into the RAM buffer. In this instance, this block would be $80A048 to $81A047. It adjusts the memory reference as shown:

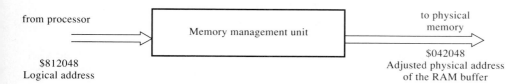

A detailed listing of the TRAP #2 routine is very complex; hence, we have chosen not to include it given the constraints of the text.

At line 28, the stack is unlinked. The following RTE instruction returns the processor to the condition that existed at the time of the bus error. The processor then reruns the bus cycle that generated the bus error. It obtains the source operand from a virtual location $00812048 (which is now a physical location $00042048 in the RAM buffer) and successfully completes the faulted instruction

MOVE.W (A3),D0

If the bus error is a normal bus error, the NORMAL module between lines 31 and 33 will be executed. After unlinking the stack, the program jumps to the address contained at vector location $08. This corresponds to the bus error vector in the default vector table, and the governing operating system executes the normal bus error exception routine.

At the end of the memory-access fault correction, control is returned to the governing operating system by means of the TRAP #14 function at lines 15 and 16.

We will now present an example problem to gain further insight into the memory fault correction schemes.

Example 10.6 Memory fault correction concepts and software.
Refer to the software of Figure 10.16.

1. Describe how the virtual memory concepts are implemented and how the memory-access fault is corrected.
2. What is the difference between the default vector table and the modified (or relocated) vector table?
3. Why are the LINK and UNLK required?

Solution

1. **Memory fault correction:** The memory-access fault address has been stacked at an offset $0A. A 64-kilobyte block around that address has been moved from the backup memory into the RAM buffer and the memory reference has been readjusted. The addressed operand in the virtual address ($812048) will be found at the real physical address ($042048).

$$\text{Fault Address} = \$812048$$
$$\text{Corrected Address} = \$042048$$

2. **Default and modified vector tables:** The default table is the table at power-up reset (VBR = 0). It refers to the original (or governing) operating system exception vectors.

   The modified vector table is set up separately and is accessed with a finite value in VBR to facilitate local operating system or user-defined exception processing. In our example, VBR = $2000. All the default vectors are copied to the new vector table (refer to Section 10.1). But the bus error vector address is changed, and the bus error exception routine is different in the modified table. Initially, the processor goes to the default table; after adjusting VBR, it goes to the modified table.

3. **LINK and UNLK:** These instructions are required to access to the stack without destroying the stack pointer.

There are memory correction schemes that are more involved than those presented here. However, virtual memory implementation schemes remain the same. Because of the difference in the stack frames of the 68000 and 68010 processors, there may be some inconsistencies if a 68000-based system is upgraded to a 68010. Some of the governing operating system exception routines may have to be rewritten to maintain full functional compatibility.

10.5 SUMMARY

In this chapter we introduced the concepts of virtual memory and the virtual machine. We also examined the specific features of the 68010 and 68012 microprocessors with which these schemes are implemented.

The full addressing capability of any processor refers to the logical address space. In many instances, all the available logical address space is not filled with the memory or I/O. Only a part of the available address space, called the physical space, is filled with real and existing devices. With the help of virtual memory schemes, it is possible to realize the entire logical memory space with only a limited amount of physical memory present in the system.

Virtual memory refers to a memory reference contained in the logical space of the processor, but not contained in the physical memory around the processor. If the virtual memory reference is contained in a backup memory, such as a disk, the backup memory block can be moved into the physical memory buffer under the control of the operating system software. Moreover, the memory reference pointers are adjusted to refer to the contents in the buffer area.

At times, the hardware I/O resources may not be physically available, but software to operate them needs to be developed. Hardware resources can be emulated using virtual memory implementation principles. This embodies the concept of the virtual machine; that is, that nonexistent I/O resources can be emulated under software control. The emulated virtual machine resources are under the control of the governing operating system.

The 68010 and 68012 processors have extra registers with which to handle virtual memory and virtual machine schemes. They are the VBR (vector base register) and the SFC and DFC (source function code and destination function code registers). The stack format for the 68010 and 68012 processors is different from that of the 68000. The 68010/12 format allows for 29 words for the bus and address error exceptions.

The 68010 processor is pin compatible with the 68000 and can address 16 megabytes of logical memory. The 68012 processor has seven more address lines, and can access 2 gigabytes of logical memory. Both the 68010 and 68012 are fully software compatible with the 68000.

Memory-access faults can be corrected using virtual memory schemes, if the memory access is in the logical memory space. A bus error signal will be generated when a reference to the nonexistent physical memory is made. In response to this signal, the 68010 and 68012 processors go into bus error exception processing. Using virtual memory concepts, a block of memory is moved from the backup memory into the physical memory. The memory reference is adjusted and the memory-access fault is corrected.

There are two methods for memory-access fault correction: the restart method, and the continuation method. In the restart method, the complete instruction where the fault occurred is repeated after the fault correction. In the continuation method, the instruction is continued from the microstep within the instruction after the memory-access fault correction.

The restart method requires that all the microcoded operations of an instruction and associated operands be stored. This requires tremendous register resources, as well as other resources. The restart method, however, executes the instruction as a unit.

The continuation method is considered sufficiently accurate for most applications and does not require that all the microcoded operations of an instruction be stored. The continuation method executes the instruction in parts rather than as a single unit, however. The 68010 and 68012 processors use the continuation method.

PROBLEMS

10.1 Redefine the virtual memory and virtual machine concepts in your own terms.

(a) Give an example of virtual memory.

(b) Give an example of the virtual machine.

10.2 Explain why the virtual memory scheme cannot be implemented in the 68000 microprocessor.

      If external resources are added, can the 68000 be changed to a 68010 processor? Explain.

10.3 Can virtual memory schemes be implemented for

(a) an address error?

(b) a zero-divide error?

State your reasons in each case

10.4 Can virtual machine concepts be extended to replace real machines?

(a) If so, can the real machines be dispensed with?

(b) If not, what is the real usefulness of the virtual machine concept?

10.5 Refer to the system we considered in Examples 10.1 and 10.2. The following instruction is executed:

$$\text{ADDX.L} \quad -(\text{A1}), -(\text{A2})$$

A1 = \$080004 and A2 = \$08345C.

(a) Which memory block gets moved from the backup memory into the buffer area? Why?

(b) Where are the A1 and A2 register values stored? Why?

(c) What are the adjusted values of the A1 and A2 registers?

10.6 A printer I/O system is emulated using virtual machine concepts. The printer has a print buffer of 2,048 bytes and six different control signals, such as ready to send, clear to send, paper out, and the like. In addition, the printer has a 256-byte character buffer.

(a) To emulate the printer as a virtual machine, how much memory is required?

(b) If the printer were to send an interrupt, how would this be accomplished?

10.7 The 68000 and 68010 are pin compatible with one another.

(a) Will software written for the 68000 run completely using the 68010? Are there any instances in which a marked difference between the two processors will be evidenced?

(b) Repeat (a) if the software is intended for the 68010 and the device is then replaced by 68000.

10.8 In a multiuser environment, reconfigure

(a) the vector table for user 1 starting at $2000;
(b) the vector table for user 2 starting at $4000.

Initialize locations so that the TRAP #2 routine for user 1 starts at $1600 and for user 2 at $1800.

10.9 If the RTD instruction is not available (as is the case with the 68000),

(a) write a sequence of instructions to accomplish the task illustrated in Figure 10.9;
(b) compute the time of execution for (a) and compare this with the RTD instruction execution time.

10.10 If possible, rewrite the software of Figure 10.9

(a) to emulate an interrupt acknowledge cycle;
(b) to emulate the user I/O cycle.

10.11 Obtaining the timing information from the data sheets of the 68010,

(a) formulate the T(R/W) values for the software of Figure 10.9.
(b) compute the time of execution for (a).

10.12 In the 68010 and 68012 processors, explain how different vector tables are used for different users. For example,

> User 1   Vector table starting at $2000
> User 2   Vector table starting at $4000

Where is the default vector table for both users?

10.13 Indicate the micromodules for the following instructions:

(a) MOVE.L   (A1)+,−(A3)
(b) MOVE.L   −(A1), (A3)+

10.14 Repeat problem 10.13 for the following:

(a) ADDI.B   #$43,$14(A1,D1.W)
(b) EOR.W   D2,(A1)+

10.15 Suppose a memory-access fault occurs while accessing the source operand in the instructions that follow. Outline the sequence of events with appropriate micromodules.

(a) ADDX.L   −(A1),−(A1)
(b) ADD.L   (A1)+,D2

Compare the micromodules and specify which takes more modules and time. Explain your answer.

10.16 Can the faults occurring in the following sequence of instructions be corrected by the 68010? State all of your reasons.

(a) MOVEA.L   #$12345678,A1
     ROL.W   (A1)
(b) JMP $12345

10.17 Why is the restart method considered superior to the continuation method in the field of virtual memory? Give at least three reasons.

What additional resources are required to implement the restart method?

10.18 Are the stack structures for the 68000 and 68010 completely compatible with one another? Why or why not?

(a) If there is any incompatibility, does it create any hardware or software problems in interchanging the 68000 and 68010?

(b) Can the incompatibility, if it exists, be corrected by external hardware? Give your reasons.

10.19 Given the following software:

```
PC          Instruction

$090C       MOVE.W D0,$1003
            NOP
```

an error condition has resulted in accessing the data space at $1003.

(a) What type of error must it have been?

(b) Indicate the contents of the stack when the 68010 recognizes the error and is ready to respond with appropriate exception processing.

10.20 Repeat Problem 10.19 for the following:

```
PC          Instruction

$1000       ADDQ.W #$03,$12345678
            NOP
             :
             :
$100E       CLR.B A6
```

10.21 Specify two exception conditions in which the format code will be

(a) $0000;

(b) $1000.

10.22 Rewrite the software of Figure 10.16 so that the physical memory buffer is located between

(a) $15000 and $18000;

(b) $40000 and $44000.

10.23 Rewrite the software of Figure 10.16 to make it more efficient

(a) in terms of execution time;

(b) in terms of the program memory space.

10.24 In Example 10.6, suppose the fault-causing instruction is changed to

ADD.L   D7,(A5)+

A5 = $887766AA.

(a) Specify the sequence of events.

(b) Can the error be corrected by virtual memory schemes? If so, show how it can be done. If not, specify your reasons and validate them with practical examples.

ENDNOTES

1. Motorola, Inc. *68010 Data Book*. Phoenix, AZ: Motorola Technical Operations, 1983.

2. Motorola, Inc. *68010/68012 Data Book*. Phoenix, AZ: Motorola Technical Operations, 1985.

3. MacGregor, D., and Mothersole, D. "Virtual Memory and the 68010." *IEEE Micro* 3(10):24–39.

4. Motorola, Inc. *MTT8 68000 Course Notes*. Phoenix, AZ: Motorola Technical Operations, 1987.

5. Motorola, Inc. *M68000 16/32-Bit Microprocessor Programmer's Reference Manual, Fifth Edition*. Englewood Cliffs, NJ: Prentice-Hall, 1987.

6. MacGregor, D., and Moyer, B. "Built-in Tight Loop Mode Raises Microprocessor Performance (68010)." *Electronic Design* 31, no. 22 (1983).

7. Miller, M.A. "The 68000 Family of Microprocessors." Chap. 10 in *The 68000 Microprocessor: Architecture, Programming, and Applications*. Columbus, OH: Merrill, 1988.

68020 and 68030 Architecture, Organization, and Applications

Objectives

In this chapter we will study:

The general architecture of the 68020 and 68030 processors

The additional resources of the 68020 and 68030

Cache memory organization concepts

Functional improvements of the 68020 and 68030

11.0   INTRODUCTION

The 68020 is a 32-bit microprocessor with individual 32-bit address and data buses. It has a 4-gigabyte logical address space. In addition to all the internal resources of the 68010 and 68012 processors, it has a chip instruction cache memory. These additional features increase the overall throughput of a 68020-based system as compared to the earlier members of the 68000 family.[1]

The 68030 is an extension of the 68020 processor. Additional features of the 68030 include the data cache memory and a paged memory management unit (PMMU, or simply MMU) on the chip itself, further enhancing the throughput of 68030-based systems.

Study of the material in this chapter will provide a comprehensive introduction to the 68020 and 68030 processors, cache memory, and memory management operations.

FIGURE 11.1 General architecture of the 68020. (Courtesy of Motorola, Inc.)

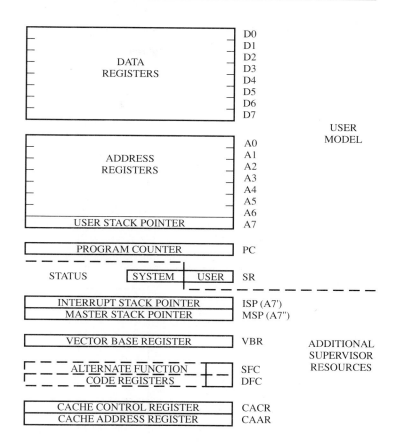

11.1 GENERAL ARCHITECTURE OF THE 68020

The 68020 is contained in a 114-pin grid-array package and is fabricated with VLSI MOS technology. Figure 11.1 illustrates the internal architecture of the 68020. It contains all the resources of the 68000, 68010, and 68012, along with some additional resources and modified resources to facilitate cache memory implementation.

Additional Resources and Modified Resources of the 68020

There are three stack pointers in the 68020: the user stack pointer USP (A7) in the user mode, the interrupt stack pointer ISP (A7′) in the supervisor mode, and the master stack pointer MSP (A7″) in the supervisor mode. The USP handles the user stack operations. The ISP handles the interrupt exceptions and the MSP handles the rest of the exceptions. Selection of the stack pointer to be used is made with the help of the S and M bits in the system byte of the status register.

The cache control and the cache address registers (CACR and CAAR) are used to control the cache memory operations. The vector base register (VBR) and the alternate

FIGURE 11.2 System byte of the 68020 status register.

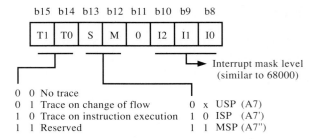

source and destination function code registers (SFC and DFC) are used in much the same way as in the 68010 processor.[2]

The user byte of the status register is similar to that of the 68000 processor. The system byte is modified, however, as shown in Figure 11.2. The T1 and T0 bits determine the trace mode of operation. The S and M bits select the stack pointer. The interrupt mask bits I2, I1, and I0 are similar to those of 68000.

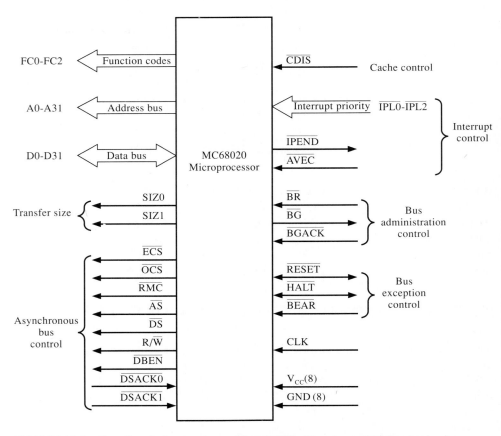

FIGURE 11.3 Functional pin structure of the 68020. (Courtesy of Motorola, Inc.)

Address, Data, and Control Buses

Figure 11.3 indicates the functional pin structure of the 68020 and Figure 11.4 describes the signals. The address and data buses are extended to 32 bits each. Eight-bit byte, 16-bit word, or 32-bit long-word data operands can be transferred in a single bus cycle. The function code outputs FC2, FC1, and FC0 specify the type of address space and the processor condition. The SIZ1 and SIZ0 outputs indicate the number of bytes to be further transferred at the beginning of each bus cycle.

The external cycle start ($\overline{ECS}$) output indicates that a bus cycle is beginning. The operand cycle start ($\overline{OCS}$) output is asserted during the first bus cycle of an operand transfer. The read-modify/write cycle ($\overline{RMC}$) output is similar to that of the 68012 processor; it indicates that the current bus cycle is an indivisible read-modify/write bus cycle.

The address strobe ($\overline{AS}$) and the data strobe ($\overline{DS}$) outputs indicate the validity of the address and the data on the respective buses. The read/write ($R/\overline{W}$) output indicates the read or write bus cycle. The data buffer enable ($\overline{DBEN}$) output is similar to the $\overline{DS}$ signal, but is used to enable the external data buffers. The $\overline{DTACK}$ input of the 68000 is

Signal Name	Mnemonic	Function
Address Bus	A0-A31	32-bit address bus used to address any of 4,294,967,296 bytes.
Data Bus	D0-D31	32-bit data bus used to transfer 8, 16, 24, or 32 bits of data per bus cycle.
Function Codes	FC0-FC2	3-bit function code used to identify the address space of each bus cycle.
Size	SIZ0 SIZ1	Indicates the number of bytes remaining to be transferred for this cycle. These signals, together with A0 and A1, define the active sections of the data bus.
Read-Modify-Write Cycle	$\overline{RMC}$	Provides an indicator that the current bus cycle is part of an indivisible read-modify-write operation.
External Cycle Start	$\overline{ECS}$	Provides an indication that a bus cycle is beginning.
Operand Cycle Start	$\overline{OCS}$	Identical operation to that of $\overline{ECS}$ except that $\overline{OCS}$ is asserted only during the first bus cycle of an operand transfer.
Address Strobe	$\overline{AS}$	Indicates that a valid address is on the bus.
Data Strobe	$\overline{DS}$	Indicates that valid data is to be placed on the data bus by an external device or has been placed on the data bus by the MC68020.
Read/Write	$R/\overline{W}$	Defines the bus transfer as an MPU read or write.
Data Buffer Enable	$\overline{DBEN}$	Provides an enable signal for external data buffers.
Data Transfer and Size Acknowledge	$\overline{DSACK0}$ $\overline{DSACK1}$	Bus response signals that indicate the requested data transfer operation is completed. In addition, these two lines indicate the size of the external bus port on a cycle-by-cycle basis.
Cache Disable	$\overline{CDIS}$	Dynamically disables the on-chip cache to assist emulator support.
Interrupt Priority Level	IPL0-IPL2	Provides an encoded interrupt level to the processor.
Autovector	$\overline{AVEC}$	Requests an autovector during an interrupt acknowledge cycle.
Interrupt Pending	$\overline{IPEND}$	Indicates that an interrupt is pending.
Bus Request	$\overline{BR}$	Indicates that an external device requires bus mastership.
Bus Grant	$\overline{BG}$	Indicates that an external device may assume bus mastership.
Bus Grant Acknowledge	$\overline{BGACK}$	Indicates that an external device has assumed bus mastership.
Reset	$\overline{RESET}$	System reset.
Halt	$\overline{HALT}$	Indicates that the processor should suspend bus activity.
Bus Error	$\overline{BERR}$	Indicates an invalid or illegal bus operation is being attempted.
Clock	$\overline{CLK}$	Clock input to the processor.
Power Supply	V_{CC}	+5 ±5% volt power supply.
Ground	GND	Ground connection.

FIGURE 11.4   The 68020 signal description. (Courtesy of Motorola, Inc.)

split into $\overline{\text{DSACK0}}$ and $\overline{\text{DSACK1}}$. These two inputs are encoded to specify byte, word, or long-word transfers on the data bus.[3]

The cache disable ($\overline{\text{CDIS}}$) input disables the internal cache memory. The interrupt priority inputs ($\overline{\text{IPL2}}$, $\overline{\text{IPL1}}$, and $\overline{\text{IPL0}}$) are similar to those of the 68000 processor. The autovector ($\overline{\text{AVEC}}$) input signifies an autovectored interrupt condition. The interrupt pending ($\overline{\text{IPEND}}$) input signifies a pending interrupt. The bus arbitration signals (the bus request ($\overline{\text{BR}}$) input, the bus grant ($\overline{\text{BG}}$) output, and the bus grant acknowledge ($\overline{\text{BGACK}}$) input) are similar to those of the 68000 processor and are used for the DMA type of transfers. The system control signals ($\overline{\text{RESET}}$, $\overline{\text{HALT}}$, and $\overline{\text{BERR}}$) are also similar to those of the 68000 processor. The device operates on 5 volts V_{DD}.

Data Formats, Memory, and I/O Interface Schemes

The 68020 is designed to facilitate byte, word, or long-word data transfers on even or odd address boundaries. However, the op.word (instruction word) fetches must be on even word boundaries to maintain code compatibility with the earlier 68000 family members. If op.word fetches are not on even word boundaries, an address error will occur.

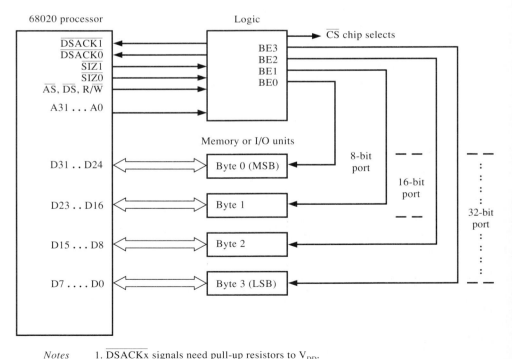

Notes   1. $\overline{\text{DSACKx}}$ signals need pull-up resistors to V_{DD}.
2. MSB $\Rightarrow$ most significant byte; LSB $\Rightarrow$ least significant byte.

FIGURE 11.5   Memory and I/O general interface scheme for the 68020.

Figure 11.5 illustrates a typical memory interface scheme and associated data formats. The 68020 uses memory-mapped I/O concepts similar to those of the other members of the family; thus, the memory and I/O interface schemes are similar. An 8-bit byte port (b7–b0) is connected to data lines D31–D24. A 16-bit word port (b15–b0) is connected to data lines D31–D16. A 32-bit long-word port (b31–b0) is connected to data lines D31–D0. The A1 and A0 address lines and the SIZ1 and SIZ0 size outputs are decoded to provide the byte enable signals BE0, BE1, BE2, and BE3. These signals enable the transfer of appropriate bytes.[4]

Figure 11.6 indicates the DSACK and SIZ signal responses for different data sizes. Depending upon the address and the alignment, there can be one, two, three, or four byte transfers in a single bus cycle.

We will now present an example problem to review basic concepts relating to the 68020 processor.

$\overline{DSACK1}$	$\overline{DSACK0}$	Data Bus Activity
1	1	not selected
1	0	byte selected
0	1	word selected
0	0	long word selected

SIZ1	SIZ0	Data Size
1	1	3 bytes more
1	0	2 bytes more
0	1	1 byte more
0	0	4 bytes more

(a)   (b)

FIGURE 11.6   Data bus activity and selection as functions of (a) DSACK and (b) SIZ signals.

Example 11.1   68020 architecture and data formats.
A 68020-based system has the following memory and I/O map:

Main memory (32-bit wide) $\Rightarrow$ $00000000 to $00FFFFFF
System I/O (16-bit wide) $\Rightarrow$ $01000000 to $0100FFFF
(8-bit wide) $\Rightarrow$ $01010000 to $010103FF

1. What are the conditions of the system byte at power-up reset? What is the default value of VBR on reset?

2. The processor is executing the following instruction:

MOVE.L   D0,(A1)

with D0 = $012A46AB; A1 = $00004000. Indicate the data transfers on the bus, along with the DSACKx and SIZx signals.

3. The processor is executing the following instruction:

$$\text{MOVE.L} \quad \text{D0,(A2)}$$

with D0 = \$012A46AB; A2 = \$01000401. Indicate the data transfers on the bus, along with the DSACKx and SIZx signals.

Solution

1. System byte and VBR on reset: In order to be compatible with the other members of the 68000 family, the system byte is set up for trace off, stack pointer ISP, and interrupt mask level 7. Similarly, the VBR is set up for the all-zero condition. The system byte and the VBR are as shown:

	b15	b14	b13	b12	b11	b10	b9	b8
System byte ⇨	T1	T0	S	M	0	I2	I1	I0
	0	0	1	0	0	1	1	1

VBR ⇨ $ 0 0 0 0 0 0 0 0

2. MOVE.L   D0,(A1): The destination effective address (A1) = \$00004000 is evenly divisible by 4; as such, it is long-word aligned. All 32 bits of data from D0 are transferred to the destination in a single bus cycle, as shown:

	MSB			LSB
	OP0	OP1	OP2	OP3
D0 ⇨	0 1	2 A	4 6	A B
	:	:	:	:
Data bus	D31–D24	D23–D16	D15–D8	D7–D0
	:	:	:	:

				DSACK1	DSACK0	SIZ1	SIZ0
\$00004000	0 1	2 A	4 6	A B	0	0	0	0

3. MOVE.L   D0,(A2): The 16-bit port is connected between data lines D31 and D16. The destination effective address (A2) = \$01000401 is at an odd byte boundary and is misaligned. However, the long-word data operand is transferred in three bus cycles. During the first bus cycle, the most significant byte (MSB) operand OP0 is transferred to location \$01000401. During the second bus cycle, byte operands OP1 and OP2 are transferred as a word to location \$01000402. During the third bus cycle, the LSB operand OP3 is transferred to location \$01000404. The sequence of operations is as shown:

	MSB			LSB				
	OP0	OP1	OP2	OP3				
D0 $\Rightarrow$	0 1	2 A	4 6	A B				

	:	:						
	D31–	D23–						
	D24	D16			$\overline{DSACK1}$	$\overline{DSACK0}$	$\overline{SIZ1}$	$\overline{SIZ0}$
$01000400	X X	0 1		$01000401	1	0	0	0
$01000402	2 A	4 6		$01000403	0	1	1	1
$01000404	A B	X X		$01000405	1	0	0	1

The DSACK and SIZ signals specify the actual bus activity. During the first bus cycle, 4 bytes were meant to be transferred, but only one could be transferred. During the second bus cycle, 3 bytes were still meant to be transferred, but only two could be transferred (as a word). During the third bus cycle, the last and remaining byte is transferred.

With the help of the DSACK and SIZ signals, it is possible to execute aligned or misaligned data transfers with equal ease. Misaligned transfers take more bus cycles, however.

To further familiarize the reader with the configuration of the 68020 processor, the internal block diagram and layout structure are presented in Figures 11.7 and 11.8.

11.2 ADDITIONAL ADDRESSING MODES AND INSTRUCTIONS FOR THE 68020

The table of Figure 11.9 (p. 316) indicates the addressing modes of the 68020. In addition to all the addressing modes of the 68000, it has memory indirect and program counter indirect addressing modes. The associated base and outer displacements (bd and od) can be up to 32 signed bits.[5]

Memory Indirection Addressing Modes and Scaling

Whenever an index register (Dn or An) is used, its contents are multiplied by a **scale factor.** In computing the effective address, the scale factor can be 1, 2, 4, or 8. The scaling enables addressing at relative displacements of the byte, word, long word, or quad word (8 bytes). The term **memory indirect addressing** is used in reference to a memory location, the contents of which form the base address of the operand. The effective address of the operand is obtained by properly adding the scaled index register

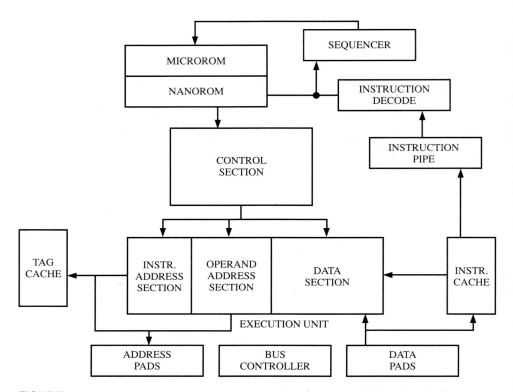

FIGURE 11.7 Internal block diagram of the 68020. (Courtesy of Motorola, Inc.)

contents and the base and outer displacements to the indirect address. This addressing scheme uses a memory location as a memory pointer.

Figure 11.10 (p. 317) indicates the results that follow from using the new addressing modes. When scaling is used, the physical value of the index register is not changed. In **memory indirect postindexing,** the contents of the memory indirect address are obtained first. The index and the outer displacements are further added to obtain the effective address of the operand. In **memory indirect preindexing,** the memory indirect address is obtained after indexing. The outer displacement is further added to obtain the EA of the operand.

In the program counter indirect and program counter memory indirect addressing modes, the program counter is used instead of an address register. These modes are suitable for relocatable code generation.

Bit-Field Type of Instructions

The bit-field instructions for the 68020 are given in Figure 11.11 (p. 318). These instructions address and manipulate a bit field of variable width (1 to 32 bits), starting from a given offset of the effective address. The syntax of the single operand instruction is

FIGURE 11.8 The 68020 internal structure and layout. (Courtesy of Motorola, Inc.)

$$BFxxx \langle ea \rangle \{offset : width\}$$

If the instruction is of the double-operand type, the other operand is a data register Dn. The offset and width fields can be specified as immediate operands or as Dn operands. For all bit-field instructions, the bit field is first tested and the N and Z flags are adjusted accordingly. The specified bit-field operation is then carried out. In Figure 11.12 (p. 319) some typical bit-field instruction operations are given in order of complexity.

The bit-field instructions are very helpful in handling bit fields of variable lengths and at any effective address location. In the absence of these instructions, a series of instructions must be written to accomplish the tasks of this type.

Addressing Modes	Syntax
Register Direct	
Data Register Direct	Dn
Address Register Direct	An
Register Indirect	
Address Register Indirect	(An)
Address Register Indirect with Postincrement	(An) +
Address Register Indirect with Predecrement	– (An)
Address Register Indirect with Displacement	(d_{16},An)
Register Indirect with Index	
Address Register Indirect with Index (8-Bit Displacement)	(d_8,An,Xn)
Address Register Indirect with Index (Base Displacement)	(bd,An,Xn)
Memory Indirect	
Memory Indirect Post-Indexed	([bd,An],Xn,od)
Memory Indirect Pre-Indexed	([bd,An,Xn],od)
Program Counter Indirect with Displacement	(d_{16},PC)
Program Counter Indirect with Index	
PC Indirect with Index (8-Bit Displacement)	(d_8,PC,Xn)
PC Indirect with Index (Base Displacement)	(bd,PC,Xn)
Program Counter Memory Indirect	
PC Memory Indirect Post-Indexed	([bd,PC],Xn,od)
PC Memory Indirect Pre-Indexed	([bd,PC,Xn],od)
Absolute	
Absolute Short	xxx.W
Absolute Long	xxx.L
Immediate	# <data>

NOTES:

Dn = Data Register, D0-D7

An = Address Register, A0-A7

d_8, d_{16} = A twos-complement, or sign-extended displacement; added as part of the effective address calculation; size is 8 or 16 bits (d_{16} and d_8 are 16- and 8-bit displacements); when omitted, assemblers use a value of zero.

Xn = Address or data register used as an index register; form is Xn.SIZE*SCALE, where SIZE is .W or .L (indicates index register size) and SCALE is 1, 2, 4, or 8 (index register is multiplied by SCALE); use of SIZE and/or SCALE is optional.

bd = A twos-complement base displacement; when present, size can be 16 or 32 bits.

od = Outer displacement, added as part of effective address calculation after any memory indirection; use is optional with a size of 16 or 32 bits.

PC = Program Counter

<data> = Immediate value of 8, 16, or 32 bits

( ) = Effective address

[ ] = Use as indirect address to long word address.

FIGURE 11.9 Addressing modes of the 68020. (Courtesy of Motorola, Inc.)

Packed and Unpacked BCD Instructions

The **PACK instruction** is used to reduce a word-sized two-digit BCD operand into a packed 8-bit two-digit BCD operand. The **UNPK instruction** increases a byte-sized two-digit BCD operand into an unpacked 16-bit two-digit BCD operand. Examples follow.

PACK   D2,D3,#$0000: The specified immediate data (0000) word is added to the source operand in the D2 register. The upper 4 bits of each byte are discarded and the lower 4 bits of each byte are packed into the destination register D3.

INITIAL CONDITIONS

A0 = $0000ABCD;	D0 = $00000004;	$00004800	0000
A1 = $00000008;	D1 = $00000200;	4802	2222
A2 = $00003000;	D2 = $0000F0F0;	4804	4444
A3 = $00004000;	D3 = $012A46AB;	4806	6666
		4808	8888
		480A	0000

1. ARI with base displacement, index, and scaling:

MOVE.L   (08, A3, D1.W * 4),D4

      :   :   :   :

     bd ARI index   scale

EA calculation:

A3.L $00004000 +
D1.W*4 $00000800 +
bd $00000008
EA = $00004808

(ARI ⇒ Address register indirect)

Long-word contents corresponding to
EA are moved into D4 register ⇒ **D4 = $88880000**

2. Memory indirect postindexed:

MOVE.L   ([$1800,A2], D1.W * 8, $15E0),D4

      :   :   :   :   :

    bd ARI index   scale od

EA calculation:

A2.L $00003000 +
bd $00001800
memory indirect address = $00004800
contents of above memory indirect address $00002222 +
D1.W*8 $00001000 +
od $000015E0
EA = $00004802

Long-word contents corresponding to
EA are moved into D4 register ⇒ **D4 = $22224444**

3. Memory indirect preindexed:

MOVE.L   ([$0800,A2, D1.W * 8], $25E4),D4

      :   :   :   :   :

    bd ARI index   scale od

EA calculation:

A2.L $00003000 +
D1.W*8 $00001000 +
bd $00000800
memory indirect address = $00004800
contents of above memory indirect address $00002222 +
od $000025E4
EA = $00004806

Long-word contents corresponding to
EA are moved into D4 register ⇒ **D4 = $66668888**

FIGURE 11.10 The 68020 scaling and memory indirect addressing modes.

Instruction	Operation
BFCHG	Test bit field and change from 1 to 0, or vice versa.
BFCLR	Test bit field and clear.
BFEXTS	Extract signed bit field from source and place into destination.
BFEXTU	Extract unsigned bit field from source and place into destination.
BFFFO	Find first one in the bit field.
BFINS	Insert bit field at specified address.
BFSET	Test bit field and set condition codes.
BFTST	Test bit field and set or reset N and Z flags.

Flag conditions: N set if the MSB of the bit field is 1.
Z set if the bit field is all-zero.
V cleared; C cleared; X unaffected.

FIGURE 11.11   Bit-field instructions for the 68020.

```
          Initially D2 =    $  x  x  x  x  3  7  3  5
      +   data element =    $              0  0  0  0
                                              :     :
          discard upper 4 bits of each byte   :     :
          and pack lower 4 bits of each byte  7     5
                                               ╲    :
          Final D3 value = $  x  x  x  x  x  x  7  5
```

The source and destination operands can also be specified by the predecrement ARI addressing mode (PACK   −(An),−(Am),#data).

UNPK   D3,D4,#$3030: The source operand in the D3 register is unpacked from 8 bits to 16 bits, with the upper 4 bits of each byte set to zero. The specified data ($3030) is added to the unpacked operand. The resulting 16-bit operand is placed in the destination register D4.

```
          Initially D3 =    $  x  x  x  x  x  x  7  5
                                               ╱╱   :
          unpacked operand                  0  7  0  5
      +   data element =    $               3  0  3  0
          Final D4 value = $  x  x  x  x  3  7  3  5
```

The source and destination operands can also be specified by the predecrement ARI addressing mode (UNPK   −(An),−(Am),#data).

In the preceding example, with a data element of $3030, the UNPK instruction has converted a normal BCD value into a corresponding ASCII value (BCD 7 ⇒ ASCII 37; BCD 5 ⇒ ASCII 35). This illustrates the usefulness of PACK and UNPK instructions in code conversions.

	bits								
	displacement	b7	b6	b5	b4	b3	b2	b1	b0	
byte address 4007	−8	1	0	1	1	1	1	0	0	$BC
base byte address 4008 ⇒	0	1	1	0	1	0	0	0	1	$D1
byte address 4009	+8	0	0	0	1	0	1	0	1	$15

1. BFTST 4008{2:6}:

Tests bit field with base address 4008, offset 2 and width 6 bits. Tests bits b5–b0 of byte at location 4008. N = 0 (MSB b5 is 0); Z = 0 (bit field is nonzero).

2. BFCLR 4008{2:6}:

Performs BFTST operation as above first and returns the N and Z values (0 and 0). Then clears bits b5–b0 of byte at 4008. (If BFSET is used, then the corresponding bits are set after returning the N and Z values).

3. BFCHG 4008{2:6}:

After performing the BFTST operation as above and returning the N and Z values (0 and 0), toggles (1 to 0 and 0 to 1) bits b5–b0 of byte 4008.

4. BFEXTU 4008{−8:16},D1:

Extracts bit field with base address 4008, offset −8, and width 16 bits. In this case, it extracts (moves) b7–b0 bits of byte at 4008 into b7–b0 bit positions of the D1 register. It further moves bits b7–b0 of byte at 4007 into bit positions b15–b8 of the D1 register. The rest of the bits of the D1 register are loaded with zeros, since the instruction is unsigned.

$$D1 = \$0000BCD1$$
$$N = 1 \text{ (MSB of the bit field (b7 of byte at 4007) = 1)}$$
$$Z = 0 \text{ (nonzero bit-field value)}$$

If BFEXTS (signed extract instruction) is used, the MSB bit of the bit field is sign extended to the higher bits of the destination register. Thus, BFEXTS 4008{−8:16} yields

$$D1 = \$FFFFBCD1$$
$$N = 1$$
$$Z = 0$$

5. BFINS D1,4008{12:4}:   (D1 = $FFFFBCD1)

Inserts into bit field with base address 4008, offset 12 the last 4 bits of the D1 register. In this case, 0 0 0 1 bits are inserted in bit positions b3–b0 of byte at 4009. N = 0 and Z = 0, since a positive nonzero value is inserted.

6. BFFFO 4008{8:8},D2:

Finds first one in the specified bit field at base address 4008 with offset 8 and field width 8 bits. Returns the effective offset value to the D2 register. In this case, the first one is found at b4 of byte at 4009. This corresponds to an effective offset of 11 = $B.

$$D2 = \$0000000B$$
$$N = 1 \text{ (1 found in the specified bit field as MSB)}$$
$$Z = 0 \text{ (nonzero effective bit field)}$$

FIGURE 11.12 Bit-field instruction applications.

Other Instructions and Enhancements

In the 68020, the divide and multiply instructions are extended to cover 32-bit operands. The TRAP instructions are further extended to operate on condition (TRAPcc). The CAS (compare and swap) instructions are of the read-modify/write type and enhance system throughput. There are also a set of coprocessor instructions (cpxxx) to control the coprocessor operation. Figure 11.13 summarizes the 68020 instruction set.

The 68020 processor has an internal 4-word pipe that holds the prefetched instructions and operands. The pipe is filled whenever there is a two-word vacancy. In the case of a change in program flow, the pipe contents are invalidated and the pipe is refilled.[6]

11.3 CACHE MEMORY CONCEPTS AND ORGANIZATION

Cache memory is a fast-access, high-speed memory designed to hold the most frequently used information. The processor copies the required information from the main memory into the cache memory. The cache memory is usually of limited size. As often as is necessary, the cached information is updated.

68020 Cache Memory Organization and Operation

The 68020 processor has a 256-byte instruction cache memory on the chip, itself. It is organized as 64 long words, as shown in Figure 11.14. Two internal registers, the CACR (cache control register) and the CAAR (cache address register), determine the operation of the cache memory. The cache memory can be disabled or enabled. When enabled, the processor fills in the cache memory with the most recently fetched instructions and uses them.

When the processor wants to fetch an instruction, it checks the cache memory to determine whether the instruction is in the cache. If it is in the cache, we have what is known as a **hit condition.** If it is not in the cache, we have what is known as a **miss condition.**

For a hit condition, the processor fetches the instruction from the cache and executes it. The typical instruction access time from cache corresponds to two clock cycles. For a miss condition, the processor fetches the instruction from the external memory and executes it. The typical instruction access time from external memory corresponds to three clock cycles. Cache memory is always updated with the most recent instructions fetched from the external memory. Figure 11.15 indicates timing under cache hit and cache miss conditions.

When the processor is obtaining instructions from the cache memory and executing them, the external bus is free. The bus interface unit accesses data operands during this time window. In addition, the prefetch mechanism of the 68000 family is operational, even with the cache memory. All of these parallel operations enhance the overall throughput of the 68020 processor.

Mnemonic	Description	Mnemonic	Description
ABCD	Add Decimal with Extend	MULS	Signed Multiply
ADD	Add	MULU	Unsigned Multiply
ADDA	Add Address	NBCD	Negate Decimal with Extend
ADDI	Add Immediate	NEG	Negate
ADDQ	Add Quick	NEGX	Negate with Extend
ADDX	Add with Extend	NOP	No Operation
AND	Logical AND	NOT	Logical Complement
ANDI	Logical AND Immediate	OR	Logical Inclusive OR
ASL, ASR	Arithmetic Shift Left and Right	ORI	Logical OR Immediate
Bcc	Branch Conditionally	PACK	Pack BCD
BCHG	Test Bit and Change	PEA	Push Effective Address
BCLR	Test Bit and Clear	RESET	Reset External Devices
BFCHG	Test Bit Field and Change	ROL, ROR	Rotate Left and Right
BFCLR	Test Bit Field and Clear	ROXL, ROXR	Rotate with Extend Left and Right
BFEXTS	Signed Bit Field Extract	RTD	Return and Deallocate
BFEXTU	Unsigned Bit Field Extract	RTE	Return from Exception
BFFFO	Bit Field Find First One	RTM	Return from Module
BFINS	Bit Field Insert	RTR	Return and Restore Conditon Codes
BFSET	Test Bit Field and Set	RTS	Return from Subroutine
BFTST	Test Bit Field	SBCD	Subtract Decimal with Extend
BRA	Branch	Scc	Set Conditionally
BSET	Test Bit and Set	STOP	Stop
BSR	Branch to Subroutine	SUB	Subtract
BTST	Test Bit	SUBA	Subtract Address
CALLM	Call Module	SUBI	Subtract Immediate
CAS	Compare and Swap Operands	SUBQ	Subtract Quick
CAS2	Compare and Swap Dual Operands	SUBX	Subtract with Extend
CHK	Check Register Against Bound	SWAP	Swap Register Words
CHK2	Check Register Against Upper and Lower Bounds	TAS	Test Operand and Set
CLR	Clear	TRAP	Trap
CMP	Compare	TRAPcc	Trap Conditionally
CMPA	Compare Address	TRAPV	Trap on Overflow
CMPI	Compare Immediate	TST	Test Operand
CMPM	Compare Memory to Memory	UNLK	Unlink
CMP2	Compare Register Against Upper and Lower Bounds	UNPK	Unpack BCD

COPROCESSOR INSTRUCTIONS

Mnemonic	Description	Mnemonic	Description
DBcc	Test Condition, Decrement and Branch	cpBcc	Branch Conditionally
DIVS, DIVSL	Signed Divide	cpDBcc	Test Coprocessor Condition, Decrement, and Branch
DIVU, DIVUL	Unsigned Divide	cpGEN	Coprocessor General Instruction
EOR	Logical Exclusive OR	cpRESTORE	Restore Internal State of Coprocessor
EORI	Logical Exclusive OR Immediate	cpSAVE	Save Internal State of Coprocessor
EXG	Exchange Registers	cpScc	Set Conditionally
EXT	Sign Extend	cpTRAPcc	Trap Conditionally
JMP	Jump		
JSR	Jump to Subroutine		
LEA	Load Effective Address		
LINK	Link and Allocate		
LSL, LSR	Logical Shift Left and Right		
MOVE	Move		
MOVEA	Move Address		
MOVE CCR	Move Condition Code Register		
MOVE SR	Move Status Register		
MOVE USP	Move User Stack Pointer		
MOVEC	Move Control Register		
MOVEM	Move Multiple Registers		
MOVEP	Move Peripheral		
MOVEQ	Move Quick		
MOVES	Move Alternate Address Space		

FIGURE 11.13 Instruction set summary for the 68020. (Courtesy of Motorola, Inc.)

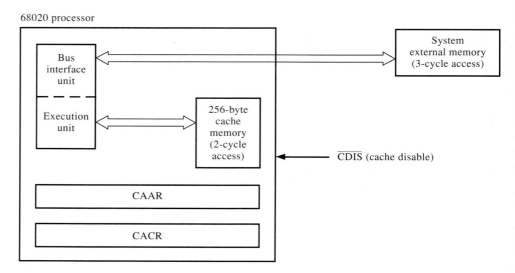

FIGURE 11.14 The 68020 cache memory organization and operation.

Cache Control and Cache Address Registers

The cache memory operation is controlled by the cache control (CACR) and cache address (CAAR) registers. These are illustrated in Figure 11.16. Using the CACR, the cache memory can be disabled or enabled, the cache entry can be cleared or frozen, or the cache memory can be completely cleared. These operations are required during initialization or when the processor is changing tasks.

The 6-bit index field of the CAAR specifies one of the 64 long words of the cache memory. The 24-bit tag, filed along with FC2 function code bit, specifies the address

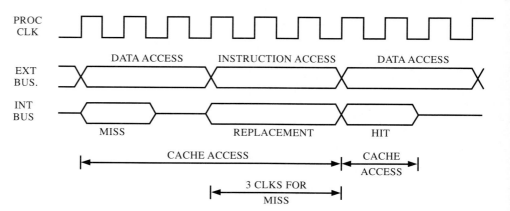

FIGURE 11.15 Cache hit and cache miss timing of the 68020. (Courtesy of Motorola, Inc.)

FIGURE 11.16 (a) Cache control register (CACR) and (b) cache address register (CAAR) formats of the 68020.

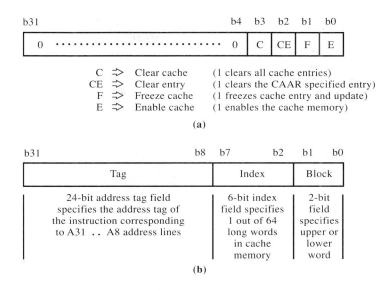

	C $\Rightarrow$	Clear cache	(1 clears all cache entries)
	CE $\Rightarrow$	Clear entry	(1 clears the CAAR specified entry)
	F $\Rightarrow$	Freeze cache	(1 freezes cache entry and update)
	E $\Rightarrow$	Enable cache	(1 enables the cache memory)

(a)

(b)

tag field of the instruction. FC2 is required to distinguish between supervisor and user space. In addition, there is a V bit associated with each of the address tag fields in the cache memory address area. If the V bit is 1, the corresponding cached instruction is valid.

At power-up reset, the CACR is cleared to the all-zero condition and the cache is disabled. The cache needs to be properly initialized as a part of the system reset routine. The cache registers CACR and CAAR can be accessed only in the supervisor mode (using the MOVEC instruction).

Sometimes it is necessary to hardware disable the cache memory for debugging purposes. This is accomplished by activating the $\overline{\text{CDIS}}$ signal to a low level, as shown in Figure 11.14.

We will now present an example problem to review what we have learned about cache memory.

Example 11.2   68020 cache memory and performance.
Consider a 68020-based system.

1. Why is the cache memory disabled on power-up reset?

2. How much additional tag address and other space is required for each long-word cache entry?

3. Assume the following code is being executed while the cache memory is disabled:

```
MOVE.L (A2)+,D2
ADD.L  D2, D0
NOP
MOVE.L D0, (A3)+
```

With 32-bit aligned access, how many total read and write bus cycles take place on the external bus, including the instruction prefetches?

4. Answer the preceding question, assuming the cache is enabled and the code is in the cache memory.

Solution

1. **Cache disable on reset:** The information contained in the cache memory at the time of power-up reset does not correspond to any valid code. The cache memory should be disabled to prevent the processor from running invalid code from it.

2. **Additional cache space:** Each long-word cache entry has a 25-bit effective tag address field (A31–A8 and FC2 values). Each long-word entry also has an associated V bit. Thus, 26 bits of additional cache space is required for each long-word entry.

3. **Bus cycles when cache is disabled:** Each of the instructions is a single op.word instruction. To prefetch four op.words, two read bus cycles are required on the 32-bit aligned access. In addition, the instruction MOVE.L (A2)+,D2 requires a read cycle to obtain the source operand and the instruction MOVE.L D0,(A3)+ requires a write bus cycle to write the destination operand. Thus, the total number of bus cycles required is four.

4. **Bus cycles when cache is enabled:** When the instructions are already in the cache and the cache memory is enabled, the instruction fetches will be from the cache. The external bus activity is only for the source and the destination operands. Thus, the total number of bus cycles required is two.

In the preceding example, the benefits of the cache memory and aligned access are apparent. The external bus cycles are greatly reduced, enhancing the throughput. However, depending upon the alignment, the port size, and the cache memory condition, actual bus activity varies.

11.4 GENERAL ARCHITECTURE OF THE 68030

The 68030 is an enhanced 32-bit microprocessor contained in a 128-pin grid-array package. It is fabricated with VLSI HMOS technology. It has all the resources of the 68020 processor. In addition, it contains the data cache and the memory management units on the chip.[7]

Instruction and Data Cache Memory Organization

The 68030 processor contains a 256-byte instruction cache memory and a separate 256-byte data cache memory on the chip. The instruction cache is similar to that of the 68020 processor, but is organized as a bank of 16 rows of 4 long words. There are 16 address tag fields for the 16 rows, consisting of FC2 output and address lines A31–A8.

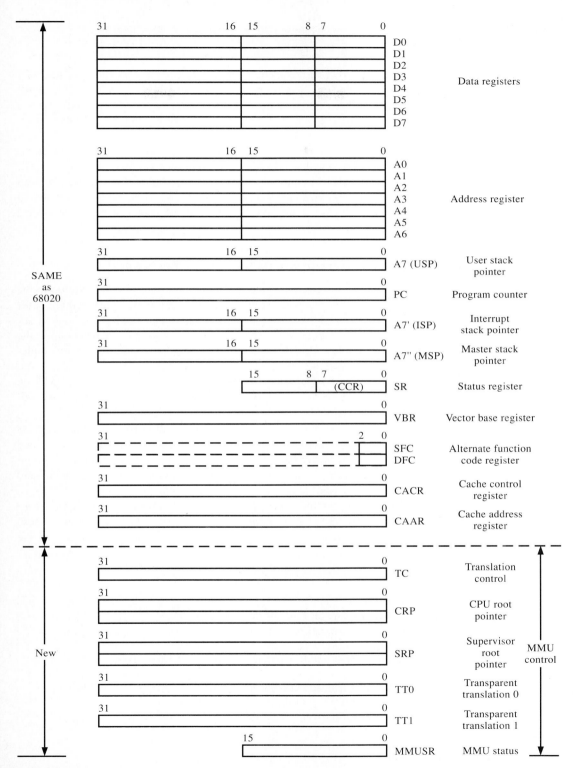

FIGURE 11.17 General architecture of the 68030. (Courtesy of Motorola, Inc.)

Selection of one of the 16 rows of the cache bank is accomplished by address lines A7–A4. Selection of one of the long words of a row is accomplished by the A3 and A2 address lines. The A1 address line is used to select the upper or lower word within a long word. Each long word is associated with a V bit. The operation of the 68030 instruction cache is similar to that of the 68020 processor.

Data cache organization in the 68030 is similar to instruction cache organization. In the address tag field, however, the FC1 and FC0 function code bits are also included. The processor reads the cached data in the case of a hit condition. When there is a hit condition for writing data, the processor writes the data in the cache memory and also in the external memory. This is necessary to eliminate any stale data in the external data memory.

Additional Software Resources of the 68030 Processor

Figure 11.17 specifies the register architecture of the 68030 processor. In addition to the 68020 resources, it has extra registers related to the **memory management unit (MMU).** These registers can be handled only in the supervisor mode. The logical address space for the 68030 is 4 gigabytes. The physical address space depends upon the available hardware and is much less than the logical space. In virtual memory implementation, the MMU translates a logical address into an existing physical address. Associated with the MMU, there is also an address translation cache (ATC) memory on board for the 68030. The ATC has 22 entries consisting of the most recently used address translations.

Whenever there is a requirement for an address translation from a logical address to a physical address, the ATC is checked for a hit. For a hit condition, the cached translation address is used to locate the instruction or the data operand. For a miss condition, 68030 goes to the external memory to locate the address translation tables and obtains the required information.

Figure 11.18 summarizes the functions of the MMU registers and Figure 11.19 summarizes the additional 68030 instructions to support the MMU functions. These MMU instructions are privileged. In Figure 11.20, the relative performance of the 68020 and 68030 processors is indicated.

TC	⇒ **Translation control:** Controls the translation process.
CRP	⇒ **CPU root pointer:** Locates the root pointer in memory for user-level operating systems.
SRP	⇒ **Supervisor root pointer:** Locates the root pointer in memory for the governing operating system.
TT0 and **TT1**	⇒ **Transparent translation registers 0 and 1:** The entries here will be transparent to the ATC and will not be cached.
MMUSR	⇒ **MMU status register:** Contains the status of the MMU operations.

FIGURE 11.18 68030 MMU register functions.

PMOVE	⇒ Move to and from MMU registers. (Moves contents between the MMU registers and the EA.)
PLOAD	⇒ Load page descriptor into the ATC from the EA.
PTEST	⇒ Test translation. (Tests the ATC and updates the MMU status register.)
PFLUSH	⇒ Flush selected ATC entries as specified by the EA.
PFLUSHA	⇒ Flush all ATC entries.

FIGURE 11.19   MMU-related instructions for the 68030.

FIGURE 11.20   Relative performance of the 68020 and 68030 processors.

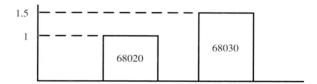

Additional Hardware Resources of the 68030 Processor

In Figures 11.21 and 11.22 the 68030 functional signal groups and associated signal descriptions are given. There are additional cache control signals to assist instruction and data cache management.

The **synchronous termination input ($\overline{\text{STERM}}$)** is of particular importance. It controls synchronous transfers between the processor and the external memory and I/O. Synchronous transfers take only two clock cycles, as compared to three clock cycles for normal asynchronous transfers. The processor terminates the bus cycle upon receiving $\overline{\text{STERM}}$. If $\overline{\text{STERM}}$ is not received, the processor assumes the normal asynchronous operation and looks for the $\overline{\text{DSACK}}$ signals. In synchronous operation, only 32-bit aligned transfers are allowed. The other hardware resources of the 68030 function in basically the same manner as in the 68020 processor.

We will now present an example problem to review what we have learned about the 68030.

Example 11.3   The 68030 microprocessor.
With regard to the 68030 microprocessor,

1. why is it useful to have a data cache?
2. why is it useful to have the MMU on board?
3. what are the disadvantages of the data cache and MMU?

Solution

1. **Data cache:** In the case of a cache hit for read operations, only two clock cycle data transfers are required, as compared to three clock cycle data transfers for external

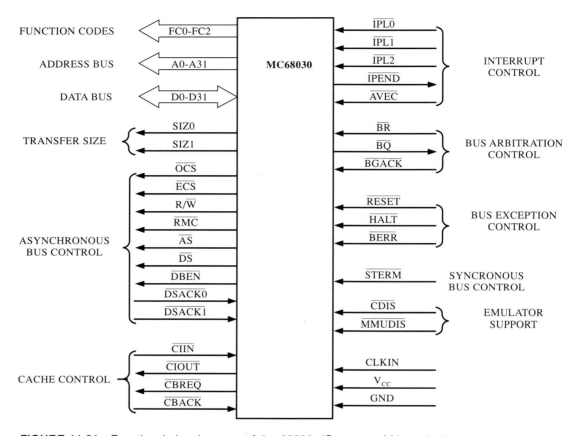

FIGURE 11.21   Functional signal groups of the 68030. (Courtesy of Motorola, Inc.)

memory access. This increases the throughput by 33.3 percent for read operations.

For write operations, since data are also written into the external memory, there is no speed advantage. However, the updated data may be used for other read operations, ultimately resulting in a speed advantage.

2. **MMU on board:** The MMU and the associated ATC provide internal 2-cycle access, as compared to external 3-cycle access. This, in turn, affords a speed advantage of 33.3 percent.

3. **Disadvantages of on-board cache and MMU:** Each of the units takes silicon real estate and complicates semiconductor processing. Thus, the cost of the unit is increased. Also, the integrated functionality makes debugging and testing difficult.

Figure 11.23 illustrates the internal structure of the very powerful 68030 processor. As of this writing, considerable system development is still taking place. The concepts we have presented are elementary; for more detailed information, additional references should be consulted.[8,9]

Signal Name	Mnemonic	Function
Function Codes	FC0-FC2	3-bit function code used to identify the address space of each bus cycle.
Address Bus	A0-A31	32-bit address bus used to address any of 4,294,967,296 bytes.
Data Bus	D0-D31	32-bit data bus used to transfer 8, 16, 24, or 32 bits of data per bus cycle.
Size	SIZ0/SIZ1	Indicates the number of bytes remaining to be transferred for this cycle. These signals, together with A0 and A1, define the active sections of the data bus.
Operand Cycle Start	$\overline{OCS}$	Identical operation to that of $\overline{ECS}$ except that $\overline{OCS}$ is asserted only during the first bus cycle of an operand transfer.
External Cycle Start	$\overline{ECS}$	Provides an indication that a bus cycle is beginning.
Read/Write	R/$\overline{W}$	Defines the bus transfer as an MPU read or write.
Read-Modify-Write Cycle	$\overline{RMC}$	Provides an indicator that the current bus cycle is part of an indivisible read-modify-write operation.
Address Strobe	$\overline{AS}$	Indicates that a valid address is on the bus.
Data Strobe	$\overline{DS}$	Indicates that valid data is to be placed on the data bus by an external device or has been placed on the data bus by the MC68030.
Data Buffer Enable	$\overline{DBEN}$	Provides an enable signal for external data buffers.
Data Transfer and Size Acknowledge	$\overline{DSACK0}/\overline{DSACK1}$	Bus response signals that indicate the requested data transfer operation is completed. In addition, these two lines indicate the size of the external bus port on a cycle-by-cycle basis.
Cache Inhibit In	$\overline{CIIN}$	Prevents data from being loaded into the MC68030 instruction and data caches.
Cache Inhibit Out	$\overline{CIOUT}$	Reflects the CI bit in ATC entries or a transparent translation register; indicates that external caches should ignore these accesses.
Cache Burst Request	$\overline{CBREQ}$	Indicates a miss in either the instruction or data cache for cachable accesses.
Cache Burst Acknowledge	$\overline{CBACK}$	Indicates that accessed device can operate in burst mode.
Interrupt Priority Level	$\overline{IPL0}$-$\overline{IPL2}$	Provides an encoded interrupt level to the processor.
Interrupt Pending	$\overline{IPEND}$	Indicates that an interrupt is pending.
Autovector	$\overline{AVEC}$	Requests an autovector during an interrupt acknowledge cycle.
Bus Request	$\overline{BR}$	Indicates that an external device requires bus mastership.
Bus Grant	$\overline{BG}$	Indicates that an external device may assume bus mastership.
Bus Grant Acknowledge	$\overline{BGACK}$	Indicates that an external device has assumed bus mastership.
Reset	$\overline{RESET}$	System reset.
Halt	$\overline{HALT}$	Indicates that the processor should suspend bus activity.
Bus Error	$\overline{BERR}$	Indicates an invalid or illegal bus operation is being attempted.
Synchronous Termination	$\overline{STERM}$	Bus response signal that indicates a port size of 32 bits and that data may be latched on the next falling clock edge.
Cache Disable	$\overline{CDIS}$	Dynamically disables the on-chip cache to assist emulator support.
MMU Disable	$\overline{MMUDIS}$	Dynamically disables the translation mechanism of the MMU.
Microsequencer Status	$\overline{STATUS}$	Status indications for debug purposes.
Pipe Refill	$\overline{REFILL}$	Indicates when the instruction pipe is beginning to refill
Clock	CLK	Clock input to the processor.
Power Supply	V_{CC}	+5 volt ± 5% power supply.
Ground	GND	Ground connection.

FIGURE 11.22 Signal descriptions for the 68030. (Courtesy of Motorola, Inc.)

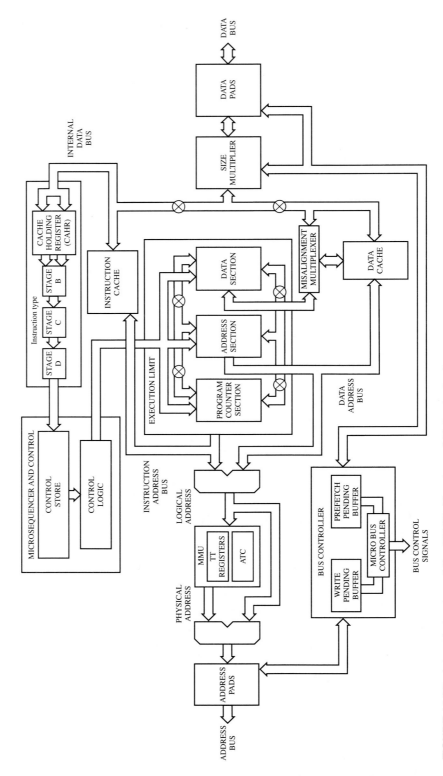

FIGURE 11.23 Internal structure of the 68030. (Courtesy of Motorola, Inc.)

11.5 FUNCTIONAL IMPROVEMENTS IN THE 68020 AND 68030 PROCESSORS

Even though the 68020 and 68030 are based on the prototype architecture of the 68000 processor, they far exceed the functional capabilities of the 68000. This is primarily due to their memory indirect addressing capability, extended instructions for 32-bit operand manipulations (such as multiply and divide), cache memory and virtual memory implementation capabilities, and their enhanced 32-bit data and address buses.

For routine 16/32 bit applications, the 68000 processor with 16-megabyte address space is usually sufficient and is widely used. For applications requiring fast operations, large memory space (up to 4-gigabyte), and cache memory implementation schemes, the 68020 and 68030 processors are preferred. If a data cache and memory management are also required, the 68030 is the processor of choice.

Memory Indirect Addressing Capability

The 68020 and 68030 processors have the additional memory indirect addressing mode as we discussed earlier in the chapter. This addressing mode uses any memory location as a memory pointer register, which provides unlimited pointer resources in addition to the internal registers. The 68000 processor does not have the memory indirect addressing scheme; therefore, it must use one of the seven address registers (A0–A6) for any register indirect addressing scheme.

32-Bit Extended Instructions

For the 68020 and 68030 processors, some instructions, such as the multiply (MULU, MULS) and divide (DIVU, DIVS), are extended to handle 32-bit operands, producing a 64-bit result. For the 68000 processor, these instructions operate on 16-bit operands and produce 32-bit results. To obtain a 64-bit effective result with the 68000 processor, a software routine must be written and executed.

Cache Memory and the Concept of Tag Field

Both the 68020 and 68030 processors have an instruction cache on board, organized as 64 long words as discussed earlier. The 68030 processor has an additional data cache on board. The upper 24-bit address reference (A31–A8) for the instruction cache memory is called the **address tag.** The next 6-bit address reference (A7–A2) is called the **address index,** which selects one out of the 64 cache locations on board.

Each cache location has a **tag field,** in which tag information is stored, and an **instruction field,** in which information corresponding to the tag field is stored. If a memory reference is made, the stored tag is checked against the current tag for a hit. In the event of a hit, the information from the cache is read by the processor. In the event of a miss, the processor goes to the external memory, obtains the instruction, copies it into the cache memory, and executes it.

The 68000 and 68010 processors do not have cache memory capability; hence, the tag field concept does not apply to them.

The 68020 and 68030 Additional Signal Groups

The 68020 and 68030 processors have all the signal groups of the 68000 processor. In the 68020 and 68030, the data bus is extended to 32 bits compared to the 16-bit data bus of the 68000. The address bus is extended to 32 bits compared to the 24-bit effective address bus of the 68000. The control bus of the 68020 and 68030 processors is extended to include two data acknowledge signals ($\overline{DSACK0}$ and $\overline{DSACK1}$), size signals (SIZ0 and SIZ1), and bus interface signals ($\overline{OCS}$, $\overline{ECS}$, and $\overline{RMC}$).

In addition, the 68020 processor has a cache disable ($\overline{CDIS}$) input signal. The 68030 has four cache-related signals to handle the data and instruction cache on board. All of these additional resources increase the throughput of the 68020/30-based system.

Software Considerations for the 68020 and 68030 Processors

The assembly language programming techniques for the 68020 and 68030 processors are similar to those for the 68000. Due to additional and enhanced instructions, the efficiency of the software routines for the 68020 and 68030 processors can be increased. In case of loop-type operations, for example, instructions are copied into the cache memory, which further reduces the execution time of the program.

The following example problem deals with the software capabilities of the 68020 and 68030.

Example 11.4   68020/30-processor software.
Suppose a 68020/30-based system is used in a control system application with a software routine as shown in Figure 11.24.

1. Assuming the cache is disabled, analyze the software and specify the contents of the affected registers after the MULU and DIVU instructions.

2. Assume that the NOP instruction is replaced by the DBRA   D3,AGAIN instruction. Consider the cache to be enabled. How many times is the AGAIN loop run? How many times is the code obtained from the cache memory?

3. Can the same software function on a 68000-based system?

Solution

1. **Software and contents of the registers:** The software initializes

$$A0 \Rightarrow \$00004000; \quad D0 \Rightarrow \$22224444; \quad D1 \Rightarrow \$00000000$$
$$D2 \Rightarrow \$00000000; \quad D3 \Rightarrow \$\$0000200; \quad D4 \Rightarrow \$00000200$$

```
;68020/30 based software
;
            CHIP      68020
            OPT       A
            ORG       $00002000
;initialize registers
;A0 is memory pointer for memory
;indirect addressing mode
;D0 is the data register for multiply and divide
;
START       MOVEA.L   #$00004000,A0
            MOVE.L    #$22224444,D0
            CLR.L     D1              ;clear D1
            CLR.L     D2              ;clear D2
            MOVE.L    #$00000200,D3
            MOVE.L    D3,D4
;perform long word multiplication and division
;multiplication is unsigned
;division is unsigned
;all numbers are hex decimal
;
AGAIN       MULU.L    #$00000020,D1,D0
            DIVU.L    #$00000100,D2,D0
            MOVE.L    D0,([0,A0,D3.W*4],0)
            NOP
            JMP       START
```

FIGURE 11.24 68020/30-based software for the control system application (Example 11.4).

The MULU.L #$00000020,D1,D0 instruction multiplies the 32-bit contents of the D0 register with the 32-bit multiplier $20, and puts the 64-bit result in the D1 and D0 pair as shown.

$$
\begin{array}{rl}
\text{D0 (before)} & \$\,2\,2\,2\,2\,4\,4\,4\,4 \\
\times \quad \text{multiplier} & \$\,0\,0\,0\,0\,0\,0\,2\,0 \\
\hline
\text{result} \quad\; & \$\,0\,0\,0\,0\,0\,0\,0\,4\,4\,4\,4\,8\,8\,8\,8\,0
\end{array}
$$

The upper 8-digit (32-bit) result is put in the D1 register and the lower 8-digit result is put in the D0 register. Thus, after the multiplication;

$$\mathbf{D1 \Rightarrow \$\,0\,0\,0\,0\,0\,0\,0\,4}$$

$$\mathbf{D0 \Rightarrow \$\,4\,4\,4\,8\,8\,8\,8\,0}$$

The DIVU.L #$00000100,D2,D0 instruction divides the 64-bit operand contained in the D2 and D0 registers by the dividend $00000100. The 32-bit quotient is put in the D0 register and the 32-bit remainder is put in the D2 register, as shown.

$$
\begin{array}{rl}
\text{D2 and D0 (before)} & \$\ 0\ 0\ 0\ 0\ 0\ 0\ 0\ 0\ 4\ 4\ 4\ 8\ 8\ 8\ 8\ 0 \\
\text{divided by dividend} \$ & \underline{0\ 0\ 0\ 0\ 0\ 1\ 0\ 0} \\
\text{quotient} & \$\ 0\ 0\ 4\ 4\ 4\ 8\ 8\ 8 \\
\text{remainder} & \underline{\$\ 0\ 0\ 0\ 0\ 0\ 0\ 8\ 0}
\end{array}
$$

Thus, after the division,

$$\text{D0} \Rightarrow \$\ 0\ 0\ 4\ 4\ 4\ 8\ 8\ 8$$

$$\text{D2} \Rightarrow \$\ 0\ 0\ 0\ 0\ 0\ 0\ 8\ 0$$

2. **DBRA D3,AGAIN instruction:** When the NOP is replaced by the DBRA instruction, the software goes into the AGAIN loop until the D3 register is decremented to -1 (from its initial value of \$200). The code is obtained first from the external memory and is copied into the cache. Subsequently, the code is obtained from the cache. Thus, the AGAIN loop is run \$201 times and the code is obtained from the cache \$200 times.

3. **68000-based system:** The code will not function on the 68000 system, since the 32-bit multiply and divide instructions and the memory indirect addressing modes of the software are not defined for the 68000 processor.

11.6 SUMMARY

In this chapter we introduced the 68020 and 68030 32-bit microprocessors with on-board cache memory. Both these processors are extensions of the earlier members of the 68000 family. Both have all the resources of the 68010 and 68012 processors. In addition, they have 32-bit address and 32-bit data buses. Both processors also have additional control lines to handle the coprocessor interface.

The 68020 and 68030 have a 4-gigabyte logical address space. They can transfer up to 32 bits of information in one bus cycle. The data bus can be dynamically sized to hold byte, word, or long-word data. This is accomplished by having two data acknowledge signals ($\overline{\text{DSACK0}}$ and $\overline{\text{DSACK1}}$) and two additional SIZ control signals.

The 68020 has an on-chip 256-byte instruction cache memory organized as 64 long words. The cache memory also contains 64 address tag fields consisting of address lines A31–A8. Whenever a program memory reference is made, the processor examines the address tag entries for a hit condition. In the event of a hit, the processor fetches the instructions from the internal cache. This enhances the overall throughput of the system. In the event of a miss, the processor obtains the instruction code from the external memory for execution and also copies it into the internal cache for subsequent use. A typical cache bus cycle corresponds to two clock cycles, compared to three clock cycles for the external bus cycle for the 68020 and 68030 processors. By contrast, the 68000 takes four clock cycles for a single bus cycle without any wait states.

For the 68020 and 68030 processors, instructions such as multiply and divide are extended to operate on 32-bit operands and provide a 64-bit result. These processors use an addressing scheme known as memory indirect addressing. In this scheme, any valid memory location can serve as a memory pointer. This greatly enhances the addressing capabilities of the 68020 and 68030. There are several variations of the memory indirect addressing scheme.

In our discussion of the bit-field instructions for the 68020 and 68030 processors, we explained how they are used to address bit fields of varying size and operate on them.

The 68030 processor is a further enhancement of the 68020 processor. The 68030 has an additional 256-byte data cache memory. To prevent the problem of stale data, whenever new data are written into the cache memory they are also written into the external memory. A speed advantage is realized when the data cache is used for obtaining source operands. The 68030 also has an on-chip memory management unit for implementing address translations and virtual memory schemes. This further increases the throughput.

The 68020 and 68030 are not pin compatible with one another. Separate hardware must be designed for each. However, they do have similar microcomputer configurations.

PROBLEMS

11.1 Indicate the contents of the system byte of the 68020 processor

(a) during power-up system reset;
(b) when the processor is servicing interrupt 5 in the supervisor mode;
(c) under the conditions of (b), when a bus error condition occurs.

11.2 Which stack pointer is used in the 68020

(a) when the processor is executing a reset system routine?
(b) when the processor is executing user programs?

11.3 State the conditions of the system byte

(a) when an interrupt 7 routine is being executed and there is a trace on each instruction;
(b) when a bus error routine is being executed with a trace on change of flow.

11.4 What is the functional difference between the $\overline{ECS}$ and $\overline{OCS}$ signals? Where are they used?

11.5 What should be the condition of the $\overline{CDIS}$ signal

(a) if the 68020 internal cache is to be disabled continuously?
(b) if the 68020 internal cache is to be disabled for instruction fetches above a certain address?

11.6 The 68020 has the memory map given in Figure 11.25.
Specify the conditions of the DSACKx and SIZx signals and the data bus activity when the following instructions are executed individually:

(a) MOVE.L (A1),D1: A1 = $0000FFFF; long word is $1234AABB
(b) ADD.L (A1),D1: A1 = $0000FFFF; long word is $1234AABB

(c) ADD.L   D1,D2:   D1 = $1234AABB; D2 = $FFFFFFFF
(d) MOVE.L   D2,(A4):   D2 = $FFFFFFFF; A4 = $01010001

---

main memory (32-bit wide) ⇒$00000000 to $00FFFFFF

system I/O (16-bit wide) ⇒$01000000 to $0100FFFF

(8-bit wide) ⇒$01010000 to $010103FF

FIGURE 11.25   Memory and I/O map (for Problem 11.6).

11.7 Repeat Problem 11.6, assuming that the instructions are executed in sequence, as a program.

11.8 If the VBR is loaded with $00003000 as a part of a reset routine, specify where the autovectors are located for interrupts 6 and 2.

11.9 Consider the initial conditions given in Figure 11.26.
Indicate the effective address and the data operand in each of the following individual operations:

(a) MOVE.W   (08,A3,D1.L*8),D4
(b) MOVEP.L   (08,A3,D1.L*4),D5

A0 = $0000ABCD; D0 = $00000004;	$00004800	0000
A1 = $00000008; D1 = $00000200;	4802	4802
A2 = $00003000; D2 = $0000F0F0;	4804	0000
A3 = $00004000; D3 = $012A46AB;	4806	4806
	:	:
	$0000A000	0000
	A002	A002
	:	:

FIGURE 11.26   Initial conditions (for Problem 11.9).

11.10 Use the initial conditions of Figure 11.26. Indicate the results of the following operations:

(a) ADD.L   ([$1800,A3],D1.W,$0400),D2
(b) ADD.L   ([$1800,A3,D0.W*8],$0A00),D0

11.11 Write appropriate instructions to move long-word contents from location $00008000 to the D6 register using each of the following addressing modes and proper displacement values:

(a) EA ⇒ (bd,A0,D0.W*8)
(b) EA ⇒ ([$6000,A3],D2.W,od)

11.12 Repeat Problem 11.11 using all possible addressing modes. Use A3 as the ARI register and D1 as the index register.

11.13 Consider the bit-field memory values given in Figure 11.27.
Specify the operation for each of the following, including the results of the operation and the contents of the XNZVC flags:

   (a) BFTST   4008{6:8}
   (b) BFCLR   4008{8:6}
   (c) BFSET   4008{8:6}

	bits									
displacement	b7	b6	b5	b4	b3	b2	b1	b0	
−16	0	0	0	0	0	0	0	1	$01
−8	1	0	1	1	1	1	0	0	$BC
base address 4008 ⇒ 0	1	1	0	1	0	0	0	1	$D1
+8	0	0	0	1	0	1	0	1	$15
+16	0	1	1	1	1	0	0	1	$79

FIGURE 11.27   Bit-field memory map (for Problem 11.13).

11.14 Using the bit map of Figure 11.27, specify the operation for each of the following, including the results of the operation and the contents of the XNZVC flags:

   (a) BFCHG   4009{7:7}
   (b) BFEXTU   4008{−16:22},D1
   (c) BFEXTS   4008{−16:22},D1

11.15 Repeat Problem 11.14 for the following:

   (a) BFINS   D4,4007{12:12};   D4 = $047689AB
   (b) BFFFO   4006{5:12},D5

11.16 Perform the following PACK and UNPK operations. Initially, D3 = $ x x x x 4 8 4 3; D4 = $ x x x x x x 2 1.

   (a) PACK   D3,D5,#$0000
   (b) PACK   D3,D5,#$1010
   (c) UNPK   D4,D5,#$3030

11.17 D3 = $ x x x x 4 8 4 3; D4 = $ x x x x x x 2 1. Write a sequence of instructions, using PACK and UNPK, to pack the number in D3, convert it into an ASCII code, and place it in the D5 register.

11.18 Suppose it is required to clear an instruction cache entry at address $0010004C for the 68020 processor. What are the contents of the CACR and CAAR registers?

11.19 What would happen if the CAAR and CACR were addressed in the user mode? Why?

11.20 The following interrupt routine is being run by the 68020 processor. A4 = $0000A000. Assume a 32-bit memory port.

```
Loop        MOVEP.L  ($0400,A4),D4
            ADD.L    #$00000200,D4
            BFTST    (A4){0:17}
            BNE      Loop
            RTE
```

Consider the cache memory is disabled. Indicate the total number of bus cycles, including instruction prefetches, required to execute the preceding program.

11.21 Repeat Problem 11.20, assuming the cache memory is enabled.

11.22 Explain the concept of stale data. How does stale data affect system performance?

11.23 Suppose the program of Problem 11.20 is run on a 68030-based system with the instruction and the data cache units disabled. Compute the total number of bus cycles under the following conditions:

(a) asynchronous memory interface;
(b) synchronous memory interface.

11.24 Repeat Problem 11.23, assuming the instruction and data cache units are enabled.

11.25 List three areas in which the 68030 processor can outperform the 68020 processor.

11.26 In the software of Figure 11.24, what is the effective address of the operand in the MOVE.L   D0,([0,A0,D3.W*4].0) operation?

11.27 What are the contents of the affected registers in Example 11.4 if the MULU and DIVU instructions are replaced by the MULS and DIVS instructions when the AGAIN loop is run the first time?

ENDNOTES

1. Motorola, Inc. *MC68020 32-Bit Microprocessor User's Manual*. Phoenix, AZ: Motorola Technical Operations, 1987.

2. Motorola, Inc. *MTT20 68020 Course Notes*. Phoenix, AZ: Motorola Technical Operations, 1988.

3. Motorola, Inc. *MC68020 Technical Summary*. Austin, TX: Motorola Microprocessor Group, 1984.

4. Miller, M.A. "MC68020 32-Bit Processor." Chap. 11 in *The 68000 Microprocessor: Architecture, Programming, and Applications*. Columbus, OH: Merrill, 1988.

5. MacGregor, D.; Mothersole, D.; and Moyer, B. "The Motorola 68020." *IEEE Micro* 4(4):101–118.

6. Beims, B. *Multiprocessing Capabilities of the 68020 32-Bit Microprocessor*. App. Note #AR 220. Austin, TX: Motorola Microprocessor Group, 1984.

7. Motorola, Inc. *MC68030 32-Bit Microprocessor User's Manual*. Phoenix, AZ: Motorola Technical Operations, 1988.

8. Motorola, Inc. *MC68030 Technical Summary*. Austin, TX: Motorola Microprocessor Group, 1986.

9. Motorola, Inc. *Performance Report: 68020 and 68030 32-Bit Microprocessors*. App. Note #BR 705/D. Phoenix, AZ: Motorola Technical Operations, 1988.

Number Systems: Binary and BCD Operations

The digital field deals with the binary number system in which any number is expressed to the base 2 as a string of binary ones and zeros. The most popular number system is the decimal system, in which any number is expressed to the base 10. The binary numbers can be further expressed in the form of hex codes.

BINARY AND HEX NUMBER SYSTEMS

A binary number is expressed as a collection of 1s and 0s. Each digit to the left is multiplied by the corresponding power of two. The addition of these values results in the appropriate value for the number string.

> MSB: Most Significant Bit   LSB: Least Significant Bit

Conversion from Binary to Decimal and Hex Decimal Systems

bit position	7	6	5	4	3	2	1	0	
(MSB)	0	0	1	1	1	0	1	1	(LSB)
binary value	—	—	2^5	2^4	2^3	—	2^1	2^0	
	0	0	32	16	8	0	2	1	$\Rightarrow$ 59 decimal

Expressing larger binary strings can be very tedious. Four binary bits are grouped together to form a hex (or hexadecimal) code or a BCD (binary coded decimal) as

TABLE A.1 Decimal, Binary, Hex, and BCD Number Systems

Decimal Number	Binary Number				Hex Number Code	BCD Number Code
	b_3	b_2	b_1	b_0		
0	0	0	0	0	0	0
1	0	0	0	1	1	1
2	0	0	1	0	2	2
3	0	0	1	1	3	3
4	0	1	0	0	4	4
5	0	1	0	1	5	5
6	0	1	1	0	6	6
7	0	1	1	1	7	7
8	1	0	0	0	8	8
9	1	0	0	1	9	9
10	1	0	1	0	A	X
11	1	0	1	1	B	X
12	1	1	0	0	C	X
13	1	1	0	1	D	X
14	1	1	1	0	E	X
15	1	1	1	1	F	X

X => invalid code.

shown in Table A.1. The hex code goes from 0 to F for decimal numbers 0 to 15. The BCD code is valid for decimal numbers 0 to 9, as shown.

Binary number

$$0\ 0\ 1\ 1\ 1\ 0\ 1\ 1$$
$$3 \qquad B$$

is equivalent to hex decimal value 3B, as shown. We will use a dollar sign (\$) to represent the hex numbers.

Conversion from Decimal to Hex Decimal and Binary Systems By successively dividing the decimal number by the descending powers of 16, it is possible to obtain the hex decimal number as shown.

$$16 \vert 59 \qquad \$3 \text{ (quotient)}$$
$$\underline{48}$$
$$11 \Rightarrow \$B \text{ (remainder)}$$

Decimal value 59 is equal to \$3B. Converting \$3B to the binary number is relatively easy and is given by

$$\$3B \Rightarrow 0\ 0\ 1\ 1\ 1\ 0\ 1\ 1$$

Binary and Hex Decimal Arithmetic Operations The binary and hex addition and subtraction operations are similar to decimal operations involving carry and borrow concepts. In the binary arithmetic operations, the following identities are used:

$$0 + 0 = 0; \quad 0 + 1 = 1; \quad 1 + 0 = 1; \quad 1 + 1 = 0 \text{ with carry;}$$
$$0 - 0 = 0; \quad 0 - 1 = 1 \text{ with borrow;} \quad 1 - 0 = 1; \quad 1 - 1 = 0.$$

In hex decimal arithmetic, when the sum of addition exceeds a value of 16, carry to the next higher hex digit results. Similarly, borrow from the next higher hex digit results in the case of subtraction. The value of borrow to the lower digit equals 16.

Examples
Addition of $FB and $3A using the hex and binary arithmetic:

```
$ F B ⇒  1 1 1 1 1 0 1 1
$ 3 A ⇒  0 0 1 1 1 0 1 0
$ 1 3 5 ⇒ 1 0 0 1 1 0 1 0 1
      ┊        ┊
   carry     carry
```

Subtraction of $3A from $2B using the hex and binary arithmetic:

```
$ 2 B ⇒  0 0 1 0 1 0 1 1
$ 3 A ⇒  0 0 1 1 1 0 1 0
$ 1 F 1   1 1 1 1 1 0 0 0 1
    ┊        ┊
 borrow    borrow
```

Multiplication of $3A by $03 using the hex and binary arithmetic:

```
$ 3 A ⇒  0 0 1 1 1 0 1 0
$   3 ⇒         0 0 1 1
$ A E    0 0 1 1 1 0 1 0
         0 0 1 1 1 0 1 0
         0 1 0 1 0 1 1 1 0
```

Binary multiplication involves successive left-shift and addition operations, as shown. Hex multiplication is similar to decimal multiplication and is simpler than binary multiplication. The hex division operation is similar to decimal division and is left to the reader to practice.

B

68000/10/12 Instruction Set and Condition Codes

INSTRUCTION SET DETAILS

B.1 INTRODUCTION

This appendix contains detailed information about each instruction in the M68000 instruction set. They are arranged in alphabetical order with the mnemonic heading set in large bold type for easy reference.

B.2 ADDRESSING CATEGORIES

Effective address modes may be categorized by the ways in which they may be used. The following classifications will be used in the instruction definitions.

Data   If an effective address mode may be used to refer to data operands, it is considered a data addressing effective address mode.

Memory If an effective address mode may be used to refer to memory operands, it is considered a memory addressing effective address mode.

Alterable If an effective address mode may be used to refer to alterable (writeable) operands, it is considered an alterable addressing effective address mode.

Control If an effective address mode may be used to refer to memory operands without an associated size, it is considered a control addressing effective address mode.

B.4 OPERATION DESCRIPTION DEFINITIONS

The following definitions are used for the operation description in the details of the instruction set.

OPERANDS:

An	— address register
Dn	— data register
Rn	— any data or address register
PC	— program counter
SR	— status register
CCR	— condition codes (lower order byte of status register)
SSP	— supervisor stack pointer
USP	— user stack pointer
SP	— active stack pointer (equivalent to A7)
X	— extend operand (from condition codes)
N	— negative condition code
Z	— zero condition code
V	— overflow condition code
C	— carry condition code
Immediate Data	— immediate data from the instruction
d	— address displacement
Source	— source contents
Destination	— destination contents
Vector	— location of exception vector
ea	— any valid effective address

SUBFIELDS AND QUALIFIERS:

<bit>of<operand>	selects a single bit of the operand
(<operand>)	the contents of the referenced location
<operand>10	the operand is binary coded decimal; operations are to be performed in decimal.
(<address register>) –(<address register>) (<address register>)+	the register indirect operator which indicates that the operand register points to the memory location of the instruction operand.
#xxx or #<data>	immediate data located with the instruction is the operand.

OPERATIONS: Operations are grouped into binary, unary, and other.

Binary—These operations are written <operand> <op> <operand> where <op> is one of the following:

↑	the left operand is moved to the right operand
↕	the two operands are exchanged
+	the operands are added
−	the right operand is subtracted from the left operand
*	the operands are multiplied
_	the first operand is divided by the second operand
∧	the operands are logically ANDed
∨	the operands are logically ORed
⊕	the operands are logically exclusively ORed
<	relational test, true if left operand is less than right operand
>	relational test, true if left operand is greater than right operand
shifted by	the left operand is shifted or rotated by the number of positions
rotated by	specified by the right operand

Unary:

~ <operand>	the operand is logically complemented
<operand> sign-extended	the operand is sign extended, all bits of the upper portion are made equal to high order bit of the lower portion
<operand> tested	the operand is compared to 0, the results are used to set the condition codes

Other:

TRAP	equivalent to SSP − 2 → SSP; Format/Offset Word→(SSP); SSP − 2 → SSP; PC→(SSP); SSP − 4 → SSP; SR→(SSP); (vector)→PC
STOP	enter the stopped state, waiting for interrupts

If <condition> then <operations> else <operations>. The condition is tested. If true, the operations after the "then" are performed. If the condition is false and the optional "else" clause is present, the operations after the "else" are performed. If the condition is false and the optional "else" clause is absent, the instruction performs no operation.

; Semicolon is used to separate operations and terminate the if/then/else operation.

ABCD   Add Decimal with Extend   ABCD

Operation: $Source_{10} + Destination_{10} + X \rightarrow Destination$

Assembler ABCD Dy,Dx
Syntax: ABCD −(Ay), −(Ax)

Attributes: Size = (Byte)

Description: Add the source operand to the destination operand along with the extend bit, and store the result in the destination location. The addition is performed using binary coded decimal arithmetic. The operands may be addressed in two different ways:

1. Data register to data register: The operands are contained in the data registers specified in the instruction.
2. Memory to memory: The operands are addressed with the predecrement addressing mode using the address registers specified in the instruction.

This operation is a byte operation only.

Condition Codes:

X	N	Z	V	C
*	U	*	U	*

N Undefined.
Z Cleared if the result is non-zero. Unchanged otherwise.
V Undefined.
C Set if a carry (decimal) was generated. Cleared otherwise.
X Set the same as the carry bit.

NOTE

Normally the Z condition code bit is set via programming before the start of an operation. This allows successful tests for zero results upon completion of multiple-precision operations.

Instruction Format:

15	14	13	12	11	10	9	8	7	6	5	4	3	2	1	0
1	1	0	0	Register Rx			1	0	0	0	0	R/M	Register Ry		

Instruction Fields:

Register Rx field — Specifies the destination register:
If R/M = 0, specifies a data register
If R/M = 1, specifies an address register for the predecrement addressing mode
R/M field — Specifies the operand addressing mode:
0 — The operation is data register to data register
1 — The operation is memory to memory
Register Ry field — Specifies the source register:
If R/M = 0, specifies a data register
If R/M = 1, specifies an address register for the predecrement addressing mode

ADD
Add
ADD

Operation: Source + Destination → Destination

Assembler
Syntax: ADD <ea>,Dn
ADD Dn,<ea>

Attributes: Size = (Byte, Word, Long)

Description: Add the source operand to the destination operand using binary addition, and store the result in the destination location. The size of the operation may be specified to be byte, word, or long. The mode of the instruction indicates which operand is the source and which is the destination as well as the operand size.

Condition Codes:

X	N	Z	V	C
*	*	*	*	*

N Set if the result is negative. Cleared otherwise.
Z Set if the result is zero. Cleared otherwise.
V Set if an overflow is generated. Cleared otherwise.
C Set if a carry is generated. Cleared otherwise.
X Set the same as the carry bit.

The condition codes are not affected when the destination is an address register.

Instruction Format:

15	14	13	12	11	10	9	8	7	6	5	4	3	2	1	0
1	1	0	1		Register Dn			Op-Mode			Effective Address Mode			Register	

Instruction Fields:

Register field — Specifies any of the eight data registers.

Op-Mode field —

Byte	Word	Long	Operation
000	001	010	<ea> + <Dn> → <Dn>
100	101	110	<Dn> + <ea> → <ea>

Effective Address Field — Determines addressing mode:

a. If the location specified in a source operand, the all addressing modes are allowed as shown:

Addr. Mode	Mode	Register
Dn	000	reg. number:Dn
An*	001	reg. number:An
(An)	010	reg. number:An
(An)+	011	reg. number:An
-(An)	100	reg. number:An
(d16,An)	101	reg. number:An
(d8,An,Xn)	110	reg. number:An

Addr. Mode	Mode	Register
(xxx).W	111	000
(xxx).L	111	001
#<data>	111	100
(d16,PC)	111	010
(d8,PC,Xn)	111	011

*Word and Long only.

b. If the location specified is a destination operand, then only alterable memory addressing modes are allowed as shown:

Addr. Mode	Mode	Register
Dn	—	—
An	—	—
(An)	010	reg. number:An
(An)+	011	reg. number:An
-(An)	100	reg. number:An
(d16,An)	101	reg. number:An
(d8,An,Xn)	110	reg. number:An

Addr. Mode	Mode	Register
(xxx).W	111	000
(xxx).L	111	001
#<data>	—	—
(d16,PC)	—	—
(d8,PC,Xn)	—	—

Notes:
1. If the destination is a data register, then it cannot be specified by using the destination <ea> mode, but must use the destination Dn mode instead.
2. ADDA is used when the destination is an address register. ADDI and ADDQ are used when the source is immediate data. Most assemblers automatically make this distinction.

346

ADDA

Add Address

Operation: Source + Destination → Destination

Assembler Syntax: ADDA <ea>,An

Attributes: Size = (Word, Long)

Description: Add the source operand to the destination address register, and store the result in the address register. The size of the operation may be specified to be word or long. The entire destination address register is used regardless of the operation size.

Condition Codes: Not affected.

Instruction Format:

15	14	13	12	11	10	9	8	7	6	5	4	3	2	1	0
1	1	0	1	Register An			Op-Mode			Effective Address Mode			Register		

Instruction Fields:

Register field — Specifies any of the eight address registers. This is always the destination.

Op-Mode field — Specifies the size of the operation:
011—word operation. The source operand is sign-extended to a long operand and the operation is performed on the address register using all 32 bits.
111—long operation.

Effective Address field — Specifies the source operand. All addressing modes are allowed as shown:

Addr. Mode	Mode	Register
Dn	000	reg. number:Dn
An	001	reg. number:An
(An)	010	reg. number:An
(An)+	011	reg. number:An
−(An)	100	reg. number:An
(d16,An)	101	reg. number:An
(d8,An,Xn)	110	reg. number:An

Addr. Mode	Mode	Register
(xxx).W	111	000
(xxx).L	111	001
#<data>	111	100
(d16,PC)	111	010
(d8,PC,Xn)	111	011

ADDX

Add Extended

Operation: Source + Destination + X → Destination

Assembler Syntax: ADDX Dy,Dx
ADDX −(Ay),−(Ax)

Attributes: Size = (Byte, Word, Long)

Description: Add the source operand to the destination operand along with the extend bit and store the result in the destination location. The operands may be addressed in two different ways:
1. Data register to data register: the operands are contained in data registers specified in the instruction.
2. Memory to memory: the operands are addressed with the predecrement addressing mode using the address registers specified in the instruction.
The size of the operation may be specified to be byte, word, or long.

Condition Codes:

X	N	Z	V	C
*	*	*	*	*

N Set if the result is negative. Cleared otherwise.
Z Cleared if the result is non-zero. Unchanged otherwise.
V Set if an overflow is generated. Cleared otherwise.
C Set if a carry is generated. Cleared otherwise.
X Set the same as the carry bit.

NOTE

Normally the Z condition code bit is set via programming before the start of an operation. This allows successful tests for zero results upon completion of multiple-precision operations.

Instruction Format:

15	14	13	12	11	10	9	8	7	6	5	4	3	2	1	0
1	1	0	1	Register Rx			1	Size		0	0	R/M	Register Ry		

ADDX

Add Extended

Instruction Fields:

Register Rx field — Specifies the destination register:
  If R/M = 0, specifies a data register.
  If R/M = 1, specifies an address register for the predecrement addressing mode.

Size field — Specifies the size of the operation:
  00—byte operation.
  01—word operation.
  10—long operation.

R/M field — Specifies the operand address mode:
  0—The operation is data register to data register.
  1—The operation is memory to memory.

Register Ry field — Specifies the source register:
  If R/M = 0, specifies a data register.
  If R/M = 1, specifies an address register for the predecrement addressing mode.

AND

AND Logical

Operation: Source∧Destination → Destination

Assembler   AND <ea>,Dn
Syntax: AND Dn,<ea>

Attributes: Size = (Byte, Word, Long)

Description: AND the source operand to the destination operand and store the result in the destination location. The size of the operation may be specified to be byte, word, or long. The contents of an address register may not be used as an operand.

Condition Codes:

X	N	Z	V	C
—	*	*	0	0

N   Set if the most significant bit of the result is set. Cleared otherwise.
Z   Set if the result is zero. Cleared otherwise.
V   Always cleared.
C   Always cleared.
X   Not affected.

Instruction Format:

15	14	13	12	11	10	9	8	7	6	5	4	3	2	1	0
1	1	0	0	Register Dn			Op-Mode			Effective Address Mode			Register		

Instruction Fields:

Register field — Specifies any of the eight data registers.
Op-Mode field —

Byte	Word	Long	Operation
000	001	010	(<ea>)∧(<Dn>) → Dn
100	101	110	(<Dn>)∧(<ea>) → ea

Effective Address field — Determines a source operand addressing mode:
If the location specified is a source operand then only data addressing modes are allowed as shown:

AND

AND Logical

Addr. Mode	Mode	Register
Dn	000	reg. number:Dn
An	—	—
(An)	010	reg. number:An
(An)+	011	reg. number:An
-(An)	100	reg. number:An
(d16,An)	101	reg. number:An
(d8,An,Xn)	110	reg. number:An

Addr. Mode	Mode	Register
(xxx).W	111	000
(xxx).L	111	001
#<data>	111	100
(d16,PC)	111	010
(d8,PC,Xn)	111	011

If the location specified is a destination operand then only alterable memory addressing modes are allowed as shown:

Addr. Mode	Mode	Register
Dn	—	—
An	—	—
(An)	010	reg. number:An
(An)+	011	reg. number:An
-(An)	100	reg. number:An
(d16,An)	101	reg. number:An
(d8,An,Xn)	110	reg. number:An

Addr. Mode	Mode	Register
(xxx).W	111	000
(xxx).L	111	001
#<data>	—	—
(d16,PC)	—	—
(d8,PC,Xn)	—	—

Notes:
1. If the destination is a data register, then it cannot be specified by using the destination <ea> mode, but must use the destination Dn mode instead.
2. ANDI is used when the source is immediate data. Most assemblers automatically make this distinction.

ANDI

AND Immediate

Operation: Immediate Data ∧ Destination → Destination

Assembler Syntax: ANDI #<data>, <ea>

Attributes: Size = (Byte, Word, Long)

Description: AND the immediate data to the destination operand and store the result in the destination location. The size of the operation may be specified to be byte, word, or long. The size of the immediate data matches the operation size.

Condition Codes:

X	N	Z	V	C
-	*	*	0	0

N Set if the most significant bit of the result is set. Cleared otherwise.
Z Set if the result is zero. Cleared otherwise.
V Always cleared.
C Always cleared.
X Not affected.

Instruction Format:

15	14	13	12	11	10	9	8	7	6	5	4	3	2	1	0
0	0	0	0	0	0	1	0		Size			Effective Address		Mode	Register
		Word Data											Byte Data		
					Long Data (Includes Previous Word)										

Instruction Fields:

Size field — Specifies the size of the operation:
00—byte operation.
01—word operation.
10—long operation.

Effective Address field — Specifies the destination operand. Only data alterable addressing modes are allowed as shown:

Addr. Mode	Mode	Register
Dn	000	reg. number:Dn
An	—	—
(An)	010	reg. number:An
(An)+	011	reg. number:An
-(An)	100	reg. number:An
(d16,An)	101	reg. number:An
(d8,An,Xn)	110	reg. number:An

Addr. Mode	Mode	Register
(xxx).W	111	000
(xxx).L	111	001
#>data>	—	—
(d16,PC)	—	—
(d8,PC,Xn)	—	—

Immediate field — (Data immediately following the instruction):
If size = 00, then the data is the low order byte of the immediate word.
If size = 01, then the data is the entire immediate word.
If size = 10, then the data is the next two immediate words.

ANDI to CCR

AND Immediate to Condition Codes

Operation: Source ∧ CCR → CCR

Assembler Syntax: ANDI #<data>,CCR

Attributes: Size = (Byte)

Description: AND the immediate operand with the condition codes and store the result in the low-order byte of the status register.

Condition Codes:

X	N	Z	V	C
*	*	*	*	*

N Cleared if bit 3 of immediate operand is zero. Unchanged otherwise.
Z Cleared if bit 2 of immediate operand is zero. Unchanged otherwise.
V Cleared if bit 1 of immediate operand is zero. Unchanged otherwise.
C Cleared if bit 0 of immediate operand is zero. Unchanged otherwise.
X Cleared if bit 4 of immediate operand is zero. Unchanged otherwise.

Instruction Format:

15	14	13	12	11	10	9	8	7	6	5	4	3	2	1	0
0	0	0	0	0	0	1	0	0	0	1	1	1	1	0	0
0	0	0	0	0	0	0	0	Byte Data (8 Bits)							

ANDI to SR

AND Immediate to the Status Register (Privileged Instruction)

Operation: If supervisor state
then Source ∧ SR → SR
else TRAP;

Assembler Syntax: ANDI #<data>,SR

Attributes: Size = (Word)

Description: AND the immediate operand with the contents of the status register and store the result in the status register. All bits of the status register are affected.

Condition Codes:

X	N	Z	V	C
*	*	*	*	*

N Cleared if bit 3 of immediate operand is zero. Unchanged otherwise.
Z Cleared if bit 2 of immediate operand is zero. Unchanged otherwise.
V Cleared if bit 1 of immediate operand is zero. Unchanged otherwise.
C Cleared if bit 0 of immediate operand is zero. Unchanged otherwise.
X Cleared if bit 4 of immediate operand is zero. Unchanged otherwise.

Instruction Format:

15	14	13	12	11	10	9	8	7	6	5	4	3	2	1	0
0	0	0	0	0	0	1	0	0	1	1	1	1	1	0	0
Word Data (16 Bits)															

ASL, ASR   Arithmetic Shift   ASL, ASR

Operation: Destination Shifted by < count> → Destination

Assembler Syntax:
ASd Dx,Dy
ASd #< data>,Dy
ASd < ea>
where d is direction, L or R

Attributes: Size = (Byte, Word, Long)

Description: Arithmetically shift the bits of the operand in the direction (L or R) specified. The carry bit receives the last bit shifted out of the operand. The shift count for the shifting of a register may be specified in two different ways:

1. Immediate: the shift count is specified in the instruction (shift range, 1-8).
2. Register: the shift count is contained in a data register specified in the instruction (shift count is modulo 64).

The size of the operation may be specified to be byte, word, or long. The content of memory may be shifted one bit only, and the operand size is restricted to a word.

For ASL, the operand is shifted left; the number of positions shifted is the shift count. Bits shifted out of the high order bit go to both the carry and the extend bits; zeroes are shifted into the low order bit. The overflow bit indicates if any sign changes occur during the shift.

ASL:

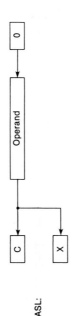

For ASR, the operand is shifted right; the number of positions shifted is the shift count. Bits shifted out of the low order bit go to both the carry and the extend bits; the sign bit (MSB) is replicated into the high order bit.

ASR:

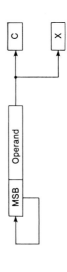

Condition Codes:

X	N	Z	V	C
*	*	*	*	*

N   Set if the most significant bit of the result is set. Cleared otherwise.
Z   Set if the result is zero. Cleared otherwise.
V   Set if the most significant bit is changed at any time during the shift operation. Cleared otherwise.
C   Set according to the last bit shifted out of the operand. Cleared for a shift count of zero.
X   Set according to the last bit shifted out of the operand. Unaffected for a shift count of zero.

Instruction Format (Register Shifts):

15	14	13	12	11	10	9	8	7	6	5	4	3	2	1	0
1	1	1	0	Count Register			dr	Size		i/r	0	0	Register		

Instruction Fields (Register Shifts):

Count/Register field — Specifies shift count or register where count is located:
If i/r=0, the shift count is specified in this field. The values 0, 1-7 represent a range of 8, 1 to 7 respectively.
If i/r=1, the shift count (modulo 64) is contained in the data register specified in this field.

dr field — Specifies the direction of the shift:
0—shift right.
1—shift left.

Size field — Specifies the size of the operation:
00—byte operation.
01—word operation.
10—long operation.

i/r field —
If i/r=0, specifies immediate shift count.
If i/r=1, specifies register shift count.
Register field — Specifies a data register whose content is to be shifted.

ASL, ASR   Arithmetic Shift   ASL, ASR

Instruction Format (Memory Shifts):

15	14	13	12	11	10	9	8	7	6	5	4	3	2	1	0
1	1	0	0	0	dr	1	1			Effective Address Mode			Register		

Instruction Fields (Memory Shifts):

dr field — Specifies the direction of the shift:
0—shift right
1—shift left

Effective Address field — Specifies the operand to be shifted. Only memory alterable addressing modes are allowed as shown:

Addr. Mode	Mode	Register
Dn	—	—
An	—	—
(An)	010	reg. number:An
(An)+	011	reg. number:An
-(An)	100	reg. number:An
(d16,An)	101	reg. number:An
(d8,An,Xn)	110	reg. number:An

Addr. Mode	Mode	Register
(xxx).W	111	000
(xxx).L	111	001
#<data>	—	—
(d16,PC)	—	—
(d8,PC,Xn)	—	—

Bcc   Branch Conditionally   Bcc

Operation: If (condition true) then PC + d → PC;

**Assembler
Syntax:**   Bcc <label>

Attributes: Size = (Byte, Word)

Description: If the specified condition is met, program execution continues at location (PC) + displacement. The displacement is a twos complement integer which counts the relative distance in bytes. The value in the PC is the sign-extended instruction location plus two. If the 8-bit displacement in the instruction word is zero, then the 16-bit displacement (word immediately following the instruction) is used. "cc" may specify the following conditions:

CC	carry clear	0100	$\bar{C}$		LS	low or same	0011	$C + Z$
CS	carry set	0101	C		LT	less than	1101	$N \cdot \bar{V} + \bar{N} \cdot V$
EQ	equal	0111	Z		MI	minus	1011	N
GE	greater or equal	1100	$N \cdot V + \bar{N} \cdot \bar{V}$		NE	not equal	0110	$\bar{Z}$
GT	greater than	1110	$N \cdot V \cdot \bar{Z} + \bar{N} \cdot \bar{V} \cdot \bar{Z}$		PL	plus	1010	$\bar{N}$
HI	high	0010	$\bar{C} \cdot \bar{Z}$		VC	overflow clear	1000	$\bar{V}$
LE	less or equal	1111	$Z + N \cdot \bar{V} + \bar{N} \cdot V$		VS	overflow set	1001	V

Condition Codes: Not affected.

Instruction Format:

15	14	13	12	11	10	9	8	7	6	5	4	3	2	1	0
0	1	1	0		Condition						8-Bit Displacement				
							16-Bit Displacement If 8-Bit Displacement = $00								

Instruction Fields:

Condition field — One of fourteen conditions discussed in description.

8-Bit Displacement field — Twos complement integer specifying the relative distance (in bytes) between the branch instruction and the next instruction to be executed if the condition is met.

16-Bit Displacement field — Allows a larger displacement than 8 bits. Used only if the 8-bit displacement is equal to $00.

Note: A short branch to the immediately following instruction cannot be generated, because it would result in a zero offset, which forces a word branch instruction definition.

352

Reprinted by permission of Motorola, Inc.

BCHG

Test a Bit and Change

BCHG

Operation: ~(<bit number> of Destination) → Z;
~(<bit number> of Destination) → <bit number> of Destination

Assembler Syntax: BCHG Dn,<ea>
BCHG #<data>,<ea>

Attributes: Size = (Byte, Long)

Description: A bit in the destination operand is tested and the state of the specified bit is reflected in the Z condition code. After the test, the state of the specified bit is changed in the destination. If a data register is the destination, then the bit numbering is modulo 32 allowing bit manipulation on all bits in a data register. If a memory location is the destination, a byte is read from that location, the bit operation is performed using the bit number, modulo 8, and the byte is written back to the location. In all cases, bit zero refers to the least significant bit. The bit number for this operation may be specified in two different ways:

1. Immediate — the bit number is specified in a second word of the instruction.
2. Register — the bit number is contained in a data register specified in the instruction.

Condition Codes:

X	N	Z	V	C
-	-	*	-	-

N Not affected.
Z Set if the bit tested is zero. Cleared otherwise.
V Not affected.
C Not affected.
X Not affected.

Instruction Format (Bit Number Dynamic specified by a register):

15	14	13	12	11	10	9	8	7	6	5	4	3	2	1	0
0	0	0	0	Register Dn			1	0	1	Effective Address					
										Mode			Register		

Instruction Fields (Bit Number Dynamic):
Register field — Specifies the data register whose content is the bit number.
Effective Address field — Specifies the destination location. Only data alterable addressing modes are allowed as shown:

Addr. Mode	Mode	Register		Addr. Mode	Mode	Register
Dn*	000	reg. number:Dn		(xxx).W	111	000
An	-	-		(xxx).L	111	001
(An)	010	reg. number:An		#<data>	-	-
(An)+	011	reg. number:An				
-(An)	100	reg. number:An		(d16,PC)	-	-
(d16,An)	101	reg. number:An		(d8,PC,Xn)	-	-
(d8,An,Xn)	110	reg. number:An				

*Long only; all others are byte only.

BCHG

Test a Bit and Change

BCHG

Instruction Format (Bit Number Static, specified as immediate data):

15	14	13	12	11	10	9	8	7	6	5	4	3	2	1	0
0	0	0	0	1	0	0	0	0	1	Effective Address					
										Mode			Register		
0	0	0	0	0	0	0	0	Bit Number							

Instruction Fields (Bit Number Static):
Effective Address field — Specifies the destination location. Only data alterable addressing modes are allowed as shown:

Addr. Mode	Mode	Register		Addr. Mode	Mode	Register
Dn*	000	reg. number:Dn		(xxx).W	111	000
An	-	-		(xxx).L	111	001
(An)	010	reg. number:An		#<data>	-	-
(An)+	011	reg. number:An				
-(An)	100	reg. number:An		(d16,PC)	-	-
(d16,An)	101	reg. number:An		(d8,PC,Xn)	-	-
(d8,An,Xn)	110	reg. number:An				

*Long only; all others are byte only.

Bit Number field — Specifies the bit number.

BCLR

BCLR

BCLR

Test a Bit and Clear

Test a Bit and Clear

BCLR

Operation: ~(<bit number> of Destination) → Z;
0 → <bit number> of Destination

Assembler
Syntax: BCLR Dn,<ea>
BCLR #<data>,<ea>

Attributes: Size = (Byte, Long)

Description: A bit in the destination operand is tested and the state of the specified bit is reflected in the Z condition code. After the test, the specified bit is cleared in the destination. If a data register is the destination, then the bit numbering is modulo 32 allowing bit manipulation on all bits in a data register. If a memory location is the destination, a byte is read from that location, the bit operation performed using the bit number, modulo 8, and the byte written back to the location. In all cases, bit zero refers to the least significant bit. The bit number for this operation may be specified in two different ways:

1. Immediate — the bit number is specified in a second word of the instruction.
2. Register — the bit number is contained in a data register specified in the instruction.

Condition Codes:

X	N	Z	V	C
—	—	*	—	—

N Not affected.
Z Set if the bit tested is zero. Cleared otherwise.
V Not affected.
C Not affected.
X Not affected.

Instruction Format (Bit Number Dynamic, specified in a register):

15	14	13	12	11	10	9	8	7	6	5	4	3	2	1	0
0	0	0	0	Register Dn			1	1	0	Effective Address Mode			Register		

Instruction Fields (Bit Number Dynamic):
Register field — Specifies the data register whose content is the bit number.
Effective Address field — Specifies the destination location. Only data alterable addressing modes are allowed as shown:

Addr. Mode	Mode	Register
Dn*	000	reg. number:Dn
An	—	—
(An)	010	reg. number:An
(An)+	011	reg. number:An
−(An)	100	reg. number:An
(d₁₆,An)	101	reg. number:An
(d₈,An,Xn)	110	reg. number:An

Addr. Mode	Mode	Register
(xxx).W	111	000
(xxx).L	111	001
#<data>	—	—
(d₁₆,PC)	—	—
(d₈,PC,Xn)	—	—

*Long only; all others are byte only

Instruction Format (Bit Number Static, specified as immediate data):

15	14	13	12	11	10	9	8	7	6	5	4	3	2	1	0
0	0	0	0	1	0	0	0	1	0	Effective Address Mode			Register		
0	0	0	0	0	0	0	0			Bit Number					

Instruction Fields (Bit Number Static):
Effective Address field — Specifies the destination location. Only data alterable addressing modes are allowed as shown:

Addr. Mode	Mode	Register
Dn*	000	reg. number:Dn
An	—	—
(An)	010	reg. number:An
(An)+	011	reg. number:An
−(An)	100	reg. number:An
(d₁₆,An)	101	reg. number:An
(d₈,An,Xn)	110	reg. number:An

Addr. Mode	Mode	Register
(xxx).W	111	000
(xxx).L	111	001
#<data>	—	—
(d₁₆,PC)	—	—
(d₈,PC,Xn)	—	—

*Long only; all others are byte only.

Bit Number field — Specifies the bit number.

354

BKPT

Breakpoint

BKPT

Operation: Execute breakpoint acknowledge bus cycle;
Trap as illegal instruction

Assembler
Syntax: BKPT #<data>

Attributes: Unsized

Description: This instruction is used to support the program breakpoint function for debug monitors and real-time hardware emulators, and the operation will be dependent on the implementation. Execution of this instruction will cause the MC68010/MC68012 to run a breakpoint acknowledge bus cycle (all function codes driven high) and zeros on all address lines.

Whether the breakpoint acknowledge bus cycle is terminated with DTACK, BERR, or VPA, the processor always takes an illegal instruction exception. During exception processing, a debug monitor can distinguish eight different software breakpoints by decoding the field in the BKPT instruction.

For the MC68000 and MC68008, this instruction causes an illegal instruction exception but does not run the breakpoint acknowledge bus cycle.

Condition Codes: Not affected.

Instruction Format:

15	14	13	12	11	10	9	8	7	6	5	4	3	2	1	0
0	1	0	0	1	0	0	0	0	1	0	0	1	BKPT #		

Instruction Fields:

BKPT # = Immediate data (value = 0—7), encodes 8 software breakpoints.

BRA

Branch Always

BRA

■ **Operation:** PC + d → PC

Assembler
Syntax: BRA <label>

Attributes: Size = (Byte, Word)

Description: Program execution continues at location (PC) + displacement. The displacement is a twos complement integer, which counts the relative distance in bytes. The value in the PC is the instruction location plus two. If the 8-bit displacement in the instruction word is zero, then the 16-bit displacement (word immediately following the instruction) is used.

Condition Codes: Not affected.

Instruction Format:

15	14	13	12	11	10	9	8	7	6	5	4	3	2	1	0
0	1	1	0	0	0	0	0	8-Bit Displacement							
16-Bit Displacement if 8-Bit Displacement = $00															

Instruction Fields:

8-Bit Displacement field — Two complement integer specifying the relative distance (in bytes) between the branch instruction and the next instruction to be executed.
16-Bit Displacement field — Allows a larger displacement than 8 bits. Used only if the 8-bit displacement is equal to $00.

Note: A short branch to the immediately following instruction cannot be generated because it would result in a zero offset, which forces a word branch instruction definition.

BSET

Test a Bit and Set

Operation: ~(<bit number> of Destination) → Z;
1 → <bit number> of Destination

Assembler
Syntax: BSET Dn,<ea>
BSET #<data>,<ea>

Attributes: Size = (Byte, Long)

Description: A bit in the destination operand is tested, and the state of the specified bit is reflected in the Z condition code. After the test, the specified bit is set in the destination. If a data register is the destination, then the bit numbering is modulo 32, allowing bit manipulation on all bits in a data register. If a memory location is the destination, a byte is read from that location, the bit operation performed using the bit number, modulo 8, and the byte written back to the location. Bit zero refers to the least significant bit. The bit number for this operation may be specified in two different ways:

1. Immediate — the bit number is specified in a second word of the instruction.
2. Register — the bit number is contained in a data register specified in the instruction.

Condition Codes:

X	N	Z	V	C
-	-	*	-	-

N Not affected.
Z Set if the bit tested is zero. Cleared otherwise.
V Not affected.
C Not affected.
X Not affected.

Instruction Format (Bit Number Dynamic, specified in a register):

15	14	13	12	11	10	9	8	7	6	5	4	3	2	1	0
0	0	0	0	Register			1	1	1	Effective Address					
										Mode			Register		

Instruction Fields (Bit Number Dynamic):
Register field — Specifies the data register whose content is the bit number.
Effective Address field — Specifies the destination location. Only data alterable addressing modes are allowed as shown:

Addr. Mode	Mode	Register
Dn*	000	reg. number:Dn
An	—	—
(An)	010	reg. number:An
(An)+	011	reg. number:An
-(An)	100	reg. number:An
(d16,An)	101	reg. number:An
(d8,An,Xn)	110	reg. number:An

Addr. Mode	Mode	Register
(xxx).W	111	000
(xxx).L	111	001
#<data>	—	—
(d16,PC)	—	—
(d8,PC,Xn)	—	—

*Long only; all others are byte only.

BSET

Test a Bit and Set

Instruction Format (Bit Number Static, specified as immediate data):

15	14	13	12	11	10	9	8	7	6	5	4	3	2	1	0
0	0	0	0	1	0	0	0	1	1	Effective Address					
										Mode			Register		
0	0	0	0	0	0	0	0	Bit Number							

Instruction Fields (Bit Number Static):
Effective Address field — Specifies the destination location. Only data alterable addressing modes are allowed as shown:

Addr. Mode	Mode	Register
Dn*	000	reg. number:Dn
An	—	—
(An)	010	reg. number:An
(An)+	011	reg. number:An
-(An)	100	reg. number:An
(d16,An)	101	reg. number:An
(d8,An,Xn)	110	reg. number:An

Addr. Mode	Mode	Register
(xxx).W	111	000
(xxx).L	111	001
#<data>	—	—
(d16,PC)	—	—
(d8,PC,Xn)	—	—

*Long only; all others are byte only.

Bit Number field — Specifies the bit number.

BSR

Branch to Subroutine

Operation: SP − 4 → SP; PC → (SP); PC + d → PC

Assembler Syntax: BSR <label>

Attributes: Size = (Byte, Word)

Description: The long word address of the instruction immediately following the BSR instruction is pushed onto the system stack. Program execution then continues at location (PC) + displacement. The displacement in a twos complement integer which counts the relative distances in the bytes. The value in the PC is the instruction location plus two. If the 8-bit displacement in the instruction word is zero, then the 16-bit displacement (word immediately following the instruction) is used.

Condition Codes: Not affected.

Instruction Format:

15	14	13	12	11	10	9	8	7	6	5	4	3	2	1	0
0	1	1	0	0	0	0	1			8-Bit Displacement					
				16-Bit Displacement If 8-Bit Displacement = $00											

Instruction Fields:

8-Bit Displacement field — Twos complement integer specifying the relative distance (in bytes) between the branch instruction and the next instruction to be executed.

16-Bit Displacement field — Allows a larger displacement than 8 bits. Used only if the 8-bit displacement is equal to $00.

Note: A short subroutine branch to the immediately following instruction cannot be generated because it would result in a zero offset, which forces a word branch instruction definition.

BTST

Test a Bit

Operation: ∼(<bit number> of Destination) → Z;

Assembler Syntax:
BTST Dn,<ea>
BTST #<data>,<ea>

Attributes: Size = (Byte, Long)

Description: A bit in the destination operand is tested, and the state of the specified bit is reflected in the Z condition code. If a data register is the destination, then the bit numbering is modulo 32, allowing bit manipulation on all bits in a data register. If a memory location is the destination, a byte is read from that location, and the bit operation performed using the bit number, modulo 8, with zero referring to the least significant bit. The bit number for this operation may be specified in two different ways:

1. Immediate — the bit number is specified in a second word of the instruction.
2. Register — the bit number is contained in a data register specified in the instruction.

Condition Codes:

X	N	Z	V	C
—	—	*	—	—

N Not affected.
Z Set if the bit tested is zero. Cleared otherwise.
V Not affected.
C Not affected.
X Not affected.

Instruction Format (Bit Number Dynamic, specified in a register):

15	14	13	12	11	10	9	8	7	6	5	4	3	2	1	0
0	0	0	0		Register Dn		1	0	0		Effective Address				
										Mode			Register		

Instruction Fields (Bit Number Dynamic):

Register field — Specifies the data register whose content is the bit number.
Effective Address field — Specifies the destination location. Only data addressing modes are allowed as shown:

BTST

BTST

Test a Bit

Addr. Mode	Mode	Register
(xxx).W	111	000
(xxx).L	111	001
#<data>	111	100
(d16,PC)	111	010
(d8,An,Xn)	111	011

*Long only; all others are byte only.

Instruction Format (Bit Number Static, specified as immediate data):

15	14	13	12	11	10	9	8	7	6	5	4	3	2	1	0
											Effective Address				
												Mode		Register	
0	0	0	0	1	0	0	0	0	0						
0	0	0	0	0	0	0	0			Bit Number					

Instruction Fields (Bit Number Static):
Effective Address field — Specifies the destination location. Only data addressing modes are allowed as shown:

Addr. Mode	Mode	Register
Dn*	000	reg. number:Dn
An	—	—
(An)	010	reg. number:An
(An)+	011	reg. number:An
-(An)	100	reg. number:An
(d16,An)	101	reg. number:An
(d8,An,Xn)	110	reg. number:An

Addr. Mode	Mode	Register
(xxx).W	111	000
(xxx).L	111	001
#<data>	111	—
(d16,PC)	111	010
(d8,PC,Xn)	111	011

*Long only; all others are byte only.

Bit Number field — Specifies the bit number.

CHK

CHK

Check Register Against Bounds

Operation: If Dn<0 or Dn> Source then TRAP;

Assembler Syntax: CHK <ea>,Dn

Attributes: Size = (Word)

Description: The content of the low order word in the data register specified in the instruction is examined and compared to the upper bound. The upper bound is a twos complement integer. If the register value is less than zero or greater than the upper bound, then the processor initiates exception processing. The vector number is generated to reference the CHK instruction exception vector.

Condition Codes:

X	N	Z	V	C
-	*	U	U	U

N Set if Dn< 0; cleared if Dn> Source. Undefined otherwise.
Z Undefined.
V Undefined.
C Undefined.
X Not affected.

Instruction Format:

15	14	13	12	11	10	9	8	7	6	5	4	3	2	1	0
											Effective Address				
												Mode		Register	
0	1	0	0		Register Dn			1	1	0					

Instruction Fields:
Register field — Specifies the data register whose content is checked.
Effective Address field — Specifies the upper bound operand word. Only data addressing modes are allowed as shown:

Addr. Mode	Mode	Register
Dn	000	reg. number:Dn
An	—	—
(An)	010	reg. number:An
(An)+	011	reg. number:An
-(An)	100	reg. number:An
(d16,An)	101	reg. number:An
(d8,An,Xn)	110	reg. number:An

Addr. Mode	Mode	Register
(xxx).W	111	000
(xxx).L	111	001
#<data>	111	100
(d16,PC)	111	010
(d8,PC,Xn)	111	011

CLR

Clear an Operand

Operation: 0 → Destination

Assembler Syntax: CLR <ea>

Attributes: Size = (Byte, Word, Long)

Description: The destination is cleared to all zero. The size of the operation may be specified to be byte, word, or long.

Condition Codes:

X	N	Z	V	C
—	0	1	0	0

N Always cleared.
Z Always set.
V Always cleared.
C Always cleared.
X Not affected.

Instruction Format:

15	14	13	12	11	10	9	8	7	6	5	4	3	2	1	0
0	1	0	0	0	0	1	0	Size		— Effective Address Mode			Register		

Instruction Fields:

Size field — Specifies the size of the operation.
00—byte operation.
01—word operation.
10—long operation.

Effective Address field — Specifies the destination location. Only data alterable addressing modes are allowed as shown:

Addr. Mode	Mode	Register
Dn*	000	reg. number:Dn
An	—	—
(An)	010	reg. number:An
(An)+	011	reg. number:An
−(An)	100	reg. number:An
(d₁₆,An)	101	reg. number:An
(d₈,An,Xn)	110	reg. number:An

Addr. Mode	Mode	Register
(xxx).W	111	000
(xxx).L	111	001
#<data>	—	—
(d₁₆,PC)	—	—
(d₈,PC,Xn)	—	—

CMP

Compare

Operation: Destination − Source

Assembler Syntax: CMP <ea>,Dn

Attributes: Size = (Byte, Word, Long)

Description: Subtract the source operand from the specified data register and set the condition codes according to the result; the data register is not changed. The size of the operation may be byte, word, or long.

Condition Codes:

X	N	Z	V	C
—	*	*	*	*

N Set if the result is negative. Cleared otherwise.
Z Set if the result is zero. Cleared otherwise.
V Set if an overflow is generated. Cleared otherwise.
C Set if a borrow is generated. Cleared otherwise.
X Not affected.

Instruction Format:

15	14	13	12	11	10	9	8	7	6	5	4	3	2	1	0
1	0	1	1	Register Dn			Op-Mode			— Effective Address Mode			Register		

Instruction Fields:

Register field — Specifies the destination data register.
Op-Mode field —

	Byte	Word	Long	Operation
	000	001	010	Dn−(<ea>)

Effective Address field — Specifies the source operand. All addressing modes are allowed as shown:

Addr. Mode	Mode	Register
Dn	000	reg. number:Dn
An*	001	reg. number:An
(An)	010	reg. number:An
(An)+	011	reg. number:An
−(An)	100	reg. number:An
(d₁₆,An)	101	reg. number:An
(d₈,An,Xn)	110	reg. number:An

Addr. Mode	Mode	Register
(xxx).W	111	000
(xxx).L	111	001
#<data>	111	100
(d₁₆,PC)	111	010
(d₈,PC,Xn)	111	011

*Word and Long only.

Note: CMPA is used when the destination is an address register. CMPI is used when the source is immediate data. CMPM is used for memory to memory compares. Most assemblers automatically make this distinction.

CMPA

Compare Address

Operation: Destination − Source

**Assembler
Syntax:** CMPA <ea>,An

Attributes: Size = (Word, Long)

Description: Subtract the source operand from the destination address register and set the condition codes according to the result; the address register is not changed. The size of the operation may be specified to be word or long. Word length source operands are sign extended to 32-bit quantities before the operation is done.

Condition Codes:

X	N	Z	V	C
−	*	*	*	*

N   Set if the result is negative. Cleared otherwise.
Z   Set if the result is zero. Cleared otherwise.
V   Set if an overflow is generated. Cleared otherwise.
C   Set if a borrow is generated. Cleared otherwise.
X   Not affected.

Instruction Format:

15	14	13	12	11	10	9	8	7	6	5	4	3	2	1	0
1	0	1	1		Register An				Op-Mode			Effective Address Mode			Register

Instruction Fields:

Register field — Specifies the destination data register.
Op-Mode field — Specifies the size of the operation:
011—word operation. The source operand is sign-extended to a long operand and the operation is performed on the address register using all 32 bits.
111—long operation.
Effective Address field — Specifies the source operand. All addressing modes are allowed as shown:

Addr. Mode	Mode	Register
Dn	000	reg. number:Dn
An	001	reg. number:An
(An)	010	reg. number:An
(An)+	011	reg. number:An
−(An)	100	reg. number:An
(d16,An)	101	reg. number:An
(d8,An,Xn)	110	reg. number:An

Addr. Mode	Mode	Register
(xxx).W	111	000
(xxx).L	111	001
#<data>	111	100
(d16,PC)	111	010
(d8,PC,Xn)	111	011

CMPI

Compare Immediate

Operation: Destination − Immediate Data

**Assembler
Syntax:** CMPI #<data>,<ea>

Attributes: Size = (Byte, Word, Long)

Description: Subtract the immediate data from the destination operand and set the condition codes according to the result; the destination location is not changed. The size of the operation may be specified to be byte, word, or long. The size of the immediate data matches the operation size.

Condition Codes:

X	N	Z	V	C
−	*	*	*	*

N   Set if the result is negative. Cleared otherwise.
Z   Set if the result is zero. Cleared otherwise.
V   Set if an overflow is generated. Cleared otherwise.
C   Set if a borrow is generated. Cleared otherwise.
X   Not affected.

Instruction Format:

15	14	13	12	11	10	9	8	7	6	5	4	3	2	1	0
0	0	0	0	1	1	0	0		Size			Effective Address Mode			Register
		Word Data										Byte Data			
		Long Data													

Instruction Fields:

Size field — Specifies the size of the operation:
00—byte operation.
01—word operation.
10—long operation.
Effective Address field — Specifies the destination operand. Only data alterable addressing modes are allowed as shown:

Reprinted by permission of Motorola, Inc.

CMPI

Compare Immediate

Addr. Mode	Mode	Register
Dn	000	reg. number:Dn
An	–	–
(An)	010	reg. number:An
(An) +	011	reg. number:An
– (An)	100	reg. number:An
(d₁₆,An)	101	reg. number:An
(d₈,An,Xn)	110	reg. number:An

Addr. Mode	Mode	Register
(xxx).W	111	000
(xxx).L	111	001
#<data>	–	–
(d₁₆,PC)	–	–
(d₈,PC,Xn)	–	–

Immediate field — (Data immediately following the instruction):
If size = 00, then the data is the low order byte of the immediate word.
If size = 01, then the data is the entire immediate word.
If size = 10, then the data is the next two immediate words.

CMPM

Compare Memory

Operation: Destination – Source

Assembler Syntax: CMPM (Ay) + ,(Ax) +

Attributes: Size = (Byte, Word, Long)

Description: Subtract the source operand from the destination operand, and set the condition codes according to the results; the destination location is not changed. The operands are always addressed with the postincrement addressing mode, using the address registers specified in the instruction. The size of the operation may be specified to be byte, word, or long.

Condition Codes:

X	N	Z	V	C
–	*	*	*	*

N Set if the result is negative. Cleared otherwise.
Z Set if the result is zero. Cleared otherwise.
V Set if an overflow is generated. Cleared otherwise.
C Set if a borrow is generated. Cleared otherwise.
X Not affected.

Instruction Format:

15	14	13	12	11	10	9	8	7	6	5	4	3	2	1	0
1	0	1	1		Register Ax		1		Size	0	0	1		Register Ay	

Instruction Fields:

Register Ax field — (always the destination) Specifies an address register for the postincrement addressing mode.
Size field — Specifies the size of the operation:
00—byte operation.
01—word operation.
10—long operation.
Register Ay field — (always the source) Specifies an address register for the postincrement addressing mode.

DBcc

Test Condition, Decrement, and Branch

DBcc

Operation: If condition false then (Dn − 1→Dn; If Dn ≠ − 1 then PC + d→PC);

Assembler
Syntax: DBcc Dn,<label>

Attributes: Size=(Word)

Description: This instruction is a looping primitive of three parameters: a condition, a counter (data register), and a displacement. The instruction first tests the condition to determine if the termination condition for the loop has been met, and if so, no operation is performed. If the termination condition is not true, the low order 16 bits of the counter data register are decremented by one. If the result is − 1, the counter is exhausted and execution continues with the next instruction. If the result is not equal to − 1, execution continues at the location indicated by the current value of the PC plus the sign-extended 16-bit displacement. The value in the PC is the current instruction location plus two.

"cc" may specify the following conditions:

CC	carry clear	0100	$\overline{C}$		LS	low or same	0011	$C + Z$
CS	carry set	0101	C		LT	less than	1101	$N \cdot \overline{V} + \overline{N} \cdot V$
EQ	equal	0111	Z		MI	minus	1011	N
F	never true	0001	0		NE	not equal	0110	$\overline{Z}$
GE	greater or equal	1100	$N \cdot V + \overline{N} \cdot \overline{V}$		PL	plus	1010	$\overline{N}$
GT	greater than	1110	$N \cdot V \cdot \overline{Z} + \overline{N} \cdot \overline{V} \cdot \overline{Z}$		T	always true	0000	1
HI	high	0010	$\overline{C} \cdot \overline{Z}$		VC	overflow clear	1000	$\overline{V}$
LE	less or equal	1111	$Z + N \cdot \overline{V} + \overline{N} \cdot V$		VS	overflow set	1001	V

Condition Codes: Not affected.

Instruction Format:

15	14	13	12	11	10	9	8	7	6	5	4	3	2	1	0
0	1	0	1		Condition			1	1	0	0	1		Register	
								Displacement							

Instruction Fields:
Condition field — One of the sixteen conditions discussed in description.
Register field — Specifies the data register which is the counter.
Displacement field — Specifies the distance of the branch (in bytes).

Notes: 1. The terminating condition is like that defined by the UNTIL loop constructs of high-level languages. For example: DBMI can be stated as "decrement and branch until minus".

DBcc

Test Condition, Decrement, and Branch

DBcc

2. Most assemblers accept DBRA for DBF for use when no condition is required for termination of a loop.

3. There are two basic ways of entering a loop: at the beginning or by branching to the trailing DBcc instruction. If a loop structure terminated with DBcc is entered at the beginning, the control index count must be one less than the number of loop executions desired. This count is useful for indexed addressing modes and dynamically specified bit operations. However, when entering a loop by branching directly to the trailing DBcc instruction, the control index should equal the loop execution count. In this case, if a zero count occurs, the DBcc instruction will not branch, causing a complete bypass of the main loop.

Reprinted by permission of Motorola, Inc.

DIVS

Signed Divide

DIVS

Operation: Destination/Source→Destination

Assembler
Syntax: DIVS <ea>,Dn   32/16→16r:16q

Attributes: Size = (Word)

Description: Divide the destination operand by the source and store the result in the destination. The operation is performed using signed arithmetic.

The destination operand is a long word and the source operand is a word. The result is 32-bits, such that the quotient is in the lower word (least significant 16 bits) of the destination and the remainder is in the upper word (most significant 16 bits) of the destination. Note that the sign of the remainder is the same as the sign of the dividend.

Two special conditions may arise during the operation:
1. Division by zero causes a trap.
2. Overflow may be detected and set before completion of the instruction. If overflow is detected, the condition is flagged but the operands are unaffected.

Condition Codes:

X	N	Z	V	C
–	*	*	*	0

N   Set if the quotient is negative. Cleared otherwise. Undefined if overflow or divide by zero.
Z   Set if the quotient is zero. Cleared otherwise. Undefined if overflow or divide by zero.
V   Set if division overflow is detected. Cleared otherwise.
C   Always cleared.
X   Not affected..

Instruction Format:

15	14	13	12	11	10	9	8	7	6	5	4	3	2	1	0
1	0	0	0	Register Dn			1	1	1	Effective Address				Register		
										Mode						

DIVS DIVS

Signed Divide

DIVS

Instruction Fields:
  Register field — Specifies any of the eight data registers. This field always specifies the destination operand.
  Effective Address field — Specifies the source operand. Only data addressing modes are allowed as shown:

Addr. Mode	Mode	Register
Dn	000	reg. number:Dn
An	–	–
(An)	010	reg. number:An
(An)+	011	reg. number:An
–(An)	100	reg. number:An
(d₁₆,An)	101	reg. number:An
(d₈,An,Xn)	110	reg. number:An

Addr. Mode	Mode	Register
(xxx).W	111	000
(xxx).L	111	001
#<data>	111	100
(d₁₆,PC)	111	010
(d₈,PC,Xn)	111	011

Note: Overflow occurs if the quotient is larger than a 16-bit signed integer.

363

DIVU   Unsigned Divide   DIVU

Operation: Destination/Source→Destination

**Assembler
Syntax:** DIVU <ea>,Dn $32/16 \rightarrow 16r:16q$

Attributes: Size = (Word)

Description: Divide the destination operand by the source and store the result in the destination. The operation is performed using unsigned arithmetic.

The destination operand is a long word and the source operand is a word. The result is 32-bits, such that the quotient is in the lower word (least significant 16 bits) of the destination and the remainder is in the upper word (most significant 16 bits) of the destination. Note that the sign of the remainder is the same as the sign of the dividend.

Two special conditions may arise:
1. Division by zero causes a trap.
2. Overflow may be detected and set before completion of the instruction. If overflow is detected, the condition is flagged but the operands are unaffected.

Condition Codes:

X	N	Z	V	C
—	*	*	*	0

N Set if the quotient is negative. Cleared otherwise. Undefined if overflow or divide by zero.
Z Set if the quotient is zero. Cleared otherwise. Undefined if overflow or divide by zero.
V Set if division overflow is detected. Cleared otherwise.
C Always cleared.
X Not affected.

DIVU   Unsigned Divide   DIVU

Instruction Fields:
Register field — Specifies any of the eight data registers. This field always specifies the destination operand.
Effective Address field — Specifies the source operand. Only data addressing modes are allowed as shown:

Addr. Mode	Mode	Register
Dn	000	reg. number:Dn
An	—	—
(An)	010	reg. number:An
(An)+	011	reg. number:An
-(An)	100	reg. number:An
(d16,An)	101	reg. number:An
(d8,An,Xn)	110	reg. number:An

Addr. Mode	Mode	Register
(xxx).W	111	000
(xxx).L	111	001
#<data>	111	100
(d16,PC)	111	010
(d8,PC,Xn)	111	011

Note: Overflow occurs if the quotient is larger than a 16-bit unsigned integer.

Instruction Format:

15	14	13	12	11	10	9	8	7	6	5	4	3	2	1	0
1	0	0	0	Register Dn			0	1	1	Effective Address Mode			Register		

EOR

Exclusive OR Logical

Operation: Source ⊕ Destination → Destination

Assembler Syntax: EOR Dn,<ea>

Attributes: Size = (Byte, Word, Long)

Description: Exclusive OR the source operand to the destination operand and store the result in the destination location. The size of the operation may be specified to be byte, word, or long. This operation is restricted to data registers as the source operand. The destination operand is specified in the effective address field.

Condition Codes:

X	N	Z	V	C
—	*	*	0	0

N Set if the most significant bit of the result is set. Cleared otherwise.
Z Set if the result is zero. Cleared otherwise.
V Always cleared.
C Always cleared.
X Not affected.

Instruction Format (word form):

15	14	13	12	11	10	9	8	7	6	5	4	3	2	1	0
1	0	1	1	Register Dn			Op-Mode			Effective Address Mode			Register		

Instruction Fields:

Register field — Specifies any of the eight data registers.
Op-Mode field —

Byte	Word	Long	Operation
100	101	110	<ea> ⊕ <Dx> → <ea>

Effective Address field — Specifies the destination operand. Only data alterable addressing modes are allowed as shown:

Addr. Mode	Mode	Register
Dn	000	reg. number:Dn
An	—	—
(An)	010	reg. number:An
(An)+	011	reg. number:An
-(An)	100	reg. number:An
(d₁₆,An)	101	reg. number:An
(d₈,An,Xn)	110	reg. number:An

Addr. Mode	Mode	Register
(xxx).W	111	000
(xxx).L	111	001
#<data>	—	—
(d₁₆,PC)	—	—
(d₈,PC,Xn)	—	—

EOR   EORI

Exclusive OR Immediate

Operation: Immediate Data ⊕ Destination → Destination

Assembler Syntax: EORI #<data>, <ea>

Attributes: Size = (Byte, Word, Long)

Description: Exclusive OR the immediate data to the destination operand and store the result in the destination location. The size of the operation may be specified to be byte, word, or long. The immediate data matches the operation size.

Condition Codes:

X	N	Z	V	C
—	*	*	0	0

N Set if the most significant bit of the result is set. Cleared otherwise.
Z Set if the result is zero. Cleared otherwise.
V Always cleared.
C Always cleared.
X Not affected.

Instruction Format:

15	14	13	12	11	10	9	8	7	6	5	4	3	2	1	0
0	0	0	0	1	0	1	0	Size		Effective Address Mode			Register		

Word Data (16 Bits)	Byte Data (8 Bits)
Long Data (32 Bits, including Previous Word)	

Instruction Fields:

Size field — Specifies the size of the operation:
00—byte operation.
01—word operation.
10—long operation.

Effective Address field — Specifies the destination operand. Only data alterable addressing modes are allowed as shown:

Addr. Mode	Mode	Register
Dn	000	reg. number:Dn
An	—	—
(An)	010	reg. number:An
(An)+	011	reg. number:An
-(An)	100	reg. number:An
(d₁₆,An)	101	reg. number:An
(d₈,An,Xn)	110	reg. number:An

Addr. Mode	Mode	Register
(xxx).W	111	000
(xxx).L	111	001
#<data>	—	—
(d₁₆,PC)	—	—
(d₈,PC,Xn)	—	—

Immediate field — (Data immediately following the instruction):
If size = 00, then the data is the low order byte of the immediate word.
If size = 01, then the data is the entire immediate word.
If size = 10, then the data is next two immediate words.

Note: Memory to data register operations are not allowed. EORI is used when the source is immediate data. Most assemblers automatically make this distinction.

EORI to CCR

Exclusive OR Immediate to Condition Code

Operation: Source ⊕ CCR → CCR

**Assembler
Syntax:** EORI #<data>,CCR

Attributes: Size = (Byte)

Description: Exclusive OR the immediate operand with the condition codes and store the result in the low-order byte of the status register.

Condition Codes:

X	N	Z	V	C
*	*	*	*	*

N   Changed if bit 3 of immediate operand is one. Unchanged otherwise.
Z   Changed if bit 2 of immediate operand is one. Unchanged otherwise.
V   Changed if bit 1 of immediate operand is one. Unchanged otherwise.
C   Changed if bit 0 of immediate operand is one. Unchanged otherwise.
X   Changed if bit 4 of immediate operand is one. Unchanged otherwise.

Instruction Format:

15	14	13	12	11	10	9	8	7	6	5	4	3	2	1	0
0	0	0	0	1	0	1	0	0	0	1	1	1	1	0	0
								Byte Data (8 Bits)							

EORI to SR

**Exclusive OR Immediate to the Status Register
(Privileged Instruction)**

Operation: If supervisor state
then Source ⊕ SR → SR
else TRAP;

**Assembler
Syntax:** EORI #<data>,SR

Attributes: Size = (Word)

Description: Exclusive OR the immediate operand with the contents of the status register and store the result in the status register. All bits of the status register are affected.

Condition Codes:

X	N	Z	V	C
*	*	*	*	*

N   Changed if bit 3 of immediate operand is one. Unchanged otherwise.
Z   Changed if bit 2 of immediate operand is one. Unchanged otherwise.
V   Changed if bit 1 of immediate operand is one. Unchanged otherwise.
C   Changed if bit 0 of immediate operand is one. Unchanged otherwise.
X   Changed if bit 4 of immediate operand is one. Unchanged otherwise.

Instruction Format:

15	14	13	12	11	10	9	8	7	6	5	4	3	2	1	0
0	0	0	0	1	0	1	0	0	1	1	1	1	1	0	0
								Word Data (16 Bits)							

EXG

Exchange Registers

Operation: Rx ⟷ Ry

Assembler Syntax:
EXG Dx,Dy
EXG Ax,Ay
EXG Dx,Ay

Attributes: Size = (Long)

Description: Exchange the contents of two registers. This exchange is always a long (32 bit) operation. Exchange works in three modes:
1. Exchange data registers.
2. Exchange address registers.
3. Exchange a data register and an address register.

Condition Codes: Not affected.

Instruction Format:

15	14	13	12	11	10	9	8	7	6	5	4	3	2	1	0
1	1	0	0	Register Rx			1	Op-Mode				Register Ry			

Instruction Fields:

Register Rx field — Specifies either a data register or an address register depending on the mode. If the exchange is between data and address registers, this field always specifies the data register.

Op-Mode field — Specifies whether exchanging:
01000—data registers.
01001—address registers.
10001—data register and address register.

Register Ry field — Specifies either a data register or an address register depending on the mode. If the exchange is between data and address registers, this field always specifies the address register.

EXT

Sign Extend

Operation: Destination Sign-extended→Destination

Assembler Syntax: EXT Dn

Attributes: Size = (Word, Long)

Description: Extend the sign bit of a data register from a byte to a word, or from a word to a long word, depending on the size selected. If the operation is word, bit [7] of the designated data register is copied to bits [15:8] of that data register. If the operation is long, bit [15] of the designated data register is copied to bits [31:16] of the data register.

Condition Codes:

X	N	Z	V	C
–	*	*	0	0

N Set if the result is negative. Cleared otherwise.
Z Set if the result is zero. Cleared otherwise.
V Always cleared.
C Always cleared.
X Not affected.

Instruction Format:

15	14	13	12	11	10	9	8	7	6	5	4	3	2	1	0
0	1	0	0	1	0	0	0	Op-Mode			0	0	0	Register Dn	

Instruction Fields:

Op-Mode field — Specifies the size of the sign-extension operation:
010—Sign-extend low order byte of data register to word.
011—Sign-extend low order word of data register to long.

Register field — Specifies the data register whose content is to be sign-extended.

ILLEGAL

Take Illegal Instruction Trap

Operation: SSP – 2 → SSP; Vector Offset → (SSP);
SSP – 4 → SSP; PC → (SSP);
SSP – 2 → SSP; SR → (SSP);
Illegal Instruction Vector Address → PC

**Assembler
Syntax:** ILLEGAL

Attributes: Unsized

Description: This bit pattern causes an illegal instruction exception. All other illegal instruction bit patterns are reserved for future extension of the instruction set.

The MC68010/012 will first write the exception vector offset and format code to the system stack followed by the PC and SR to complete a 4-word exception stack frame.

Condition Codes: Not affected.

Instruction Format:

15	14	13	12	11	10	9	8	7	6	5	4	3	2	1	0
0	1	0	0	1	0	1	0	1	1	1	1	1	1	0	0

ILLEGAL

JMP

Jump

JMP

Operation: Destination Address → PC

**Assembler
Syntax:** JMP <ea>

Attributes: Unsized

Description: Program execution continues at the effective address specified by the instruction. The address is specified by the control addressing modes.

Condition Codes: Not affected.

Instruction Format:

15	14	13	12	11	10	9	8	7	6	5	4	3	2	1	0
0	1	0	0	1	1	1	0	1	1	\multicolumn{3}{c}{Mode}	\multicolumn{3}{c}{Register}

				Effective Address				
				Mode		Register		

Instruction Fields:

Effective Address field — Specifies the address of the next instruction. Only control addressing modes are allowed as shown:

Addr. Mode	Mode	Register
Dn	–	–
An	–	–
(An)	010	reg. number:An
(An)+	–	–
–(An)	–	–
(d$_{16}$,An)	101	reg. number:An
(d$_8$,An,Xn)	110	reg. number:An

Addr. Mode	Mode	Register
(xxx).W	111	000
(xxx).L	111	001
#<data>	–	–
(d$_{16}$,PC)	111	010
(d$_8$,PC,Xn)	111	011

JSR

Jump to Subroutine

JSR

Operation: SP − 4 → SP; PC → (SP);
Destination Address → PC

**Assembler
Syntax:** JSR <ea>

Attributes: Unsized

Description: The long word address of the instruction immediately following the JSR instruction is pushed onto the system stack. Program execution then continues at the address specified in the instruction.

Condition Codes: Not affected.

Instruction Format:

15	14	13	12	11	10	9	8	7	6	5	4	3	2	1	0
0	1	0	0	1	1	1	0	1	0		Mode			Register	
										Effective Address					

Instruction Fields:
Effective Address field — Specifies the address of the next instruction. Only control addressing modes are allowed as shown:

Addr. Mode	Mode	Register
Dn	—	—
An	—	—
(An)	010	reg. number:An
(An)+	—	—
−(An)	—	—
(d₁₆,An)	101	reg. number:An
(d₈,An,Xn)	110	reg. number:An

Addr. Mode	Mode	Register
(xxx).W	111	000
(xxx).L	111	001
#<data>	—	—
(d₁₆,PC)	111	010
(d₈,PC,Xn)	111	011

LEA

Load Effective Address

LEA

Operation: <ea> → An

**Assembler
Syntax:** LEA <ea>,An

Attributes: Size = (Long)

Description: The effective address is loaded into the specified address register. All 32 bits of the address register are affected by this instruction.

Condition Codes: Not affected.

Instruction Format:

15	14	13	12	11	10	9	8	7	6	5	4	3	2	1	0
0	1	0	0		Register		1	1	1		Mode			Register	
					An					Effective Address					

Instruction Fields:
Register field — Specifies the address register which is to be loaded with the effective address.
Effective Address field — Specifies the address to be loaded into the address register. Only control addressing modes are allowed as shown:

Addr. Mode	Mode	Register
Dn	—	—
An	—	—
(An)	010	reg. number:An
(An)+	—	—
−(An)	—	—
(d₁₆,An)	101	reg. number:An
(d₈,An,Xn)	110	reg. number:An

Addr. Mode	Mode	Register
(xxx).W	111	000
(xxx).L	111	001
#<data>	—	—
(d₁₆,PC)	111	010
(d₈,PC,Xn)	111	011

LINK

Link and Allocate

Operation: SP − 4 → SP; An → (SP);
SP → An; SP + d → SP

**Assembler
Syntax:** LINK An, #<displacement>

Attributes: Size = Unsized

Description: The current content of the specified address register is pushed onto the stack. After the push, the address register is loaded from the updated stack pointer. Finally, the 16-bit sign-extended displacement operand is added to the stack pointer. The content of the address register occupies one long word on the stack. A negative displacement is specified to allocate stack area.

Condition Codes: Not affected.

Instruction Format:

15	14	13	12	11	10	9	8	7	6	5	4	3	2	1	0
0	1	0	0	1	1	1	0	0	1	0	1	0	Register		

Word Displacement

Instruction Fields:
Register field — Specifies the address register through which the link is to be constructed.
Displacement field — Specifies the twos complement integer which is to be added to the stack pointer.

Note: LINK and UNLK can be used to maintain a linked list of local data and parameter areas on the stack for nested subroutine calls.

LSL, LSR

Logical Shift

Operation: Destination Shifted by<count> → Destination

**Assembler
Syntax:** LSd Dx,Dy
LSd #<data>,Dy
LSd <ea>
where d is direction, L or R

Attributes: Size = (Byte, Word, Long)

Description: Shift the bits of the operand in the direction (L or R) specified. The carry bit receives the last bit shifted out of the operand. The shift count for the shifting of a register may be specified in two different ways:
1. Immediate — the shift count is specified in the instruction (shift range 1-8).
2. Register — the shift count is contained in a data register specified in the instruction (shift count modulo 64).

The size of the operation may be specified to be byte, word, or long. The content of memory may be shifted one bit only, and the operand size is restricted to a word.

For LSL, the operand is shifted left; the number of positions shifted is the shift count. Bits shifted out of the high order bit go to both the carry and the extend bits; zeroes are shifted into the low order bit.

LSL:

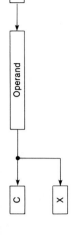

For LSR, the operand is shifted right; the number of positions shifted is the shift count. Bits shifted out of the low order bit go to both the carry and the extend bits; zeroes are shifted into the high order bit.

LSR:

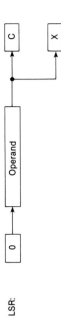

Logical Shift

Condition Codes:

X	N	Z	V	C
*	*	*	0	*

N   Set if the result is negative. Cleared otherwise.
Z   Set if the result is zero. Cleared otherwise.
V   Always cleared.
C   Set according to the last bit shifted out of the operand. Cleared for a shift count of zero.
X   Set according to the last bit shifted out of the operand. Unaffected for a shift count of zero.

Instruction Format (Register Shifts):

15	14	13	12	11	10	9	8	7	6	5	4	3	2	1	0
1	1	1	0	Count/Register			dr	Size		i/r	0	1	Register		

Instruction Field (Register Shifts):

Count/Register field —
If i/r = 0, the shift count is specified in this field. The values 0, 1-7 represent a range of 8, 1 to 7 respectively.
If i/r = 1, the shift count (modulo 64) is contained in the data register specified in this field.

dr field — Specifies the direction of the shift:
0—shift right.
1—shift left.

Size field — Specifies the size of the operation:
00—byte operation.
01—word operation.
10—long operation.

i/r field —
If i/r = 0, Specifies immediate shift count.
If i/r = 1, Specifies register shift count.

Register field — Specifies a data register whose content is to be shifted.

Instruction Format (Memory Shifts):

15	14	13	12	11	10	9	8	7	6	5	4	3	2	1	0
1	1	1	0	0	0	1	dr	1	1	Effective Address					
										Mode			Register		

Instruction Fields (Memory Shifts):

dr field — Specifies the direction of the shift:
0—shift right.
1—shift left.

Effective Address field — Specifies the operand to be shifted. Only memory alterable addressing modes are allowed as shown:

LSL, LSR

Addr. Mode	Mode	Register
Dn	—	—
An	—	—
(An)	010	reg. number:An
(An)+	011	reg. number:An
-(An)	100	reg. number:An
(d$_{16}$,An)	101	reg. number:An
(d$_8$,An,Xn)	110	reg. number:An

LSL, LSR

Logical Shift

Addr. Mode	Mode	Register
(xxx).W	111	000
(xxx).L	111	001
#<data>	—	—
(d$_{16}$,PC)	—	—
(d$_8$,PC,Xn)	—	—

MOVE
Move Data from Source to Destination

Operation: Source → Destination

**Assembler
Syntax:** MOVE <ea>, <ea>

Attributes: Size = (Byte, Word, Long)

Description: Move the content of the source to the destination location. The data is examined as it is moved, and the condition codes set accordingly. The size of the operation may be specified to be byte, word, or long.

Condition Codes:

X	N	Z	V	C
—	*	*	0	0

N Set if the result is negative. Cleared otherwise.
Z Set if the result is zero. Cleared otherwise.
V Always cleared.
C Always cleared.
X Not affected.

Instruction Format:

15	14	13	12	11	10	9	8	7	6	5	4	3	2	1	0
0	0	Size		Destination			Mode			Source			Mode		Register

Destination: Register / Mode ; Source: Mode / Register

Instruction Fields:

Size field — Specifies the size of the operand to be moved:
01—byte operation.
11—word operation.
10—long operation.

Destination Effective Address field — Specifies the destination location. Only data alterable addressing modes are allowed as shown:

Addr. Mode	Mode	Register
Dn	000	reg. number:An
An	—	—
(An)	010	reg. number:An
(An)+	011	reg. number:An
−(An)	100	reg. number:An
(d₁₆,An)	101	reg. number:An
(d₈,An,Xn)	110	reg. number:An

Addr. Mode	Mode	Register
(xxx).W	111	000
(xxx).L	111	001
#<data>	—	—
(d₁₆,PC)	—	—
(d₈,PC,Xn)	—	—

MOVE
Move Data from Source to Destination

Source Effective Address field — Specifies the source operand. All addressing modes are allowed as shown:

Addr. Mode	Mode	Register
Dn	000	reg. number:Dn
An*	001	reg. number:An
(An)	010	reg. number:An
(An)+	011	reg. number:An
−(An)	100	reg. number:An
(d₁₆,An)	101	reg. number:An
(d₈,An,Xn)	110	reg. number:An

Addr. Mode	Mode	Register
(xxx).W	111	000
(xxx).L	111	001
#<data>	111	100
(d₁₆,PC)	111	010
(d₈,PC,Xn)	111	011

*For byte size operation, address register direct is not allowed.

Notes: 1. MOVEA is used when the destination is an address register. Most assemblers automatically make this distinction.
2. MOVEQ can also be used for certain operations on data registers.

MOVE

372

MOVEA

Move Address

Operation: Source → Destination

Assembler Syntax: MOVEA <ea>,An

Attributes: Size = (Word, Long)

Description: Move the content of the source to the destination address register. The size of the operation may be specified to be word or long. Word size source operands are sign extended to 32 bit quantities before the operation is done.

Condition Codes: Not affected.

Instruction Format:

15	14	13	12	11	10	9	8	7	6	5	4	3	2	1	0
0	0	Size		Destination Register			0	0	1	Source					
										Mode			Register		

Instruction Fields:

Size field — Specifies the size of the operand to be moved:
11 — Word operation. The source operand is sign-extended to a long operand and all 32 bits are loaded into the address register.
10 — Long operation.

Destination Register field — Specifies the destination address register.

Source Effective Address field — Specifies the location of source operand. All addressing modes are allowed as shown:

Addr. Mode	Mode	Register
Dn	000	reg. number:Dn
An	001	reg. number:An
(An)	010	reg. number:An
(An)+	011	reg. number:An
-(An)	100	reg. number:An
(d16,An)	101	reg. number:An
(d8,An,Xn)	110	reg. number:An

Addr. Mode	Mode	Register
(xxx).W	111	000
(xxx).L	111	001
#<data>	111	100
(d16,PC)	111	010
(d8,PC,Xn)	111	011

MOVE from CCR

Move from the Condition Code Register

Operation: CCR → Destination

Assembler Syntax: MOVE CCR,<ea>

Attributes: Size = (Word)

Description: The content of the status register is moved to the destination location. The source operand is a word, but only the low order byte contains the condition codes. The upper byte is all zeroes.

Condition Codes: Not affected.

Instruction Format:

15	14	13	12	11	10	9	8	7	6	5	4	3	2	1	0
0	1	0	0	0	0	1	0	1	1	Effective Address					
										Mode			Register		

Instruction Fields:

Effective Address field — Specifies the destination location. Only data alterable addressing modes are allowed as shown:

Addr. Mode	Mode	Register
Dn	000	reg. number:Dn
An	—	—
(An)	010	reg. number:An
(An)+	011	reg. number:An
-(An)	100	reg. number:An
(d16,An)	101	reg. number:An
(d8,An,Xn)	110	reg. number:An

Addr. Mode	Mode	Register
(xxx).W	111	000
(xxx).L	111	001
#<data>	—	—
(d16,PC)	—	—
(d8,PC,Xn)	—	—

Note: MOVE from CCR is a word operation. ANDI, ORI, and EORI to CCR are byte operations.

MOVE to CCR

Move to the Condition Code Register

Operation: Source → CCR

Assembler Syntax: MOVE <ea>,CCR

Attributes: Size = (Word)

Description: The content of the source operand is moved to the condition codes. The source operand is a word, but only the low order byte is used to update the condition codes. The upper byte is ignored.

Condition Codes:

X	N	Z	V	C
*	*	*	*	*

N Set the same as bit 3 of the source operand.
Z Set the same as bit 2 of the source operand.
V Set the same as bit 1 of the source operand.
C Set the same as bit 0 of the source operand.
X Set the same as bit 4 of the source operand.

Instruction Format:

15	14	13	12	11	10	9	8	7	6	5	4	3	2	1	0
0	1	0	0	0	1	0	0	1	1		Effective Address				
											Mode			Register	

Instruction Fields:

Effective Address field — Specifies the location of the source operand. Only data addressing modes are allowed as shown:

Addr. Mode	Mode	Register
Dn	000	reg. number:Dn
An	—	—
(An)	010	reg. number:An
(An)+	011	reg. number:An
-(An)	100	reg. number:An
(d16,An)	101	reg. number:An
(d8,An,Xn)	110	reg. number:An

Addr. Mode	Mode	Register
(xxx).W	111	000
(xxx).L	111	001
#<data>	111	100
(d16,PC)	111	010
(d8,PC,Xn)	111	011

Note: MOVE to CCR is a word operation. ANDI, ORI, and EORI to CCR are byte operations.

MOVE from SR

Move from the Status Register

Operation: SR → Destination

Assembler Syntax: MOVE SR,<ea>

Attributes: Size = (Word)

Description: The content of the status register is moved to the destination location. The operand size is a word.

Condition Codes: Not affected.

Instruction Format:

15	14	13	12	11	10	9	8	7	6	5	4	3	2	1	0
0	1	0	0	0	0	0	0	1	1		Effective Address				
											Mode			Register	

Instruction Fields:

Effective Address field — Specifies the destination location. Only data alterable addressing modes are allowed as shown:

Addr. Mode	Mode	Register
Dn	000	reg. number:Dn
An	—	—
(An)	010	reg. number:An
(An)+	011	reg. number:An
-(An)	100	reg. number:An
(d16,An)	101	reg. number:An
(d8,An,Xn)	110	reg. number:An

Addr. Mode	Mode	Register
(xxx).W	111	000
(xxx).L	111	001
#<data>	—	—
(d16,PC)	—	—
(d8,PC,Xn)	—	—

Note: A memory destination is read before it is written to.

MOVE from SR

Move from the Status Register
(Privileged Instruction)

Operation: If supervisor state
then SR→Destination
else TRAP;

Assembler Syntax: MOVE SR,<ea>

Attributes: Size = (Word)

Description: The content of the status register is moved to the destination location. The operand size is a word.

Condition Codes: Not affected.

Instruction Format:

15	14	13	12	11	10	9	8	7	6	5	4	3	2	1	0
0	1	0	0	0	0	0	0	1	1		Effective Address				
											Mode			Register	

Instruction Fields:
Effective Address field — Specifies the destination location. Only data alterable addressing modes are allowed as shown:

Addr. Mode	Mode	Register
Dn	000	reg. number:Dn
An	–	–
(An)	010	reg. number:An
(An)+	011	reg. number:An
-(An)	100	reg. number:An
(d16,An)	101	reg. number:An
(d8,An,Xn)	110	reg. number:An

Addr. Mode	Mode	Register
(xxx).W	111	000
(xxx).L	111	001
#<data>	–	–
(d16,PC)	–	–
(d8,PC,Xn)	–	–

Note: Use the MOVE from CCR instruction to access only the condition codes.

MOVE to SR

Move to the Status Register
(Privileged Instruction)

Operation: If supervisor state
then Source→SR
else TRAP;

Assembler Syntax: MOVE <ea>,SR

Attributes: Size = (Word)

Description: The content of the source operand is moved to the status register. The source operand is a word and all bits of the status register are affected.

Condition Codes: Set according to the source operand.

Instruction Format:

15	14	13	12	11	10	9	8	7	6	5	4	3	2	1	0
0	1	0	0	0	1	1	0	1	1		Effective Address				
											Mode			Register	

Instruction Fields:
Effective Address field — Specifies the location of the source operand. Only data addressing modes are allowed as shown:

Addr. Mode	Mode	Register
Dn	000	reg. number:Dn
An	–	–
(An)	010	reg. number:An
(An)+	011	reg. number:An
-(An)	100	reg. number:An
(d16,An)	101	reg. number:An
(d8,An,Xn)	110	reg. number:An

Addr. Mode	Mode	Register
(xxx).W	111	000
(xxx).L	111	001
#<data>	111	100
(d16,PC)	111	010
(d8,PC,Xn)	111	011

MOVE USP

Move User Stack Pointer
(Privileged Instruction)

Operation: If supervisor state
then USP→An or An→USP
else TRAP;

Assembler
Syntax: MOVE USP,An
Move An,USP

Attributes: Size = (Long)

Description: The contents of the user stack pointer are transferred to or from the specified address register.

Condition Codes: Not affected.

Instruction Format:

15	14	13	12	11	10	9	8	7	6	5	4	3	2	1	0
0	1	0	0	1	1	1	0	0	1	1	0	dr	Register		

Instruction Fields:

dr field — Specifies the direction of transfer:
0—transfer the address register to the USP.
1—transfer the USP to the address register.
Register field — Specifies the address register to or from which the user stack pointer is to be transferred.

MOVEC

Move Control Register
(Privileged Instruction)

Operation: If supervisor state
then Rc→Rn or Rn→Rc
else TRAP;

Assembler
Syntax: MOVEC Rc,Rn
MOVEC Rn,Rc

Attributes: Size = (Long)

Description: Copy the contents of the specified control register (Rc) to the specified general register or copy the contents of the specified general register to the specified control register. This is always a 32-bit transfer even though the control register may be implemented with fewer bits. Unimplemented bits are read as zeros.

Condition Codes: Not affected.

Instruction Format:

15	14	13	12	11	10	9	8	7	6	5	4	3	2	1	0
0	1	0	0	1	1	1	0	0	1	1	1	1	1	0	1
A/D	Register			Control Register											dr

Instruction Fields:

dr field — Specifies the direction of the transfer:
0—control register to general register.
1—general register to control register.
A/D field — Specifies the type of general register:
0—data register.
1—address register.
Register field — Specifies the register number.
Control Register field — Specifies the control register.

Hex	Control Register
000	Source Function Code (SFC) register.
001	Destination Function Code (DFC) register.
800	User Stack Pointer (USP).
801	Vector Base Register (VBR).

All other codes cause an illegal instruction exception.

MOVEM

Move Multiple Registers

MOVEM

Operation: Registers → Destination
Source → Registers

Assembler MOVEM register list,<ea>
Syntax: MOVEM <ea>,register list

Attributes: Size = (Word, Long)

Description: Selected registers are transferred to or from consecutive memory locations starting at the location specified by the effective address. A register is transferred if the bit corresponding to that register is set in the mask field. The instruction selects how much of each register is transferred; either the entire long word can be moved or just the low order word. In the case of a word transfer to the registers, each word is sign-extended to 32 bits (including data registers) and the resulting long word loaded into the associated register.

MOVEM allows three forms of address modes: the control modes, the predecrement mode, or the postincrement mode. If the effective address is in one of the control modes, the registers are transferred starting at the specified address and up through higher addresses. The order of transfer is from data register 0 to data register 7, then from address register 0 to address register 7.

If the effective address is the predecrement mode, only a register to memory operation is allowed. The registers are stored starting at the specified address minus the operand length (2 or 4) and down through lower addresses. The order of storing is from address register 7 to address register 0, then from data register 7 to data register 0. The decremented address register is updated to contain the address of the last word stored.

If the effective address is the postincrement mode, only a memory to register operation is allowed. The registers are loaded starting at the specified address and up through higher addresses. The order of loading is the same as for the control mode addressing. The incremented address register is updated to contain the address of the last word loaded plus the operand length (2 or 4).

Condition Codes: Not affected.

Instruction Format:

15	14	13	12	11	10	9	8	7	6	5	4	3	2	1	0
0	1	0	0	1	dr	0	0	1	Sz			Mode			Register
												Effective Address			

Register List Mask

MOVEM

Move Multiple Registers

MOVEM

Instruction Fields:

dr field — Specifies the direction of the transfer:
0—register to memory.
1—memory to register.

Sz field — Specifies the size of the registers being transferred:
0—word transfer.
1—long transfer.

Effective Address field — Specifies the memory address to or from which the registers are to be moved.

For register to memory transfers, only control alterable addressing modes or the predecrement addressing mode are allowed as shown:

Addr. Mode	Mode	Register
Dn	—	—
An	—	—
(An)	010	reg. number:An
(An)+	—	—
-(An)	100	reg. number:An
(d₁₆,An)	101	reg. number:An
(d₈,An,Xn)	110	reg. number:An

Addr. Mode	Mode	Register
(xxx).W	111	000
(xxx).L	111	001
#<data>	—	—
(d₁₆,PC)	—	—
(d₈,PC,Xn)	—	—

For memory to register transfers, only control addressing modes or the postincrement addressing mode are allowed as shown:

Addr. Mode	Mode	Register
Dn	—	—
An	—	—
(An)	010	reg. number:An
(An)+	011	reg. number:An
-(An)	—	—
(d₁₆,An)	101	reg. number:An
(d₈,An,Xn)	110	reg. number:An

Addr. Mode	Mode	Register
(xxx).W	111	000
(xxx).L	111	001
#<data>	—	—
(d₁₆,PC)	111	010
(d₈,PC,Xn)	111	011

Register List Mask field — Specifies which registers are to be transferred. The low order bit corresponds to the first register to be transferred; the high bit corresponds to the last register to be transferred. Thus, both for control modes and for the postincrement mode addresses, the mask correspondence is

15	14	13	12	11	10	9	8	7	6	5	4	3	2	1	0
A7	A6	A5	A4	A3	A2	A1	A0	D7	D6	D5	D4	D3	D2	D1	D0

while for the predecrement mode addresses, the mask correspondence is

15	14	13	12	11	10	9	8	7	6	5	4	3	2	1	0
D0	D1	D2	D3	D4	D5	D6	D7	A0	A1	A2	A3	A4	A5	A6	A7

Note: An extra read bus cycle occurs for memory operands. This accesses an operand at one address higher than the last register image required.

377

MOVEP

Move Peripheral Data

MOVEP

Operation: Source → Destination

Assembler
Syntax: MOVEP Dx,(d,Ay)
MOVEP (d,Ay)Dx

Attributes: Size = (Word, Long)

Description: Data is transferred between a data register and alternate bytes of memory, starting at the location specified and incrementing by two. The high order byte of the data register is transferred first and the low order byte is transferred last. The memory address is specified using the address register indirect plus 16-bit displacement addressing mode. This instruction is designed to work with 8-bit peripherals on a 16-bit data bus. If the address is even, all the transfers are made on the high order half of the data bus; if the address is odd, all the transfers are made on the low order half of the data bus. On an 8- or 32-bit bus, the instruction still accesses every other byte.

Example: Long transfer to/from an even address.

Byte organization in register

31		24 23		16 15		8 7		0
Hi-Order		Mid-Upper		Mid-Lower		Low-Order		

Byte organization in memory (low address at top)

15		8 7		0
Hi-Order				
Mid-Upper				
Mid-Lower				
Low-Order				

Example: Word transfer to/from an odd address.

Byte organization in register

31		24 23		16 15		8 7		0
				Hi-Order		Low-Order		

Byte organization in memory (low address at top)

15		8 7		0
		Hi-Order		
		Low-Order		

MOVEP

Move Peripheral Data

MOVEP

Condition Codes: Not affected.

Instruction Format:

15	14	13	12	11	10	9	8	7	6	5	4	3	2	1	0
0	0	0	0	Data Register			Op-Mode			0	0	1	Address Register		

Displacement

Instruction Fields:

Data Register field — Specifies the data register to or from which the data is to be transferred.

Op-Mode field — Specifies the direction and size of the operation:
100—transfer word from memory to register.
101—transfer long from memory to register.
110—transfer word from register to memory.
111—transfer long from register to memory.

Address Register field — Specifies the address register which is used in the address register indirect plus displacement addressing mode.

Displacement field — Specifies the displacement which is used in calculating the operand address.

378

MOVEQ

Move Quick

Operation: Immediate Data → Destination

Assembler Syntax: MOVEQ #<data>,Dn

Attributes: Size = (Long)

Description: Move immediate data to a data register. The data is contained in an 8-bit field within the operation word. The data is sign-extended to a long operand and all 32 bits are transferred to the data register.

Condition Codes:

X	N	Z	V	C
—	*	*	0	0

N   Set if the result is negative. Cleared otherwise.
Z   Set if the result is zero. Cleared otherwise.
V   Always cleared.
C   Always cleared.
X   Not affected.

Instruction Format:

15	14	13	12	11	10	9	8	7	6	5	4	3	2	1	0
0	1	1	1	Register			0	Data							

Instruction Fields:
Register field — Specifies the data register to be loaded.
Data field — 8 bits of data which are sign extended to a long operand.

MOVES

Move Address Space (Privileged Instruction)

Operation: If supervisor state
then Rn→Destination [DFC] or Source [SFC]→Rn
else TRAP;

Assembler Syntax: MOVES Rn,<ea>
MOVES <ea>,Rn

Attributes: Size = (Byte, Word, Long)

Description: Move the byte, word, or long operand from the specified general register to a location within the address space specified by the destination function code (DFC) register. Or, move the byte, word, or long operand from a location within the address space specified by the source function code (SFC) register to the specified general register.

If the destination is a data register, the source operand replaces the corresponding low-order bits of that data register. If the destination is an address register, the source operand is sign-extended to 32 bits and then loaded into that address register.

Condition Codes: Not affected.

Instruction Format:

15	14	13	12	11	10	9	8	7	6	5	4	3	2	1	0
0	0	0	0	1	1	1	0	Size			Mode			Register	
A/D	Register			dr	0	0	0				0	0	0	0	0

(Effective Address: Mode, Register)

Instruction Fields:
Size field — Specifies the size of the operation:
00—byte operation.
01—word operation.
10—long operation.
Effective Address field — Specifies the source or destination location within the alternate address space. Only alterable memory addressing modes are allowed as shown:

MOVES

MOVES

Move Address Space (Privileged Instruction)

Addr. Mode	Mode	Register
Dn	–	–
An	–	–
(An)	010	reg. number:An
(An)+	011	reg. number:An
–(An)	100	reg. number:An
(d16,An)	101	reg. number:An
(d8,An,Xn)	110	reg. number:An

Addr. Mode	Mode	Register
(xxx).W	111	000
(xxx).L	111	001
#<data>	–	–
(d16,PC)	–	–
(d8,PC,Xn)	–	–

A/D field — Specifies the type of general register:
0—data register.
1—address register.
Register field — Specifies the register number.
dr field — Specifies the direction of the transfer:
0—from <ea> to general register.
1—from general register to <ea>.

MOVES.x An,(An)+
  or
MOVES.x An,–(An)

where An is the same address register for both source and destination and is an undefined operation. The value stored in memory is undefined.

NOTE

On the MC68010 and MC68020 implementations, the value stored is the incremented or the decremented value of An. This implementation may not appear on future devices.

MULS

MULS

Signed Multiply

Operation: Source·Destination→Destination

Assembler Syntax: MULS<ea>,Dn   16×16→32

Attributes: Size = (Word)

Description: Multiply two signed operands yielding a signed result. The operation is performed using signed arithmetic.

The multiplier and multiplicand are both word operands and the result is long word operand. A register operand is taken from the low order word, the upper word is unused. All 32 bits of the product are saved in the destination data register.

Condition Codes:

X	N	Z	V	C
–	*	*	0	0

N Set if the result is negative. Cleared otherwise.
Z Set if the result is zero. Cleared otherwise.
V Set if overflow. Cleared otherwise.
C Always cleared.
X Not affected.

Instruction Format:

15	14	13	12	11	10	9	8	7	6	5	4	3	2	1	0
1	1	0	0	Register Dn			1	1	1	Effective Address					
										Mode			Register		

Instruction Fields:
Register field — Specifies one of the data registers. This field always specifies the destination.
Effective Address field — Specifies the source operand. Only data addressing modes are allowed as shown:

Addr. Mode	Mode	Register
Dn	000	reg. number:Dn
An	–	–
(An)	010	reg. number:An
(An)+	011	reg. number:An
–(An)	100	reg. number:An
(d16,An)	101	reg. number:An
(d8,An,Xn)	110	reg. number:An

Addr. Mode	Mode	Register
(xxx).W	111	000
(xxx).L	111	001
#<data>	111	100
(d16,PC)	111	010
(d8,PC,Xn)	111	011

MULU
Unsigned Multiply

Operation: Source•Destination→Destination

**Assembler
Syntax:** MULS<ea>,Dn   16 × 16→32

Attributes: Size = (Word)

Description: Multiply two unsigned operands yielding a unsigned result. The operation is performed using unsigned arithmetic.

The multiplier and multiplicand are both word operands and the result is a long word operand. A register operand is taken from the low order word, the upper word is unused. All 32 bits of the product are saved in the destination data register.

Condition Codes:

X	N	Z	V	C
–	*	*	0	0

N Set if the result is negative. Cleared otherwise.
Z Set if the result is zero. Cleared otherwise.
V Set if overflow. Cleared otherwise.
C Always cleared.
X Not affected.

Instruction Format:

15	14	13	12	11	10	9	8	7	6	5	4	3	2	1	0
1	1	0	0		Register Dn		0	1	1			Effective Address Mode			Register

Instruction Fields:
Register field — Specifies one of the data registers. This field always specifies the destination.
Effective Address field — Specifies the source operand. Only data addressing modes are allowed as shown:

Addr. Mode	Mode	Register
Dn	000	reg. number:Dn
An	–	–
(An)	010	reg. number:An
(An)+	011	reg. number:An
–(An)	100	reg. number:An
(d16,An)	101	reg. number:An
(d8,An,Xn)	110	reg. number:An

Addr. Mode	Mode	Register
(xxx).W	111	000
(xxx).L	111	001
#<data>	111	100
(d16,PC)	111	010
(d8,PC,Xn)	111	011

NBCD
Negate Decimal with Extend

Operation: 0 – Destination₁₀ – X → Destination

**Assembler
Syntax:** NBCD <ea>

Attributes: Size = (Byte)

Description: The operand addressed as the destination and the extend bit are subtracted from zero. The operation is performed using decimal arithmetic. The result is saved in the destination location. This instruction produces the tens complement of the destination if the extend bit is clear, the nines complement if the extend bit is set. This is a byte operation only.

Condition Codes:

X	N	Z	V	C
*	U	*	U	*

N Undefined.
Z Cleared if the result is non-zero. Unchanged otherwise.
V Undefined.
C Set if a borrow (decimal) was generated. Cleared otherwise.
X Set the same as the carry bit.

NOTE

Normally the Z condition code bit is set via programming before the start of an operation. This allows successful tests for zero results upon completion of multiple precision operations.

Instruction Format:

15	14	13	12	11	10	9	8	7	6	5	4	3	2	1	0
0	1	0	0	1	0	0	0	0	0			Effective Address Mode			Register

Instruction Fields:
Effective Address field — Specifies the destination operand. Only data alterable addressing modes are allowed as shown:

Addr. Mode	Mode	Register
Dn	000	reg. number:Dn
An	–	–
(An)	010	reg. number:An
(An)+	011	reg. number:An
–(An)	100	reg. number:An
(d16,An)	101	reg. number:An
(d8,An,Xn)	110	reg. number:An

Addr. Mode	Mode	Register
(xxx).W	111	000
(xxx).L	111	001
#<data>	–	–
(d16,PC)	–	–
(d8,PC,Xn)	–	–

NEG

Negate

Operation: 0 – Destination → Destination

Assembler Syntax: NEG <ea>

Attributes: Size = (Byte, Word, Long)

Description: The operand addressed as the destination is subtracted from zero. The result is stored in the destination location. The size of the operation may be specified to be byte, word, or long.

Condition Codes:

X	N	Z	V	C
*	*	*	*	*

N Set if the result is negative. Cleared otherwise.
Z Set if the result is zero. Cleared otherwise.
V Set if an overflow is generated. Cleared otherwise.
C Cleared if the result is zero. Set otherwise.
X Set the same as the carry bit.

Instruction Format:

15	14	13	12	11	10	9	8	7	6	5	4	3	2	1	0
0	1	0	0	0	1	0	0		Size		Effective Address Mode			Register	

Instruction Fields:
Size field — Specifies the size of the operation.
00—byte operation.
01—word operation.
10—long operation.
Effective Address field — Specifies the destination operand. Only data alterable addressing modes are allowed as shown:

Addr. Mode	Mode	Register
Dn	000	reg. number:Dn
An	–	–
(An)	010	reg. number:An
(An)+	011	reg. number:An
-(An)	100	reg. number:An
(d$_{16}$,An)	101	reg. number:An
(d$_8$,An,Xn)	110	reg. number:An

Addr. Mode	Mode	Register
(xxx).W	111	000
(xxx).L	111	001
#<data>	–	–
(d$_{16}$,PC)	–	–
(d$_8$,PC,Xn)	–	–

NEGX

Negate with Extend

Operation: 0 – Destination – X → Destination

Assembler Syntax: NEGX <ea>

Attributes: Size = (Byte, Word, Long)

Description: The operand addressed as the destination and the extend bit are subtracted from zero. The result is stored in the destination location. The size of the operation may be specified to be byte, word, or long.

Condition Codes:

X	N	Z	V	C
*	*	*	*	*

N Set if the result is negative. Cleared otherwise.
Z Cleared if the result is non-zero. Unchanged otherwise.
V Set if an overflow is generated. Cleared otherwise.
C Set if a borrow is generated. Cleared otherwise.
X Set the same as the carry bit.

NOTE

Normally the Z condition code bit is set via programming before the start of an operation. This allows successful tests for zero results upon completion of multiple-precision operations.

Instruction Format:

15	14	13	12	11	10	9	8	7	6	5	4	3	2	1	0
0	1	0	0	0	0	0	0		Size		Effective Address Mode			Register	

Instruction Fields:
Size field — Specifies the size of the operation.
00—byte operation.
01—word operation.
10—long operation.
Effective Address field — Specifies the destination operand. Only data alterable addressing modes are allowed as shown:

Addr. Mode	Mode	Register
Dn	000	reg. number:Dn
An	–	–
(An)	010	reg. number:An
(An)+	011	reg. number:An
-(An)	100	reg. number:An

Addr. Mode	Mode	Register
(xxx).W	111	000
(xxx).L	111	001
#<data>	–	–

382

NOP

No Operation

Operation: None

Assembler Syntax: NOP

Attributes: Unsized

Description: No operation occurs. The processor state, other than the program counter, is unaffected. Execution continues with the instruction following the NOP instruction. The NOP instruction does not complete execution until all pending bus cycles are completed. This allows synchronization of the pipeline to be accomplished, and prevents instruction overlap.

Condition Codes: Not affected.

Instruction Format:

15	14	13	12	11	10	9	8	7	6	5	4	3	2	1	0
0	1	0	0	1	1	1	0	0	1	1	1	0	0	0	1

NOT

Logical Complement

Operation: ~ Destination → Destination

Assembler Syntax: NOT <ea>

Attributes: Size = (Byte, Word, Long)

Description: The ones complements of the destination operand is taken and the result is stored in the destination location. The size of the operation may be specified to be byte, word, or long.

Condition Codes:

X	N	Z	V	C
—	*	*	0	0

N Set if the result is negative. Cleared otherwise.
Z Set if the result is zero. Cleared otherwise.
V Always cleared.
C Always cleared.
X Not affected.

Instruction Format:

15	14	13	12	11	10	9	8	7	6	5	4	3	2	1	0
0	1	0	0	0	1	1	0	Size		Effective Address					
										Mode			Register		

Instruction Fields:

Size field — Specifies the size of the operation.
  00—byte operation.
  01—word operation.
  10—long operation.
Effective Address field — Specifies the destination operand. Only data alterable addressing modes are allowed as shown:

Addr. Mode	Mode	Register	Addr. Mode	Mode	Register
Dn	000	reg. number:Dn	(xxx).W	111	000
An	—	—	(xxx).L	111	001
(An)	010	reg. number:An	#<data>	—	—
(An)+	011	reg. number:An			
−(An)	100	reg. number:An			
(d$_{16}$,An)	101	reg. number:An	(d$_{16}$,PC)	—	—
(d$_8$,An,Xn)	110	reg. number:An	(d$_8$,PC,Xn)	—	—

383

OR

Inclusive OR Logical

OR

Operation: Source v Destination → Destination

Assembler
Syntax: OR <ea>,Dn
OR Dn,<ea>

Attributes: Size = (Byte, Word, Long)

Description: Inclusive OR the source operand to the destination operand and store the result in the destination location. The size of the operation may be specified to be byte, word, or long. The contents of an address register may not be used as an operand.

Condition Codes:

X	N	Z	V	C
—	*	*	0	0

N Set if the most significant bit of the result is set. Cleared otherwise.
Z Set if the result is zero. Cleared otherwise.
V Always cleared.
C Always cleared.
X Not affected.

Instruction Format:

15	14	13	12	11	10	9	8	7	6	5	4	3	2	1	0
1	0	0	0		Register			Op-Mode			Effective Address				
											Mode			Register	

Instruction Fields:
Register field — Specifies any of the eight data registers.
Op-Mode field —

Byte	Word	Long	Operation
000	001	010	(<ea>)v(<Dn>)→<Dn>
100	101	110	(<Dn>)v(<ea>)→<ea>

Effective Address field —
If the location specified is a source operand then only data addressing modes are allowed as shown:

Addr. Mode	Mode	Register
Dn	000	reg. number:Dn
An	—	—
(An)	010	reg. number:An
(An)+	011	reg. number:An
-(An)	100	reg. number:An
(d16,An)	101	reg. number:An
(d8,An,Xn)	110	reg. number:An

Addr. Mode	Mode	Register
(xxx).W	111	000
(xxx).L	111	001
#<data>	111	100
(d16,PC)	111	010
(d8,PC,Xn)	111	011

OR

OR

Inclusive OR Logical

If the location specified is a destination operand then only memory alterable addressing modes are allowed as shown:

Addr. Mode	Mode	Register
Dn	—	—
An	—	—
(An)	010	reg. number:An
(An)+	011	reg. number:An
-(An)	100	reg. number:An
(d16,An)	101	reg. number:An
(d8,An,Xn)	110	reg. number:An

Addr. Mode	Mode	Register
(xxx).W	111	000
(xxx).L	111	001
#<data>	—	—
(d16,PC)	—	—
(d8,PC,Xn)	—	—

Notes: 1. If the destination is a data register, then it cannot be specified by using the destination <ea> mode, but must use the destination Dn mode instead.
2. ORI is used when the source is immediate data. Most assemblers automatically make this distinction.

Inclusive OR Immediate

Operation: Immediate Data v Destination → Destination

Assembler Syntax: ORI #<data>,<ea>

Attributes: Size = (Byte, Word, Long)

Description: Inclusive OR the immediate data to the destination operand and store the result in the destination location. The size of the operation may be specified to be byte, word, or long. The size of the immediate data matches the operation size.

Condition Codes:

X	N	Z	V	C
–	*	*	0	0

N   Set if the most significant bit of the result is set. Cleared otherwise.
Z   Set if the result is zero. Cleared otherwise.
V   Always cleared.
C   Always cleared.
X   Not affected.

Instruction Format:

15	14	13	12	11	10	9	8	7	6	5	4	3	2	1	0
0	0	0	0	0	0	0	0	Size		Effective Address		Mode			Register

15 ... 0
Word Data
Long Data
Byte Data

Instruction Fields:

Size field — Specifies the size of the operation.
00—byte operation.
01—word operation.
10—long operation.

Effective Address field — Specifies the destination operand. Only data alterable addressing modes are allowed as shown:

Addr. Mode	Mode	Register
Dn	000	reg. number:Dn
An	–	–
(An)	010	reg. number:An
(An)+	011	reg. number:An
–(An)	100	reg. number:An
(d16,An)	101	reg. number:An
(d8,An,Xn)	110	reg. number:An

Addr. Mode	Mode	Register
(xxx).W	111	000
(xxx).L	111	001
#<data>	–	–
(d16,PC)	–	–
(d8,PC,Xn)	–	–

Immediate field — (Data immediately following the instruction):
If size = 00, then the data is the low order byte of the immediate word.
If size = 01, then the data is the entire immediate word.
If size = 10, then the data is the next two immediate words.

Inclusive OR Immediate to Condition Codes

Operation: Source v CCR → CCR

Assembler Syntax: ORI #<data>,CCR

Attributes: Size = (Byte)

Description: Inclusive OR the immediate operand with the condition codes and store the result in the low-order byte of the status register.

Condition Codes:

X	N	Z	V	C
*	*	*	*	*

N   Set if bit 3 of immediate operand is one. Unchanged otherwise.
Z   Set if bit 2 of immediate operand is one. Unchanged otherwise.
V   Set if bit 1 of immediate operand is one. Unchanged otherwise.
C   Set if bit 0 of immediate operand is one. Unchanged otherwise.
X   Set if bit 4 of immediate operand is one. Unchanged otherwise.

Instruction Format:

15	14	13	12	11	10	9	8	7	6	5	4	3	2	1	0
0	0	0	0	0	0	0	0	0	0	1	1	1	1	0	0
0	0	0	0	0	0	0	0	Byte Data (8 Bits)							

ORI to SR

Inclusive OR Immediate to the Status Register
(Privileged Instruction)

Operation: If supervisor state
then Source v SR→SR
else TRAP;

Assembler
Syntax: ORI #<data>,SR

Attributes: Size=(Word)

Description: Inclusive OR the immediate operand with the contents of the status register and store the result in the status register. All bits of the status register are affected.

Condition Codes:

X	N	Z	V	C
*	*	*	*	*

N Set if bit 3 of immediate operand is one. Unchanged otherwise.
Z Set if bit 2 of immediate operand is one. Unchanged otherwise.
V Set if bit 1 of immediate operand is one. Unchanged otherwise.
C Set if bit 0 of immediate operand is one. Unchanged otherwise.
X Set if bit 4 of immediate operand is one. Unchanged otherwise.

Instruction Format:

15	14	13	12	11	10	9	8	7	6	5	4	3	2	1	0
0	0	0	0	0	0	0	0	0	1	1	1	1	1	0	0

Word Data (16 Bits)

PEA

Push Effective Address

Operation: SP − 4 →SP; EA→(SP)

Assembler
Syntax: PEA <ea>

Attributes: Size=(Long)

Description: The effective address is computed and pushed onto the stack. A long word address is pushed onto the stack.

Condition Codes: Not affected.

Instruction Format:

15	14	13	12	11	10	9	8	7	6	5	4	3	2	1	0
0	1	0	0	1	0	0	0	0	1			Mode			Register

Effective Address

Instruction Fields:

Effective Address field — Specifies the address to be pushed onto the stack. Only control addressing modes are allowed as shown:

Addr. Mode	Mode	Register	Addr. Mode	Mode	Register
Dn	–	–	(xxx).W	111	000
An	–	–	(xxx).L	111	001
(An)	010	reg. number:An	#<data>	–	–
(An)+	–	–		–	–
–(An)	–	–	(d16,PC)	111	010
(d16,An)	101	reg. number:An	(d8,PC,Xn)	111	011
(d8,An,Xn)	110	reg. number:An			

RESET

RESET

Reset External Devices
(Privileged Instruction)

Operation: If supervisor state
then Assert RESET Line
else TRAP;

**Assembler
Syntax:** RESET

Attributes: Unsized

Description: The reset line is asserted for 124 clocks, causing all external devices to be reset. The processor state, other than the program counter, is unaffected and execution continues with the next instruction.

Condition Codes: Not affected.

Instruction Format:

15	14	13	12	11	10	9	8	7	6	5	4	3	2	1	0
0	1	0	0	1	1	1	0	0	1	1	1	0	0	0	0

ROL
ROR

Rotate (Without Extend)

Operation: Destination Rotated by <count> → Destination

**Assembler
Syntax:** ROd Dx,Dy
ROd #<data>,Dy
ROd <ea>
where d is direction, L or R

Attributes: Size = (Byte, Word, Long)

Description: Rotate the bits of the operand in the direction (L or R) specified. The extend bit is not included in the rotation. The rotate count for the rotation of a register may be specified in two different ways:
1. Immediate — the rotate count is specified in the instruction (rotate range, 1-8).
2. Register → the rotate count is contained in a data register specified in the instruction.

The size of the operation may be specified to be byte, word, or long. The content of memory may be rotated by one bit only and the operand size is restricted to a word.

For ROL, the operand is rotated left; the number of positions rotated is the rotate count. Bits rotated out of the high order bit go to both the carry bit and back into the low order bit. The extend bit is not modified or used.

ROL:

For ROR, the operand is rotated right; the number of positions rotated is the rotate count. Bits shifted out of the low order bit go to both the carry bit and back into high order bit. The extend bit is not modified or used.

ROR:

Condition Codes:

X	N	Z	V	C
—	*	*	0	*

N Set if the most significant bit of the result is set. Cleared otherwise.
Z Set if the result is zero. Cleared otherwise.
V Always cleared.
C Set according to the last bit rotated out of the operand. Cleared for a rotate count of zero.
X Not affected.

ROXL
ROXR

Rotate (Without Extend)

ROXL / ROXR

Rotate with Extend

Operation: Destination Rotated with X by <count> → Destination

Assembler
Syntax:
ROXd Dx,Dy
ROXd #<data>,Dy
ROXd <ea>

Attributes: Size = (Byte, Word, Long)

Description: Rotate the bits of the destination operand in the direction specified. The extend bit (X) is included in the rotation. The rotate count for the rotation of a register may be specified in two different ways:

1. Immediate — the rotate count is specified in the instruction (rotate range, 1-8).
2. Register — the rotate count (modulo 64) is contained in a data register specified in the instruction.

The size of the operation may be specified to be byte, word, or long. The content of memory may be rotated one bit only and the operand size is restricted to a word.

For ROXL, the operand is rotated left; the number of positions rotated is the rotate count. Bits rotated out of the high order bit go to both the carry and extend bits; the previous value of the extend bit is rotated into the low order bit.

ROXL:

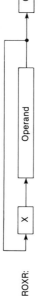

For ROXR, the operand is rotated right; the number of positions shifted is the rotate count. Bits rotated out of the low order bit go to both the carry and extend bits; the previous value of the extend bit is rotated into the high order bit.

ROXR:

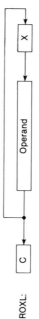

Condition Codes:

X	N	Z	V	C
*	*	*	0	*

N Set if the most significant bit of the result is set. Cleared otherwise.
Z Set if the result is zero. Cleared otherwise.
V Always cleared.
C Set according to the last bit rotated out of the operand. Set to the value of the extend bit for a rotate count of zero.
X Set according to the last bit rotated out of the operand. Unaffected for a rotate count of zero.

Instruction Format (Register Rotate):

15	14	13	12	11	10	9	8	7	6	5	4	3	2	1	0
1	1	1	0	Rotate/ Register			dr	Size		i/r	1	1	Register		

Instruction Fields (Register Rotate):

Rotate/Register field —
If i/r = 0, the rotate count is specified in this field. The values 0, 1-7 represent a range of 8, 1 to 7 respectively.
If i/r = 1, the rotate count (modulo 64) is contained in the data register specified in this field.

dr field — Specifies the direction of the rotate:
0—rotate right.
1—rotate left.

Size field — Specifies the size of the operation:
00—byte operation.
01—word operation.
10—long operation.

i/r field —
If i/r = 0, specifies immediate rotate count.
If i/r = 1, specifies register rotate count.

Register field — Specifies a data register whose content is to be rotated.

Instruction Format (Memory Rotate):

15	14	13	12	11	10	9	8	7	6	5	4	3	2	1	0
1	1	1	0	0	1	1	dr	1	1	Effective Address					
										Mode			Register		

Instruction Fields (Memory Rotate):

dr field — Specifies the direction of the rotate:
0—rotate right.
1—rotate left.

Effective Address field — Specifies the operand to be rotated. Only memory alterable addressing modes are allowed as shown:

Addr. Mode	Mode	Register
Dn	—	—
An	—	—
(An)	010	reg. number:An
(An)+	011	reg. number:An
-(An)	100	reg. number:An
(d16,An)	101	reg. number:An
(d8,An,Xn)	110	reg. number:An

Addr. Mode	Mode	Register
(xxx).W	111	000
(xxx).L	111	001
#<data>	—	—
(d16,PC)	—	—
(d8,PC,Xn)	—	—

ROXL
ROXR

Rotate with Extend

Instruction Format (Register Rotate):

15	14	13	12	11	10	9	8	7	6	5	4	3	2	1	0
1	1	1	0	Rotate/Register			dr	Size		i/r	1	0	Register		

Instruction Fields (Register Rotate):

Rotate/Register field —
If i/r = 0, the rotate count is specified in this field. The values 0, 1-7 represent a range of 8, 1 to 7 respectively.
If i/r = 1, the rotate count (modulo 64) is contained in the data register specified in this field.

dr field — Specifies the direction of the rotate:
0—rotate right.
1—rotate left.

Size field — Specifies the size of the operation:
00—byte operation.
01—word operation.
10—long operation.

i/r field —
If i/r = 0, specifies immediate rotate count.
If i/r = 1, specifies register rotate count.

Register field — Specifies a data register whose content is to be rotated.

Instruction Format (Memory Rotate):

15	14	13	12	11	10	9	8	7	6	5	4	3	2	1	0
1	1	1	0	0	1	0	dr	1	1	Mode			Register		
												Effective Address			

Instruction Fields (Memory Rotate):

dr field — Specifies the direction of the rotate:
0—rotate right.
1—rotate left.

Effective Address field — Specifies the operand to be rotated. Only memory alterable addressing modes are allowed as shown:

Addr. Mode	Mode	Register
Dn	—	—
An	—	—
(An)	010	reg. number:An
(An)+	011	reg. number:An
-(An)	100	reg. number:An
(d16,An)	101	reg. number:An
(d8,An,Xn)	110	reg. number:An

Addr. Mode	Mode	Register
(xxx).W	111	000
(xxx).L	111	001
#<data>	—	—
(d16,PC)	—	—
(d8,PC,Xn)	—	—

RTD

Return and Deallocate Parameters

Operation: (SP) → PC; SP + 4 + d → SP

Assembler Syntax: RTD #<displacement>

Attributes: Unsized

Description: The program counter is pulled from the stack. The previous program counter value is lost. After the program counter is read from the stack, the displacement value (16 bits) is sign-extended to 32 bits and added to the stack pointer.

Condition Codes: Not affected.

Instruction Format:

15	14	13	12	11	10	9	8	7	6	5	4	3	2	1	0
0	1	0	0	1	1	1	0	0	1	1	1	0	1	0	0
							Displacement								

Instruction Field:

Displacement field — Specifies the twos complement integer which is to be sign-extended and added to the stack pointer.

RTE

Return from Exception
(Privileged Instruction)

Operation: If supervisor state
then ((SP)→SR; SP + 2→SP; (SP)→PC; SP + 4→SP;
restore state and deallocate
stack according to (SP))
else TRAP;

Assembler
Syntax: RTE

Attributes: Unsized

Description: The processor state information in the exception stack frame on top of the stack is loaded into the processor. The stack format field in the format/offset word is examined to determine how much information must be restored.

Condition Codes: Set according to the content of the word on the stack.

Instruction Format:

15	14	13	12	11	10	9	8	7	6	5	4	3	2	1	0
0	1	0	0	1	1	1	0	0	1	1	1	0	0	1	1

Format/Offset Word (in stack frame):

15	14	13	12	11	10	9	8	7	6	5	4	3	2	1	0
Format	0	0							Vector Offset						

Instruction Fields:

Format field — This 4-bit field defines the amount of information to be restored.
0000—Short Format, only four words are to be removed from the top of the stack. The status register and program counter are loaded from the stack frame.
1000—MC68010 Long Format, 29 words are removed from the top of the stack. Any others — the processor takes a format error exception.

RTR

Return and Restore Condition Codes

Operation: (SP)→CCR; SP + 2→SP;
(SP)→PC; SP + 4→SP

Assembler
Syntax: RTR

Attributes: Unsized

Description: The condition codes and program counter are pulled from the stack. The previous condition codes and program counter are lost. The supervisor portion of the status register is unaffected.

Condition Codes: Set according to the content of the word on the stack.

Instruction Format:

15	14	13	12	11	10	9	8	7	6	5	4	3	2	1	0
0	1	0	0	1	1	1	0	0	1	1	1	0	1	1	1

RTS

Return from Subroutine

Operation: $(SP) \to PC$; $SP + 4 \to SP$

Assembler Syntax: RTS

Attributes: Unsized

Description: The program counter is pulled from the stack. The previous program counter is lost.

Condition Codes: Not affected.

Instruction Format:

15	14	13	12	11	10	9	8	7	6	5	4	3	2	1	0
0	1	0	0	1	1	1	0	0	1	1	1	0	1	0	1

SBCD

Subtract Decimal with Extend   **SBCD**

Operation: Destination$_{10}$ - Source$_{10}$ - X $\to$ Destination

Assembler Syntax: SBCD Dx,Dy
SBCD -(Ax),-(Ay)

Attributes: Size = (Byte)

Description: Subtract the source operand from the destination operand with the extend bit and store the result in the destination location. The subtraction is performed using decimal arithmetic. The operands may be addressed in two different ways:
1. Data register to data register: The operands are contained in the data registers specified in the instruction.
2. Memory to memory: The operands are addressed with the predecrement addressing mode using the address registers specified in the instruction.

This operation is a byte operation only.

Condition Codes:

X	N	Z	V	C
*	U	*	U	*

N Undefined.
Z Cleared if the result is non-zero. Unchanged otherwise.
V Undefined.
C Set if a borrow (decimal) is generated. Cleared otherwise.
X Set the same as the carry bit.

NOTE

Normally the Z condition code bit is set via programming before the start of an operation. This allows successful tests for zero results upon completion of multiple-precision operations.

Instruction Format:

15	14	13	12	11 10 9	8	7	6	5	4	3	2 1 0
1	0	0	0	Register Dy/Ay	1	0	0	0	0	R/M	Register Dx/Ax

Instruction Fields:

Register Dy/Ay field — Specifies the destination register.
If R/M = 0, specifies a data register.
If R/M = 1, specifies an address register for the predecrement addressing mode.

R/M field — Specifies the operand addressing mode:
0—The operation is data register to data register.
1—The operation is memory to memory.

Register Dx/Ax field — Specifies the source register:
If R/M = 0, specifies a data register.
If R/M = 1, specifies an address register for the predecrement addressing mode.

STOP

Load Status Register and Stop
(Privileged Instruction)

Operation: If supervisor state
then (Immediate Data → SR; STOP)
else TRAP;

Assembler
Syntax: STOP #<data>

Attributes: Unsized

Description: The immediate operand is moved into the entire status register; the program counter is advanced to point to the next instruction and the processor stops fetching and executing instructions. Execution of instructions resumes when a trace, interrupt, or reset exception occurs. A trace exception will occur if the trace state is on when the STOP instruction begins execution. If an interrupt request is asserted with a priority higher than the priority level set by the immediate data, an interrupt exception occurs, otherwise, the interrupt request has no effect. If the bit of the immediate data corresponding to the S-bit is off, execution of the instruction will cause a privilege violation. External reset will always initiate reset exception processing.

Condition Codes: Set according to the immediate operand.

Instruction Format:

15	14	13	12	11	10	9	8	7	6	5	4	3	2	1	0
0	1	0	0	1	1	1	0	0	1	1	1	0	0	1	0
						Immediate Data									

Instruction Fields:
Immediate field — Specifies the data to be loaded into the status register.

Scc

Set According to Condition

Operation: If Condition True
then 1s → Destination
else 0s → Destination;

Assembler
Syntax: Scc <ea>

Attributes: Size = (Byte)

Description: The specified condition code is tested; if the condition is true, the byte specified by the effective address is set to TRUE (all ones), otherwise that byte is set to FALSE (all zeroes). "cc" may specify the following conditions:

CC	carry clear	0100	$\bar{C}$		LS	low or same	0011	$C + Z$
CS	carry set	0101	C		LT	less than	1101	$N \cdot \bar{V} + \bar{N} \cdot V$
EQ	equal	0111	Z		MI	minus	1011	N
F	never true	0001	0		NE	not equal	0110	$\bar{Z}$
GE	greater or equal	1100	$N \cdot V + \bar{N} \cdot \bar{V}$		PL	plus	1010	$\bar{N}$
GT	greater than	1110	$N \cdot V \cdot \bar{Z} + \bar{N} \cdot \bar{V} \cdot \bar{Z}$		T	always true	0000	1
HI	high	0010	$\bar{C} \cdot \bar{Z}$		VC	overflow clear	1000	$\bar{V}$
LE	less or equal	1111	$Z + N \cdot \bar{V} + \bar{N} \cdot V$		VS	overflow set	1001	V

Condition Codes: Not affected.

Instruction Format:

15	14	13	12	11	10	9	8	7	6	5	4	3	2	1	0
0	1	0	1		Condition			1	1			Effective Address			
											Mode			Register	

Instruction Fields:
Condition field — One of sixteen conditions discussed in description.
Effective Address field — Specifies the location in which the true/false byte is to be stored. Only data alterable addressing modes are allowed as shown:

Addr. Mode	Mode	Register
Dn	000	reg. number:Dn
An	—	—
(An)	010	reg. number:An
(An)+	011	reg. number:An
-(An)	100	reg. number:An
(d16,An)	101	reg. number:An
(d8,An,Xn)	110	reg. number:An

Addr. Mode	Mode	Register
(xxx).W	111	000
(xxx).L	111	001
#<data>	—	—
(d16,PC)	—	—
(d8,PC,Xn)	—	—

Note: 1. An arithmetic one and zero result may be generated by following the Scc instruction with a NEG instruction.

SUB

Subtract Binary

Operation: Destination − Source → Destination

Assembler Syntax: SUB <ea>,Dn
SUB Dn,<ea>

Attributes: Size = (Byte, Word, Long)

Description: Subtract the source operand from the destination operand and store the result in the destination. The size of the operation may be specified to be byte, word, or long. The mode of the instruction indicates which operand is the source and which is the destination as well as the operand size.

Condition Codes:

X	N	Z	V	C
*	*	*	*	*

N Set if the result is negative. Cleared otherwise.
Z Set if the result is zero. Cleared otherwise.
V Set if an overflow is generated. Cleared otherwise.
C Set if a borrow is generated. Cleared otherwise.
X Set the same as the carry bit.

The condition codes are not affected if a subtraction from an address register is made.

Instruction Format:

15	14	13	12	11	10	9	8	7	6	5	4	3	2	1	0
1	0	0	1		Register			Op-Mode			Effective Address				
											Mode			Register	

Instruction Fields:

Register field — Specifies any of the eight data registers.

Op-Mode field —

Byte	Word	Long	Operation
000	001	010	<Dn> − <ea> → <Dn>
100	101	110	<ea> − <Dn> → <ea>

Effective Address field — Determines addressing mode:
If the location specified is a source operand, then all addressing modes are allowed as shown:

Addr. Mode	Mode	Register
Dn	000	reg. number:Dn
An*	001	reg. number:An
(An)	010	reg. number:An
(An)+	011	reg. number:An
−(An)	100	reg. number:An
(d16,An)	101	reg. number:An
(d8,An,Xn)	110	reg. number:An

Addr. Mode	Mode	Register
(xxx).W	111	000
(xxx).L	111	001
#<data>	111	100
(d16,PC)	111	010
(d8,PC,Xn)	111	011

*For byte size operation, address register direct is not allowed.

SUB SUB

Subtract Binary

If the location specified is a destination operand, then only alterable memory addressing modes are allowed as shown:

Addr. Mode	Mode	Register
Dn	—	—
An	—	—
(An)	010	reg. number:An
(An)+	011	reg. number:An
−(An)	100	reg. number:An
(d16,An)	101	reg. number:An
(d8,An,Xn)	110	reg. number:An

Addr. Mode	Mode	Register
(xxx).W	111	000
(xxx).L	111	001
#<data>	—	—
(d16,PC)	—	—
(d8,PC,Xn)	—	—

Notes: 1. If the destination is a data register, then it cannot be specified by using the destination <ea> mode, but must use the destination Dn mode instead.
2. SUBA is used when the destination is an address register. SUBI and SUBQ are used when the source is immediate data. Most assemblers automatically make this distinction.

SUBA

Subtract Address

SUBA

Operation: Destination − Source → Destination

Assembler Syntax: SUBA <ea>,An

Attributes: Size = (Word, Long)

Description: Subtract the source operand from the destination address register and store the result in the address register. The size of the operation may be specified to be word or long. Word size source operands are sign extended to 32 bit quantities before the operation is done.

Condition Codes: Not affected.

Instruction Format:

15	14	13	12	11	10	9	8	7	6	5	4	3	2	1	0
1	0	0	1	Register			Op-Mode			Effective Address					
										Mode			Register		

Instruction Fields:

Register field — Specifies any of the eight address registers. This is always the destination.

Op-Mode field — Specifies the size of the operation:
011—Word operation. The source operand is sign-extended to a long operand and the operation is performed on the address register using all 32 bits.
111—Long operations.

Effective Address field — Specifies the source operand. All addressing modes are allowed as shown:

Addr. Mode	Mode	Register
Dn	000	reg. number:Dn
An	001	reg. number:An
(An)	010	reg. number:An
(An)+	011	reg. number:An
−(An)	100	reg. number:An
(d16,An)	101	reg. number:An
(d8,An,Xn)	110	reg. number:An

Addr. Mode	Mode	Register
(xxx).W	111	000
(xxx).L	111	001
#<data>	111	100
(d16,PC)	111	010
(d8,PC,Xn)	111	011

SUBI

Subtract Immediate

SUBI

Operation: Destination − Immediate Data → Destination

Assembler Syntax: SUBI #<data>,<ea>

Attributes: Size = (Byte, Word, Long)

Description: Subtract the immediate data from the destination operand and store the result in the destination location. The size of the operation may be specified to be byte, word, or long. The size of the immediate data matches the operation size.

Condition Codes:

X	N	Z	V	C
*	*	*	*	*

N Set if the result is negative. Cleared otherwise.
Z Set if the result is zero. Cleared otherwise.
V Set if an overflow is generated. Cleared otherwise.
C Set if a borrow is generated. Cleared otherwise.
X Set the same as the carry bit.

Instruction Format:

15	14	13	12	11	10	9	8	7	6	5	4	3	2	1	0
0	0	0	0	0	1	0	0	Size		Effective Address					
										Mode			Register		
Word Data										Byte Data					
Long Data															

Instruction Fields:

Size field — Specifies the size of the operation.
00—byte operation.
01—word operation.
10—long operation.

Effective Address field — Specifies the destination operand. Only data alterable addressing modes are allowed as shown:

Addr. Mode	Mode	Register
Dn	000	reg. number:Dn
An	—	—
(An)	010	reg. number:An
(An)+	011	reg. number:An
−(An)	100	reg. number:An
(d16,An)	101	reg. number:An
(d8,An,Xn)	110	reg. number:An

Addr. Mode	Mode	Register
(xxx).W	111	000
(xxx).L	111	001
#<data>	—	—
(d16,PC)	—	—
(d8,PC,Xn)	—	—

Immediate field — (Data immediately following the instruction)
If size = 00, then the data is the low order byte of the immediate word.
If size = 01, then the data is the entire immediate word.
If size = 10, then the data is the next two immediate words.

SUBQ

Subtract Quick

Operation: Destination − Immediate Data → Destination

**Assembler
Syntax:** SUBQ #<data>,<ea>

Attributes: Size = (Byte, Word, Long)

Description: Subtract the immediate data from the destination operand. The data range is from 1-8. The size of the operation may be specified to be byte, word, or long. Word and long operations are also allowed on the address registers and the condition codes are not affected. When subtracting from address registers, the entire destination address register is used, regardless of the operation size.

Condition Codes:

X	N	Z	V	C
*	*	*	*	*

N Set if the result is negative. Cleared otherwise.
Z Set if the result is zero. Cleared otherwise.
V Set if an overflow is generated. Cleared otherwise.
C Set if a borrow is generated. Cleared otherwise.
X Set the same as the carry bit.

The condition codes are not affected if a subtraction from an address register is made.

Instruction Format:

15	14	13	12	11	10	9	8	7	6	5	4	3	2	1	0
0	1	0	1		Data		1		Size			Effective Address			
												Mode			Register

Instruction Fields:

Data field — Three bits of immediate data, 0, 1-7 representing a range of 8, 1 to 7 respectively.
Size field — Specifies the size of the operation:
  00—byte operation.
  01—word operation.
  10—long operation.
Effective Address field — Specifies the destination location. Only alterable addressing modes are allowed as shown:

Addr. Mode	Mode	Register
Dn	000	reg. number:Dn
An*	001	reg. number:An
(An)	010	reg. number:An
(An)+	011	reg. number:An
−(An)	100	reg. number:An
(d16,An)	101	reg. number:An
(d8,An,Xn)	110	reg. number:An

*Word and long only.

SUBX

Subtract with Extend

Operation: Destination − Source − X → Destination

**Assembler
Syntax:** SUBX Dx,Dy
          SUBX −(Ax), −(Ay)

Attributes: Size = (Byte, Word, Long)

Description: Subtract the source operand from the destination operand along with the extend bit and store the result in the destination location. The operands may be addressed in two different ways:
1. Data register to data register: The operands are contained in data registers specified in the instruction.
2. Memory to memory. The operands are contained in memory and addressed with the predecrement addressing mode using the address registers specified in the instruction.
The size of the operand may be specified to be byte, word, or long.

Condition Codes:

X	N	Z	V	C
*	*	*	*	*

N Set if the result is negative. Cleared otherwise.
Z Cleared if the result is non-zero. Unchanged otherwise.
V Set if an overflow is generated. Cleared otherwise.
C Set if a carry is generated. Cleared otherwise.
X Set the same as the carry bit.

NOTE

Normally the Z condition code bit is set via programming before the start of an operation. This allows successful tests for zero results upon completion of multiple-precision operations.

Instruction Format:

15	14	13	12	11	10	9	8	7	6	5	4	3	2	1	0
1	0	0	1		Register Dy/Ay		1		Size		0	0	R/M		Register Dx/Ax

Instruction Fields:

Register Dy/Ay field — Specifies the destination register:
  If R/M = 0, specifies a data register.
  If R/M = 1, specifies an address register for the predecrement addressing mode.
Size field — Specifies the size of the operation:
  00—byte operation.
  01—word operation.
  10—long operation.

Addr. Mode	Mode	Register
(xxx).W	111	000
(xxx).L	111	001
#<data>	—	—
(d16,PC)	—	—
(d8,PC,Xn)	—	—

395

SUBX

Subtract with Extend

R/M field — Specifies the operand addressing mode:
0—The operation is data register to data register.
1—The operation is memory to memory.
Register Dx/Ax field — Specifies the source register:
If R/M = 0, specifies a data register.
If R/M = 1, specifies an address register for the predecrement addressing mode.

SWAP

Swap Register Halves

Operation: Register [31:16] ↔ Register [15:0]

Assembler Syntax: SWAP Dn

Attributes: Size = (Word)

Description: Exchange the 16-bit halves of a data register.

Condition Codes:

X	N	Z	V	C
—	*	*	0	0

N Set if the most significant bit of the 32-bit result is set. Cleared otherwise.
Z Set if the 32-bit result is zero. Cleared otherwise.
V Always cleared.
C Always cleared.
X Not affected.

Instruction Format:

15	14	13	12	11	10	9	8	7	6	5	4	3	2	1	0
0	1	0	0	1	0	0	0	0	1	0	0	0	Register		

Instruction Fields:
Register field — Specifies the data register to swap.

TAS

Test and Set an Operand

TAS

Operation: Destination Tested → Condition Codes; 1→bit 7 of Destination

Assembler Syntax: TAS <ea>

Attributes: Size = (Byte)

Description: Test and set the byte operand addressed by the effective address field. The current value of the operand is tested and N and Z are set accordingly. The high order bit of the operand is set. The operation is indivisible (using a read-modify-write memory cycle) to allow synchronization of several processors.

Condition Codes:

X	N	Z	V	C
—	*	*	0	0

N   Set if the most significant bit of the operand was set. Cleared otherwise.
Z   Set if the operand was zero. Cleared otherwise.
V   Always cleared.
C   Always cleared.
X   Not affected.

Instruction Format:

15	14	13	12	11	10	9	8	7	6	5	4	3	2	1	0
0	1	0	0	1	0	1	0	1	1		Mode			Register	
												Effective Address			

Instruction Fields:

Effective Address field — Specifies the location of the tested operand. Only data alterable addressing modes are allowed as shown:

Addr. Mode	Mode	Register
Dn	000	reg. number:Dn
An	—	—
(An)	010	reg. number:An
(An)+	011	reg. number:An
−(An)	100	reg. number:An
(d$_{16}$,An)	101	reg. number:An
(d$_8$,An,Xn)	110	reg. number:An

Addr. Mode	Mode	Register
(xxx).W	111	000
(xxx).L	111	001
#<data>	—	—
(d$_{16}$,PC)	—	—
(d$_8$,PC,Xn)	—	—

NOTE: Bus error retry is inhibited on the read portion of the TAS read-modify-write bus cycle to ensure system integrity. The bus error exception is always taken.

TRAP

Trap

TRAP

Operation: SSP − 2→SSP; Format/Vector Offset→(SSP); SSP − 4→4→SSP; PC→(SSP); SSP − 2→SSP; SR→(SSP); Vector Address→PC

Assembler Syntax: TRAP #<vector>

Attributes: Unsized

Description: The processor initiates exception processing. The vector number is generated to reference the TRAP instruction exception vector specified by the low order four bits of the instruction. Sixteen TRAP instruction vectors (0-15) are available.

Condition Codes: Not affected.

Instruction Format:

15	14	13	12	11	10	9	8	7	6	5	4	3	2	1	0
0	1	0	0	1	1	1	0	0	1	0	0		Vector		

Instruction Fields:

Vector field — Specifies which trap vector contains the new program counter to be loaded.

TRAPV

Trap on Overflow

Operation: If V then TRAP

Assembler Syntax: TRAPV

Attributes: Unsized

Description: If the overflow condition is set, the processor initiates exception processing. The vector number is generated to reference the TRAPV exception vector. If the overflow condition is clear, no operation is performed and execution continues with the next instruction in sequence.

Condition Codes: Not affected.

Instruction Format:

15	14	13	12	11	10	9	8	7	6	5	4	3	2	1	0
0	1	0	0	1	1	1	0	0	1	1	1	0	1	1	0

TST

Test an Operand

Operation: Destination Tested → Condition Codes

Assembler Syntax: TST <ea>

Attributes: Size = (Byte, Word, Long)

Description: Compare the operand with zero. No results are saved; however, the condition codes are set according to results of the test. The size of the operation may be specified to be byte, word, or long.

Condition Codes:

X	N	Z	V	C
–	*	*	0	0

N Set if the operand is negative. Cleared otherwise.
Z Set if the operand is zero. Cleared otherwise.
V Always cleared.
C Always cleared.
X Not affected.

Instruction Format:

15	14	13	12	11	10	9	8	7	6	5	4	3	2	1	0
0	1	0	0	1	0	1	0	Size		Mode			Register		
										Effective Address					

Instruction Fields:

Size field — Specifies the size of the operation:
00—byte operation.
01—word operation.
10—long operation.

Effective Address field — Specifies the destination operand. Only data alterable addressing modes are allowed as shown:

Addr. Mode	Mode	Register
Dn	000	reg. number:Dn
An	–	–
(An)	010	reg. number:An
(An)+	011	reg. number:An
–(An)	100	reg. number:An
(d16,An)	101	reg. number:An
(d8,An,Xn)	110	reg. number:An

Addr. Mode	Mode	Register
(xxx).W	111	000
(xxx).L	111	001
#<data>	–	–
(d16,PC)	–	–
(d8,PC,Xn)	–	–

UNLK UNLK

Unlink

Operation: An→SP; (SP)→An; SP + 2→SP

**Assembler
Syntax:** UNLK An

Attributes: Unsized

Description: The stack pointer is loaded from the specified address register. The address register is then loaded with the long word pulled from the top of the stack.

Condition Codes: Not affected.

Instruction Format:

15	14	13	12	11	10	9	8	7	6	5	4	3	2	1	0
0	1	0	0	1	1	1	0	0	1	0	1	1	Register		

Instruction Fields:
Register field — Specifies the address register through which the unlinking is to be done.

C

Analog and Digital Converter Devices for Interface

National Semiconductor

Analog-to-Digital Converters

ADC0816, ADC0817 8-Bit μP Compatible A/D Converters with 16-Channel Multiplexer

General Description

The ADC0816, ADC0817 data acquisition component is a monolithic CMOS device with an 8-bit analog-to-digital converter, 16-channel multiplexer and microprocessor compatible control logic. The 8-bit A/D converter uses successive approximation as the conversion technique. The converter features a high impedance chopper stabilized comparator, a 256R voltage divider with analog switch tree and a successive approximation register. The 16-channel multiplexer can directly access any one of 16-single-ended analog signals, and provides the logic for additional channel expansion. Signal conditioning of any analog input signal is eased by direct access to the multiplexer output, and to the input of the 8-bit A/D converter.

The device eliminates the need for external zero and full-scale adjustments. Easy interfacing to microprocessors is provided by the latched and decoded multiplexer address inputs and latched TTL TRI-STATE® outputs.

The design of the ADC0816, ADC0817 has been optimized by incorporating the most desirable aspects of several A/D conversion techniques. The ADC0816, ADC0817 offers high speed, high accuracy, minimal temperature dependence, excellent long-term accuracy and repeatability, and consumes minimal power. These features make this device ideally suited to applications from process and machine control to consumer and automotive applications. For similar performance in an 8-channel, 28-pin,

8-bit A/D converter, see the ADC0808, ADC0809 data sheet.

Features

- Resolution — 8-bits
- Total unadjusted error — ± 1/2 LSB and ± 1 LSB
- No missing codes
- Conversion time — 100 μs
- Single supply — 5 V_{DC}
- Operates ratiometrically or with 5 V_{DC} or analog span adjusted voltage reference
- 16-channel multiplexer with latched control logic
- Easy interface to all microprocessors, or operates "stand alone"
- Outputs meet T²L voltage level specifications
- 0V to 5V analog input voltage range with single 5V supply
- No zero or full-scale adjust required
- Standard hermetic or molded 40-pin DIP package
- Temperature range −40°C to +85°C or −55°C to +125°C
- Low power consumption — 15 mW
- Latched TRI-STATE® output
- Direct access to "comparator in" and "multiplexer out" for signal conditioning

Block Diagram

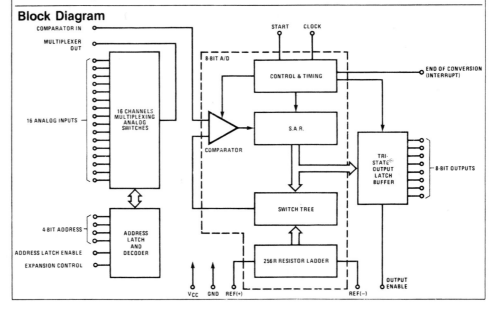

Absolute Maximum Ratings (Notes 1 and 2)

Supply Voltage (V$_{CC}$) (Note 3)	6.5V
Voltage at Any Pin Except Control Inputs	−0.3V to (V$_{CC}$ + 0.3V)
Voltage at Control Inputs (START, OE, CLOCK, ALE, EXPANSION CONTROL, ADD A, ADD B, ADD C, ADD D)	−0.3V to 15V
Storage Temperature Range	−65°C to +150°C
Package Dissipation at T$_A$ = 25°C	875 mW
Lead Temperature (Soldering, 10 seconds)	300°C

Operating Ratings (Notes 1 and 2)

Temperature Range (Note 1)	T$_{MIN}$ ≤ T$_A$ ≤ T$_{MAX}$
ADC0816CJ	−55°C ≤ T$_A$ ≤ +125°C
ADC0816CCJ, ADC0816CCN, ADC0817CCN	−40°C ≤ T$_A$ ≤ +85°C
Range of V$_{CC}$ (Note 1)	4.5 V$_{DC}$ to 6.0 V$_{DC}$
Voltage at Any Pin Except Control Inputs	0V to V$_{CC}$
Voltage at Control Inputs (START, OE, CLOCK, ALE, EXPANSION CONTROL, ADD A, ADD B, ADD C, ADD D)	0V to 15V

Electrical Characteristics

Converter Specifications: V$_{CC}$ = 5 V$_{DC}$ = V$_{REF(+)}$, V$_{REF(-)}$ = GND, V$_{IN}$ = V$_{COMPARATOR\,IN}$, T$_{MIN}$ ≤ T$_A$ ≤ T$_{MAX}$ and f$_{CLK}$ = 640 kHz unless otherwise stated.

Parameter		Conditions	Min	Typ	Max	Units
	ADC0816					
	Total Unadjusted Error	25°C			± 1/2	LSB
	(Note 5)	T$_{MIN}$ to T$_{MAX}$			± 3/4	LSB
	ADC0817					
	Total Unadjusted Error	0°C to 70°C			± 1	LSB
	(Note 5)	T$_{MIN}$ to T$_{MAX}$			± 1 1/4	LSB
	Input Resistance	From Ref(+) to Ref(−)	1.0	4.5		kΩ
	Analog Input Voltage Range	(Note 4) V(+) or V(−)	GND−0.10		V$_{CC}$+0.10	V$_{DC}$
V$_{REF(+)}$	Voltage, Top of Ladder	Measured at Ref(+)		V$_{CC}$	V$_{CC}$+0.1	V
$\frac{V_{REF(+)} + V_{REF(-)}}{2}$	Voltage, Center of Ladder		V$_{CC}$/2−0.1	V$_{CC}$/2	V$_{CC}$/2 + 0.1	V
V$_{REF(-)}$	Voltage, Bottom of Ladder	Measured at Ref(−)	−0.1	0		V
	Comparator Input Current	f$_c$ = 640 kHz, (Note 6)	−2	± 0.5	2	μA

Electrical Characteristics

Digital Levels and DC Specifications: ADC0816CJ 4.5V ≤ V$_{CC}$ ≤ 5.5V, −55°C ≤ T$_A$ ≤ +125°C unless otherwise noted. ADC0816CCJ, ADC0816CCN, ADC0817CCN 4.75V ≤ V$_{CC}$ ≤ 5.25V, −40°C ≤ T$_A$ ≤ +85°C unless otherwise noted.

Parameter		Conditions	Min	Typ	Max	Units
ANALOG MULTIPLEXER						
R$_{ON}$	Analog Multiplexer ON	(Any Selected Channel)				
	Resistance	T$_A$ = 25°C, R$_L$ = 10k		1.5	3	kΩ
		T$_A$ = 85°C			6	kΩ
		T$_A$ = 125°C			9	kΩ
ΔR$_{ON}$	Δ ON Resistance Between Any	(Any Selected Channel)				
	2 Channels	R$_L$ = 10k		75		Ω
I$_{OFF(+)}$	OFF Channel Leakage Current	V$_{CC}$ = 5V, V$_{IN}$ = 5V,				
		T$_A$ = 25°C		10	200	nA
		T$_{MIN}$ to T$_{MAX}$			1.0	μA
I$_{OFF(-)}$	OFF Channel Leakage Current	V$_{CC}$ = 5V, V$_{IN}$ = 0,				
		T$_A$ = 25°C	−200			nA
		T$_{MIN}$ to T$_{MAX}$	−1.0			μA
CONTROL INPUTS						
V$_{IN(1)}$	Logical "1" Input Voltage		V$_{CC}$−1.5			V
V$_{IN(0)}$	Logical "0" Input Voltage				1.5	V
I$_{IN(1)}$	Logical "1" Input Current (The Control Inputs)	V$_{IN}$ = 15V			1.0	μA
I$_{IN(0)}$	Logical "0" Input Current (The Control Inputs)	V$_{IN}$ = 0	−1.0			μA
I$_{CC}$	Supply Current	f$_{CLK}$ = 640 kHz		0.3	3.0	mA

Electrical Characteristics (Continued)

Digital Levels and DC Specifications: ADC0816CJ 4.5V ≤ V_{CC} ≤ 5.5V, −55°C ≤ T_A ≤ +125°C unless otherwise noted. ADC0816CCJ, ADC0816CCN, ADC0817CCN 4.75V ≤ V_{CC} ≤ 5.25V, −40°C ≤ T_A ≤ +85°C unless otherwise noted.

Parameter		Conditions	Min	Typ	Max	Units
DATA OUTPUTS AND EOC (INTERRUPT)						
$V_{OUT(1)}$	Logical "1" Output Voltage	$I_O = -360\ \mu A$	$V_{CC}-0.4$			V
$V_{OUT(0)}$	Logical "0" Output Voltage	$I_O = 1.6$ mA			0.45	V
$V_{OUT(0)}$	Logical "0" Output Voltage EOC	$I_O = 1.2$ mA			0.45	V
I_{OUT}	TRI-STATE Output Current	$V_O = V_{CC}$			3	μA
		$V_O = 0$	−3			μA

Electrical Characteristics

Timing Specifications: $V_{CC} = V_{REF(+)} = 5V$, $V_{REF(-)} = GND$, $t_r = t_f = 20$ ns and $T_A = 25°C$ unless otherwise noted.

Symbol	Parameter	Conditions	Min	Typ	Max	Units
t_{WS}	Minimum Start Pulse Width	(Figure 5)		100	200	ns
t_{WALE}	Minimum ALE Pulse Width	(Figure 5)		100	200	ns
t_s	Minimum Address Set-Up Time	(Figure 5)		25	50	ns
t_H	Minimum Address Hold Time	(Figure 5)		25	50	ns
t_D	Analog MUX Delay Time From ALE	$R_S = 0\Omega$ (Figure 5)		1	2.5	μs
t_{H1}, t_{H0}	OE Control to Q Logic State	$C_L = 50$ pF, $R_L = 10k$ (Figure 8)		125	250	ns
t_{1H}, t_{0H}	OE Control to Hi-Z	$C_L = 10$ pF, $R_L = 10k$ (Figure 8)		125	250	ns
t_c	Conversion Time	$f_c = 640$ kHz, (Figure 5) (Note 7)	90	100	116	μs
f_c	Clock Frequency		10	640	1280	kHz
t_{EOC}	EOC Delay Time	(Figure 5)	0		$8 + 2\ \mu s$	Clock Periods
C_{IN}	Input Capacitance	At Control Inputs		10	15	pF
C_{OUT}	TRI-STATE Output Capacitance	At TRI-STATE Outputs, (Note 7)		10	15	pF

Note 1: Absolute maximum ratings are those values beyond which the life of the device may be impaired.

Note 2: All voltages are measured with respect to GND, unless otherwise specified.

Note 3: A zener diode exists, internally, from V_{CC} to GND and has a typical breakdown voltage of 7 V_{DC}.

Note 4: Two on-chip diodes are tied to each analog input which will forward conduct for analog input voltages one diode drop below ground or one diode drop greater than the V_{CC} supply. The spec allows 100 mV forward bias of either diode. This means that as long as the analog V_{IN} does not exceed the supply voltage by more than 100 mV, the output code will be correct. To achieve an absolute 0 V_{DC} to 5 V_{DC} input voltage range will therefore require a minimum supply voltage of 4.900 V_{DC} over temperature variations, initial tolerance and loading.

Note 5: Total unadjusted error includes offset, full-scale, and linearity errors. See Figure 3. None of these A/Ds requires a zero or full-scale adjust. However, if an all zero code is desired for an analog input other than 0.0V, or if a narrow full-scale span exists (for example: 0.5V to 4.5V full-scale) the reference voltages can be adjusted to achieve this. See Figure 13.

Note 6: Comparator input current is a bias current into or out of the chopper stabilized comparator. The bias current varies directly with clock frequency and has little temperature dependence (Figure 6). See paragraph 4.0.

Note 7: The outputs of the data register are updated one clock cycle before the rising edge of EOC.

Functional Description

Multiplexer: The device contains a 16-channel single-ended analog signal multiplexer. A particular input channel is selected by using the address decoder. Table I shows the input states for the address line and the expansion control line to select any channel. The address is latched into the decoder on the low-to-high transition of the address latch enable signal.

TABLE I

SELECTED ANALOG CHANNEL	ADDRESS LINE				EXPANSION CONTROL
	D	C	B	A	
IN0	L	L	L	L	H
IN1	L	L	L	H	H
IN2	L	L	H	L	H
IN3	L	L	H	H	H
IN4	L	H	L	L	H
IN5	L	H	L	H	H
IN6	L	H	H	L	H
IN7	L	H	H	H	H
IN8	H	L	L	L	H
IN9	H	L	L	H	H
IN10	H	L	H	L	H
IN11	H	L	H	H	H
IN12	H	H	L	L	H
IN13	H	H	L	H	H
IN14	H	H	H	L	H
IN15	H	H	H	H	H
All Channels OFF	X	X	X	X	L

X = don't care

Additional single-ended analog signals can be multiplexed to the A/D converter by disabling all the multiplexer inputs using the expansion control. The additional external signals are connected to the comparator input and the device ground. Additional signal conditioning (i.e., prescaling, sample and hold, instrumentation amplification, etc.) may also be added between the analog input signal and the comparator input.

CONVERTER CHARACTERISTICS

The Converter

The heart of this single chip data acquisition system is its 8-bit analog-to-digital converter. The converter is designed to give fast, accurate, and repeatable conversions over a wide range of temperatures. The converter is partitioned into 3 major sections: the 256R ladder network, the successive approximation register, and the comparator. The converter's digital outputs are positive true.

The 256R ladder network approach *(Figure 1)* was chosen over the conventional R/2R ladder because of its inherent monotonicity, which guarantees no missing digital codes. Monotonicity is particularly important in closed loop feedback control systems. A non-monotonic relationship can cause oscillations that will be catastrophic for the system. Additionally, the 256R network does not cause load variations on the reference voltage.

The bottom resistor and the top resistor of the ladder network in *Figure 1* are not the same value as the remainder of the network. The difference in these resistors causes the output characteristic to be symmetrical with the zero and full-scale points of the transfer curve. The first output transition occurs when the analog signal has reached + 1/2 LSB and succeeding output transitions occur every 1 LSB later up to full-scale.

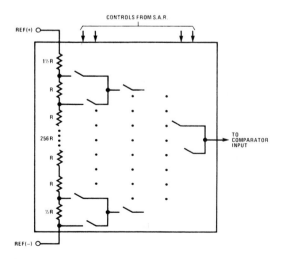

FIGURE 1. Resistor Ladder and Switch Tree

Functional Description (Continued)

The successive approximation register (SAR) performs 8 iterations to approximate the input voltage. For any SAR type converter, n-iterations are required for an n-bit converter. In the ADC0816, ADC0817, the approximation technique is extended to 8 bits using the 256R network.

The A/D converter's successive approximation register (SAR) is reset on the positive edge of the start conversion (SC) pulse. The conversion is begun on the falling edge of the start conversion pulse. A conversion in process will be interrupted by receipt of a new start conversion pulse. Continuous conversion may be accomplished by tying the end-of-conversion (EOC) output to the SC input. If used in this mode, an external start conversion pulse should be applied after power up. End-of-conversion will go low between 0 and 8 clock pulses after the rising edge of start conversion.

The most important section of the A/D converter is the comparator. It is this section which is responsible for the ultimate accuracy of the entire converter. It is also the comparator drift which has the greatest influence on the repeatability of the device. A chopper-stabilized comparator provides the most effective method of satisfying all the converter requirements.

The chopper-stabilized comparator converts the DC input signal into an AC signal. This signal is then fed through a high gain AC amplifier and has the DC level restored. This technique limits the drift component of the amplifier since the drift is a DC component which is not passed by the AC amplifier. This makes the entire A/D converter extremely insensitive to temperature, long term drift and input offset errors.

Figure 4 shows a typical error curve for the ADC0816 as measured using the procedures outlined in AN-179.

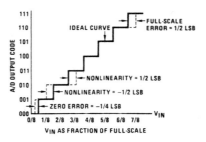

FIGURE 2. 3-Bit A/D Transfer Curve

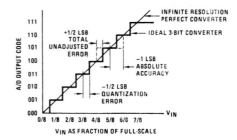

FIGURE 3. 3-Bit A/D Absolute Accuracy Curve

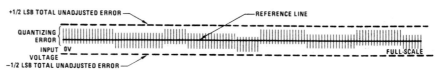

FIGURE 4. Typical Error Curve

Connection Diagram

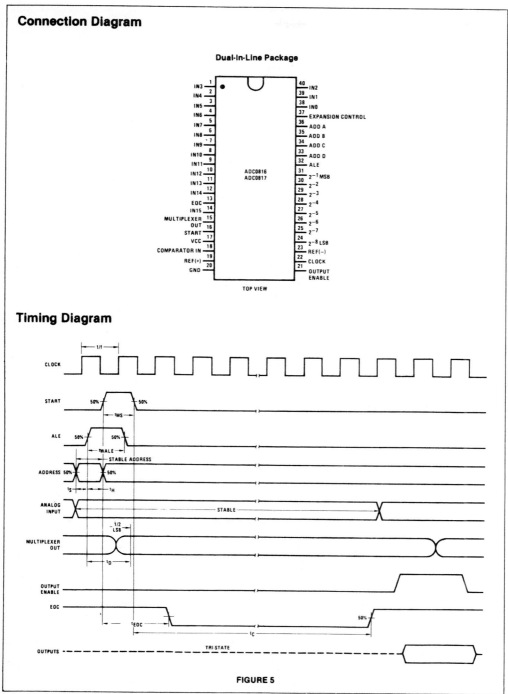

Dual-In-Line Package

```
          IN3   1        40  IN2
          IN4   2        39  IN1
          IN5   3        38  IN0
          IN6   4        37  EXPANSION CONTROL
          IN7   5        36  ADD A
          IN8   6        35  ADD B
          IN9   7        34  ADD C
         IN10   8        33  ADD D
         IN11   9        32  ALE
         IN12  10        31  2⁻¹ MSB
         IN13  11   ADC0816   30  2⁻²
         IN14  12   ADC0817   29  2⁻³
          EOC  13        28  2⁻⁴
         IN15  14        27  2⁻⁵
  MULTIPLEXER  15        26  2⁻⁶
         OUT   16        25  2⁻⁷
        START  17        24  2⁻⁸ LSB
          VCC  18        23  REF(−)
COMPARATOR IN  19        22  CLOCK
       REF(+)  20        21  OUTPUT ENABLE
          GND
```

TOP VIEW

Timing Diagram

FIGURE 5

Typical Performance Characteristics

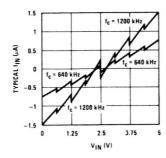

FIGURE 6. Comparator I_{IN} vs V_{IN}
($V_{CC} = V_{REF} = 5V$)

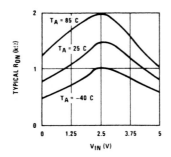

FIGURE 7. Multiplexer R_{ON} vs V_{IN}
($V_{CC} = V_{REF} = 5V$)

TRI-STATE® Test Circuits and Timing Diagrams

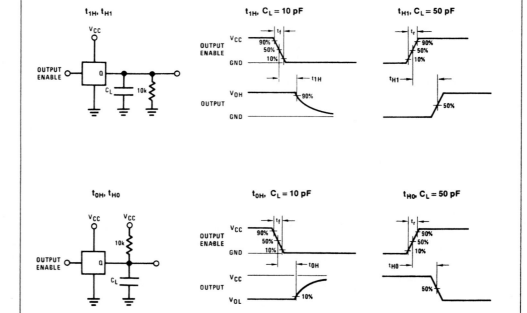

FIGURE 8

Applications Information

OPERATION

1.0 Ratiometric Conversion

The ADC0816, ADC0817 is designed as a complete Data Acquisition System (DAS) for ratiometric conversion systems. In ratiometric systems, the physical variable being measured is expressed as a percentage of full-scale which is not necessarily related to an absolute standard. The voltage input to the ADC0816 is expressed by the equation

$$\frac{V_{IN}}{V_{fs} - V_Z} = \frac{D_X}{D_{MAX} - D_{MIN}} \qquad (1)$$

V_{IN} = Input voltage into the ADC0816
V_{fs} = Full-scale voltage
V_Z = Zero voltage
D_X = Data point being measured
D_{MAX} = Maximum data limit
D_{MIN} = Minimum data limit

A good example of a ratiometric transducer is a potentiometer used as a position sensor. The position of the wiper is directly proportional to the output voltage which is a ratio of the full-scale voltage across it. Since the data is represented as a proportion of full-scale, reference requirements are greatly reduced, eliminating a large source of error and cost for many applications. A major advantage of the ADC0816, ADC0817 is that the input voltage range is equal to the supply range so the transducers can be connected directly across the supply and their outputs connected directly into the multiplexer inputs, *(Figure 9)*.

Ratiometric transducers such as potentiometers, strain gauges, thermistor bridges, pressure transducers, etc., are suitable for measuring proportional relationships; however, many types of measurements must be referred to an absolute standard such as voltage or current. This means a system reference must be used which relates the full-scale voltage to the standard volt. For example, if $V_{CC} = V_{REF} = 5.12V$, then the full-scale range is divided into 256 standard steps. The smallest standard step is 1 LSB which is then 20 mV.

2.0 Resistor Ladder Limitations

The voltages from the resistor ladder are compared to the selected input 8 times in a conversion. These voltages are coupled to the comparator via an analog switch tree which is referenced to the supply. The voltages at the top, center and bottom of the ladder must be controlled to maintain proper operation.

The top of the ladder, Ref(+), should not be more positive than the supply, and the bottom of the ladder, Ref(−), should not be more negative than ground. The center of the ladder voltage must also be near the center of the supply because the analog switch tree changes from N-channel switches to P-channel switches. These limitations are automatically satisfied in ratiometric systems and can be easily met in ground referenced systems.

Figure 10 shows a ground referenced system with a separate supply and reference. In this system, the supply must be trimmed to match the reference voltage. For instance, if a 5.12V reference is used, the supply should be adjusted to the same voltage within 0.1V.

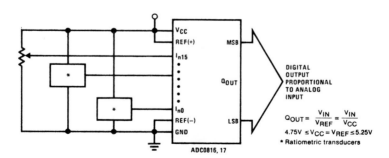

FIGURE 9. Ratiometric Conversion System

Applications Information (Continued)

The ADC0816 needs less than a milliamp of supply current so developing the supply from the reference is readily accomplished. In *Figure 11* a ground referenced system is shown which generates the supply from the reference. The buffer shown can be an op amp of sufficient drive to supply the milliamp of supply current and the desired bus drive, or if a capacitive bus is driven by the outputs a large capacitor will supply the transient supply current as seen in *Figure 12*. The LM301 is overcompensated to insure stability when loaded by the 10 μF output capacitor.

The top and bottom ladder voltages cannot exceed V_{CC} and ground, respectively, but they can be symmetrically less than V_{CC} and greater than ground. The center of the ladder voltage should always be near the center of the supply. The sensitivity of the converter can be increased, (i.e., size of the LSB steps decreased) by using a symmetrical reference system. In *Figure 13*, a 2.5V reference is symmetrically centered about $V_{CC}/2$ since the same current flows in identical resistors. This system with a 2.5V reference allows the LSB to be half the size of the LSB in a 5V reference system.

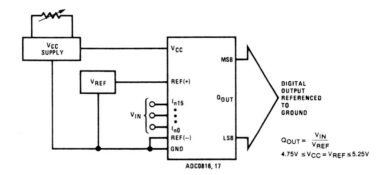

FIGURE 10. Ground Referenced
Conversion System Using Trimmed Supply

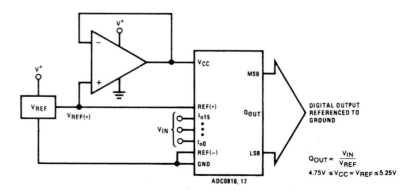

FIGURE 11. Ground Referenced Conversion System with
Reference Generating V_{CC} Supply

410

Applications Information (Continued)

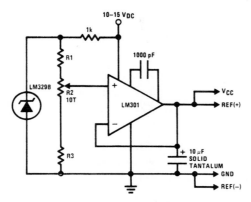

FIGURE 12. Typical Reference and Supply Circuit

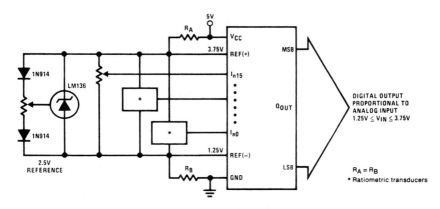

FIGURE 13. Symmetrically Centered Reference

3.0 Converter Equations

The transition between adjacent codes N and N + 1 is given by:

$$V_{IN} = \left\{ (V_{REF(+)} - V_{REF(-)}) \left[\frac{N}{256} + \frac{1}{512} \right] \pm V_{TUE} \right\} + V_{REF(-)} \quad (2)$$

The center of an output code N is given by:

$$V_{IN} = \left\{ (V_{REF(+)} - V_{REF(-)}) \left[\frac{N}{256} \right] \pm V_{TUE} \right\} + V_{REF(-)} \quad (3)$$

The output code N for an arbitrary input are the integers within the range:

$$N = \frac{V_{IN} - V_{REF(-)}}{V_{REF(+)} - V_{REF(-)}} \times 256 \pm \text{Absolute Accuracy} \quad (4)$$

where: V_{IN} = Voltage at comparator input
$V_{REF(+)}$ = Voltage at Ref(+)
$V_{REF(-)}$ = Voltage at Ref(−)
V_{TUE} = Total unadjusted error voltage (typically $V_{REF(+)} + 512$)

411

DAC0800 8-Bit Digital-to-Analog Converter

General Description

The DAC08 is a monolithic 8-bit high-speed current-output digital-to-analog converter (DAC) featuring typical settling times of 100 ns. When used as a multiplying DAC, monotonic performance over a 40 to 1 reference current range is possible. The DAC08 also features high compliance complementary current outputs to allow differential output voltages of 20 Vp-p with simple resistor loads as shown in *Figure 1*. The reference-to-full-scale current matching of better than ±1 LSB eliminates the need for full scale trims in most applications while the nonlinearities of better than ±0.1% over temperature minimizes system error accumulations.

The noise immune inputs of the DAC08 will accept TTL levels with the logic threshold pin, V_{LC}, pin 1 grounded. Simple adjustments of the V_{LC} potential allow direct interface to all logic families. The performance and characteristics of the device are essentially unchanged over the full ±4.5V to ±18V power supply range; power dissipation is only 33 mW with ±5V supplies and is independent of the logic input states.

The DAC0800L, DAC0802L, DAC0800LC, DAC0801LC and DAC0802LC are a direct replacement for the DAC08, DAC08A, DAC08C, DAC08E and DAC08H, respectively.

Features

- Fast settling output current   100 ns
- Full scale error   ±1 LSB
- Nonlinearity over temperature   ±0.1%
- Full scale current drift   ±10 ppm/°C
- High output compliance   −10V to +18V
- Complementary current outputs
- Interface directly with TTL, CMOS, PMOS and others
- 2 quadrant wide range multiplying capability
- Wide power supply range   ±4.5V to ±18V
- Low power consumption   33 mW at ±5V
- Low cost

Typical Applications

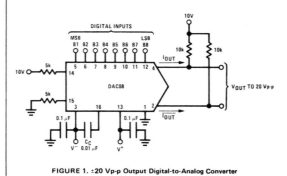

FIGURE 1. ±20 Vp-p Output Digital-to-Analog Converter

Connection Diagram

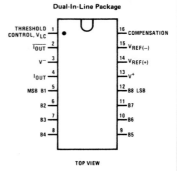

Dual-In-Line Package

TOP VIEW

Ordering Information

NON LINEARITY	TEMPERATURE RANGE	D PACKAGE (D16C)		J PACKAGE (J16A)		N PACKAGE (N16A)	
±0.1% FS	$-55°C \leq T_A \leq +125°C$	DAC0802LD	LMDAC08AD				
±0.1% FS	$0°C \leq T_A \leq +70°C$			DAC0802LCJ	LMDAC08HJ	DAC0802LCN	LMDAC08HN
±0.19% FS	$-55°C \leq T_A \leq +125°C$	DAC0800LD	LMDAC08D				
±0.19% FS	$0°C \leq T_A \leq +70°C$			DAC0800LCJ	LMDAC08EJ	DAC0800LCN	LMDAC08EN
±0.39% FS	$0°C \leq T_A \leq +70°C$			DAC0801LCJ	LMDAC08CJ	DAC0801LCN	LMDAC08CN

*Note. Devices may be ordered by using either order number.

Absolute Maximum Ratings

Supply Voltage	±18V or 36V
Power Dissipation (Note 1)	500 mW
Reference Input Differential Voltage (V14 to V15)	V^- to V^+
Reference Input Common-Mode Range (V14, V15)	V^- to V^+
Reference Input Current	5 mA
Logic Inputs	V^- to V^- plus 36V
Analog Current Outputs	*Figure 24*
Storage Temperature	$-65°$C to $+150°$C
Lead Temperature (Soldering, 10 seconds)	$300°$C

Operating Conditions

	MIN	MAX	UNITS
Temperature (T_A)			
DAC0802LA, LMDAC08A	-55	$+125$	$°$C
DAC0800L, LMDAC08	-55	$+125$	$°$C
DAC0800LC, LMDAC08E	0	$+70$	$°$C
DAC0801LC, LMDAC08C	0	$+70$	$°$C
DAC0802LC, LMDAC08H	0	$+70$	$°$C

Electrical Characteristics

($V_S = \pm15$V, I_{REF} = 2 mA, $T_{MIN} \le T_A \le T_{MAX}$ unless otherwise specified. Output characteristics refer to both I_{OUT} and $\overline{I_{OUT}}$.)

PARAMETER		CONDITIONS	DAC0802L/ DAC0802LC MIN	TYP	MAX	DAC0800L/ DAC0800LC MIN	TYP	MAX	DAC0801LC MIN	TYP	MAX	UNITS
	Resolution		8	8	8	8	8	8	8	8	8	Bits
	Monotonicity		8	8	8	8	8	8	8	8	8	Bits
	Nonlinearity				±0.1			±0.19			±0.39	%FS
t_s	Settling Time	To $\pm1/2$ LSB, All Bits Switched "ON" or "OFF", $T_A = 25°$C		100	135					100	150	ns
		DAC0800L					100	135				ns
		DAC0800LC					100	150				ns
t_{PLH}, t_{PHL}	Propagation Delay	$T_A = 25°$C										
	Each Bit			35	60		35	60		35	60	ns
	All Bits Switched			35	60		35	60		35	60	ns
TCI_{FS}	Full Scale Tempco			±10	±50		±10	±50		±10	±80	ppm/$°$C
V_{OC}	Output Voltage Compliance	Full Scale Current Change < 1/2 LSB, $R_{OUT} > 20$ MΩ Typ	-10		18	-10		18	-10		18	V
I_{FS4}	Full Scale Current	V_{REF} = 10.000V, R14 = 5.000 kΩ R15 = 5.000 kΩ, $T_A = 25°$C	1.984	1.992	2.000	1.94	1.99	2.04	1.94	1.99	2.04	mA
I_{FSS}	Full Scale Symmetry	$I_{FS4} - I_{FS2}$		±0.5	±4.0		±1	±8.0		±2	±16	μA
I_{ZS}	Zero Scale Current			0.1	1.0		0.2	2.0		0.2	4.0	μA
I_{FSR}	Output Current Range	$V^- = -5$V	0	2.0	2.1	0	2.0	2.1	0	2.0	2.1	mA
		$V^- = -8$V to -18V	0	2.0	4.2	0	2.0	4.2	0	2.0	4.2	mA
	Logic Input Levels											
V_{IL}	Logic "0"	$V_{LC} = 0$V			0.8			0.8			0.8	V
V_{IH}	Logic "1"		2.0			2.0			2.0			V
	Logic Input Current	$V_{LC} = 0$V										
I_{IL}	Logic "0"	-10V $\le V_{IN} \le +0.8$V		-2.0	-10		-2.0	-10		-2.0	-10	μA
I_{IH}	Logic "1"	2V $\le V_{IN} \le +18$V		0.002	10		0.002	10		0.002	10	μA
V_{IS}	Logic Input Swing	$V^- = -15$V	-10		18	-10		18	-10		18	V
V_{THR}	Logic Threshold Range	$V_S = \pm15$V	-10		13.5	-10		13.5	-10		13.5	V
I_{15}	Reference Bias Current			-1.0	-3.0		-1.0	-3.0		-1.0	-3.0	μA
dI/dt	Reference Input Slew Rate	*(Figure 24)*		8.0			8.0			8.0		mA/μs
$PSSI_{FS+}$	Power Supply Sensitivity	4.5V $\le V^+ \le 18$V		0.0001	0.01		0.0001	0.01		0.0001	0.01	%/%
$PSSI_{FS-}$		-4.5V $\le V^- \le 18$V		0.0001	0.01		0.0001	0.01		0.0001	0.01	%/%
		$I_{REF} = 1$ mA										
	Power Supply Current	$V_S = \pm5$V, $I_{REF} = 1$ mA										
$I+$				2.3	3.8		2.3	3.8		2.3	3.8	mA
$I-$				-4.3	-5.8		-4.3	-5.8		-4.3	-5.8	mA
		$V_S = 5$V, -15V, $I_{REF} = 2$ mA										
$I+$				2.4	3.8		2.4	3.8		2.4	3.8	mA
$I-$				-6.4	-7.8		-6.4	-7.8		-6.4	-7.8	mA
		$V_S = \pm15$V, $I_{REF} = 2$ mA										
$I+$				2.5	3.8		2.5	3.8		2.5	3.8	mA
$I-$				-6.5	-7.8		-6.5	-7.8		-6.5	-7.8	mA
P_D	Power Dissipation	±5V, $I_{REF} = 1$ mA		33	48		33	48		33	48	mW
		5V, -15V, $I_{REF} = 2$ mA		108	136		108	136		108	136	mW
		±15V, $I_{REF} = 2$ mA		135	174		135	174		135	174	mW

Note 1: The maximum junction temperature of the DAC0800, DAC0801 and DAC0802 is 100$°$C. For operating at elevated temperatures, devices in the dual-in-line J or D package must be derated based on a thermal resistance of 100$°$C/W, junction to ambient, 175$°$C/W for the molded dual-in-line N package.

Block Diagram

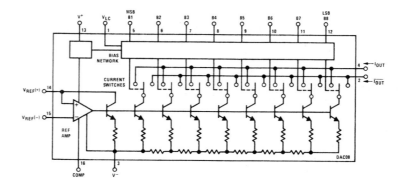

Equivalent Circuit

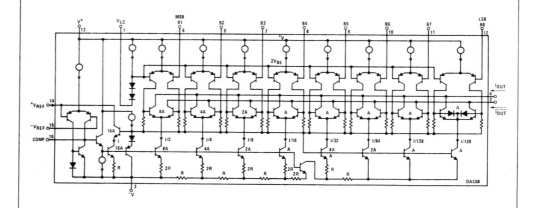

FIGURE 2

DAC0800

Typical Performance Characteristics

Full Scale Current
vs Reference Current

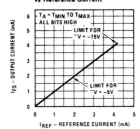

FIGURE 3

LSB Propagation Delay vs I_{FS}

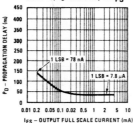

FIGURE 4

Reference Input
Frequency Response

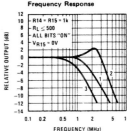

Curve 1: C_C = 15 pF, V_{IN} = 2 Vp-p
centered at 1V.

Curve 2: C_C = 15 pF, V_{IN} = 50 mVp-p
centered at 200 mV.

Curve 3: C_C = 0 pF, V_{IN} = 100 mVp-p
at 0V and applied through 50 Ω connected to pin 14. 2V applied to R14.

FIGURE 5

Reference Amp
Common-Mode Range

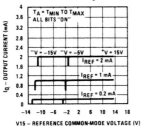

Note. Positive common-mode range is
always (V+) − 1.5V.

FIGURE 6

Logic Input Current
vs Input Voltage

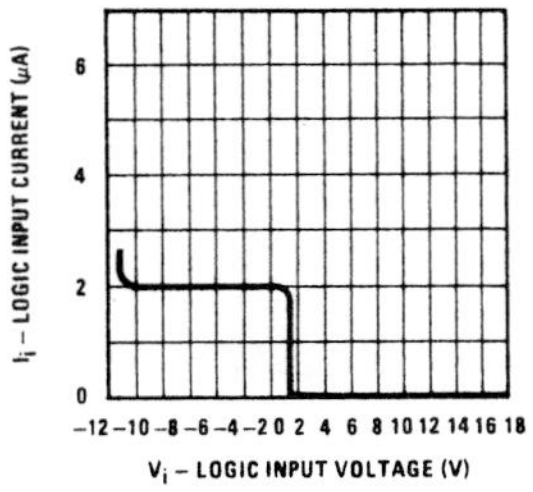

FIGURE 7

$V_{TH} - V_{LC}$ vs Temperature

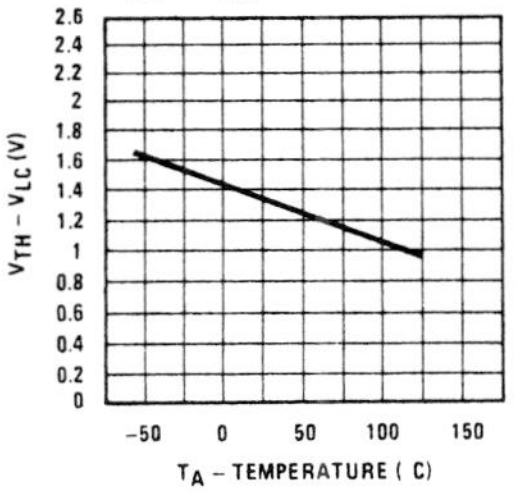

FIGURE 8

Output Current vs Output
Voltage (Output Voltage
Compliance)

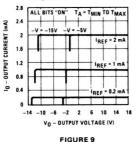

FIGURE 9

Output Voltage Compliance
vs Temperature

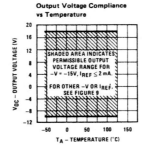

FIGURE 10

Bit Transfer Characteristics

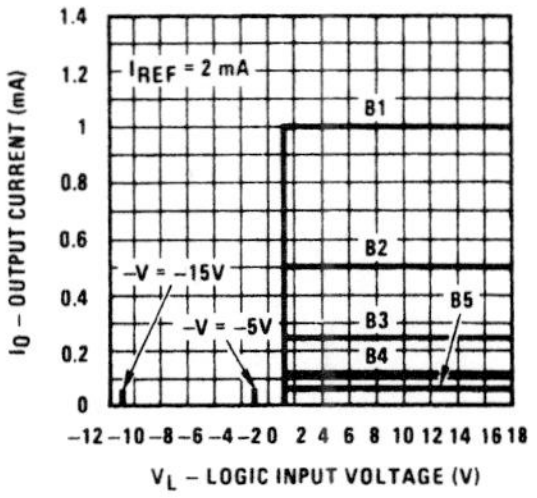

Note. B1—B8 have identical transfer
characteristics. Bits are fully switched
with less than 1/2 LSB error, at less than
±100 mV from actual threshold. These
switching points are guaranteed to lie
between 0.8 and 2V over the operating
temperature range (V_{LC} = 0V).

FIGURE 11

415

Typical Performance Characteristics (Continued)

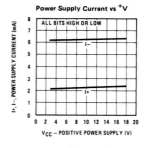

Power Supply Current vs +V

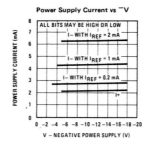

Power Supply Current vs −V

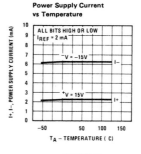

Power Supply Current vs Temperature

FIGURE 12   FIGURE 13   FIGURE 14

Typical Applications (Continued)

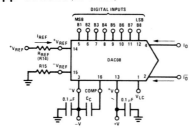

$$I_{FS} \approx \frac{+V_{REF}}{R_{REF}} \times \frac{255}{256}$$

$I_O + \overline{I_O} = I_{FS}$ for all logic states

For fixed reference, TTL operation, typical values are:

$V_{REF} = 10.000V$
$R_{REF} = 5.000k$
$R15 \approx R_{REF}$
$C_C = 0.01 \ \mu F$
$V_{LC} = 0V$ (Ground)

FIGURE 15. Basic Positive Reference Operation

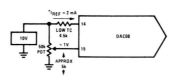

FIGURE 16. Recommended Full Scale Adjustment Circuit

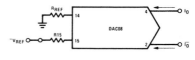

$$I_{FS} \approx \frac{-V_{REF}}{R_{REF}} \times \frac{255}{256}$$

Note. R_{REF} sets I_{FS}; R15 is for bias current cancellation

FIGURE 17. Basic Negative Reference Operation

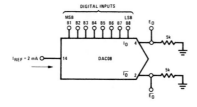

	B1	B2	B3	B4	B5	B6	B7	B8	I_O mA	$\overline{I_O}$ mA	E_O	$\overline{E_O}$
Full Scale	1	1	1	1	1	1	1	1	1.992	0.000	−9.960	0.000
Full Scale−LSB	1	1	1	1	1	1	1	0	1.984	0.008	−9.920	−0.040
Half Scale+LSB	1	0	0	0	0	0	0	1	1.008	0.984	−5.040	−4.920
Half Scale	1	0	0	0	0	0	0	0	1.000	0.992	−5.000	−4.960
Half Scale−LSB	0	1	1	1	1	1	1	1	0.992	1.000	−4.960	−5.000
Zero Scale+LSB	0	0	0	0	0	0	0	1	0.008	1.984	−0.040	−9.920
Zero Scale	0	0	0	0	0	0	0	0	0.000	1.992	0.000	−9.960

FIGURE 18. Basic Unipolar Negative Operation

Typical Applications (Continued)

	B1	B2	B3	B4	B5	B6	B7	B8	E_O	$\overline{E_O}$
Pos. Full Scale	1	1	1	1	1	1	1	1	−9.920	+10.000
Pos. Full Scale−LSB	1	1	1	1	1	1	1	0	−9.840	+9.920
Zero Scale+LSB	1	0	0	0	0	0	0	1	−0.080	+0.160
Zero Scale	1	0	0	0	0	0	0	0	0.000	+0.080
Zero Scale−LSB	0	1	1	1	1	1	1	1	+0.080	0.000
Neg. Full Scale+LSB	0	0	0	0	0	0	0	1	+9.920	−9.840
Neg. Full Scale	0	0	0	0	0	0	0	0	+10.000	−9.920

FIGURE 19. Basic Bipolar Output Operation

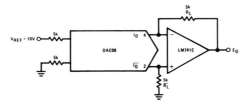

If $R_L = \overline{R_L}$ within ±0.05%, output is symmetrical about ground

	B1	B2	B3	B4	B5	B6	B7	B8	E_O
Pos. Full Scale	1	1	1	1	1	1	1	1	+9.920
Pos. Full Scale−LSB	1	1	1	1	1	1	1	0	+9.840
(+) Zero Scale	1	0	0	0	0	0	0	0	+0.040
(−) Zero Scale	0	1	1	1	1	1	1	1	−0.040
Neg. Full Scale+LSB	0	0	0	0	0	0	0	1	−9.840
Neg. Full Scale	0	0	0	0	0	0	0	0	−9.920

FIGURE 20. Symmetrical Offset Binary Operation

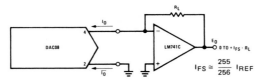

For complementary output (operation as negative logic DAC), connect inverting input of op amp to $\overline{I_O}$ (pin 2), connect I_O (pin 4) to ground.

FIGURE 21. Positive Low Impedance Output Operation

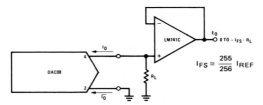

For complementary output (operation as a negative logic DAC) connect non-inverting input of op amp to $\overline{I_O}$ (pin 2); connect I_O (pin 4) to ground.

FIGURE 22. Negative Low Impedance Output Operation

Typical Applications (Continued)

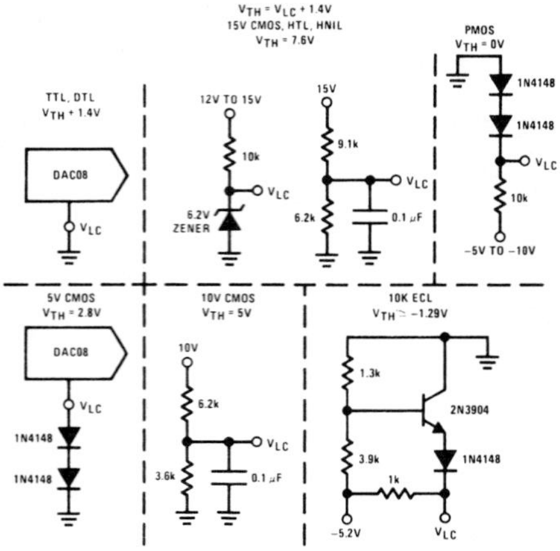

FIGURE 23. Interfacing with Various Logic Families

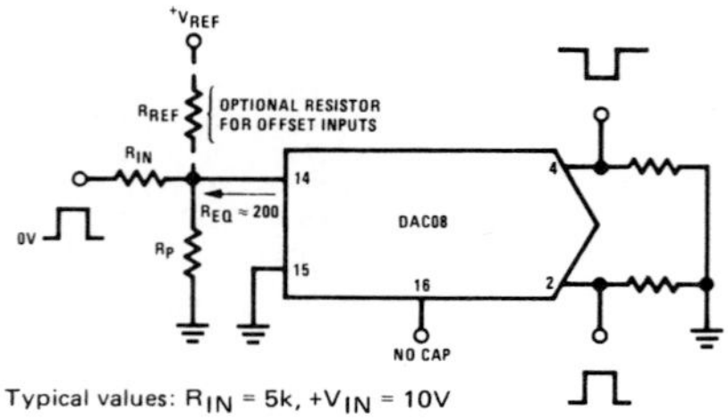

Note. Do not exceed negative logic input range of DAC.

Typical values: R_{IN} = 5k, $+V_{IN}$ = 10V

FIGURE 24. Pulsed Reference Operation

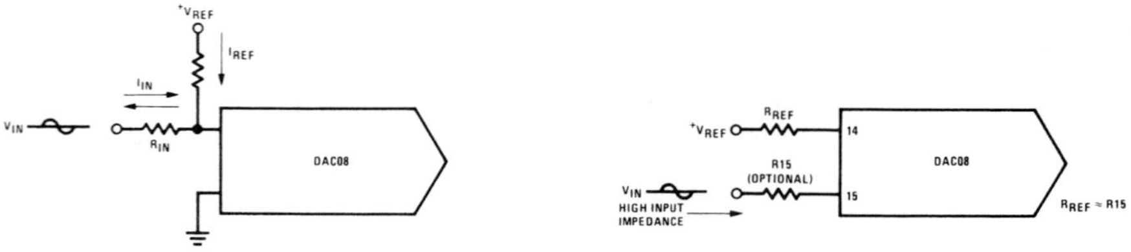

(a) $I_{REF} \geq$ peak negative swing of I_{IN}

(b) $+V_{REF}$ must be above peak positive swing of V_{IN}

FIGURE 25. Accommodating Bipolar References

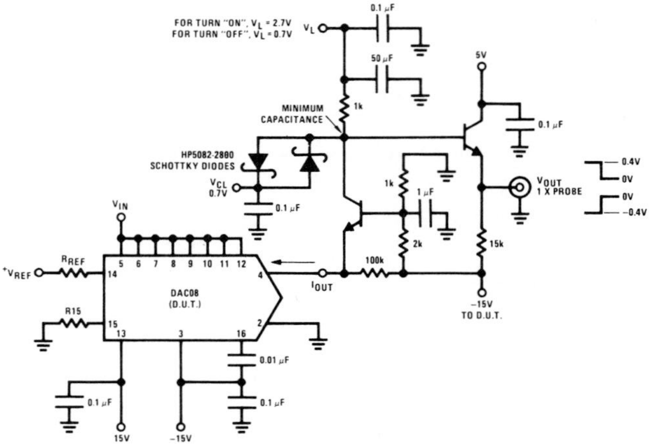

FIGURE 26. Settling Time Measurement

418

Typical Applications (Continued)

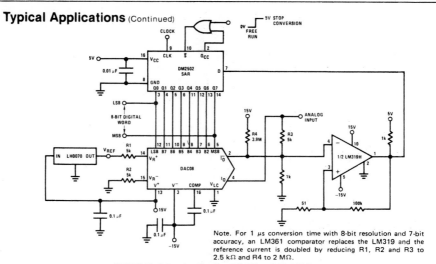

Note. For 1 μs conversion time with 8-bit resolution and 7-bit accuracy, an LM361 comparator replaces the LM319 and the reference current is doubled by reducing R1, R2 and R3 to 2.5 kΩ and R4 to 2 MΩ.

FIGURE 27. A Complete 2 μs Conversion Time, 8-Bit A/D Converter

419

Instruction Timing
for the 68000/10 Processors

MC68000 INSTRUCTION EXECUTION TIMES

D.1 INTRODUCTION

This Appendix contains listings of the instruction execution times in terms of external clock (CLK) periods. In this data, it is assumed that both memory read and write cycle times are four clock periods. A longer memory cycle will cause the generation of wait states which must be added to the total instruction time.

The number of bus read and write cycles for each instruction is also included with the timing data. This data is enclosed in parenthesis following the number of clock periods and is shown as: (r/w) where r is the number of read cycles and w is the number of write cycles included in the clock period number. Recalling that either a read or write cycle requires four clock periods, a timing number given as 18(3/1) relates to 12 clock periods for the three read cycles, plus 4 clock periods for the one write cycle, plus 2 cycles required for some internal function of the processor.

NOTE
The number of periods includes instruction fetch and all applicable operand fetches and stores.

D.2 OPERAND EFFECTIVE ADDRESS CALCULATION TIMING

Table D-1 lists the number of clock periods required to compute an instruction's effective address. It includes fetching of any extension words, the address computation, and fetching of the memory operand. The number of bus read and write cycles is shown in parenthesis as (r/w). Note there are no write cycles involved in processing the effective address.

Table D-1. Effective Address Calculation Times

Addressing Mode		Byte, Word	Long
	Register		
Dn	Data Register Direct	0(0/0)	0(0/0)
An	Address Register Direct	0(0/0)	0(0/0)
	Memory		
(An)	Address Register Indirect	4(1/0)	8(2/0)
(An) +	Address Register Indirect with Postincrement	4(1/0)	8(2/0)
− (An)	Address Register Indirect with Predecrement	6(1/0)	10(2/0)
d_{16}(An)	Address Register Indirect with Displacement	8(2/0)	12(3/0)
d_8(An, Xn)*	Address Register Indirect with Index	10(2/0)	14(3/0)
(xxx).W	Absolute Short	8(2/0)	12(3/0)
(xxx).L	Absolute Long	12(3/0)	16(4/0)
d_8(PC)	Program Counter with Displacement	8(2/0)	12(3/0)
d_{16}(PC, Xn)*	Program Counter with Index	10(2/0)	14(3/0)
#<data>	Immediate	4(1/0)	8(2/0)

*The size of the index register (Xn) does not affect execution time.

Reprinted by permission of Motorola, Inc.

D.3 MOVE INSTRUCTION EXECUTION TIMES

Tables D-2 and D-3 indicate the number of clock periods for the move instruction. This data includes instruction fetch, operand reads, and operand writes. The number of bus read and write cycles is shown in parenthesis as (r/w).

Table D-2. Move Byte and Word Instruction Execution Times

Source	Destination								
	Dn	An	(An)	(An) +	− (An)	d_{16}(An)	d_8(An,Xn)*	(xxx).W	(xxx).L
Dn	4(1/0)	4(1/0)	8(1/1)	8(1/1)	8(1/1)	12(2/1)	14(2/1)	12(2/1)	16(3/1)
An	4(1/0)	4(1/0)	8(1/1)	8(1/1)	8(1/1)	12(2/1)	14(2/1)	12(2/1)	16(3/1)
(An)	8(2/0)	8(2/0)	12(2/1)	12(2/1)	12(2/1)	16(3/1)	18(3/1)	16(3/1)	20(4/1)
(An) +	8(2/0)	8(2/0)	12(2/1)	12(2/1)	12(2/1)	16(3/1)	18(3/1)	16(3/1)	20(4/1)
− (An)	10(2/0)	10(2/0)	14(2/1)	14(2/1)	14(2/1)	18(3/1)	20(3/1)	18(3/1)	22(4/1)
d_{16}(An)	12(3/0)	12(3/0)	16(3/1)	16(3/1)	16(3/1)	20(4/1)	22(4/1)	20(4/1)	24(5/1)
d_8(An,Xn)*	14(3/0)	14(3/0)	18(3/1)	18(3/1)	18(3/1)	22(4/1)	24(4/1)	22(4/1)	26(5/1)
(xxx).W	12(3/0)	12(3/0)	16(3/1)	16(3/1)	16(3/1)	20(4/1)	22(4/1)	20(4/1)	24(5/1)
(xxx).L	16(4/0)	16(4/0)	20(4/1)	20(4/1)	20(4/1)	24(5/1)	26(5/1)	24(5/1)	28(6/1)
d_{16}(PC)	12(3/0)	12(3/0)	16(3/1)	16(3/1)	16(3/1)	20(4/1)	22(4/1)	20(4/1)	24(5/1)
d_8(PC, Xn)*	14(3/0)	14(3/0)	18(3/1)	18(3/1)	18(3/1)	22(4/1)	24(4/1)	22(4/1)	26(5/1)
#<data>	8(2/0)	8(2/0)	12(2/1)	12(2/1)	12(2/1)	16(3/1)	18(3/1)	16(3/1)	20(4/1)

*The size of the index register (Xn) does not affect execution time.

Table D-3. Move Long Instruction Execution Times

Source	Destination								
	Dn	An	(An)	(An) +	− (An)	d_{16}(An)	d_8(An,Xn)*	(xxx).W	(xxx).L
Dn	4(1/0)	4(1/0)	12(1/2)	12(1/2)	12(1/2)	16(2/2)	18(2/2)	16(2/2)	20(3/2)
An	4(1/0)	4(1/0)	12(1/2)	12(1/2)	12(1/2)	16(2/2)	18(2/2)	16(2/2)	20(3/2)
(An)	12(3/0)	12(3/0)	20(3/2)	20(3/2)	20(3/2)	24(4/2)	26(4/2)	24(4/2)	28(5/2)
(An) +	12(3/0)	12(3/0)	20(3/2)	20(3/2)	20(3/2)	24(4/2)	26(4/2)	24(4/2)	28(5/2)
− (An)	14(3/0)	14(3/0)	22(3/2)	22(3/2)	22(3/2)	26(4/2)	28(4/2)	26(4/2)	30(5/2)
d_{16}(An)	16(4/0)	16(4/0)	24(4/2)	24(4/2)	24(4/2)	28(5/2)	30(5/2)	28(5/2)	32(6/2)
d_8(An,Xn)*	18(4/0)	18(4/0)	26(4/2)	26(4/2)	26(4/2)	30(5/2)	32(5/2)	30(5/2)	34(6/2)
(xxx).W	16(4/0)	16(4/0)	24(4/2)	24(4/2)	24(4/2)	28(5/2)	30(5/2)	28(5/2)	32(6/2)
(xxx).L	20(5/0)	20(5/0)	28(5/2)	28(5/2)	28(5/2)	32(6/2)	34(6/2)	32(6/2)	36(7/2)
d(PC)	16(4/0)	16(4/0)	24(4/2)	24(4/2)	24(4/2)	28(5/2)	30(5/2)	28(5/2)	32(5/2)
d(PC,Xn)*	18(4/0)	18(4/0)	26(4/2)	26(4/2)	26(4/2)	30(5/2)	32(5/2)	30(5/2)	34(6/2)
#<data>	12(3/0)	12(3/0)	20(3/2)	20(3/2)	20(3/2)	24(4/2)	26(4/2)	24(4/2)	28(5/2)

*The size of the index register (Xn) does not affect execution time.

D.4 STANDARD INSTRUCTION EXECUTION TIMES

The number of clock periods shown in Table D-4 indicates the time required to perform the operations, store the results, and read the next instruction. The number of bus read and write cycles is shown in parenthesis as (r/w). The number of clock periods and the number of read and write cycles must be added respectively to those of the effective address calculation where indicated.

In Table D-4 the headings have the following meanings: An = address register operand, Dn = data register operand, ea = an operand specified by an effective address, and M = memory effective address operand.

Table D-4. Standard Instruction Execution Times

Instruction	Size	op<ea>, An†	op<ea>, Dn	op Dn, <M>
ADD/ADDA	Byte, Word	8(1/0) +	4(1/0) +	8(1/1) +
	Long	6(1/0) + * *	6(1/0) + * *	12(1/2) +
AND	Byte, Word	—	4(1/0) +	8(1/1) +
	Long	—	6(1/0) + * *	12(1/2) +
CMP/CMPA	Byte, Word	6(1/0) +	4(1/0) +	—
	Long	6(1/0) +	6(1/0) +	—
DIVS	—	—	158(1/0) + *	—
DIVU	—	—	140(1/0) + *	—
EOR	Byte, Word	—	4(1/0) * * *	8(1/1) +
	Long	—	8(1/0) * * *	12(1/2) +
MULS	—	—	70(1/0) + *	—
MULU	—	—	70(1/0) + *	—
OR	Byte, Word	—	4(1/0) +	8(1/1) +
	Long	—	6(1/0) + * *	12(1/2) +
SUB	Byte, Word	8(1/0) +	4(1/0) +	8(1/1) +
	Long	6(1/0) + * *	6(1/0) + * *	12(1/2) +

NOTES:
+ add effective address calculation time
† word or long only
* indicates maximum basic value added to word effective address time.
* * The base time of six clock periods is increased to eight if the effective address mode is register direct or immediate (effective address time should also be added).
* * * Only available effective address mode is data register direct.
DIVS, DIVU — The divide algorithm used by the MC68000 provides less than 10% difference between the best and worst case timings.
MULS, MULU — The multiply algorithm requires 38 + 2n clocks where n is defined as:
MULU: n = the number of ones in the <ea>
MULS: n = concatanate the <ea> with a zero as the LSB; n is the resultant number of 10 or 01 patterns in the 17-bit source; i.e., worst case happens when the source is $5555.

D.5 IMMEDIATE INSTRUCTION EXECUTION TIMES

The number of clock periods shown in Table D-5 includes the time to fetch immediate operands, perform the operations, store the results, and read the next operation. The number of bus read and write cycles is shown in parenthesis as (r/w). The number of clock periods and the number of read and write cycles must be added respectively to those of the effective address calculation where indicated.

In Table D-5, the headings have the following meanings: # = immediate operand, Dn = data register operand, An = address register operand, and M = memory operand. SR = status register.

Table D-5. Immediate Instruction Execution Times

Instruction	Size	op #, Dn	op #, An	op #, M
ADDI	Byte, Word	8(2/0)	—	12(2/1) +
	Long	16(3/0)	—	20(3/2) +
ADDQ	Byte, Word	4(1/0)	8(1/0) *	8(1/1) +
	Long	8(1/0)	8(1/0)	12(1/2) +
ANDI	Byte, Word	8(2/0)	—	12(2/1) +
	Long	16(3/0)	—	20(3/1) +
CMPI	Byte, Word	8(2/0)	—	8(2/0) +
	Long	14(3/0)	—	12(3/0) +
EORI	Byte, Word	8(2/0)	—	12(2/1) +
	Long	16(3/0)	—	20(3/2) +
MOVEQ	Long	4(1/0)	—	—
ORI	Byte, Word	8(2/0)	—	12(2/1) +
	Long	16(3/0)	—	20(3/2) +
SUBI	Byte, Word	8(2/0)	—	12(2/1) +
	Long	16(3/0)	—	20(3/2) +
SUBQ	Byte, Word	4(1/0)	8(1/0) *	8(1/1) +
	Long	8(1/0)	8(1/0)	12(1/2) +

+ add effective address calculation time
* word only

D.6 SINGLE OPERAND INSTRUCTION EXECUTION TIMES

Table D-6 indicates the number of clock periods for the single operand instructions. The number of bus read and write cycles is shown in parenthesis as (r/w). The number of clock periods and the number of read and write cycles must be added respectively to those of the effective address calculation where indicated.

Table D-6. Single Operand Instruction Execution Times

Instruction	Size	Register	Memory
CLR	Byte, Word	4(1/0)	8(1/1) +
	Long	6(1/0)	12(1/2) +
NBCD	Byte	6(1/0)	8(1/1) +
NEG	Byte, Word	4(1/0)	8(1/1) +
	Long	6(1/0)	12(1/2) +
NEGX	Byte, Word	4(1/0)	8(1/1) +
	Long	6(1/0)	12(1/2) +
NOT	Byte, Word	4(1/0)	8(1/1) +
	Long	6(1/0)	12(1/2) +
Scc	Byte, False	4(1/0)	8(1/1) +
	Byte, True	6(1/0)	8(1/1) +
TAS	Byte	4(1/0)	10(1/1) +
TST	Byte, Word	4(1/0)	4(1/0) +
	Long	4(1/0)	4(1/0) +

+ add effective address calculation time

D.7 SHIFT/ROTATE INSTRUCTION EXECUTION TIMES

Table D-7 indicates the number of clock periods for the shift and rotate instructions. The number of bus read and write cycles is shown in parenthesis as (r/w). The number of clock periods and the number of read and write cycles must be added respectively to those of the effective address calculation where indicated.

Table D-7. Shift/Rotate Instruction Execution Times

Instruction	Size	Register	Memory
ASR, ASL	Byte, Word	6 + 2n(1/0)	8(1/1) +
	Long	8 + 2n(1/0)	—
LSR, LSL	Byte, Word	6 + 2n(1/0)	8(1/1) +
	Long	8 + 2n(1/0)	—
ROR, ROL	Byte, Word	6 + 2n(1/0)	8(1/1) +
	Long	8 + 2n(1/0)	—
ROXR, ROXL	Byte, Word	6 + 2n(1/0)	8(1/1) +
	Long	8 + 2n(1/0)	—

+ add effective address calculation time for word operands
n is the shift count

D.8 BIT MANIPULATION INSTRUCTION EXECUTION TIMES

Table D-8 indicates the number of clock periods required for the bit manipulation instructions. The number of bus read and write cycles is shown in parenthesis as (r/w). The number of clock periods and the number of read and write cycles must be added respectively to those of the effective address calculation where indicated.

Table D-8. Bit Manipulation Instruction Execution Times

Instruction	Size	Dynamic		Static	
		Register	Memory	Register	Memory
BCHG	Byte	—	8(1/1) +	—	12(2/1) +
	Long	8(1/0) *	—	12(2/0) *	—
BCLR	Byte	—	8(1/1) +	—	12(2/1) +
	Long	10(1/0) *	—	14(2/0) *	—
BSET	Byte	—	8(1/1) +	—	12(2/1) +
	Long	8(1/0) *	—	12(2/0) *	—
BTST	Byte	—	4(1/0) +	—	8(2/0) +
	Long	6(1/0)	—	10(2/0)	—

+ add effective address calculation time
*indicates maximum value; data addressing mode only

D.9 CONDITIONAL INSTRUCTION EXECUTION TIMES

Table D-9 indicates the number of clock periods required for the conditional instructions. The number of bus read and write cycles is indicated in parenthesis as (r/w). The number of clock periods and the number of read and write cycles must be added respectively to those of the effective address calculation where indicated.

Table D-9. Conditional Instruction Execution Times

Instruction	Displacement	Branch Taken	Branch Not Taken
Bcc	Byte	10(2/0)	8(1/0)
	Word	10(2/0)	12(2/0)
BRA	Byte	10(2/0)	—
	Word	10(2/0)	—
BSR	Byte	18(2/2)	—
	Word	18(2/2)	—
DBcc	cc true	—	12(2/0)
	cc false, Count Not Expired	10(2/0)	—
	cc false, Counter Expired	—	14(3/0)

+ add effective address calculation time
*indicates maximum base value

Reprinted by permission of Motorola, Inc.

D.10 JMP, JSR, LEA, PEA, AND MOVEM INSTRUCTION EXECUTION TIMES

Table D-10 indicates the number of clock periods required for the jump, jump-to-subroutine, load effective address, push effective address, and move multiple registers instructions. The number of bus read and write cycles is shown in parenthesis as (r/w).

Table D-10. JMP, JSR, LEA, PEA, and MOVEM Instruction Execution Times

Instruction	Size	(An)	(An) +	– (An)	d_{16}(An)	d_8(An,Xn)+	(xxx).W	(xxx).L	d_{16}(PC)	d_8(PC,Xn) *
JMP	–	8(2/0)	–	–	10(2/0)	14(3/0)	10(2/0)	12(3/0)	10(2/0)	14(3/0)
JSR	–	16(2/2)	–	–	18(2/2)	22(2/2)	18(2/2)	20(3/2)	18(2/2)	22(2/2)
LEA	–	4(1/0)	–	–	8(2/0)	12(2/0)	8(2/0)	12(3/0)	8(2/0)	12(2/0)
PEA	–	12(1/2)	–	–	16(2/2)	20(2/2)	16(2/2)	20(3/2)	16(2/2)	20(2/2)
MOVEM M → R	Word	12 + 4n (3 + n/0)	12 + 4n (3 + n/0)	–	16 + 4n (4 + n/0)	18 + 4n (4 + n/0)	16 + 4n (4 + n/0)	20 + 4n (5 + n/0)	16 + 4n (4 + n/0)	18 + 4n (4 + n/0)
	Long	12 + 8n (3 + 2n/0)	12 + 8n (3 + 2n/0)	–	16 + 8n (4 + 2n/0)	18 + 8n (4 + 2n/0)	16 + 8n (4 + 2n/0)	20 + 8n (5 + 2n/0)	16 + 8n (4 + 2n/0)	18 + 8n (4 + 2n/0)
MOVEM R → M	Word	8 + 4n (2/n)	–	8 + 4n (2/n)	12 + 4n (3/n)	14 + 4n (3/n)	12 + 4n (3/n)	16 + 4n (4/n)	–	–
	Long	8 + 8n (2/2n)	–	8 + 8n (2/2n)	12 + 8n (3/2n)	14 + 8n (3/2n)	12 + 8n (3/2n)	16 + 8n (4/2n)	–	–

n is the number of registers to move
* is the size of the index register (Xn) does not affect the instruction's execution time

D.11 MULTI-PRECISION INSTRUCTION EXECUTION TIMES

Table D-11 indicates the number of clock periods for the multi-precision instructions. The number of clock periods includes the time to fetch both operands, peform the operations, store the results, and read the next instructions. The number of read and write cycles is shown in parenthesis as (r/w).

In Table D-11, the headings have the following meanings: Dn = data register operand and M = memory operand.

Table D-11. Multi-Precision Instruction Execution Times

Instruction	Size	op Dn, Dn	op M, M
ADDX	Byte, Word	4(1/0)	18(3/1)
	Long	8(1/0)	30(5/2)
CMPM	Byte, Word	–	12(3/0)
	Long	–	20(5/0)
SUBX	Byte, Word	4(1/0)	18(3/1)
	Long	8(1/0)	30(5/2)
ABCD	Byte	6(1/0)	18(3/1)
SBCD	Byte	6(1/0)	18(3/1)

Reprinted by permission of Motorola, Inc.

D.12 MISCELLANEOUS INSTRUCTION EXECUTION TIMES

Tables D-12 and D-13 indicate the number of clock periods for the following miscellaneous instructions. The number of bus read and write cycles is shown in parenthesis as (r/w). The number of clock periods plus the number of read and write cycles must be added to those of the effective address calculation where indicated.

Table D-12. Miscellaneous Instruction Execution Times

Instruction	Size	Register	Memory
ANDI to CCR	Byte	20(3/0)	—
ANDI to SR	Word	20(3/0)	—
CHK (No Trap)	—	10(1/0) +	—
EORI to CCR	Byte	20(3/0)	—
EORI to SR	Word	20(3/0)	—
ORI to CCR	Byte	20(3/0)	—
ORI to SR	Word	20(3/0)	—
MOVE from SR	—	6(1/0)	8(1/1) +
MOVE to CCR	—	12(1/0)	12(1/0) +
MOVE to SR	—	12(1/0)	12(1/0) +
EXG	—	6(1/0)	—
EXT	Word	4(1/0)	—
EXT	Long	4(1/0)	—
LINK	—	16(2/2)	—
MOVE from USP	—	4(1/0)	—
MOVE to USP	—	4(1/0)	—
NOP	—	4(1/0)	—
RESET	—	132(1/0)	—
RTE	—	20(5/0)	—
RTR	—	20(5/0)	—
RTS	—	16(4/0)	—
STOP	—	4(0/0)	—
SWAP	—	4(1/0)	—
TRAPV	—	4(1/0)	—
UNLK	—	12(3/0)	—

+ add effective address calculation time

Table D-13. Move Peripheral Instruction Execution Times

Instruction	Size	Register → Memory	Memory → Register
MOVEP	Word	16(2/2)	16(4/0)
MOVEP	Long	24(2/4)	24(6/0)

D.13 EXCEPTION PROCESSING EXECUTION TIMES

Table D-14 indicates the number of clock periods for exception processing. The number of clock periods includes the time for all stacking, the vector fetch, and the fetch of the first two instruction words of the handler routine. The number of bus read and write cycles is shown in parenthesis as (r/w).

Table D-14. Exception Processing Execution Times

Exception	Periods
Address Error	**50**(4/7)
Bus Error	**50**(4/7)
CHK Instruction	**40**(4/3) +
Divide by Zero	**38**(4/3) +
Illegal Instruction	**34**(4/3)
Interrupt	**44**(5/3) *
Privilege Violation	**34**(4/3)
RESET**	**40**(6/0)
Trace	**34**(4/3)
TRAP Instruction	**34**(4/3)
TRAPV Instruction	**34**(5/3)

+ add effective address calculation time

* The interrupt acknowledge cycle is assumed to take four clock periods.

** Indicates the time from when RESET and HALT are first sampled as negated to when instruction execution starts.

Access Memory   All RAM location can be accessed in the same amount of time. Also known as *Read/Write Memory (R/WM)*.

accumulator   A special purpose register that holds one of the data elements going into the ALU and the result from the ALU.

ACIA   Asynchronous Communications Interface Adapter. A serial communication device belonging to the 6800 family. It has standard RS-232 properties.

A/D   Analog-to-digital converter. An electronic circuit that converts an analog input voltage into a digital equivalent word.

address bus   A collection of address signals.

address error   An error condition that results when the processor attempts to access instructions or word or long-word operands at an odd address.

ALU   Arithmetic Logic Unit. It performs the arithmetic and logical operations of the operands.

architecture   The arrangement of the processor's internal resources.

arithmetic operations   Operations that deal with operands as numbers. They change the number values of the operands.

arithmetic shift   A shift operation in which the sign of the operand is maintained.

$\overline{\text{AS}}$ Address strobe output signifying that the contents of the address bus are valid and stable.

ASCII   American Standard Code for Information Interchange. A 7-bit code that represents alphanumeric characters. ASCII code is widely used in data communications.

assembler directives   Commands associated with the assembler to guide the assembly process.

assemblers   Programmed utilities that convert programs written in assembly language, using the mnemonic instructions of the processor, into the corresponding machine code.

asynchronous events   Events that occur at irregular intervals; that is, not in time with a clock signal.

autovectors   Dedicated vector locations for interrupts in the exception table.

base address   The reference address that forms the basis for effective address calculation.

base displacement   The displacement added to an address register or program counter before indexing.

baud rate   The rate of serial data transfer given in bits per second (bps).

BCD   Binary Coded Decimal. In BCD format, each decimal digit is represented by four binary bits.

$\overline{\text{BERR}}$ Active low bus error input to the processor. Asserting a $\overline{\text{BERR}}$ causes a bus error exception routine to be run by the processor.

bidirectional   A term used to refer to a signal line that can be input or output.

binary   A system of number representation using logic 1 and 0.

binary integers   Numbers that are regarded as integer values in the binary convention.

bit field   Designated portion of memory that holds bits of data.

bit-field width   The number of bits in the field.

bit manipulation   Data manipulation at the bit level. Bit-manipulation instructions are very useful in I/O applications in which a single bit needs to be tested or changed.

break condition   A condition that results when an all-zero data frame is encountered without the stop bits. In communications, a break condition is used for special events.

buffer   An electrical circuit used as a go-between when the circuits on either side have different voltage or current requirements. It is also used for holding and/or isolation applications.

bus   A collection of signals with common properties.

bus arbitration   Exchange of information between two or more units, such as a processor and DMA controller, to gain control of the bus.

bus error   A condition that results when the processor attempts to access nonexistent memory or I/O.

bus master   The device or unit that has control over the system buses.

byte   An 8-bit binary data structure; the fundamental unit in data structures.

cache memory   High-speed fast-access memory, designed to hold frequently used instructions and operands.

$\overline{\text{CAS}}$ Column Address Strobe. A signal used to latch the column address into a dynamic RAM device. It also acts as a chip select.

CHK   A 68000 instruction that checks the boundaries of a specified data register.

cold start   Starting from a power-up condition in which complete initialization of the system is required. Enough time must be allotted for the system electronics to stabilize.

comment directive   An assembler directive for introducing comments to clarify the program. The assembler will not convert a comment into machine code.

compiler   A programming utility that converts programs written in higher level languages, such as PASCAL, into the corresponding machine code of the processor.

condition codes (flags):   Codes containing information concerning the operation of a program on an instruction-by-instruction basis.

CRA and **CRB**   Control registers A and B of the PIA. These registers must be configured for any I/O handshake application.

cross assembler   An assembler utility that uses one computer to develop software designed to be used on a different computer.

crystal oscillator   An electronic circuit in which a crystal produces oscillations. It is frequently used for timing generation.

CTS   Clear to Send. A control signal from the DCE to the DTE indicating that the data transfer is about to take place.

cutoff frequency   The value at which the system response will be at approximately 70 percent of its maximum value. Also known as *corner frequency*.

D/A   Digital-to-analog converter. An electronic circuit that converts a digital word into a corresponding analog voltage.

daisy chain   A cascading mechanism to increase the number of effective inputs onto a single input line.

data bus   A collection of data signals.

data movement instructions   Instructions used to move byte, word, and long-word data between data registers, address registers, and memory. Usually these instructions do not affect the value of the operand moved.

$\overline{\text{DCD}}$ Data Carrier Detect. A control signal to the DTE from the RS-232 interface, indicating that the carrier signal is in progress.

DC directive   Define constant assembler directive. It defines constant values, including characters. These values will be put into the memory.

DCE   Data Communication Equipment. The unit that interfaces with an intelligent system (usually a DTE) for data transfers.

DDRA and **DDRB**   Data direction registers A and B of the PIA. The contents of these registers determine whether the port bits are input or output.

debounce   An electronic circuit that removes oscillations due to mechanical vibrations when a mechanical switch closes or opens.

delimiters   Special characters used by the assembler to specify certain types of operations.

destination operand   The location at which the results of an operation should be placed.

DFC   Destination Function Code. A 3-bit register in 68010 and 68012 processors that contains destination function code information.

displacement   A value added to the base address to obtain an effective address.

DMA   Direct Memory Access. A mechanism by which data transfers take place between memory and I/O without processor intervention. DMA is used for high-speed data transfers.

double bus fault   A catastrophic failure condition in which the processor comes to a complete halt. This condition results from nested error conditions involving bus errors, reset vector fetches, address errors, or privilege violation errors.

DRAM   Dynamic Random Access Memory. DRAM devices store information in the form of dynamic charge. They are about four times denser than static RAMs.

DS directive   Define storage assembler directive. It defines the memory area for general-purpose or stack storage.

$\overline{\text{DTACK}}$ Data acknowledge signal from the selected memory or I/O signifying that the data transfer during the bus cycle has successfully taken place.

DTE   Data Terminal Equipment. An intelligent system that commands other units interfaced with it (usually DCE) for data transfers.

DTR   Data Terminal Ready. A control signal to the DCE from the RS-232 interface indicating that the DTE is ready for data transfer.

EBCDIC   Enhanced Binary Coded Decimal Interchange Code. An 8-bit code standardized by IBM for information exchange.

effective address   Actual physical address where the source or destination operands are located.

emulation   The mimicking of certain properties and conditions by the operating system that do not actually exist in the operating system conditions.

END directive   End assembler directive. It tells the assembler to terminate the assembly process.

EQU directive   Equate assembler directive. It equates the defined symbol with the value specified on the right-hand side.

even memory byte   The byte located at an even address, such as $000000, $000002.

exception   A special condition, such as an interrupt, error, or reset, that moves the 68000 family of processors into a higher level of operation and control.

exception vector   A number from 0 to 255 used to point to a group of memory locations that contain the address of the routine that will handle the exception.

FIFO   First In First Out. A data structure in memory in which the first element stored will be the first one retrieved.

frame   Start and end of a character or message.

frame error   An error condition that results when the stop bits of a data frame are missing.

frame pointer   One of the address registers containing the stack address information. It is used to access information from the work area of the stack.

function control outputs   Outputs from the processor that specify its status during the current bus cycle.

giga   One billion units (10^9).

governing operating system   The actual operating system that controls the local operating systems and users. The governing operating system is truly operational in the supervisor mode and corresponds to the default vector table.

handshake   A method of exchanging control information during data transfer between devices or stations.

hardware   A term referring to the physical electronics, the associated circuitry, and the electronic packaging associated with microcomputer systems.

hex   A system of number representation to the base 16. Each hex digit takes four binary bits. Representation of numbers 0–9 is similar to the decimal system. Decimal numbers 10–15 are represented by alphabet letters A, B, C, D, E, and F.

host system   The computer system containing the utilities. It is used for program development and storage.

IC   Integrated Circuit. It refers to semiconductor circuitry on a single wafer and packaged together.

illegal instruction error   An error condition that results when the processor attempts to use instruction codes that are not legal and valid.

index   A parameter value in one of the registers that is added to the base address to obtain the effective address.

index register   The register holding the index value. In the 68000, it can be a data or an address register.

inductive transients   Voltage spikes across inductive windings that occur when there is a sudden change in current.

initialization   The part of a program that sets the register and memory contents to their starting values.

input/output (I/O) devices   Peripheral devices, such as keyboards, displays, and disk drives, used to input or take data from a computer. All external data enters through the input section; all output data exits through the output section.

instruction time   The time it takes to execute a given instruction without any wait states.

interrupt   A hardware signal from the I/O device to the processor to obtain the attention of the processor.

interrupt mask level   Mask level in the system byte of the status register. Only interrupts above this level are recognized.

I/O-mapped I/O   A technique whereby the I/O devices are grouped in a separate address range and serviced by I/O instructions.

labels   Symbolic representations of addresses in assembly language programming. The assembler replaces labels with corresponding numbers when the assembly process takes place.

LDS   Lower Data Strobe. When active (low), it validates the lower data byte connected to the D0–D7 lines of the data bus. The lower data byte is also known as the *odd byte*.

LED   Light Emitting Diode. It is usually used as an optical display or source.

LIFO   Last In First Out. A data structure in memory in which the last element stored will be the first element retrieved.

linker   A programming utility of the host system used to link several machine code files and generate the final machine code program.

LINK   An operation used to allocate stack space and implement linked lists. One of the address registers holds stack-access information. Work area is created on the stack in the linking process.

list file   A file that contains the machine code, the mnemonics, and the actual program location addresses.

loader   A programming utility of the host system used to format a machine code file to be transferred to the target system.

local operating system   An intermittent operating system between the user and the governing operating system. It looks like a user to the governing operating system, and like a governing operating system to the user.

logical address space   The complete address space that can be directly addressed by the address bus of the processor.

logical memory space   The memory space that can be addressed by the processor in real time with its address bus.

long word   For the 68000, 32-bit binary data consisting of four 8-bit bytes or two 16-bit words.

long-word aligned address   An address evenly divisible by 4.

loop   A repetitive process in which the same series of instructions is executed over and over until the loop terminates.

LPF   Low-Pass Filter. It attenuates the high frequencies above the cutoff frequency, but allows low-frequency signals to pass through without attenuation. An LPF is used to remove switching transients in the digital world.

LSB   Least Significant Bit. The binary bit in the lowest position of a binary string. It has a value of 1 or 0.

LSD   Least Significant Digit. The lowest valued digit in a hex decimal or a BCD string.

machine code   A string of binary 1s and 0s residing in memory, representing the operation to be performed. Also known as *object code*.

macros   User-defined functions that consist of processor instructions. Software can be developed using these functions.

mask   A method of preventing information from being recognized. In the context of interrupt handling, a mask prevents the processor from detecting an interrupt request.

memory   The area in which the processor's data are stored externally. Semiconductor memory consists of integrated circuit devices with a large array of flip-flops. Backup memory consists of disks, bubble memory, and the like.

memory indexing Providing an extra number to be added to the base address, resulting in an effective address of the memory or I/O location.

memory-mapped I/O A technique whereby all instructions dealing with memory also apply to input and output ports. A memory-mapped I/O device is treated as a memory location in the memory map.

MFP MultiFunction Peripheral. The 68901 MFP is an interface device that supports multifunctions, such as serial and parallel I/O, timing, interrupts, and DMA.

microcomputer An integrated system consisting of a microprocessor, memory, I/O, and other support circuitry.

microprocessor An integrated circuit device consisting of internal registers, flip-flops, an ALU, data paths, and other circuitry.

MMU Memory Management Unit. A hardware unit that performs functions such as address translation and data buffering. It operates under the control of the processor.

mnemonic A symbolic representation of an operation. An assembly program is written using mnemonics.

modems Electronic equipment that modulates and demodulates information for serial communications. Remote computers and systems communicate via modems and telephone lines through an RS-232 interface.

monostable An electronic circuit that produces a fixed-width pulse when it is triggered.

MOS technology Metal Oxide Semiconductor technology. The current processing technology. with which high-density integrated circuit devices are fabricated.

MSB Most Significant Bit. For a binary string with n digits, it has a value of 2^{n-1}.

MSD Most Significant Digit. The highest valued digit in a hex decimal or a BCD string.

multiprecision operations Operations on strings of data requiring continuity from one operation to the next.

multiprocessing An activity in which more than one processor is operational.

nest Operations within similar operations, subroutines within subroutines, exceptions within exceptions, and so forth.

NMI Nonmaskable Interrupt. An interrupt condition that cannot be masked out by the mask level. It has to be recognized. For NMI, processor must respond.

object code See **machine code.**

odd memory byte The byte located at an odd address, such as $000001, $000003.

operand The data element or the address of the data element. This term is frequently used in the microcomputer field to refer to any data or address elements other than the program code.

operating system The system-level programs that control the operation of the computer and associated I/O. These programs usually cannot be altered by the user.

optoisolators A combination of LED and photodetector. Optoisolators eliminate any electrical noise from being coupled.

op.word The word containing the machine code, with reference to the operation to be performed.

ORA and **ORB** Output registers A and B of the PIA. These registers communicate with the external I/O units.

ORG directive Origin assembler directive. It provides information to the assembler about the starting address of the program.

outer displacement   The final displacement value that is added to obtain the effective address, EA.

overrun error   An error condition that results when a new frame of information is overwritten on the old frame that has not yet been used.

parallel data transfer   A mode of transfer in which all signals are connected simultaneously.

parity error   An error condition that results when an even-parity word is detected instead of an expected odd-parity word, or vice versa.

PIA   Peripheral Interface Adapter. The 6821 PIA is an 8-bit parallel I/O device belonging to the 6800 family.

pipe   First-in-first-out register structure.

PI/T   Parallel Interface/Timer. The 68230 PI/T is a multiport parallel interface device belonging to the 68000 family.

PMMU   Paged Memory Management Unit. Similar to MMU, except the memory translations and transfers are based on a memory page of 256 bytes to 32 kilobytes.

pointers   Counter and register combinations, the contents of which address a location. Pointer contents change in a predetermined manner.

popping or **pulling**   Retrieving the stored data from the stack.

postincrement   One of the 68000 addressing modes, in which the address register is incremented after addressing the operand.

predecrement   One of the 68000 addressing modes, in which the address register is decremented before addressing the operand.

prefetch   The process of obtaining the next instruction during the execution of the current instruction; typical of the 68000 family of processors.

privilege violation error   An error condition that results when the processor attempts to use privileged instructions while in the user mode.

pushing   Storing data on the stack.

queue   An arrangement of operands in FIFO sequence.

RAM   Random Access Memory. All RAM locations can be accessed in the same amount of time. Also known as *Read/Write Memory (R/WM)*.

RAS   Row Address Strobe. A signal used to latch the row address into the DRAM device. When RAS is activated, the corresponding row of the DRAM is refreshed.

read bus cycle   A bus cycle during which the processor reads data from memory or I/O.

read-modify/write   An operation in which the processor reads data content from a given location, modifies it, and writes it back at the same location.

receiver   The electronic circuit that receives, decodes, and restores information sent to it by the transmitter.

register   An array of flip-flops and gates.

relocation   A process by which the program code is made to reside at different locations, yet remain operational.

reset input   A hardware signal to the processor, forcing system initialization.

reset vectors   Locations in the vector table containing the values to be loaded into the supervisor stack pointer and the program counter on reset condition.

response time   The time taken by the addressed device to provide data during the read cycle or to accept data during the write cycle.

ROM   Read-Only Memory. Also a random access memory, but one that cannot be written into during normal operation.

RS-232 interface An industry standard asynchronous interface for serial data communications.

RTE Return from interrupt instruction of the 68000 processor. An RTE is always the last instruction in an exception routine.

RTS Ready to Send. A control signal from the DTE signifying that the DTE is ready for data transfers.

R/W̄ Read/write strobe signifying a read operation when it is at a high logic level and a write operation when it is at a low level.

serial data transfer A mode of transfer in which data are transmitted and received one bit at a time on a single signal line.

SFC Source Function Code. A 3-bit register within the 68010 and 68012 processors that contains the source function code information.

sign extension Replication of the most significant bit of an operand to all higher order bits in the data string. This helps to preserve the numeric value of the operand and also the sign, if the operand is only a part of the complete string.

software The actual programming sequence, program code, and the associated resources. This term is frequently used in connection with writing the programs and using the system resident programs.

source operand A term used to refer to the data or the address of the data element on which the operations are to be performed.

source program The version of the program written in assembly language, with comments included. Programs written in higher languages are also known as source programs. The source program cannot be executed by a computer without first being assembled into an object, or machine language, program.

special status word An additional word included in the long stack that defines the type of operation in process at the time of occurrence of a bus or address error condition.

spurious interrupt error An error condition that results from the occurrence of a bus error while the processor is fetching the interrupt vectors during the interrupt acknowledge cycle.

stack LIFO data structure in memory in which the processor registers are stored whenever there is a change in program flow due to subroutines and exceptions.

stepper motors Magnetically coupled motors that advance one step at a time when the code on the windings changes in sequence. Stepper motors may be thought of as digital motors.

strings A collection of data elements arranged in sequential order.

subroutines Subprograms called by other programs to perform certain dedicated operations and provide results.

supervisor mode The mode of the 68000 family of processors in which to handle exception conditions. Operating system programs are handled in this mode.

symbol table A table generated at the end of the assembly process that shows all the symbols used in the program and their corresponding values.

symbols Alphabetical or alphanumeric representations of numbers used in assembly language programming to enhance a program's readability.

synchronous events Events that occur in time with a clock cycle in a definite sequence.

target system The actual hardware system on which the assembled code will run.

terminals A loosely used term to specify keyboard and CRT display in data communications.

throughput The overall performance of a unit; a measure of how efficient and effective the unit is.

trace A procedure by which to obtain information about the processor's internal condition.

transmitter   An electronic circuit that codes, conditions, and transmits information to the receiving end.

TRAPs   Software instructions similar to interrupts that cause the 68000 processor to move into the supervisor mode.

tristate   A high-impedance state in which the devices are virtually disconnected from the bus.

$\overline{\text{UDS}}$ Upper Data Strobe. When active (low), it validates the upper data byte connected to the D8–D15 lines of the data bus. The upper data byte is also known as the *even byte*.

unidirectional   A signal line that can function as an input or an output, but not both.

unimplemented instructions   68000 instructions that have not yet been defined. These may refer to coprocessor-type instructions or new instructions that may be defined in the future.

uninitialized interrupt condition   A condition that occurs if the vector number for a user interrupt is not initialized. The user device provides a default vector number (#15) for the uninitialized interrupt error.

unlink   A process whereby the work area is removed from the stack and the frame pointer decoupled from the stack.

USART   Universal Synchronous and Asynchronous Receiver and Transmitter. An electronic unit used for synchronous or asynchronous serial data communications, depending upon the mode of operation.

user mode   A lower level of processor operation that deals with user programs. Some instructions and resources are not permitted in this mode.

user vector   A vector number supplied by the user for a given interrupt in response to an interrupt acknowledge condition.

VBR   Vector base register. A 32-bit register within the 68010, 68012, 68020, and 68030 processors that contains the base address for the relocated vector table.

vector location   A location in the vector table containing the starting address of the corresponding exception routine.

vector number   The number corresponding to the memory location holding the starting address of the exception routine selected to be run.

vector table   Dedicated memory between $000000 and $0003FF. It holds the starting addresses of all the exception routines.

virtual machine   A term used to refer to nonexistent hardware resources, the properties of which are mimicked by the operating system.

virtual memory   Physically nonexistent memory, but logically addressable memory, possibly contained in the backup memory.

$\overline{\text{VMA}}$ Valid memory address signal from the 68000 that validates the address bus during synchronous data transfers.

$\overline{\text{VPA}}$ Valid peripheral address signal from the memory or I/O to inform the 68000 that it has addressed a 6800 peripheral, and that the data transfer should be synchronized with the E clock.

wait state   The equivalent of a clock period. It is introduced by the 68000 processor during a bus cycle, while waiting for the $\overline{\text{DTACK}}$ to occur.

warm start   System reinitialization via a pushbutton type of reset activation. No extra time is necessary for stabilization of the system electronics.

word aligned   Always in increments of words.

word extensions   Additional words in an instruction containing additional information about the instruction, data, or the address of the data.

word organized   The condition in which all 16 bits of the data bus are physically active, providing for 16-bit data transfer activity.

word-aligned address   An address evenly divisible by 2.

word   A 16-bit data structure, consisting of two 8-bit bytes.

write bus cycle   A bus cycle during which the processor writes data into memory or I/O.

zero-divide error   An error condition that results when division by zero is attempted during the execution of DIVIDE instructions.

INDEX